Hollywood in the Age of Television

Hollywood in the Age of Television

EDITED BY TINO BALIO

Boston
UNWIN HYMAN
London   Sydney   Wellington

© 1990 by Unwin Hyman, Inc.

Unwin Hyman, Inc.
955 Massachusetts Avenue, Cambridge, Mass. 02138, USA

Published by the Academic Division of
Unwin Hyman Ltd
15/17 Broadwick Street, London W1V 1FP, UK

Allen & Unwin (Australia) Ltd,
8 Napier Street, North Sydney, NSW 2060, Australia

Allen & Unwin (New Zealand) Ltd in association with the
Port Nicholson Press Ltd,
Compusales Building, 75 Ghuznee Street, Wellington 1, New Zealand

First published in 1990.

Library of Congress Cataloging-in-Publication Data
Hollywood in the age of television / (edited) by Tino Balio.
    p. cm.
    ISBN 0-04-445837-1. – ISBN 0-04-445836-3 (pbk.)
    1. Motion pictures and television—United States.   2. Motion
picture industry—United States.   3. Television broadcasting—
United States.   I. Balio, Tino.
PN1992.63.H65   1990
384'.8'0973—dc20   90-12200
                                                              CIP

British Library Cataloguing in Publication Data
Hollywood in the age of television.–Boston, Mass ed.
    1. United States. Television services, history 2.
    California. Los Angeles. Hollywood. Cinema industries,
    history
    I. Balio, Tino
    384.5540973

    ISBN 0-04-445837-1
    ISBN 0-04-445836-3 pbk

Typeset in 10 on 12 point Palatino
by Falcon Typographic Art Ltd and
printed in Great Britain by The University Press, Cambridge

Contents

Part II   Responding to New Television Technologies

List of Tables

Editor's Acknowledgments

I wish to thank Thomas Schatz, Brian Winston, and David Marc for reading this book in manuscript and for offering many valuable suggestions to improve it.

I am indebted to my colleague Vance Kepley for his advice and encouragement during all stages of this project.

My gratitude to the College of Letters and Science of the University of Wisconsin for a sabbatical leave that enabled me to start the book and to the Vilas Trust for summer salary support and research support that helped me to complete it.

Hollywood in the Age
of Television

Part I

Responding to Network Television

Introduction to Part I

Tino Balio

*A*fter World War II, things were never the same for the motion picture industry. Beginning in 1947, Hollywood entered a recession that lasted for ten years; movie attendance dropped by half, four thousand theaters closed their doors, and profits plummeted. In foreign markets, governments erected trade barriers to limit the importation of motion pictures. Thus, instead of enjoying sustained prosperity after the war, which many had predicted, Hollywood retrenched. Production was severely cut back; "B" pictures, shorts, cartoons, and newsreels were dropped and the studios concentrated their efforts on fewer and fewer "A" pictures. The studio system went by the board as companies disposed of their back lots, film libraries, and other assets and pared producers, directors, and stars from the payrolls.

Television is usually identified as the main culprit for this state of affairs, but TV did not make significant inroads into moviegoing until the mid-fifties; rather, the postwar recession in Hollywood was caused in large part by the migration to the suburbs and the baby boom, which focused consumer spending on appliances, automobiles, and new housing. For entertainment, suburbanites with small children, far removed from the downtown location of movie palaces, found a substitute for the movies in radio, which enjoyed unprecedented growth in the late forties.

Even after suburban families substituted television for radio, other nonmedia factors still influenced moviegoing. During the fifties, shorter working hours, paid vacations and holidays, and general prosperity started a middle-class spending spree on leisure—domestic and foreign pleasure travel, vacation homes, athletics, hunting and fishing, gardening, boating, games and toys, records and hi-fi's, and do-it-yourself projects around the home. The challenge facing Hollywood

3

therefore was not just the rise of television but changing demographics and audience tastes as well.

REORGANIZATION

Impact of the Paramount Case

Agitation over the monopolistic trade practices of the indus-try by Congress, organized religion, and the education establish-ment prompted the Justice Department to file ·an antitrust action against the eight major motion picture companies in 1938, known as *United States v. Paramount Pictures, Inc. et al*—the *Paramount* case for short. The defendants consisted of the Big Five—Para-mount, Warner Bros., Loew's, Inc. (MGM), Twentieth Century–Fox, and RKO—and the Little Three—Universal, Columbia, and United Artists. The Big Five were fully integrated; they owned studios, operated worldwide distribution facilities, and controlled chains of theaters where their pictures were guaranteed a showing. With sta-bles of stars, writers, directors, producers, cameramen, and the rest, each of these companies produced from 40 to 60 pictures a year. Although in total their productions represented at most 50 percent of the industry's annual output, about three-fourths of the class-A features, the ones that played in the best theaters and received top billing, were made and distributed by the Big Five. The Big Five's greatest strength, however, was in exhibition. Of the twenty-three thousand theaters operating in the United States in 1930, the five majors either owned or controlled only three thousand, but this number represented the largest and best first-run houses in the metropolitan areas that accounted for 50 percent of domestic film rentals.

The Little Three operated in a sort of symbiotic relationship to the Big Five: Universal and Columbia had their own studios and distri-bution facilities and were useful to the majors in supplying low-cost pictures for frequent program changes and double features; United Artists functioned solely as a distributor for a small number of elite independent producers.

Poverty Row existed on the bottom rung of the industry. Tiny studios such as Monogram, Republic, Grand National, and Producers' Releasing Corporation serviced the lesser theaters in small towns and

TABLE I.1

The Big Five and Successor Companies After the Consent Decrees

Successor Motion Picture Company (Theaters before divestiture)	Successor Theater Company (Theaters after divestiture)
Paramount Pictures (1,424)	United Paramount Theatres (650)
Twentieth Century–Fox (549)	National Theatres (321)
Warner Bros. (436)	Stanley Warner (297)
Metro-Goldwyn-Mayer (129)	Loew's Theatres (100)
RKO Pictures (124)	RKO Theatres (82)

rural areas by churning out scores of low-budget Westerns and formula crime melodramas. As a group, they had a marginal impact on the industry.

The *Paramount* case reached the Supreme Court in 1948, after thousands of pages of testimony and exhibits, consent decrees, two lower-court decisions, and appeals. In a landmark decision, the court held that the Big Five conspired to monopolize motion picture exhibition. Trade practices such as block booking, whereby the majors rented their pictures to independent exhibitors in groups on an all-or-nothing basis, unfair clearances and runs that prolonged the time independent theaters had to wait to receive new films, and preferential arrangements among members of the Big Five were declared illegal restraints of trade. To remedy the monopoly in exhibition, the Supreme Court remanded the matter to the district court, which insisted that the Big Five divorce their theater chains from their production and distribution branches.

Paramount and RKO were the first to enter into consent decrees in 1949, and by 1959 the remaining majors had followed suit. The consent decrees contained these provisions: (1) the prohibition of unfair distribution trade practices so that each picture would be rented on an individual basis, theater by theater, without regard to other pictures or exhibitor affiliation; (2) the divorcement of the theater chains of the Big Five companies from their production and distribution operations; (3) the divestiture of all jointly owned theaters or theaters in closed towns—that is, where an exhibition chain had no competitors; and (4) the establishment of voting trusts to prevent stockholders in the former integrated companies from exercising common control of both successor companies (see table I.1).

As far as the Little Three were concerned, some economists have argued that they should not have been made defendants in the case, because they owned no theaters. Nonetheless, the court subjected the companies to the same price-fixing and trade-practice prohibitions as it had the Big Five.

The motion picture industry underwent many changes during the postwar period, and it is difficult to separate the effects of the decrees from the shifts in audience demand and the rise of television. But this much is certain. Although divorcement and divestiture restructured the industry, these provisions by no means reduced the importance of the majors. In 1954, the Big Five and the Little Three plus two minor companies collected most of the domestic film rentals, as did ten companies (not all the same ones) 20 years later. Overseas, the majors fared just as well. Despite trade restrictions and stiffer competition from foreign producers, U.S. film companies continued to dominate foreign screens; they distributed the biggest box office attractions and captured the lion's share of the gross. Before the war, about a third of their revenue came from abroad; during the fifties, the proportion rose to one-half.

By allowing the defendants to retain their distribution arms, the court, wittingly or not, gave them the means to retain control of the market. The reason, simply stated, is that decreasing demand for motion picture entertainment during the fifties foreclosed the distribution market to newcomers. Distribution presents high barriers to entry. To operate efficiently, a distributor requires a worldwide sales force and capital to finance 20 to 30 pictures a year. During the fifties, annual overhead costs of a major distributor amounted to over $25 million, and financing a full roster of pictures came to more than twice that amount. Since the market absorbed less and less product during this period, it could support only a limited number of distributors—about the same as existed at the time of the *Paramount* case. Without new competition, the film rentals collected by the majors represented a market share of 90 percent in 1972, the same share they collected during the halcyon days of the thirties and forties.

After the consent decrees, the divorced theater circuits also fared well. The successor companies—United Paramount Theatres, National Theatres, Stanley Warner, Loew's, and RKO Theatres—still owned considerable holdings and were assured a dominant role in the business throughout the fifties and sixties. As a result of divestiture, they sold off their weaker houses in small towns while retaining their large first-run houses. During the fifties, the big houses in the big cities, which accounted for 20 percent of the theaters, still generated the bulk of the business. As will be discussed later, the major companies concentrated their efforts on producing blockbusters to win back audiences. Only the first-run houses had the seating capacity, the location, and the bargaining power to successfully bid on new pictures. Thus, despite the impact of television, revenues per theater for many of the circuits actually increased. Moreover, their buying power guaranteed their prominence in the exhibition field.

The independent exhibitor, on the other hand—the supposed beneficiary of the decrees—fared less well. Outside the first-run market, conditions were disastrous. By the time the exhibition market bottomed out in 1963, the number of four-wall theaters had dropped an astounding 48 percent since 1947. To carve a niche for itself in the market, some independent theaters converted to art films. In adjusting to the new business climate of the fifties and sixties, the marginal theaters faced a dilemma. On the one hand, the inner-city and neighborhood houses found it difficult to lure suburbanites back to the city: public transportation was inadequate, parking was expensive, and business districts were starting to deteriorate. On the other hand, a chronic product shortage existed, the result of the phaseout of B and medium-budget pictures by the majors.

To stay alive, one option was to convert to art films by targeting the "Lost Audience." As described by *Variety*, the Lost Audience consisted of

mature, adult, sophisticated people who read good books and magazines, who attend lectures and concerts, who are politically and socially aware and alert. . . . These people have been literally driven out of the motion picture theatre by the industry's insistence on aiming most of its product at the lowest level.

The size of this audience, estimated the trade paper, was around 25 million.[1] The number of art houses in 1950 was only 83 theaters, but by 1966 the number had grown to 664. A smallish, intimate theater typically seating around five hundred, the art house was located at first in the inner city and neighborhoods of metropolitan areas and later in college and university communities and in the suburbs. Most of these theaters were individually owned, although several small chains operated in New England, the Midwest, and on the West Coast. New York City, with 25 houses, was the most prestigious market for imports and served as the launching pad for new releases. Los Angeles, with an equal number of art theaters, was the second most important hub.

To create an attractive and comfortable ambience for the adult sophisticated audience, exhibitors remodeled the interiors of their theaters, installed comfortable seats, and, in the lobbies, exhibited works of local artists, sold specialized film books and magazines, and served freshly brewed coffee, fine teas, and Swiss chocolates. The exhibition policy of these houses varied. Some showed foreign films only occasionally; some presented a mix of avant-garde shorts, documentaries, classic American films, and imports; while others specialized in a few award-winning art films.

Significant demand existed for foreign films during the sixties, but their share of the total market remained remarkably stable. Every year one or two foreign pictures achieved the status of art-house blockbusters whose grosses compared favorably with domestic product. In addition, several others each year did moderate business, enough to turn a small profit. However, it was a volatile market and one that could not be sustained using traditional means.

The one bright spot in independent exhibition during this period was the drive-in. As conventional four-wall theaters closed their doors, a new type of theater, the drive-in, rescued exhibition from the full impact of television. At the end of World War II, the number of "ozoners," the industry term for drive-ins, was estimated at between 60 and 300; by 1958, the number had grown to 4,700, or nearly a third of all the theaters in the country. Drive-ins ranged in size from a 200 to 2,500 car capacity and were located in every state. Although drive-ins were limited to a 30-week season in most parts of the country because of winter weather, those in the South and Southwest operated throughout the year. Generating a mere trickle of revenue in 1948, drive-ins accounted for 20 percent of all film rentals ten years later and more than made up for the total seats lost through the closing down of theaters.

The drive-in boom resulted from the rise in automobile sales, the high level of general prosperity, and the marketing strategies of drive-in owners. Automobile production had stopped during the war, to resume in 1946. Afterward, car ownership, and gasoline consumption, grew until, by 1954, 60 percent of the nation's 54 million families owned cars. Car ownership accounted, in part, for the migration to the suburbs. In 1929, 60 percent of Americans lived in big cities or on farms; in 1953, the same percentage lived in suburbs and in small towns. Fueling the suburbanization trend was the growth in real income. In 1929, 29 percent of American families had a real income of three thousand to ten thousand dollars; in 1953, 58 percent achieved that level. In these new areas of population growth, the drive-in theater found its place.

The drive-in entrepreneur was typically an amateur showman, with a background in real estate development, construction, farming, or small business. Ozoners cost only a fraction of the price of a new four-wall theater—around a quarter of a million—and the return on investment could be high. (The divorced theater circuits were restrained from branching out into the drive-in business by the provisions of the *Paramount* case.) Movies provided only part of the attraction of the drive-in. Patrons could attend without having to dress up, paid somewhat lower admission prices, and were spared parking fees and baby-sitting problems. Located mainly on the fringes of the suburbs, drive-ins offered a total entertainment service for the family. At different drive-ins one could find such attractions as playgrounds, picnic areas, bingo, laundromats, miniature golf courses, bottle-warming services, open-air dance floors for teenagers, and concession stands. Given the nature of these gimmicks, it is easy to understand the appeal of the drive-in for married couples with small children, teenagers, and dating couples.

Those exhibitors who neither owned favorably situated theaters nor had the capital to acquire drive-ins found little shelter in the decrees from the vicissitudes of the business brought about by television, shortages of product, and higher rentals. Shifting population trends isolated many houses in run-down, out-of-the-way places. Theaters that were old and tired simply closed their doors.

Independent Production

Divorcement has been hailed as a charter of freedom for independent production. It is true that by abolishing block booking and other unfair trade practices, the *Paramount* case gave independents freer access to theaters, but if producers wanted entree to the best houses, they had to come up with pictures that compared favorably with anything on the market. The antitrust action was no panacea for independents, but it was one of many factors in the transition to fewer and better-quality pictures in the postwar period.

Clearly, the most important factor in the rise of independent production was the decreased demand for motion pictures, which made the venerable studio system an outmoded form of production. Before television, when moviegoing was a natural pastime, Hollywood's fine-honed method of mass-producing pictures was ideal to meet audience demand. Back then, studios divided the production process into discrete tastes—such as script development, scene and costume design, direction and cinematography—and organized the studio into corresponding departments that supplied talent and material at appropriate points. In this fashion, the studios churned out a whole range of genres from crime films, musicals, and screwball comedies to Westerns, including both high- and low-quality product, to satisfy every taste and pocketbook.

But as I have pointed out, television and changing audience tastes forced the majors to retrench. The majors pink-slipped contract personnel, reduced overhead wherever possible, and concentrated on making big-budget pictures. The most efficient means of operating under these circumstances was to organize production units to tailor-make individual motion pictures. In this way, the personnel best-suited for a project could be hired to contribute their talents and afterward let go. A studio, as a result, would not be burdened with high fixed salary costs, the largest component of which was studio overhead.

By the sixties, every studio, with the notable exception of Universal, had opened their doors to independents. Independents produced around 20 percent of the 234 pictures released by the eight majors in 1949; in 1957, the majors released 291 productions, of which 170 (58 percent) were produced by independents. The ranks of independent producers contained a mix of creative producers, packagers, talent, and combinations thereof. The packager was the most typical. A packager assembled the ingredients of a picture, but unlike the creative producer or star, typically took a secondary position in the production. More often than not the packager was also a talent agent. During the fifties, styles, genres, and even screen size changed, but a constant in the motion picture business was the insurance value of proven stars. Stars, in fact, became more important than ever; in this era of retrenchment, financing a picture of any consequence without a name of proven box office worth would have been unthinkable. Talent agents were quick to capitalize on the situation.

During the era of the studio system, talent agents played a marginal role in the industry. At best, they succeeded in negotiating higher salaries for their clients. It was the studio that nurtured talent, selected properties to develop, and took the long view in developing screen careers. But by dismantling the studio system, the studios abrogated these functions, and in so doing relinquished power to the talent brokers. Agencies such as William Morris and MCA took over the traditional studio function of scientifically putting together packages consisting of stars, literary properties, directors, and other ingredients. By the sixties, it was estimated that of the 125 or so films made each year, about 80, or nearly two-thirds, were prepackaged by agents for their clients.

By 1970, the majors functioned essentially as bankers supplying financing and landlords renting studio space. Distribution now became the name of the game. As independent production became assimilated by the majors as an alternative to the studio system method of production, the term "independent" no longer had meaning in the new context (see chapter 6). The majors accorded talent more creative freedom that it had ever enjoyed, but as financiers, the studios were able to retain ultimate discretionary power by exercising approval rights over the basic ingredients of a production and by establishing tight fiscal controls. In the age of television, the term independent is best used to describe the producer of low-budget features, documentaries, and experimental films that are handled outside the channels of mainstream Hollywood.

Demise of the Production Code

Before television, the industry produced a wide range of genres that appealed to an undifferentiated mass audience. Although certain genres might be more popular with segments of the audience—melodramas obviously appealed to women and crime and adventure films appealed to men—Hollywood considered itself a purveyor of family entertainment. Critics of the industry accused Hollywood of hiding behind the Production Code to avoid any serious treatment of significant social, political, and moral issues that might stir up trouble from pressure groups. Hollywood's timidity was self-serving, without a doubt. Moreover, the enforcement mechanism behind the code guaranteed that the screen would remain noncontroversial; for a picture to play in a theater owned by the majors, it had to have a seal of approval from the Production Code Administration. In essence, the majors exercised censorship over the entire industry. An independent producer who hoped to establish his name and business by treating such pressing issues as race relations or extremist politics would find access to the important theaters blocked.

Hollywood assumed that after the war audiences would be receptive to films that addressed social problems or contained adult themes. Hadn't the United States successfully fought a campaign to defeat totalitarianism in Europe and Japan? And hadn't these totalitarian regimes thrived on racism of the worst sort? After the war several studios produced films that treated the issues of anti-Semitism, racism, and demagoguery. Some of these films had been critical and box office hits—*Gentleman's Agreement, Crossfire, All the King's Men,* and *Home of the Brave,* for example.

However, the Red Scare put a stop to Hollywood's foray into social criticism and any thought the industry might have had to differentiate its product from television's by producing pictures aimed exclusively at the so-called "Lost Audience." Beginning in 1947, Hollywood was traumatized by the House Committee on Un-American Activities (HUAC). In 1947 and 1951, HUAC conducted hearings to investigate the alleged Communist infiltration of the motion picture industry. After the 1947 hearings, the leaders of the industry found it in their best economic interests to capitulate to the Red Scare by instituting a blacklist to deny employment in the industry to anyone suspected of subversion. During the second investigation, which continued sporadically for three years, HUAC prodded prominent industry figures to name people they knew as Communists. The blacklist grew. HUAC's hold on public opinion increased in response to a series of national and international events: the fall of China to the Communists, the first successful atomic explosion by the Soviets, the outbreak of the Korean War, and the rise of Joseph McCarthy. The combined forces of these events helped the committee achieve its goal of eradicating liberalism and radicalism in the movies.

Hollywood emphasized "pure entertainment" during the HUAC investigations and in addition produced a series of anti-Communist pictures to mollify the committee. The public showed little interest in this cold war fare; nearly 40 pictures were made from 1947 to 1954, most of which lost money. As a public relations ploy, though, the effort helped appease the right-wing guardians of the industry.

Conventional wisdom has it that the 1952 Supreme Court *Miracle* decisions, coming on the heels of divorcement, weakened the Production Code and paved the way for Hollywood to produce more mature pictures. It is true that without first-run theaters, the Big Five could no longer deny playing time to pictures that did not win the seal of approval from the Production Code Administration. It is also true that the Supreme Court in the *Miracle* case read the movies into the First Amendment and extended to them the constitutional freedoms enjoyed by the press and other organs of speech. However, the industry by no means considered itself free to produce whatever it pleased. Governmental censorship boards that operated in several states and cities still had the right to function, although their licensing power was curtailed somewhat. And religious and political pressure groups still exerted considerable influence over the public.

That the industry did not want to position itself on the forefront of social change should be obvious. It preferred a prudent course that allowed other forms of expression, such as Broadway plays and novels, and more sophisticated foreign films to test the waters. Meanwhile, the liberal Supreme Court could whittle away at the authority of censors.

Not until 1968 was self-regulation replaced by the more rational classification system. Hollywood found it in its best economic self-interest to rely mainly on family fare to lure people from their TV sets.

THE RISE OF COMMERCIAL TELEVISION

The first big push to launch commercial television service in the United States began on April 30, 1939. After investing in television research and development for more than a decade, RCA decided to promote the sale of home television sets by inaugurating regular daily broadcasts from its experimental station W2XBS (later WNBC) in New York. To kick off the event, NBC, the broadcasting arm of RCA, covered the opening of the New York World's Fair. Broadcast from NBC's powerful transmitter atop the Empire State Building on Sunday at 12:30 P.M., the single-camera program opened with a panoramic sweep of the Trylon and Perisphere (the symbols of the fair) and covered addresses by President Franklin Roosevelt and David Sarnoff, the president of RCA and the mastermind behind the company's move into television. About 200 television sets in the New York area and 12 special receivers at the RCA Pavilion at the fair were tuned into the event.

The Radio Corporation of America was practically the only company in the country capable of mounting such a campaign. A communications giant founded after World War I, RCA was organized at the behest of the U.S. government to ensure the nation a U.S.-based capability in international wireless communication. Under the leadership of David Sarnoff, RCA moved forcefully into radio by manufacturing radio receivers, beginning in 1922, and by founding the National Broadcasting Company in 1928. RCA entered motion pictures by organizing RKO Radio Pictures in 1928 and then established a strong position in the record industry by purchasing the Victor Talking Machine Company in 1929. By the mid-1930s, RCA was one of the largest corporations in the nation, with operations in two broadcasting networks, an international communications service, a manufacturing arm of components and final assemblies, and a unified research and development (R & D) organization.

Within months of NBC's television debut at the World's Fair, CBS, NBC's principal competitor in radio, started regular television programming, transmitting from atop the Chrysler Building. Joining the two networks was a newcomer to television, Allen B. DuMont Laboratories. A small manufacturer of cathode ray oscilloscopes founded in

1931, DuMont branched out into the television set market in 1938 and concurrently filed applications with the FCC for experimental television stations in New York and Washington, D.C.

Before television could expand beyond the experimental stage, however, a set of frequencies and standards had to be chosen. As early as 1929, the Radio Manufacturers Association (RMA) set up a committee to guide experimental work in TV. In 1936, the RMA proposed to the FCC a standard of 441 lines per picture and 15 frames per second. Although the FCC had yet to formally approve the RMA proposal, this was the standard NBC used for its experimental telecasts in 1939. Because sectors of the industry opposed the 441-line standard, urging that higher picture quality could be achieved with more lines, the FCC held hearings to investigate the matter in 1940.

The FCC made it clear that commercialization of television would not be permitted until the industry agreed on a single standard. The RMA therefore created the National Television Systems Committee (NTSC), comprised of technical experts from the involved companies, to evaluate the competing systems. CBS's color system offered the clearest option. However, since the color process was designed for use in the ultrahigh frequency (UHF) spectrum, which was largely undeveloped, the NTSC selected RCA's monochrome system as the national standard, because it seemed the closest to being market ready. In accepting the NTSC recommendations on April 30, 1941, the FCC gave the go-ahead to the commercialization of television and allocated spectrum space for black and white broadcasting by creating 12 VHF (very high frequency) channels, by setting a 525-line standard, and by adopting FM sound for TV.

Both NBC and CBS inaugurated regular commercial broadcasting in New York on July 1, 1941. By the end of the year, six commercial stations were in operation and ten thousand sets had been sold, mostly to New Yorkers. However, in the spring of 1942, the government suspended most television programming and manufacturing for the duration of World War II.

Increased demands on the electromagnetic spectrum by military and government users forced the FCC to reexamine the entire issue of frequency allocation. During the hearings that were held for this purpose in 1944–45, a contingent consisting of the most important members of the industry, including RCA, Philco, and DuMont, wanted TV to get off to a fast postwar start in the VHF band. An opposing group, led by CBS, Zenith, and others, advocated the development of television in the UHF band, which had four times as many channels as VHF and could accommodate CBS's field sequential color system. CBS's system was called "field sequential," explains Brad Chisholm, "because it created full-color images by rapidly filling the screen with first a red, then a green, then a blue picture. This sequence of three color fields was repeated forty times each second." The means by which colored images were rendered in this system was through the use of spinning color discs inside the receiver (see Chapter 8). Although the technology for dependable UHF service to accommodate the triple-channel bandwidth needed for color television transmission had yet to be perfected, CBS argued that a concerted industry research effort would solve the problem in a year or two. RCA, whose patents covered VHF technology, argued that if the United States waited for engineering perfection, TV would never get off the ground.

The FCC resolved the controversy in favor of the RCA group. In the process of allocating TV's place in the radio spectrum, the FCC had to assign television channels to specific markets. As a first step in establishing television throughout the United States, the FCC planned to license some 400 stations in 140 top cities. To avoid signal interference, the FCC mandated geographical separation of 85 miles for adjacent channels and 200 miles for stations on the same channel. Although the commission gave its stamp of approval to the prewar television system, it set aside a block of ultrahigh frequencies for experimental use.

After the war, new station construction and set sales languished. Uncertainty over technical standards continued to hamper the industry when CBS petitioned the FCC to reconsider its color system in 1946. Anticipating such a move, RCA unveiled its new color system midway through the FCC's hearings. A "dot sequential" process, RCA's system created color by displaying red, green, and blue dots in rapid sequence on the face of the picture tube. Unlike CBS's "mechanical" color process, RCA's utilized an all-electronic simultaneous system. Since all the color systems under consideration required channels of triple width, the FCC in 1947 elected not to authorize any system at that time. Since the decision resolved the uncertainties in the industry and in the public mind that had been raised by the color versus black and white battle, the rush to VHF television began.

The number of TV sets in use soared by more than 1,000 percent, from 14,000 in 1947 to 172,000 a year later. In 1949, the number went up to 1 million, in 1950 to 4 million, and in 1954 to 32 million. By 1955, more than half of all American homes had television.

No sooner had the rush to VHF begun, than serious faults appeared with the FCC's allocation plan. With only 50 stations built, the FCC discovered that stations had been placed too close together, both geographically and on the dial, causing interference. For example, 2 stations on the same channel in Detroit and Cleveland, more than 90 miles apart, interfered with one another to within 2 miles of the

Detroit transmitter. To sort matters out, the FCC declared a freeze on the licensing of new television stations on September 29, 1948.

Although the FCC planned to solve all technical problems within six months, the freeze lasted until April 1952 and was a crucial turning point in the development of television. The freeze by no means stopped the expansion of commercial television, as the term might imply; the FCC just halted issuing additional licenses for television stations. The 60 stations under construction were allowed to proceed, bringing the total to 108 VHF outlets by 1952. These 108 VHF stations were generally acquired by radio broadcasters already affiliated with CBS and NBC and served 63 markets in this manner: 40 markets had a single station; 11 had 2 stations; and 12 had 3 or more.

The revised channel allotment plan contained in the *Sixth Report and Order*, which the FCC issued at the conclusion of the freeze in 1952, did not change matters. Rather than moving television up to the UHF spectrum, the FCC decided to intermix VHF and UHF. The FCC maintained that to do away with the VHF assignments would have made all TV sets obsolete at a stroke. The FCC opened up the UHF spectrum because there was nowhere else for TV to expand.

The specifics of the plan reduced the number of VHF stations to widen separation and to broaden coverage. In the 50 largest markets, the top 20 were allotted three VHF channels and the next 30 a mix of VHF and UHF stations. However, UHF technology was still in the experimental stage, and when such stations were placed into service in these intermixed markets, they had to operate at a severe competitive disadvantage. For one thing, existing TV sets were equipped to receive VHF signals only; to receive UHF, owners had to buy converters. (It was not until 1964 that the FCC "solved" this problem by requiring set manufacturers to equip their sets with UHF tuners.) For another, UHF signals were weaker and had less market penetration potential than VHF. UHF stations, therefore, were unable to attract network and advertising affiliation. And without advertising revenue and popular network programs, UHF operators found it difficult to survive against their entrenched VHF competitors.

The FCC provided for 1,300 UHF stations in its allocation schedule, but by 1956 less than 400 construction permits had been applied for and approved by the FCC, and of these, a third never went on the air. In the same period, by contrast, only 4 of 276 postfreeze VHF stations went off the air. The market, as a result of the FCC order, could profitably support at best three networks—NBC and CBS and a third weak sister.

This account of the rise of television reveals that the commercial TV networks, with the aid of "a compliant regulatory agency, which seemed more content to protect the industry members than the public," in Barry Litman's words, transferred their successful radio model to the emerging industry. Networking—the ability to simultaneously transmit a program to many markets—had several economic disadvantages. According to Barry Litman, networking permitted broadcasters (1) to enhance their profits by spreading the unit costs per viewer of programming over the largest possible audience and thereby capture maximum advertising revenue; (2) to handle a large number of programs simultaneously, "thereby spreading the costs of running a large distribution network across a multiple number of shows"; and (3) to save transaction costs "by representing a large list of affiliates in the common sale of national advertising time and a substantial number of programmers in the supply of programming to affiliates." By providing these services, the networks enjoyed the benefits of vertical integration, which in turn gave them tremendous leverage in dealing with affiliates, national advertisers, and program suppliers (see chapter 4).

Network Programming Strategies

During the early fifties, nearly all prime-time programming emanated from New York and was broadcast live. By the late fifties, nearly all prime-time programming emanated from Hollywood on film. For many, the live broadcasts constituted a Golden Age, a period when network programmers adapted older media fare and experimented with new dramatic forms to entertain the public. Since the networks had their roots in radio, they borrowed heavily from the older medium. But the period is best remembered for the dramatic anthology series and the spectaculars. Dramatic anthologies consistently ranked among the most popular forms of programming. At the height of their popularity, from 1953 to 1956, the networks broadcast 20 such programs a week. Utilizing Broadway talent and with a different cast and setting each week, these shows started out adapting popular plays, but as the need for more material developed, producers turned to literary classics, short stories, well-known novels, and finally original teleplays. Spectaculars, expensive one-of-a-kind programs 90 to 120 minutes in length, typically consisted of dramatic and music hall fare.

The networks had several motives for preferring live over filmed programming. Live television, first of all, strengthened ties with affiliates by identifying the network as opposed to TV syndicators as the primary source of programming; second, live programming was cheaper to produce than filmed programming, at least in the beginning; third, live television differentiated the new medium from motion pictures; and last, the live anthology series could be pointed to by the networks when testifying before governmental investigative committees as proof that television was serving the public interest.

NBC's programming strategy reflected in part its function as a subsidiary of RCA. As a research and development organization, RCA had positioned itself in every phase of television—studio equipment, broadcasting, receivers—in the hope of enjoying the same benefits it received from radio—a substantial share of set sales and license fees from other manufacturers one every receiver they produced. Going into the freeze, NBC had acquired the FCC's limit of five owned-and-operated stations and had lined up affiliates in the most favorable one-station cities. From 1948 to 1953, a majority of television stations in the United States were NBC affiliates. Operating from this position of strength, NBC specialized in high-quality live programs and specials, which ranged from variety to drama, comedy, and talk shows, designed to boost audience size and to encourage consumers to purchase their first television sets. During the fifties, RCA held the leading market share in television set sales and earned enormous profits from the licensing of its patents. After 1956, NBC's programming radically changed to rely on the routines of series programming produced by West Coast suppliers on film. In analyzing NBC's programming strategies, Vance Kepley uses a theoretical model of a public good to explain why the network exploited "live, varied programs during its initial phase of operations but then [opted] for a regularized schedule after achieving a measure of maturity" (see chapter 1).

CBS's programming strategy resulted from its late entry into television. Because the network gambled heavily on color television and lost, CBS entered the freeze owning only one VHF station. To make a credible case for its UHF petition before the FCC, CBS encouraged its radio affiliates to apply for experimental UHF licenses and itself withdrew applications for large-market VHF licenses. After the freeze, CBS had to trade up, spending an estimated $30 million over eight years to buy out existing licenses to acquire its full complement of owned-and-operated (O&O) stations. CBS compensated for this late start in television, which deprived it of the enormous profits from station operation, by strengthening its radio network. Radio proved remarkably resistant to the onslaught of TV: for one thing, a quarter of the 105 million radio sets in the United States were in cars; for another, daytime radio, between 6:00 A.M. and 6:00 P.M., was the preferred medium of entertainment for homemakers. Beginning in 1948, CBS staged a series of talent raids on NBC by offering stars new and ingenious financial incentives. Rising radio revenues helped sustain television programming, but CBS did not have the resources of an RCA and countered NBC with a strategy of creating packaged programming strong on series situation comedy that catapulted the network to the number one position in terms of advertising sales by 1954, a position it would hold for the next 20 years (see chapter 2).

ABC's programming strategy reflected its inferior status as a broadcasting network. As previously mentioned, the FCC's rulings concerning spectrum allocation created a situation that would support two healthy networks and one weak one. In the forties, there were two contenders for the latter slot—ABC and DuMont. A latecomer on the broadcasting scene, ABC radio was formed as a result of an FCC ruling in 1941 that forced NBC to divest one of its two radio networks—named the Red and Blue—in an attempt to make radio more competitive. NBC disposed of the Blue, the weaker network, to Edward J. Noble, a wealthy entrepreneur and chief executive officer of Beech-Nut Life Savers, Inc., who organized ABC in 1943.

ABC moved into television after the war by building five VHF stations in the largest markets—the maximum permitted under FCC rules. To avoid a fight with NBC and CBS for the choicest station allocations, ABC opted for channels on the higher VHF frequencies (channel 7 and higher), which were considered technically and economically less efficient. The network hoped these O&O stations would form the nucleus of a national TV network, but during the freeze, ABC lacked the resources to produce competitive programming.

In search of fresh capital, ABC merged with United Paramount Theatres, the exhibition chain spun off by Paramount Pictures as a result of the consent decrees. At the time of the merger, ABC was heavily in debt and linked to a network consisting of only seven stations. In approving the merger in 1953, the FCC ignored Paramount's past antitrust history to conclude that the combination might improve ABC's programming and ability to attract sponsors and affiliates. In arriving at this decision, the FCC also ignored that its allocation plan was at the root of ABC's problems.

The FCC's decision permitting the ABC-UPT merger sealed the fate of the fledgling DuMont Television Network. Although DuMont succeeded in acquiring its full complement of stations, the network was unable to create a competitive line-up of affiliates, chiefly because it lacked the radio station relationships that the other networks were able to transfer to television. Consigned to be the fourth network in the industry after the ABC-UPT merger, an untenable position, DuMont ceased its national network operations in 1955.

The demise of DuMont improved ABC's fortunes, but it would be years before ABC became an equal partner with CBS and NBC. Even with the substantial resources of the Paramount theater chain, ABC faced an uphill battle in acquiring affiliates. Since there was a scarcity of three- and four-channel markets in the VHF spectrum, ABC had to link up with UHF stations with small audiences. By 1960, ABC had over 70 affiliates, but the financial and audience position of these affiliates as a group was far inferior to the 108 stations established before the freeze.

Since NBC and CBS had captured the high-priced talent and consequently the allegiance of the most powerful affiliates, ABC developed an alternative programming strategy. Instead of producing anthology dramas, spectaculars, and situation comedies live from New York, ABC turned to Hollywood for its prime-time needs. Unlike the self-production policy of the other two networks, ABC aimed to license independently produced programs; in return for financing the production of the pilot and series, the network acquired a share of the profits, the syndication rights, and the scheduling rights. The breakthrough occurred in 1954, when ABC signed a contract with Walt Disney to produce a weekly telefilm series revolving around the Disneyland theme park. The success of "Disneyland" helped convince the major motion picture companies that an opportune moment to enter television had arrived. But as Baughman points out, the majors, in entering the telefilm market, were forced to negotiate with the three networks on largely the networks' terms (see chapter 3).

ATTEMPTS AT APPROPRIATING TELEVISION

Direct Investment in Television

Myth has it that Hollywood stuck its head in the sand in the hope that television would go away. This scenario portrays the motion picture moguls as ignorant and reactionary businessmen who were so set in their ways that they watched the radio interests seize control of television. But recent research has revealed just the opposite: the industry monitored developments closely and maneuvered to get in on the ground floor of the new medium. Take the case of Paramount Pictures, for example. In his case study of the company, Timothy White (chapter 5) demonstrates that Paramount positioned itself in all the emerging markets created by television technology. In 1938, the company acquired a sizeable interest in Allen B. DuMont Laboratories to direct DuMont experimentation and research in the direction of theater television. Paramount immersed itself deeper into TV during the forties by operating the first experimental station in Chicago and the first commercial station in Los Angeles and by exploiting theater television and subscription TV. Following Paramount's lead, Warner Bros., Loew's, and Twentieth Century–Fox also filed for stations in the major markets during the war and laid plans to buy into the young television industry. Hollywood failed to move into television not because it lacked the will but because the FCC created insurmountable barriers to entry.

The short of it was that the *Paramount* antitrust case severely prejudiced the studios' reputation in the eyes of the FCC. The case had attracted the interest of the FCC from the start because the commission was about to launch an investigation of another "trust"—the radio industry. At the conclusion of the investigation in 1941, the FCC issued a set of *Chain Broadcasting Regulations* aimed at relaxing the networks' hold on affiliates and that mandated the divorcement of one of NBC's two radio networks. (As will be recalled, the divorcement of the Blue Network resulted in the creation of ABC.) Wary of possible antitrust implications behind the actions of the film industry, the FCC stymied attempts of the majors to expand further into television after the war by holding off decisions on their television station applications until the *Paramount* case had been resolved.

When the Supreme Court upheld the charges against the majors in 1948, the repercussion dashed any chance of the film industry's moving into television broadcasting. Since the FCC's intent was clear, Paramount, Warners, and the other majors withdrew their license applications by 1950.

Alternatives to Home Television

While trying to buy into television broadcasting, Hollywood simultaneously tried to create alternatives to commercial broadcast television. The first was called theater television. A form of large-screen TV designed for movie houses, theater television would show original programs shot by a regular television camera on the outside and transmitted by means of directional microwave relays or closed circuit coaxial cables to theaters equipped with special television pickups. Through their ownership of first-run theaters and theater television, the majors hoped to appropriate television as a source of profits in a period when powerful broadcasting interests led by RCA and CBS were jockeying for control of television and when the medium was in the infancy stage of commercial development.

At war's end, the exhibition branch of the industry consisted of eighteen thousand theaters with nearly 12 million seats whose box office gross regularly dwarfed all the revenues from radio advertising. With this potential for generating revenue, theater television could become the chief rival to commercial television based on the radio model. It was envisioned that theaters would form regional and national networks to present news, major league baseball, concerts, operas, Broadway plays, and even educational programs for schools.

Two theater television systems showed the greatest potential for development—RCA's direct projection system and Paramount's intermediate film system. Both were introduced to the public in early 1948. For the first year of theater TV, all events shown were available for free to the public in their own homes. However, in the fall of 1950, large-screen video started offering exclusive television programs, mostly sporting events. Although theater television had been permanently installed in only 12 theaters at the end of 1950, prospects for the innovation looked good; only 33 percent of American homes had television sets and the FCC freeze on station allocations had created a lull in the spread of television.

By 1952, the number of theaters with theater television or with plans to convert reached one hundred. Afterward, though, theater television disappeared. Several factors account for the demise, but the most important related to programming. To produce shows on a regular basis, or to outbid the networks in acquiring specials, theater television promoters had to form networks to spread the costs. They thought at the time that 50 good-sized interconnected theaters would make it possible to program exclusive television entertainment on a regular basis.

Two methods of transmission of broadcast signals were available to exhibitors—coaxial cables and local loops owned by AT&T and the airwaves, under the jurisdiction of the FCC. Intercity links provided by the telephone company were costly to lease and inefficient in many ways for video transmission. In addition, AT&T lines often could not be cleared for nationwide or even regional transmission, and when they were cleared, costs to theater owners were prohibitive.

The solution to the transmission problem lay in allocating a part of the underutilized UHF spectrum known as "movie band" to theater television. Film industry representatives petitioned the FCC in 1949 for 10 to 12 channels. Hearings were held from fall 1952 to the spring of 1953. Once again, the FCC denied a petition of the film industry on the grounds of its past monopolistic practices. But events had already made theater TV obsolete. The move to the suburbs and changing leisure-time habits of the public had already taken their toll. And after the FCC lifted the freeze in mid-1952, home television became firmly entrenched. Theater television had reached less than 1 percent of the total theaters.

Locked out of television network operation and station ownership, Hollywood investigated a second method to "better" home television called subscription television. A precursor to HBO and ESPN, subscription attempted to provide movies and sports to home television, for a fee. Paramount, once again, led the pack. Its principal competitors in the subscription television business were Zenith's Phonevision and Subscribervision, a system developed by Skiatron with the help of IBM. Two groups opposed their efforts: the broadcasters, whose defense of "free television" equated pay TV with the death of democratic choice, and the theater owners, who feared further erosion of the box office.

As White explains, the FCC protected the broadcasting industry by delaying and averting testing and operation of these systems until, by the end of the 1950s, conventional over-the-air television had saturated the market and people were reluctant to pay for what they already were getting for free.

Hollywood decided that if it wanted to lure people from their TV sets, it would have to experiment with new film technologies—3-D and widescreen processes—rather than with television technologies.

THE BIG PICTURE

To rekindle interest in the movies, Hollywood adopted the adage "We'll give them something television can't." Television viewing habits became pretty much established during the fifties; a direct connection existed between age and the amount of time spent watching the tube. The movies had lost most of the adult audience for good economic reasons: first, the cost of watching television for a consumer who had already purchased a set was negligible compared to the price of a theater ticket; second, frequent program changes provided variety; and third, television was convenient—it could be viewed in the most informal circumstances, without effort, and in the comfort of one's home. The motion picture industry, as a result, decided to differentiate its product and make the most of its natural advantages over its rival. It would adopt the policy of the big picture.

Roughly, the formula became "Make Them Big; Show Them Big; and Sell Them Big." Making them big meant investing in literary properties that were pretested and presold, such as best-selling novels, Broadway hits, and even successful television dramas. Showing them big meant presenting pictures in a spectacular fashion, using wide-screen and wide-film processes such as CinemaScope, Todd-AO, and Panavision. Selling them big meant long runs in roadshow situations, backed by custom-made exploitation and promotion campaigns.

In short, Hollywood upscaled its top product in the face of waning consumer demand and raised the price of admission. Between 1946 and 1962, the total number of moviegoers dropped 73.4 percent, but box office gross declined by only 48.3 percent. Without ticket price inflation (45.7 percent), the drop in box office would have amounted to 70.4 percent.

The transition to the big picture began in 1952, when pictures such as UA's *The African Queen*, MGM's *Quo Vadis?* and Paramount's *The Greatest Show on Earth* broke box office records. Afterward, the industry decided to make more pictures in color. Although advances in color cinematography made it technically feasible for the film industry to convert to color, television provided the economic imperative. As Chisholm points out in Chapter 8, Hollywood converted to color in the early fifties in an attempt to differentiate its product from black and white television production. When the novelty value wore off, beginning in 1955, color film production declined. It picked up again and rose steadily during the sixties to encompass nearly all feature work in response to the conversion to color broadcasting by the networks. By then, as will shortly be explained, network television had become an important secondary market for Hollywood films (see chapter 9).

To further differentiate its product from television's, Hollywood experimented with screen size and depth illusion. "The wide-screen revolution that took place during the early 1950s clearly involved more than a change in the size and shape of motion picture theater screens," says John Belton in chapter 7. "It represented a dramatic shift in the film industry's notion of the product that it was supplying to the public. During this period, the industry redefined, in part, what a motion picture should be, shifting its primary function of providing entertainment to the public to include as well another function—that of recreation."

The wide-screen revolution was launched on September 30, 1952, at the Broadway Theater with *This Is Cinerama*, a spectacular two-hour travelog with scenes ranging from a gripping roller coaster ride to a plane trip through the Grand Canyon. Cinerama created a sense of depth by projecting an image in three segments with separate projectors on a broad curved screen. Stereophonic sound heightened the realism of the experience. The handiwork of Fred Waller, former head of Paramount's special effects department, and Hazard Reeves, a sound engineer and industrial promoter, Cinerama was more than ten years in the development. Not surprisingly, the industry initially viewed the innovation as a curiosity. To convert a single theater would be expensive—anywhere from fifty to a hundred thousand dollars—and the three-camera system would radically alter conventional production methods. It remained for an outsider, Lowell Thomas, the famed radio newscaster, to take the plunge. Thomas acquired the exclusive rights to the process in 1950 and formed Cinerama Productions Corporation.

This Is Cinerama was enormously successful, eventually grossing more than $32 million. In New York, the picture played 122 weeks to an audience of 2.5 million, the longest run in the city's history. *Cinerama Holiday*, the second production, premiered in October 1953 and was just as popular. After the third production, *Seven Wonders of the World*, Cinerama hit a slump. For one thing, audiences were beginning to tire of the travelog format. For another, high conversion costs kept the number of Cinerama theaters to a mere 17, which meant that a picture had to play an incredibly long time before it could break even, let alone earn profits. Also, there were technical problems, such as jiggling dividing lines between the three panels on the screen and uneven color matches. Although Cinerama developed a single-lens projection system, which was first used in 1963 for the production of Stanley Kramer's *It's a Mad, Mad, Mad, Mad World*, other wide-screen systems had already hit the market.

In November 1952, 3-D hit the market on the heels of Cinerama with Arch Oboler's *Bwana Devil*. Devised by Milton Gunsberg, the three-dimensional process, which he dubbed Natural Vision, required two projectors for exhibiting and Polaroid glasses for viewing. This stereoscopic method, as opposed to the panoramic method of Cinerama, was supposed to provide the true three-dimensional experience.

Arch Oboler, a former radio dramatist best known for a nighttime horror and suspense series called "Lights Out," introduced Natural Vision to the public. Using his savings and whatever he could borrow, Oboler scraped together three hundred thousand dollars to produce the picture. At first, he even had to arrange his own distribution, since none of the big companies would touch it. They might have been afraid of rendering their film libraries obsolete, but then again, they might have wanted someone else to take the financial risks of promoting an untested innovation. The entrenched firms had everything to gain and little to lose following such a strategy.

Bwana Devil opened in tandem at the Los Angeles Paramount and the Hollywood Paramount in November 1952. Although the picture was ineptly made, with color mismatches and scenes out of focus, the public loved it. Oboler solicited bids for the distribution rights to the picture and the winner was United Artists. In the wake of *Bwana*

Devil, other studios jumped on the 3-D bandwagon, producing pictures in Naturescope, Panavision, Tri-Opticon, in addition to Natural Vision and other stereoscopic techniques. (Requirements for equipping a theater were minimal: a high-intensity reflective screen—or an old one painted aluminum—and an interlocking system for the projectors.) A string of 3-D hits, such as Warner's *House of Wax*, Paramount's *Sangaree*, and Universal's *It Came from Outer Space*, silenced the skeptics for a while, but as one motion picture studio head described 3-D, "It's a novelty, good for a fast dollar at the box office."[2]

It wasn't the Polaroid glasses that bothered audiences about 3-D—audiences were alienated by having things thrown at them in these movies. Producers were unwilling to experiment with the truly creative potential of this innovation. About 40 pictures were made in Natural Vision and other processes it spawned. With the exception of Alfred Hitchcock's *Dial M for Murder*, nearly all contained puerile plots of the horror or adventure types. By February 1954, *Variety* asked, "What's happened to 3-D?" A check of the major studios revealed that not a single one was making a 3-D film, nor did any of them contemplate putting one in the works.

CinemaScope was the one novelty to make a real impact on the entire industry. The innovation of Twentieth Century–Fox, Cinema-Scope made its debut in *The Robe*, which opened at the Roxy in New York on September 16, 1953. After a week of sensational business, the picture opened in a hundred other cities with the same results. Partly because of the wide-screen process and partly because of the narrative, *The Robe* set an industry record, grossing over $15 million (domestic) and $5 million (foreign). Here was the signal the industry wanted to jump on the wide-screen bandwagon. CinemaScope optics were based on an anamorphic lens system, perfected in the twenties by the French scientist Henri Chretien. With this lens a camera could compress an image horizontally; a "compensating" lens on the projector could stretch it out on the screen. As innovated by Fox, CinemaScope utilized regular 35mm film that projected an image two and a half times as wide as it was high. A curved screen and stereophonic sound on four magnetic tracks enhanced the realism. Unlike the travelog format of Cinerama that attempted to recreate the thrills of roller coaster rides and plane trips, CinemaScope features "sought to achieve a balance between narrative and spectacle, using the format to expand the range of the narrative," says Belton.

Spyros Skouras, the president of Twentieth Century–Fox, made the decision to innovate as a way to save his company. Poor earnings had forced him to institute an executive salary cut and brought charges of mismanagement from stockholders. Skouras moved fast to secure an option from Chretien, and within three months he had the lens tested, settled on the patent rights, worked out numerous complex details with equipment manufacturers here and abroad, and plunged his company into the new process, which he called CinemaScope.

Skouras realized from the outset that he could convince exhibitors to make the conversion only by guaranteeing a steady supply of product. As a result, he announced in February 1953 that Twentieth Century–Fox's future line-up would be in CinemaScope exclusively. To finance the conversion, Skouras mortgaged the entire studio, the back lot, and all the real estate the studio owned and borrowed millions from the banks. In another attempt to generate product, Skouras offered CinemaScope to all comers for a modest fee, with the result that other studios pledged to produce at least a small number of films in Scope even before *The Robe*. The provisos were that the shooting script had to be approved by Fox and the production had to be shot in color. By ensuring that all CinemaScope productions would be shot in color, Fox wanted "to convince exhibitors that CinemaScope was not a system to be reserved for occasional super specials like Cinerama, nor was it a gimmick to be exploited like 3-D." Rather, it was the system "best suited to regularly turning out the more expensive pictures necessary to reverse the decline in box office receipts."[3]

Since the cost of installing a CinemaScope system ranged from twelve to twenty-five thousand dollars, depending on the size of the theater, Fox's greatest challenge was to convince the nation's exhibitors, many of whom were in dire straits, to make the conversion. Partly to ensure quality exhibition of its films and partly to protect its interest in equipment sales, Fox required exhibitors to purchase the complete packages, consisting of lenses, screens, and speakers. The price tag on the stereophonic sound created the most resistance, especially among the smaller theaters; to stimulate sales, Fox dropped the provision on stereo sound altogether. This move, together with Skouras's persuasiveness, enabled Fox to convert virtually every theater in the United States to CinemaScope.

After the premiere of *The Robe*, Fox released 12 more Cinema-Scope pictures in as many months, generating record earnings that stablilized the operations of the company. Skouras's gamble paid off, and CinemaScope soon became the new motion picture standard. But as John Belton points out, CinemaScope was destroyed by its own success. By the end of the fifties, CinemaScope had been eclipsed as a special event process by Todd-AO, VistaVision, and other wide-screen and wide-film processes.

We need not describe the technical aspects of these other innovations; the point is that they brought people back to the movies.

TABLE I.2

Variety's Top Ten Box office Champions, 1969	
Title (distributor and date)	Domestic Distribution Gross (in thousands)
1. *The Sound of Music* (Fox; 1965)	$72,000
2. *Gone With the Wind* (MGM; 1939)	71,105
3. *The Graduate* (Avco Embassy; 1967)	43,100
4. *The Ten Commandments* (Paramount; 1956)	40,000
5. *Ben-Hur* (MGM; 1959)	39,105
6. *Doctor Zhivago* (MGM; 1965)	38,243
7. *Mary Poppins* (Disney; 1964)	31,000
8. *My Fair Lady* (Warner Bros; 1964)	30,000
9. *Thunderball* UA; 1965)	27,000
10. *Cleopatra* (Fox; 1963)	26,000

Source: *Variety*, January 7, 1970, p. 25.

The overall financial health of the industry improved markedly after 1964. The blockbuster trend accelerated. Going into the sixties, only 20 pictures had grossed over $10 million in the domestic market; by the end of the decade, nearly 80 had topped that figure. In *Variety*'s list of all-time box office champions as of 1969 (see Table I.2), 8 of the top 10 pictures were products of the sixties. (I include *Ben-Hur* since it was released at the end of 1959.)

New Marketing Techniques

Because of its high production costs, the big picture transformed the traditional methods of motion picture marketing. Before television, the industry relied on the run-clearance-zone system of distribution. A new picture opened initially in an important first-run theater in each zone (that is, metropolitan market) on an exclusive basis. After playing a week or so, the picture was withdrawn for an interval of several weeks, known as the clearance, and was then released to neighborhood houses. After a short run, the pattern was repeated until the picture played later-run theaters in the outlying areas. The merchandising pattern of movies during the thirties and forties was similar to that of other consumer goods: first, the exclusive shops; next, the general department store; and finally, the close-out sales.

This marketing strategy was designed to reach a mass undifferentiated audience, but after television, the film industry realized that motion pictures no longer had universal appeal and began targeting audience segments with special promotion campaigns and distribution techniques. Promotion took on two goals: to create a "must see" attitude and to upscale the value of the picture in the minds of the public to justify higher ticket prices. Hollywood relied on the print media to get its message across going into the fifties; afterward, television became the advertising medium of choice. The switch occurred as new shopping mall and multiplex theaters were constructed in the suburbs and as distribution patterns changed.

The turnaround in conventional theatrical exhibition began in the early sixties. Shopping centers followed the migration to the suburbs. As central cities declined, these new developments offered consumers self-enclosed mercantile communities, one-stop shopping, a safe environment, and plenty of free parking. The number of shopping centers leapt from 1,500 in 1965 to 12,500 in 1970 to 22,500 by 1980. The physical design of these theaters was perhaps the most visible change in contemporary exhibition. In comparison to the older palaces downtown, these new structures were plain and Spartan but offered the virtues of intimacy and cleanliness.

Shopping center theaters and multiplexing went hand in hand. A multiplex theater is one that contains two or more screens and is constructed so that the auditoriums share common facilities, such as lobby, box office, and concessions stand. During the sixties, multiplex theaters could be found mostly in shopping centers, but afterward these theaters were also constructed to stand alone in the suburbs or were created by subdividing older theaters downtown. Multiplex theaters had the obvious advantage of offering consumers a range of motion picture choices under one roof. And the more screens in a single setting, the greater chance an exhibitor had for coming up with a popular film. If he had the good fortune of booking a blockbuster, he had the flexibility of opening the picture at two or more screens and then cutting back over time as the popularity waned. Multiplex theaters also enjoyed economies of scale in their operations. When compared to regular four-wall theaters with a single screen, multis with two, four, or more screens cost only fractionally more to operate.

The big picture transformed the old pattern of release from a three-tier to a two-tier playoff. Typically, a blockbuster was released in each market to a few select theaters for extended runs at high admission prices and subsequently to large numbers of theaters to capture the leavings. The big picture also affected release schedules. Instead of distributing pictures at regular intervals throughout the year, companies started to release their important films during the peak seasons of Christmas, Easter, and summer.

When Hollywood started focusing on the youth audience during the seventies, this two-tier playoff, which was a slow form of release, gave way to saturation booking, which is to say a simultaneous release in several theaters in every market. The tremendous success of Universal's *Jaws*, which opened in 464 theaters during its initial release in 1975, set the pattern that the industry has followed since. Today it is not uncommon for a film to open in two thousand theaters. Saturation booking, of course, is ideally designed to take full advantage of television advertising, which reaches large numbers of people over wide areas.

To further offset the risks of producing big-budget pictures, Hollywood found creative ways to generate additional revenue from book tie-ins, merchandising, and market research. Nonetheless, blockbusters remained as speculative as their box office potential. The sixties is replete with big expensive pictures that failed to make it. As will be discussed in Part II, the blockbuster policy of the majors was partly responsible for the recession that hit the industry in 1969.

COLLABORATION

Sale of Feature Films to Syndicated Television

During the early days of television, it was obvious that the new medium—given its goal of programming a full day, every day of the week—could not exist economically without feature films. It was equally obvious during the early days of television why the majors refused to help out. Not only did the majors see television as a competitor; they also saw it as incapable of generating the advertising revenue to pay a fair price for filmed programming.

The need for filmed programming did not become acute, however, until after 1947, when television began its commercial expansion and when a nationwide coaxial cable system had yet to link all the major markets. Local broadcasters had the choice of producing live programming to fill the gaps in their schedules (which was expensive) or of searching out films to lease. The only films available to broadcasters at the time consisted of Westerns, B-features, and serials produced by Poverty Row studios; a few grade-A features produced by independents; and some foreign films.

In considering whether to unlock their film vaults, the majors encountered opposition from craft unions and exhibitors. The studios were free to dispose of the pre-1948 films in their libraries, since they controlled television performance rights and all ancillary rights to their pictures. But the Screen Actors Guild, the Writers Guild of America, and the Directors Guild of America demanded residual compensation to guild members who appeared in features made after August 1, 1948 that were leased to television. Exhibitors, however, characterized the sale of any feature to television as "unfair competition" and threatened to boycott the studios that collaborated with the enemy.

The major companies kept their vaults locked until 1955. In that year, RKO withdrew from motion picture production and sold its assets to General Teleradio, a subsidiary of General Tire & Rubber Company that operated five independent TV stations. The sale marked the first time a major motion picture library became the property of a broadcaster. Since General Teleradio wanted RKO's films primarily for its five O&O television stations, it immediately sold the television distribution rights outside these markets to C&C Television Corporation, a television syndicator, for $15 million. On the heels of the RKO sale, Warner Bros. disposed of its backlog of old films in 1956 for $21 million. Paramount, which had been holding on to its films for possible use on subscription television, finally sold its pre-1948 film library to MCA in 1958 for $50 million.

Television syndicators acquired these film libraries either through outright purchase—as was the case of the RKO and Warner libraries—or through a lease arrangement. In a lease arrangement, the syndicator received the TV rights to the package for a specific period of time and in return paid either a lump sum or a fee plus a share of the profits from TV sales. Studios that retained their old film libraries, such as Columbia and MGM, operated separate departments to handle their film rentals to television.

These pre-1948 features were used by independent stations to provide day-round programming and by affiliates to fill in nonnetwork programming hours, particularly the afternoon and late evening fringe slots. Feature films did well in the ratings, boosting the number of sets in use and occasionally giving independent stations the competitive edge in the ratings over network affiliates. Other than an occasional special, the networks did not use feature films until the sixties, when they became a prime-time staple.

Within three years, then, an estimated 3,700 features, mostly of the pre-1948 vintage, had been sold off by the majors for more than $220 million. The average price per feature rose from ten thousand to seventy-five thousand dollars in this period. Because these films had been fully amortized—that is, their production costs paid for—the sales represented windfall profits for the studios. However, increasing demand for theatrical films revealed that the majors had undervalued their libraries. Within 18 months after the RKO film library hit the market, pre-1948 features grossed an estimated $150 million in the syndication market. When the majors decided to release their post-1948 features to television in the sixties, they would not make the same mistake of undervaluing their product again.

Television Production

Having released their old films to TV, Hollywood found it easy to collaborate again by producing original television programming. Until the mid-1950s, the majors were inhibited from making such a move for reasons already discussed. Nonetheless, the yawning schedules of local stations made film programming a necessity from the start. Live programming was relatively expensive to produce. And besides, few new station managers had the technical facilities, personnel, and know-how to fill out the broadcast day on their own. To meet this demand, literally hundreds of independent telefilm producers entered the first-run syndication market, as it was called, during the late forties. Many of these independents, like their counterparts in motion pictures, were actors, directors, and producers who wanted to share in the profits of their labors. For studio space, they turned to Poverty Row, which greeted them with open arms now that the market for B films was dying.

Early telefilm production was a highly competitive and unstable business. Of the hundreds of producers who entered the first-run syndication market, only a few survived beyond one-shot projects. Since the networks controlled prime time, producers had to settle for nonnetwork fringe time, where audiences and advertising revenue were smaller. Production costs were difficult to contain because labor unions and craft guilds demanded scale wages for workers. Production financing proved almost impossible to secure from banks, which meant that independents had to put up money of their own to break into the syndication market. Faced with these barriers, independent producers specialized mostly in 30-minute, low-budget programs of the action-adventure type—Westerns, crime films, and situation comedies, among others. If the quality of the programming was middling to awful compared to network fare, the constraints of the market were partially to blame.

The major motion picture companies entered telefilm production beginning in 1955. Unlike the early syndicators, the majors supplied programming to the networks during prime time. As the proportion of live prime-time programming on all three networks declined dramatically after 1955, the working relationship between the film industry and commercial broadcasting became Hollywood (the supplier) and

New York (the exhibitor). Simultaneously, the networks repudiated the program hierarchies of influential TV critics who championed dramatic anthology series based on a theatrical model in favor of continuing-character series based on a motion picture model.

From the perspective of the networks, telefilms not only served as a form of quality control but paradoxically also as a means of maintaining their power base. Despite the prestige of the anthology drama, which had become a programming staple during the early fifties, this type of program often contained controversial subject matter and would not "clear" all the affiliates. In contrast, the "dead criticism" and non-topicality of the Hollywood-produced telefilms made them acceptable to sponsors sensitive to offending any customer taste. Telefilms, more-over, solved the time-zone problems that existed, particularly in the West, where live prime-time shows from New York aired too early to capture sizable audiences. But as will be discussed later, the most important motivation for the networks' switch to telefilms was the opportunity to shift the risks of production to outside producers while retaining control over programming.

From the perspective of the majors, telefilms had the advantage of generating revenues from reruns, spin-offs, merchandising, and foreign distribution. Unlike a live program, whose working lifetime was limited to its first network broadcast, a film series was good for endless reruns in the United States and abroad. By 1960 all the European networks were in place. Each year, more and more countries had television; set sales were growing and commercial stations were beginning to get footholds in countries where most of the networks were state owned. Market analysts were predicting that foreign markets would account for 40 percent of total revenues for telefilms, which approximated the percentage for feature films.

The entry of the majors into TV was tentative and imitated the example set by Walt Disney Productions. In signing with ABC to produce "Disneyland," a weekly hour-long series revolving around the Disney theme park, Disney secured the right to devote six minutes of each hour to promote the company's current theatrical releases. It was this concept of using programming as both product and promo-tion that the studios found alluring. After observing the overwhelming success of the "Disneyland" show, the majors began producing series with their names in the titles, such as "Warner Bros. Presents," "The MGM Parade," and "The Twentieth Century–Fox Theatre." Sponsored by the respective studios and containing commercials for forthcoming productions, these series represented advertising expenditures and not sources of profit. And they were not particularly popular.

It was not with these self-promotion vehicles but with the less glamorous television series that Hollywood slowly came to dominate broadcast schedules. The principal telefilm producers in 1960 consisted of Columbia's Screen Gems, Twentieth Century–Fox Television, Warner Bros. Television, and such independents as MCA's Revue Productions, Four Star Television, Ziv Television, and Desilu.

The largest of the group was not a Hollywood major but Revue, the television subsidiary of MCA. The most powerful talent agency in the business, MCA moved into television when studio cutbacks forced its clients out of work. After forming Revue in 1949, MCA successfully negotiated a blanket waiver from the Screen Actors Guild in 1952 that allowed the agency both to represent talent and to produce television shows in which talent appeared. The guild had a rule against agents producing programming, to prevent them simultaneously from acting as a seller and a buyer of talent. The exception made on MCA's behalf was a watershed for the company.

MCA quickly became the unchallenged giant of television production. By the end of the fifties, Revue was supplying a third of the program on prime time. Among the many hits the studio produced in this period are "Alfred Hitchcock Presents," "Bachelor Father," and "The General Electric Theater." Because of the guild waiver, MCA was able to set up its clients—mostly actors—in the TV film business and share the profits from their programs, sometimes as full partners. To further solidify its position in telefilm production, MCA developed trend-setting programming strategies, such as the long form (60- and 90-minute programs), rotating character series, rotating show series, the made-for-television movie, and mini-series.

Solidly in the black from its work in telefilm production, MCA acquired Paramount's library of old films in 1958 for $50 million, giving the company a reservoir of nearly 750 films to rent to television stations. MCA next bought the run-down Universal studio lot for $11 million and then embarked on a modernization program that ultimately cost $110 million. After coming under the scrutiny of the Justice Department, MCA agreed to divorce itself from the talent agency business in 1962. To compensate for the lost agency fees, MCA entered motion picture production the same year by purchasing Universal Pictures and its parent company, Decca Records. MCA had become the world's leading purveyor of motion pictures and television.

Of the old-line Hollywood studios, Columbia was the first to exploit television in a significant way. As a member of the Little Three, Columbia was hit hard by the decreasing demand for B films after the war. The studio had to take drastic measures to survive. Since Columbia owned no theaters, it did not feel constrained from going into television. Through its Screen Gems subsidiary, the company started out producing TV commercials in 1950. Screen Gems broke into telefilm production in 1951, when it contracted with the Ford Motor Company to produce a half-hour anthology series called "The Ford Theater" for NBC. Aired in 1952, four years ahead of shows by any other major studio, "Ford Theater" starred Hollywood names and ran for five years. Screen Gems produced its next big hit in 1954. "Father Knows Best," a comedy series starring Robert Young, also had a network run of five years. In 1956, Screen Gems absorbed two independent distributors with a combined catalog of four hundred films and in 1957 acquired the television rights to Universal's pre-1948 features. These were added to its already substantial film library of features and shorts. Thereafter, Screen Gems functioned as one of the biggest and most diversified operations in the telefilm business.

After the majors entered telefilm production the market underwent consolidation as independent producers either went out of business or merged with larger firms. The first-run syndication market had been declining since 1956, in inverse proportion to the growth of commercial television. As the TV set market became saturated, the networks competed for affiliates to increase the number of viewing homes covered by a network show. By preempting the best hours of the broadcast day, the networks foreclosed outlets for first-run syndication, which by 1964 had become virtually extinct. By the sixties, the market for filmed television programming resembled that for motion pictures, in that there were few buyers (the networks) and a pool of sellers (the producers) with unique products to sell.

Because the networks had taken control of programming, the majors had to deal with three networks largely on the networks' terms. After switching to the magazine format of program sponsorship the networks became essentially financiers of programming, and like their counterparts in motion picture distribution, they exercised their monopsony buying power "to reap the rewards associated with taking greater programming risks," in the words of Barry Litman (Chapter 4). By instituting the "pilot and series" contract, the networks locked producers into long-term contracts that stipulated a set price for the series season by season, even before the pilot was shot and before the project was accepted. This practice eliminated competitive bidding for hit shows. By instituting deficit financing, the networks paid the direct costs of production but not the producer's overhead. This practice meant that producers had to wait until their shows entered syndication before earning any money.

Since a season typically lasted 39 weeks back then, the producer had to invest a considerable amount of money to sustain a series. Even though the series might be cancelled midseason or at the end of the year because of poor ratings, the networks earned revenues from the sale of advertising, while the producer was out his investment. The major Hollywood studios had the financial resources to survive the arrangement, but not many independents did. For a producer to earn back his investment and turn a profit, he had to place his program in syndication after the network run. However, to do well in the syndication market, the series had to accumulate about a hundred episodes or some five seasons' worth of programming. Obviously, few shows could achieve this feat. Local stations preferred this number of episodes so they could "strip in" the series five days a week. At that rate a series lasting five years of prime time would be consumed in five months in syndication.

Deficit financing not only shifted the uncertainties of program development, it could also mean coproduction. In return for putting up partial financing for a series, the networks acquired the rights to share the syndication profits. Derived from network control of prime time and access to the affiliates, profit participation had several spin-off effects: it enabled the networks to enjoy the benefits of integrating upward into production while minimizing the risks; it foreclosed the syndication market to outside independent producers; and it allowed the networks to make money off of nonaffiliates.

Although the telefilm market was volatile, causing the rankings of producers to fluctuate year to year, the move to telefilm production actually saved the day for the rank and file of the film industry. In retrenching, the majors had not only cut back on production, they also began to shoot overseas in what became known as runaway production. Television production, however, opened up many jobs for Hollywood technicians and artistic personnel. For example, MCA, after expanding and renovating the Universal Pictures studio, employed 3,200 people, a number that may have matched the top job marks set by feature film studios during their most active periods during the mid-forties.

In moving into telefilm production, the majors at first opened their doors to independent producers as a means of lowering the overhead costs of their empty studios. The majors next went into telefilm production for themselves as part of a diversification strategy to offset declining revenues from feature film production and distribution. In 1955, Hollywood produced close to 20 percent of the prime-time programs and close to 40 percent of the average television station's daily schedule. Hollywood, in other words, produced ten times as much film for television as it did for theatrical motion picture exhibition. The percentage of prime-time programs originating from the West Coast climbed steadily thereafter, until by the sixties, Columbia, Warner, MGM, and the other studios earned as much as 30 percent of their total revenues from telefilm production. *Television Magazine* conducted a survey of a random week of producing in 1963 to discover that the percentage of prime-time programming from Hollywood had risen to nearly 70 percent. Thirty-one feature films were in the works, compared to 63 network or syndicated television series. These results led the magazine to conclude that "For all practical purposes motion pictures had been shoved aside and Hollywood had become a television production town."[4]

Sale of Feature Films to Network Television

Although Hollywood's oldies had demonstrated their ratings power during the fifties, the issue for the majors was how to capitalize on this potential when the time came to release their post-1948 pictures. Anticipating a boost in demand for recent vintage films when the networks converted to color television, Hollywood reached a settlement with the actors and writers in 1960. And just in time; black and white television had just about saturated the market and broadcasters and set manufacturers were looking to color as a source of new profits. Although the FCC approved RCA's color system in 1953, the company had to sustain a long and costly effort, laying out $130 million over 13 years, to overcome industry resistance to color. From 1954 to 1960, RCA was just about the only color set manufacturer in the market, selling less than one million color sets, which amounted to a tiny fraction of the sets in use. NBC's programming during the late fifties tried to do for color television what its early programming did for black and white. Since ratings for NBC's first color telecasts drew proportionately larger audiences than the audiences that watched the same program in black and white, the network therefore took the lead in color broadcasting to make black and white receivers obsolete. By 1963, NBC telecast nearly three-quarters of its prime-time schedule in color; by 1965, it had completed the conversion. ABC and the foot-dragging CBS soon followed suit.

NBC broke the ice by programming "NBC Saturday Night at the Movies," the first prime-time weekly series of post-1948 features on network television. Launched on September 23, 1961 with *How to Marry a Millionaire*, the series broadcast a package of 35 features, strong in CinemaScope, that NBC bought from Twentieth Century–Fox for $25 million.

The series solved NBC's problems competing for audiences in the Saturday evening time slot. Envious of NBC's strategy, ABC in 1962 became the second network to program a prime-time series of features by launching "Hollywood Special" to bolster Sunday nights with a package of features from United Artists. CBS, the television industry's leading network in this period, did not add a prime-time feature film program until 1965, when it moved to strengthen a weak Thursday night.

The standard arrangement worked out between film companies and networks was for a network to lease a package of 30 films for a period of one to three years, with a right to show each film once and 22 of them twice. This allowed the network to program the package 52 weeks a year. At the end of the lease period, the films reverted to the film company, which could then syndicate the packages to group television or independent TV stations in the United States and abroad. The standard leasing arrangement for syndication allowed a station to run each feature in a package 12 times over seven years. Television distribution typically began 18 months after the end of the theatrical run, first to the networks and then to individual stations.

In determining price with the networks, movie companies had greater bargaining power with features than they had for series programming. Theatrical movies "represented a different species of network programming," explains Barry Litman in Chapter 4. "Their attractiveness [to the networks] derived from knowledge concerning their value in the theatrical premarket. Hence, the risk and uncertainty were significantly lowered for all parties concerned (networks, advertisers, and movie producers) since they were dealing with a known quantity. Because of this, unexpected price wars occurred as each network sought to outbid its rival for the best pictures."

During the early 1960s, a run-of-the-mill feature leased to the networks fetched $150,000. As demand increased, the average jumped to $400,000 in 1965. The following year a new high was reached when ABC paid Columbia $2 million for *The Bridge on the River Kwai*. The picture was used by Ford Motor Company, the sole sponsor, to unveil its 1967 line. When *Kwai* aired on Sunday night, September 12, 1966, it made history; this nine-year-old film attracted an audience of 60 million, beating out the extremely popular "Bonanza" in the ratings, and opened a new era of motion picture blockbusters on TV.

Afterward, competitive bidding by the networks became hectic. In 1967, a total of $270 million had been committed by the networks for the leasing of feature films. By 1968, deals were being closed for eight hundred thousand dollars a picture, as networks scheduled movies every night of the week. This figure was the average price for a regular feature in a package. Hits and blockbusters commanded much higher prices. For example, *Cleopatra* was leased to ABC by Twentieth Century–Fox for $5 million. Thus, by the 1960s, network television had become a regular secondary market for theatrical films. Conventional theatrical exhibition had been considered the primary source of revenues, with anything from TV just "gravy." But as relations between the two industries stabilized, television income became expected and planned for. Few new film projects were put into production without assessing their potential on TV, and a TV sale was used as collateral in obtaining financing.

Demand for feature films created a new form of collaboration—the made-for-television (MFT) movie—and drew two networks into motion picture production. One innovation of long-form television programming, the MFT was designed as an inexpensive alternative to the high-priced Hollywood product, while network-produced features were supposed to compete with Hollywood head-on. The consequences of these decisions are discussed in Part II.

NEW STRUCTURES FOR OLD

Television altered not only the way the American film industry conducted its business but also the very structures of the companies. Starting out after the *Paramount* decrees primarily as producer-distributors of motion pictures, the majors diversified into every aspect of television and into allied leisure-time fields. Paramount was the first film company to take drastic measures to ensure its survival, but the other companies in turn developed strategies to stay alive. In addition to channeling its Screen Gems subsidiary into telefilm production, Columbia was one of the first majors to open its doors to independent motion picture producers. Although United Artists had difficulty breaking into telefilm production, the company made it big in distribution. In addition to distributing an expanding roster of independents each year to theaters and network television, the company consolidated its position in the syndication market by acquiring the Warner Bros. film library in 1957 and the RKO film library in 1959 and by purchasing Ziv Television Programs in 1960. Diversifying further in the fifties, UA branched out into music recording and publishing by forming United Artists Records to cross-promote its motion pictures and by forming United Artists Music to license music from its motion pictures for performance on radio, television, and records.

All the Hollywood majors diversified in similar ways, but during the sixties this diversification trend intensified as the industry entered the age of conglomerates. During the sixties, motion picture companies were either taken over by huge multifaceted corporations, absorbed into burgeoning entertainment conglomerates, or became conglomerates through diversification. The takeover of Paramount by Gulf+Western in 1966 marked the first such entry of a conglomerate into the film industry. This move was followed by the merger of United Artists with Transamerica Corporation, a full-line financial service organization, in 1967; the acquisition of Warner Bros. by Kinney National Services, a conglomerate originally engaged in building maintenance, car rentals, parking lots, and funeral homes, in 1969; and the takeover of MGM by Kirk Kerkorian, a Las Vegas hotel developer, in 1969.

Conglomerates from outside the film industry were attracted to motion picture companies for several reasons: (1) motion picture company stocks were undervalued as a result of the escalating prices features were fetching on television; (2) studios owned strategically located real estate and other valuable assets such as music publishing houses and theaters in foreign countries; and (3) film libraries had the potential of being exploited for cable and pay TV as well as for entirely new forms of exhibition by electronic means.

Although at the time observers of the industry complained Hollywood was being run by outsiders who lacked any traditional respect for their studio's history, institutions, and products, on balance the takeovers benefited the motion picture by reviving moribund managements, by stabilizing operations, and by forcing the industry to adapt to new television technologies. As will be discussed in Part II, conglomerates played and increasingly important role in the film industry in the seventies, as the industry adjusted to a new era of entertainment.

NOTES

1. Alfred Starr, "The Lost Audience Is Still Lost," *Variety*, January 16, 1954, p. 61.
2. "No Letup in 3-D's Sock Impact," *Variety*, February 4, 1953, p. 7.
3. Richard Hincha, "Selling CinemaScope: 1953–1956," *Velvet Light Trap*, 21 (Summer 1985): 46.
4. "The Hollywood Story," *Television Magazine* 20 (September 1963): 33.

Chapter 1 ───────────────────────────

From "Frontal Lobes" to the "Bob-and-Bob" Show: NBC Management and Programming Strategies, 1949–65

Vance Kepley, Jr.

───

*T*he evolution of NBC's programming strategies over the first decade and a half of the company's television service provides an overall understanding of the early development of network television. Consider how substantially NBC's service changed from the late 1940s to the middle 1960s: the company shifted from live programs to predominantly telefilms; it abandoned a schedule noted largely for its specials to implement one characterized by the routines of series programming; it established a policy of acquiring its shows from a stable set of outside program suppliers; it led the way in the move from full sponsorship to participation advertising; and it established a news division that prospered by combining journalism with show business. This reads like an inventory of the changes that redefined the entire industry, and by the end of this transition, NBC would be following practices that would remain virtually fixed among all three networks through the 1960s and 1970s and into the cable age.

Certainly the most familiar historical characterization of this transistion falls back on the hoary metaphors of "Golden Age" and "Vast Wasteland." Historians hold that the changes substantially diminished the quality of American television, that an early flush of vitality passed with the advent of standardized, homogeneous programming fare. The common charge is that a generation of bold broadcasting pioneers (Fred Friendly, Pat Weaver) who were willing to experiment with the medium gave way to more cost-conscious executives (James Aubrey, Oliver Treyz, Robert Kintner) who abandoned the pursuit of excellence for the pursuit of corporate profits. This account becomes localized around NBC's case through the apparent contrast between the programming strategies of Sylvester "Pat" Weaver in the early 1950s and those of his successors Robert Sarnoff and Robert Kintner in the late 1950s and early 1960s. Weaver's highly varied schedule of live programs and specials seemed to make a clear contrast with the succession of Westerns, quiz shows, and sitcoms that ensued. Sarnoff and Kintner have become handy villains in this saga, figures who seemed more attentive to the balance sheet than to balanced programming and who thus betrayed the medium's early promise.[1]

Establishing heroes and villains will do little to help us understand the early evolution of NBC, let alone that of the television industry as a whole. The changes effected by Sarnoff, Kintner, and others had more to do with the shifting economies of broadcasting than any personal dispositions. The industry had evolved in a way that called for routinized programming, just as a few years earlier industry relations had permitted, even encouraged, a brief period of experimentation.[2] Our best course for understanding the strategies of a Weaver, a Sarnoff, or a Kintner might be to analyze their actions in the context of the general economics of commercial television. This cast of characters can then be seen to have acted more as pragmatic corporate managers than as heroes or villains.

Most broadly put, advertiser-supported commercial television is an example of a public goods industry. As such, it follows a rather predictable developmental pattern over time, and a given firm within that industry (NBC) might realize its optimal growth potential by conforming to that pattern. As we shall see, this developmental curve militated for NBC to exploit live, varied programs during its initial phase of operations but then to opt for a regularized schedule after achieving a measure of maturity. A theoretical model of a public good like television will provide considerable explanatory power for NBC's programming strategies during the period under consideration.

PUBLIC GOODS THEORY AND NBC

The public good label, when applied to television, might create certain misconceptions. It is not to be confused with public television (PBS), which gets its name from a reliance on tax dollars. And even though commercial broadcasters are licensed by the Federal Communications Commission (FCC) to operate in the "public interest," the term *public good* has nothing to do with the various kinds of public service activities licensed broadcasters have traditionally been expected to perform. The *public good* label refers only to the industry's economic qualities.

The fundamental characteristic of a public goods industry is one in which any firm within that industry can serve at least one additional customer without consuming finite resources and without incurring any additional cost. An economist would employ more technical language, saying that the public goods firm can operate at "zero marginal cost." This seemingly minor distinction, the zero marginal cost potential of a public good, actually explains a whole host of ways in which the public goods firm is likely to behave.[3]

One way to characterize a public good more specifically would be to compare it with its opposite, a private consumption good. Economist Paul Samuelson noted that a private consumption good might be something like bread, "whose total can be parcelled out among two or more persons, with one man having a loaf more if another gets a loaf less"; by contrast, a public good might be a circus, which "is provided for all to enjoy or not according to his tastes."[4] In other words, the baker must bake a new loaf to serve another customer, and he/she makes an additional expenditure for labor and materials in the process, thus failing to realize a zero marginal cost. The circus performance is produced through a single large expenditure in advance. As particular patrons arrive and purchase their tickets for the performance, they do not force any additional operating costs on the circus, and it thus functions at zero marginal cost. A mass transportation system provides another useful example of a public good. A bus service operates through a fixed budget without particular regard to whether an individual bus is full or empty at any one time. When a given bus stops to take on another fare, the bus line's operating budget is not affected. At a certain point, in fact, each new fare can be considered pure profit because the bus company gets a full fare without experiencing any new costs.

Advertiser-supported television conforms to this mode. The principal costs of a television service are incurred up front, in the production of the shows and in the establishment of an electronic system for their distribution. Once those large expenditures are met, the service can be provided on a more-or-less stable budget, and certainly the decision of a given television viewer to tune in and enjoy the service has no effect on that budget: hence the criterion of zero marginal cost.

This situation can work to the advantage of the television broadcaster. Although the broadcaster operates at zero marginal cost, serving new viewers at no expense, the broadcaster nevertheless charges advertisers for each new viewer to the extent that advertising billings are tied to audience size. The advertiser pays the broadcaster for each additional viewer even though the broadcaster's expenditures remain constant. The broadcaster, like the mass transit company, can see pure profit after a certain point. This provides a very favorable economy of scale for the broadcaster, resulting in high profits after the break-even threshold.

This pattern can explain the growth strategies of a public goods firm such as a television company. The company might incur annual losses over the first several years of its operation while it deals with expensive start-up problems. It must be able to deficit-spend during this initial developmental phase. But those deficits might represent investments in the future if the initial spending helps to build up the company's audience and thus its potential to earn larger advertiser revenues. As the audience grows, the company will eventually pass the break-even point, after which it will be more likely to economize by regularizing its operation. In this mature phase, the company will seek to keep costs constant, striving for zero marginal costs, and it will then presumably reap the benefits of a potentially geometric yearly increase in profits.

How might NBC's situation conform to this pattern in the period 1949 to 1965? An old radio network, NBC in the late 1940s had to confront the prospect of establishing its television service virtually from scratch. In doing so, it could not even count on converting its radio talent to television, as competitor CBS planned to do; NBC had just lost its biggest names (e.g., Jack Benny, Burns and Allen) to the Columbia network when William Paley pulled off the famous "talent raid by offering imaginative financial incentives." In addition, the NBC television network only included 25 affiliates in 1949, with a coverage area that barely exceeded the East Coast industrial corridor.[5]

Weaver was hired in 1949 precisely to develop NBC's fledgling television company. Although his previous experience had been in advertising with the Young and Rubicam agency, Weaver had been in charge of developing radio talent for the firm's clients. His experience in program development recommended him for the job of running the television network, since he was going to have to build virtually an entire schedule. Daunting as the task may have seemed, Weaver and his associates could count on the enormous financial resources of NBC's parent company, RCA. The U.S. leader in electronics development and manufacturing, RCA ran NBC as a wholly owned subsidiary. RCA could specifically allocate funds to establish NBC's new television service as part of an ongoing research and development budget. It could also comfortably allow NBC to operate in the red for several years, with the expectation that the network service would boost sales of RCA television hardware until such time as the network started to turn its own profits.[6]

Weaver held several top management posts between 1949 and 1955, culminating with his being made president and chairman of NBC-TV. During this period he maintained considerable personal control over television programming no matter what office he held, and his policies translated into considerable red ink as he spent lavishly to build up the network. When he was finally removed from power in December 1955 by RCA chairman David Sarnoff, NBC had begun to show profits, but Sarnoff and the RCA board rightly judged that NBC needed to abandon growth-oriented policies in favor of operating stability. Indeed, NBC could claim 189 affiliates with considerable signal coverage by late 1955, and national set ownership stood at 64.5 percent. The time had come to run NBC on a more cost-effective basis, and a management change brought that about. Sarnoff put his son Robert in charge of the television operation, and in 1956 the younger Sarnoff had acquired the services of ABC veteran Robert Kintner. If Weaver had a record in developing new shows, Kintner at ABC had proven that he could program a network on a tight budget, and it was that credential that brought him to NBC. The two Roberts—the industry dubbed them the "Bob-and-Bob Show"—shared responsibility for the television service through 1965, with young Sarnoff handling general network policy while Kintner concentrated on the details of programming. The mandate of the Sarnoff-Kintner management team was to cut costs and to put the network on a consistent and profitable course.[7]

Rather than accusing Sarnoff and Kintner of disloyalty to Weaver's initiatives, we should note how the two regimes complemented each other. NBC needed the services of a Weaver to establish the network, and it then needed the services of a Kintner to render the company profitable. The two were merely operating at different points on the same developmental curve. To understand just how one management system complemented the other, we must examine each in greater detail.

THE WEAVER YEARS, 1949–55

Weaver joined NBC with a clear developmental plan, and he recognized that financial yield would be slow in coming. He stressed the need to extend the network's coverage by the quick acquisition of affiliates. He also insisted that only a highly varied NBC program chart would encourage private consumers to purchase their first television sets and thereby boost audience size. Only with increases in the audience and the signal coverage could the NBC service be made profitable, but NBC had to take the initiative.[8]

To these ends, Weaver never hesitated to spend NBC's (and RCA's) money. He solicited large allocations from RCA for such ventures as new program development (1949–51) and color conversion (1953–54). He urged NBC's affiliate relations department to make substantial financial concessions to new television stations in order to secure from them affiliation contracts, thereby extending NBC's coverage. He even advocated that NBC steal profits from its lucrative owned-and-operated stations to underwrite the expansion of the national network. Such policies helped NBC-TV run up $5.5 million in losses by 1953.[9]

Weaver's famed preference for live programs over telefilms can be explained as a developmental imperative. It is attributable to the priority he assigned to extending the network's coverage. He was not unaware of the technical advantages of using filmed programming. RCA engineers reported that high-quality, low-cost equipment could improve film transmission, and RCA's Joint Committee on Film Usage projected that a quick conversion to telefilms would save NBC money. And although the Hollywood majors remained on the sideline during much of the Weaver era, plenty of smaller studios, syndicators, and packagers were available to supply NBC with telefilms. In fact, NBC even dealt briefly with Disney for a production package, and the collapse of that negotiation eventually led to the important ABC-Disney contract of 1954.[10]

Despite these policy pressures, Weaver sought to maintain a schedule noted for its live performances, whether the genre be variety ("Your Show of Shows"), drama ("Goodyear/Philco Television Playhouse"), comedy ("Colgate Comedy Hour"), or talk ("Today," "Tonight"). His rationale was that NBC affiliates would not maintain their contracts if the network was not offering them a live feed. Were the network simply buying telefilms from a West Coast syndicator or packager and feeding them to local stations each night via coaxial cable, Weaver suspected that the stations would see no need to remain in the chain. Local stations could simply go to the syndicators and packagers on their own to secure their programming, without any NBC affiliation. Weaver summed up the problem in his first major policy statement: "I believe that the coaxial network structure will be undermined by film."[11]

Weaver felt that the greatest incentive for new stations to join the chain, and for old stations to remain, resided in NBC's access to high-priced New York talent that would be offered to local stations only in live feeds. His variety programs, dramas, and the like would feature talent that no syndicator, let alone local station, could hope to afford. He exploited live programs to make affiliates dependent on the Radio City feed and to differentiate television's product from that of a competitor, the film industry. "Television is not movies," Weaver insisted. "It is show business in the living room."[12]

If new stations could be expected to affiliate thanks to NBC programming, Weaver designed his schedule to increase viewership as well. Only a line-up that featured special attractions would encourage families to invest in that all-important box for the living room. Set purchases would allow NBC to raise advertising rates while benefiting RCA's consumer electronics market. A schedule that continued to rely on the routine of radio series formats would not make families change their entertainment habits, nor would it encourage advertisers to shift accounts from radio to television. Weaver served notice that variety, not the formulaic weekly series, would encourage television's quick growth, and this meant "avoiding the follow-the-formula race that was so little help to radio."[13]

Weaver mounted numerous one-time-only specials—which he labeled, with a Madison Avenue sense of hyperbole, "Spectaculars"–in order to attract viewer interest. Each special was to be heavily promoted in advance, especially on radio, with the idea that new viewers could be drawn to the medium through "event programming." The network offered a range of specials with an eye toward different audience segments: "Peter Pan" for children, "Richard III" for adults interested in prestige programming, "Satins and Spurs" for fans of the Broadway musical tradition, and "Amahl and the Night Visitors" for the holiday family trade. Weaver even made sure to rotate the times and evenings of each special in the hope of eventually reaching all audience segments no matter what their weekly schedules. The specials were intended to make first-time television viewers out of heretofore satisfied radio listeners and loyal television viewers out of heretofore indifferent ones. As one NBC executive explained: "We get them coming for the caviar, and they stick around . . . for the bread and butter."[14]

The specials took on an added dimension after David Sarnoff won the notorious "color system war" in 1953. Future NBC specials were to be mounted in color to encourage the market for RCA-patented color hardware. This boosted the already impressive production costs for the specials and the financial risks for NBC. The specials cost NBC three-to-five times the figure for standard programming on a minute-by-minute basis, and even though NBC charged advertisers the highest cost-per-household rate in the industry for commercial time on the specials, NBC always absorbed losses on the ventures. But these short-term risks could be rationalized for their contribution to broader company interests. Weaver's varied and expensive schedule operated as a "loss leader" for the company. Just as a grocer might sell some products at a loss to attract buyers into the store, Weaver's profligate ways were constructing the future market for NBC.[15]

NBC's financial risk extended into the network's regularly scheduled shows as well as its specials. As part of a plan to take programming power away from advertisers and to establish a more flexible network schedule, Weaver put NBC on a course of in-house production of its shows. The traditional radio procedure whereby sponsors produced their own programs and simply offered them to the network for distribution constrained the network's creative and scheduling authority. The sponsor enjoyed creative control over its show and held something approximating a year-long lease on its slot in the network's schedule. By producing more of its own shows, Weaver calculated, NBC could establish a more balanced program schedule. It could make sure that different programs complemented each other, and the shows could be positioned in the schedule according to some program logic. Advertising time on the network-produced shows could then be offered to several companies. Different advertisers would purchase units of time on the network shows but could not exercise creative or scheduling authority. Weaver liked to call this his "magazine concept" because it followed the common practice in the magazine industry of leaving editorial control with the magazine rather than the advertiser.[16]

The most celebrated example of how Weaver linked in-house production with scheduling balance and new sales policies was Weaver's "T-H-T Plan." The name came from a complementary set of shows Weaver conceived and developed: "Today," "Home," and "Tonight." Each was produced by NBC without benefit of prior sponsorship. Each involved somewhat loose daily formats, which could then be split in such a way that different advertisers could buy particular 15- or 30-minute segments. By offering small units of time in these and other shows, Weaver calculated that he could lower the entry costs for new television advertisers. A small manufacturer might not be able to sponsor an entire television program, especially since television production costs promised to soar above those of radio, but the manufacturer could easily buy 15-minute segments here and there in a network-produced schedule. In the case of T-H-T, NBC's sales department specifically targeted advertisers who were looking for discount time as a way of breaking into the television market. Network sales agents were instructed to ignore the Fortune 500 in locating clients and to offer potential advertisers the opportunity to buy segments of time on all three shows, so as to reach different audience segments. Participation advertising, as best demonstrated in the T-H-T arrangements, promised to enhance NBC's future market by increasing the number of advertisers involved in the medium.[17]

T-H-T contributed to network scheduling logic by virtue of the fact that the shows were designed to be distributed across the programming day, thereby enhancing viewership in each major day block. The chatty "Today" was modeled on morning radio and designed to get viewers used to the idea of watching television in the morning, to counter the assumption that television was only something to be consumed in evening prime time. Its success carried over to other morning shows through audience flow and encouraged local affiliates to maintain a full morning schedule. "Home" was calculated to appeal to housewives by offering cooking and domestic advice and was run at midday so as to sustain the middle of NBC's schedule. "Tonight" imitated night club entertainment and appropriately ran after prime time. Its function was to extend NBC's schedule into the last fringe time segment, a period previously conceded to local affiliates, and it capped off Weaver's notion that the viewing day had to extend from the time one got up in the morning until bedtime—and beyond; indeed, an apparent consequence of "Tonight" was the fact that some households purchased a second television for the master bedroom, where adults could enjoy Steve Allen from the comfort of the marriage bed.[18]

In-house production involved a high measure of risk for the network. NBC would have to absorb developmental costs while shows were being established and larger losses for shows that happened to fail. At the height of this program development, the period 1949–51, NBC took $1.25 million in losses on its own properties when ten of NBC's new productions ran in the red. But Weaver aggressively pushed home production on the expectation that neither sponsors nor outside packagers would provide the quality or balance of programming that would enhance NBC's overall schedule. To facilitate program innovation within NBC, Weaver even reorganized the company bureaucracy. He established something like a unit-producer system whereby the producer of each NBC property would enjoy considerable creative and administrative autonomy. The unit producer could control issues like hiring, firing, and salaries within the production unit without having to deal with middle-management figures in such areas as the personnel department. By the end of Weaver's reign, NBC claimed whole or part ownership of half of its program line-up.[19]

Weaver's penchant for live shows, varied programming fare, and program innovation clearly had more to do with canny developmental schemes than with any essential quest for broadcast Excellence with a capital E. The same is true, ironically, for the Weaver policy most commonly associated with pro bono broadcasting—NBC's public-service programming campaign, dubbed "Operation Frontal Lobes." With all the fanfare suggested by that slogan, Weaver announced that NBC would fund a sustained campaign of educational and informational programs aimed specifically to fulfill and even exceed NBC's public-service mandate. The programs would be produced at NBC's expense and given prominent scheduling whether or not sponsors could be found to underwrite the effort.[20]

Weaver seemed to ignore the broadcasting truism that ambitious public-affairs broadcasting discourages advertisers and drains network resources. He certainly made good on the lofty "Frontal Lobes" promise. Weaver personally conceived or supported several admirable examples of informational television. His series programs included innovative documentary work, most notably the "Victory at Sea" series. His specials included the many historical documentaries produced under the "Project XX" rubric, one-hour compilation films that dealt with particular events in U.S. and world history. He innovated a series of interviews with intellectuals and artists (Margaret Mead, Edward Steichen), which he labeled, with typical immodesty, the "Wisdom" series. Weaver even insisted that entertainment and variety shows include cultural or educational elements. Thus an entertainment vehicle like "Your Show of Shows" would have to include a Verdi aria alongside the vaudeville acts and Sid Caesar skits. Weaver ordered all unit producers to submit a regular "Responsibility Report" itemizing how each unit contributed in some way to the overall "Frontal Lobes" quota.[21]

Even these service ventures had their developmental function, however. Weaver used the programs and the beneficial image they created for NBC in his campaign to extend NBC's affiliate line-up. Potential affiliates could look to the network for some of the service programming that licensed stations would have to disseminate under the FCC's public-service mandate. Weaver also hoped that the "Frontal Lobes" PR would have a direct effect on the FCC. This seemed to be especially timely during the "Freeze" period (1948–52) when the FCC reviewed options for how to allocate new television channels. Weaver had to worry that the commission would devise an allocation plan informed by antitrust policy or the doctrine of localism, which would have precluded the establishment of coast-to-coast coverage of the network signal, thereby thwarting NBC's whole developmental program. "Frontal Lobes" would illustrate how a national network could work to the benefit of American society. Only a television organization with deep pockets—a national, commercial network—could afford to produce and distribute such ambitious public-service material. The very size, scope, and cost of "Frontal Lobes" served to demonstrate Weaver's political case for networking as the key to quality. "The FCC is supposed to represent the interests of the people," Weaver maintained. "And the interests of the people are served by a healthy, advertiser-supported television industry, operating efficently on a national basis."[22]

Public service, like Weaver's other policies of live programming, scheduling innovations, and participation advertising, served to usher NBC through its expensive developmental phase. By the middle 1950s, NBC and the television industry generally were entering a new phase, one that called for different management skills.

THE SARNOFF-KINTNER YEARS, 1956–65

When David Sarnoff announced in late 1955 that his son would take over direction of NBC's television operation, the move was initially viewed as simple nepotism, and indeed Robert proved to be on the fast track to the RCA board. But Robert's new job was part of a more fundamental policy change. NBC was moving out of its costly growth period and into a mature phase, out of product development and into product delivery. It devolved upon the younger Sarnoff to cuts costs and stabilize operations, to work toward that flattened cost curve, which is at least theoretically available to the purveyors of a public good.

RCA had initially subsidized NBC-TV by writing off losses as part of a regular research and development budget. By the middle 1950s, however, RCA was preparing to move into other areas. The company wanted to expand its consumer goods line in large appliances such as refrigerators and ranges in order to exploit the continued prosperity of America's postwar consumer economy. RCA also geared up for an ambitious and very risky venture: it would challenge IBM for control of the young but promising computer market—a move, incidentally, that would end in financial disaster some years later. RCA immediately transfered developmental monies to white goods and computers, meaning that its existing subsidiaries like NBC would have to pay their own way.[23]

The new era of economy at NBC was signaled in 1955 when David Sarnoff retained the services of the consulting firm Booz, Allen and Hamilton to review NBC's management and operations with an eye toward savings. The efficiency experts called for a thorough reorganization of NBC's management structure. Weaver's policy of autonomous production units might have been useful when the company needed to develop new shows quickly, but it provided few mechanisms for holding down costs. NBC was advised to reinsert layers of middle management, which Weaver had purged or bypassed. A more formal and stratified management system promised long-range stability for a company now interested in cost and quality controls. Meanwhile, Weaver had been removed from his one-man control of programming by being kicked upstairs to the company board; he soon took the hint and resigned. Robert Sarnoff's first major task was to establish a chain of command based on the consultant's report. He did so by inserting a new layer of vice-presidents and department heads and by dispersing much authority for day-to-day affairs through middle management. "There's no doubt that Sarnoff is boss," an NBC executive noted in describing the new system, "but so far most of the decisions have been arrived at by consensus."[24]

Under Sarnoff's new division of management labor, he would look after the general financial health of the network and find someone else to take charge of programming. He secured the services of a worthy associate by hiring Robert Kintner, who left ABC in 1956 during a management shake-up. His ABC record perfectly prepared him for the new austerity at NBC. He had supervised the smaller network's television schedule from 1950 until his departure and demonstrated that he could provide a credible program line-up on limited resources. ABC's strategy involved programming filmed series rather than big-budget live productions and specials. ABC kept its costs down by licensing outside program suppliers, most notably Warner Bros., and by keeping away from the risks of home production. Frugal as ABC's policies may have been, they resulted in the company's first significant ratings successes. The action programs ("Jim Bowie") and Westerns ("Cheyenne") that filled the ABC schedule in the middle 1950s began to attract the young viewers whose presence in front of the picture tube was of such interest to advertisers.[25]

The Sarnoff-Kintner strategy involved consolidating the gains Weaver had made in network size and competing more directly against the other two networks. Since NBC had a national signal by 1956 and since the vast majority of American homes were now television homes, market growth was no longer the paramount issue. Network television was becoming more and more a "zero-sum game" among three competitors, whereby the gains of any one network came at the expense of the other two. Under the new rules of the zero-sum game, success would be measured strictly by ratings and billings, not by how many new stations came on-line, and according to these cold measures, NBC was in big trouble in 1956, running well behind its archrival CBS. NBC had no programs in the Trendex top-ten, and it could not claim a ratings lead in any night of the week. Worse, it trailed CBS by 19 per cent in annual billings. If the company were to be put on a securely profitable footing, these things would have to change.[26]

Sarnoff and Kintner put the industry on notice that NBC was preparing to compete head-to-head. Live shows would give way to telefilms; the specials would be fewer and less expensive; and public-service programming would simply have to wait its turn. NBC's new look involved Westerns ("Wagon Train", "Restless Gun"), action series ("M Squad"), and game shows ("Twenty-One"). To describe his first complete program schedule, the fall 1957 line-up, Kintner seized on a tried culinary metaphor: "The theory of NBC is basically to create what we call a schedule of meat-and-potatoes. . . ."[27]

Live programming, particularly live drama such as the prestigious anthology tradition, was proving to be anachronistic. The relative ease and economy of shooting drama on film was long apparent to industry leaders, including, we recall, one Pat Weaver. Weaver had stuck with live formats to hold the affiliates in place. By 1956, however, the stability of the coaxial network was assured, and this only partly resulted from Weaver's doing. An unexpected ally in sustaining national networking turned out to be the FCC, through the instrument of the channel allocation plan it implemented at the end of the freeze.

The FCC virtually assured that the major networks would dominate commercial television. The allocation plan distributed precious VHF channels in a way that benefited the majors. Most markets received only two or three VHF allocations. As soon as those stations went on-line, they were offered attractive affiliation contracts by the networks, and in markets where only two VHF channels were open, the broadcasting Big Two moved in ahead of ABC and DuMont. Independent stations and ABC and DuMont affiliates were usually banished to the nether realm of UHF, where they operated at a serious disadvantage because their signals were technically inferior and because many home receiver sets were not even equipped for UHF. It might have required some time for the consequences of the allocations to become evident—Weaver never seems to have anticipated them—but they were certainly manifest by the late 1950s: 153 UHF stations began service after the freeze, but by 1956, 63 of them had folded. The major networks need not fear competition for national coverage. Clearly the power of NBC's coaxial network no longer depended on live feeds.[28]

While this last disincentive for filmed programming was being rendered obsolete by FCC action, new opportunities for film were being touted throughout the television industry. The possibilities for syndication and for the overseas sale of programming were emerging as attractive residual sources, and only filmed properties could be fully exploited in these new markets. The overseas situation held special promise as more and more foreign broadcast systems commenced operations in the late 1950s and promptly began securing U.S. product to fill air time. Industry projections held that from 1957 through 1962, 40 percent of the total revenue of U.S. television programming would come from foreign sales. The networks were not about to concede all such riches to program producers. Licensing contracts, which included a share of residuals, would represent a simple, safe way for the networks to exploit these markets.[29]

Indeed, if the Kintner era meant more film and less live work, it also meant more outside program procurement and less in-house production. Kintner explicitly advocated that his new network follow the example of ABC by cultivating good relations with a few reliable program producers and establishing durable licensing arrangements with them. As it happened, NBC's previous record of in-house production attracted the unwanted attention of the Justice Department in 1956. In the name of a more plural and open television market, NBC was advised to give more business to independent program suppliers or face the prospect of an antitrust action. Not that he needed particular urging, but Kintner did just that. By 1959, NBC's ownership of shows had dropped by 20 percent. Among other considerations, this new reliance on outside suppliers would reduce NBC's overhead and risk, thus allowing Sarnoff to trim NBC's overall operating budget. As NBC-owned shows were replaced by outside packages, NBC laid off personnel and streamlined operations.[30]

Kintner made good on his promise to cultivate relations with proven program suppliers. He dealt with MCA and its television subsidiary, Revue Productions, for such genres as Westerns ("Wagon Train") and filmed dramas ("Crisis"). To cash in on the quiz show phenomenon, NBC worked with Barry and Enright, a packager of game show entertainments, and was rewarded with the hits "Twenty-One" and "Tic Tac Dough". Such on-going relations with a few program suppliers promised to assure NBC a consistent annual supply of programming. When Sarnoff appeared at the network affiliates' meeting in 1958, he promised station owners that NBC's new acquisitions policy would assure "stability." Clearly stability had replaced innovation as the NBC watchword.[31]

Stability was certainly the essence of NBC's relationship with MCA. By the early 1960s, MCA had become for NBC what Warner Bros. had been for ABC a few years earlier, a virtual programming partner. The ratings success of certain MCA offerings, particularly the chart-topping "Wagon Train," persuaded Kintner that he could purchase new properties from MCA without the necessity of a pilot. He reportedly worked closely with MCA vice-president Sonny Werblin on planning each year's schedule, with MCA then designing packages to fit NBC's particular program needs. One famous anecdote had Kintner saying to Werblin, "Sonny, look at the schedule for next season; here are the empty shots, fill them." Whatever measure of industry apocrypha there may have been in that story, it is certain that NBC formalized a consistent, risk-free option contract with MCA. For network broadcast rights to a new property, MCA received a flat fee that only covered Revue's basic costs of production. If the show succeeded, the network's advertising billings would increase in relation to growing ratings, with no commensurate share of that increase going back to the production company. Risk was controlled; costs were controlled. NBC's investment in a show remained contractually fixed, while NBC's revenues increased with the show's ratings—a situation exactly predicted by the cost and revenue relations of a mature public goods firm.[32]

Stability would also derive from a program schedule with predictable daily and weekly offerings. Kintner dismissed Weaver's penchant for specials as a form of programming glitz that failed to cultivate the consistent viewing habits upon which ratings could be based. Entertainment specials in the Sarnoff-Kintner years were limited to particular occasions, such as holidays, or to plans by individual advertisers to support "high-impact" programs (e.g., "The Hallmark Hall of Fame" productions). Specials no longer promised to attract new viewers to the medium; television was thoroughly a part of the American domestic routine by the late 1950s. Kintner sought instead to encourage the habitual consumption of NBC shows, and that meant a consistent line-up that would not be disrupted by specials. Indeed, Kintner could cite cases where specials undermined NBC's ratings: Kintner put the popular quiz show "Twenty-One" up against CBS's ratings champ "I Love Lucy" and gradually began to narrow CBS's lead in that period. He noted that NBC lost ground, however, after the game show was preempted for previously contracted specials.[33]

Whatever the merits of these program offerings—and television critics loudly lamented NBC's abandonment of serious anthology dramas for cowboys, cops, and robbers—Kintner's strategy produced ratings and billings results. NBC quickly overtook CBS in daytime ratings and gradually whittled away at CBS's power in the all-important prime time. By the early 1960s NBC pulled even, and then edged very slightly into the lead during the 1964–65 season. In 1965, the last year of the Sarnoff-Kintner collaboration, NBC reported record billings of $470 million. Kintner's meat-and-potatoes servings seemed to benefit Sarnoff's overall household budget.[34]

NBC's table featured at least one Kintner hors d'oeuvre, however, that of a prominent news division. Kintner took special pride in NBC news, even though network journalism had never been considered lucrative and expenditures on news would seem to run counter to management's obsession with the bottom line. Kintner had been a journalist in his youth, and in fact, his journalistic credentials landed him at ABC in the first place. But his support for the news division also made corporate sense. Kintner's famous slogan of "CBS plus 30"—meaning that NBC would match CBS's weekly coverage of events and even add 30 minutes to the amount—had something of the traits of Weaver's old "Frontal Lobes" campaign, a public affairs effort that was designed to win political capital and enhance the network's image. In Kintner's case, however, he managed the campaign with an eye toward the company's balance sheet.[35]

Kintner calculated that NBC could cover special events and still find ways to cash in. He also looked to news specials to secure viewership for NBC's regular evening news broadcasts, thereby complementing his stress on habit viewing. Rather than lots of educational or cultural specials à la Weaver, Kintner's news division organized their specials around timely events, "hot topics" for which there was much immediate, and sometimes perhaps ephemeral, interest among the population. Thus when he canceled an entire day's schedule to cover Pope Paul VI's visit to New York, he banked on an intense but short-lived viewer curiosity. He also supported a three-and-one-half-hour special on American foreign policy and a three-hour report on civil rights. Those who tuned in for these topical programs were also expected to familiarize themselves with the network's news personnel and to decide to become loyal watchers of NBC's evening news report.[36]

The success of "The Huntley-Brinkley Report" bore this out. In this case, political conventions served as the specials that secured the program's regular viewership. The 1956 conventions brought the two newsmen together and led to their promotion to coanchors on the evening broadcasts, and their ratings success at the 1960 conventions carried over to nightly ratings, where they built up a formidable lead over "The CBS Evening News." Good ratings for a news broadcast in early evening could sustain subsequent prime-time programs on the principle of audience flow, Kintner calculated, and he treated the evening news as another show business problem. NBC appealed to star-system conventions in publicizing the two anchors, and it took delight in such phenomena as fan mail and autograph seekers for Huntley and Brinkley. To add flair to the evening broadcasts, NBC even commissioned composer Jacques Belasco to write a distinctive theme song. News executive Reuven Frank was quick to admit that the news program's success was "a phenomenon of show business rather than the news business."[37]

Even the allocation of precious prime time to cover news and special events, though it often meant foregoing lucrative entertainments, could be managed economically. The famous expansion of the evening news from 15 to 30 minutes, undertaken by both CBS and NBC in September 1963, worked to the financial benefit of the networks. The cost of production of a 30-minute news broadcast is not substantially more than that for 15 minutes, since many expenses are fixed in salaries and facilities. The networks could (and often did) fill the extra time with soft news features produced on a shoestring. Meanwhile, the doubling of the broadcast's length added a precious 5 minutes of commercial time, which the network could sell to advertisers, more than making up for any budgetary increase.[38]

The same canny exploitation of resources informed Kintner's policy on scheduling prime-time news specials and documentaries such as "NBC White Paper." NBC's news division was organized in such a way that up to 40 percent of the cost of any news documentary or special was already absorbed into the division's prior budget in salaries and materials. An hour-long news special could actually be produced at less overall cost to the network than the license fee for an hour-long entertainment program. When NBC ran a news documentary, they scheduled it in their weakest slots, usually up against a CBS ratings leader like "Gunsmoke" on the theory that the more expensive NBC entertainment show relegated to this time would lose money anyway. Then NBC would sell commercial time to specialized or institutional advertisers, hoping to counter-program CBS's presumably middle-brow ("Gunsmoke") fare. NBC had a standing arrangement with Gulf Oil, for example, giving them first refusal on commercial time in news documentaries, a plan that banked on the oil company's interest in image advertising. NBC could thus contain its losses through an efficient exploitation of its news resources.[39]

In this as in other policies, Sarnoff and Kintner held the line on operating expenses and established NBC's status as a mature, profitable public goods firm. If Weaver's spending pushed the company up over the threshold of profitability, Sarnoff and Kintner's stingier procedures assured the network's long-range health. Indeed, consider how fundamentally Weaver's policies prepared the way for the Sarnoff-Kintner era. If Weaver's live shows and innovations expanded NBC's potential market, Kintner's series programs secured NBC's substantial market share. If Weaver removed program power from sponsors by participation advertising and in-house production, Kintner's standardized contracts with outside suppliers completed the transfer of power while decreasing NBC's risk. If Weaver's public-service campaign won goodwill for a young network, Kintner's reorganization of the whole news division maintained that dimension while rationalizing news's functions. Far from betraying Weaver's legacy, Sarnoff and Kintner simply carried the company through its next logical stage of activity.

By the time Sarnoff and Kintner left network operations in the middle 1960s—the former to join RCA and the latter to retire from network broadcasting—NBC's future course was set.[40] It would continue to cultivate habit viewing with "least objectionable" series fare. Its news division would follow the entertainment staff's lead in securing a loyal audience. NBC would continue buying series programs from West Coast suppliers and exploiting its oligopsony power in option contracts. It would sell time to numerous advertisers through participation and use its oligopoly status to charge high prices for national coverage. It would compete head-to-head with its fellow oligopolists for market share while cooperating with them on procedures for buying programs and selling time.[41] Network practices remained substantially unchanged until the 1980s, when cable finally promised to alter the nature of the game.

NOTES

1. This familiar historical account is perhaps most prominent in Erik Barnouw, *Tube of Plenty*, rev. ed. (New York: Oxford University Press, 1982), pp. 260–65.
2. The best discussion of these changed industry relations is James L. Baughman, "Television in the 'Golden Age': An Entrepreneurial Experiment," *The Historian* 47 (1985): 175–95.
3. The following summary of public goods theory and its application to television draws from: Paul Samuelson, "Diagrammatic Exposition of a Theory of Public Expenditure," *Journal of Economics and Statistics* 37 (1955): 350–56; idem, "Aspects of Public Expenditure Theories," ibid. 40 (1958): 332–38; Jora R. Minasian, "Television Pricing and the Theory of Public Goods," *Journal of Law and Economics* 7 (1964): 71–80; Harold Demsetz, "The Private Production of Public Goods," ibid. 13 (1970): 293–306.
4. Samuelson, "Diagrammatic Exposition," p. 350.
5. On the "talent raids," see William S. Paley, *As It Happened* (New York: Doubleday, 1979), pp. 192–201; on NBC's coverage, Christopher H. Sterling and John Kittross, *Stay Tuned* (Belmont, Calif.; Wadsworth, 1978), p. 515.
6. Robert Sobel, *RCA* (New York: Stein & Day, 1986), chap. 8.
7. On the NBC management changes and David Sarnoff's influence over them, see Kenneth Bilby, *The General: David Sarnoff and the Rise of the Communications Industry* (New York: Harper & Row, 1986), pp. 252–61; on NBC coverage and set ownership, see Sterling and Kittross, *Stay Tuned*, pp. 515, 535.

8. Weaver, "Memorandum number one," September 26, 1949, Box 118, NBC Papers, State Historical Society, Madison, Wisconsin (unless otherwise noted, all internal NBC correspondence is from this collection).

9. Weaver to Charles Denny, October 3, 1949, Box 118; Leonard Hole to Weaver, December 14, 1950, Box 118; Weaver to David Sarnoff, March 31, 1953, Box 121; Charles Denny to David Sarnoff, September 8, 1953, Box 122; David Sarnoff to Joseph Heffernan, October 28, 1953, Box 121; *Business Week*, February 16, 1957, p. 100.

10. Russ Johnston to Weaver, August 4, 1949, Box 118; Minutes, Joint Committee on Film Usage, August 26, 1949, Box 118; Weaver to Roy Disney, January 27, 1953, Box 123; see also James L. Baughman, "The Weakest Chain and the Strongest Link," this volume, chap. 3.

11. Weaver, "Memorandum number one," September 26, 1949, Box 118.

12. Weaver to Charles Denny, October 3, 1949, Box 118.

13. Weaver, "Television 1953: The Case for the Networks," *Television Magazine* 10, no. 1 (1953): 17.

14. *Newsweek*, May 31, 1954, p. 7; "Color Policy Committee Statement," January 12, 1954, Box 122; quotation in *Business Week*, October 8, 1955, p. 32.

15. David Sarnoff memorandum, September 8, 1953, Box 122; *Business Week*, October 8, 1955, p. 31; *Broadcasting*, September 27, 1954, p. 5.

16. Weaver, "Memorandum number one," September 26, 1949, Box 118; "Notes on NBC Affiliates Meeting," September 12, 1953, Box 122.

17. *Advertising Age*, May 3, 1954, pp. 2, 144; *Billboard*, November 6, 1954, p. 2.

18. Weaver memorandum, July 19, 1951, Box 227; Weaver memorandum, January 25, 1955, Box 125; Robert Metz, *The Today Show* (Chicago: Playboy Press, 1977), pp. 31–39.

19. Leonard Hole to Weaver, December 14, 1950, Box 118; Weaver to J. M. Clifford, January 12, 1954, Box 123; *Time*, November 11, 1959, p. 78.

20. Weaver to James Young, May 24, 1951, Box 120.

21. Weaver memorandum, February 8, 1955, Box 323; NBC Press Release, April 7, 1954, Henry Salomon Papers, State Historical Society, Madison, Wisconsin; Vance Kepley, Jr., "The Origins of NBC's Project XX in Compilation Documentaries," *Journalism Quarterly* 61 (1984): 20–26.

22. Weaver to John McConnell, January 11, 1950, Box 118; see also Weaver's argument for networking and public service, "Television 1953," pp. 17–18, 35.

23. Sobel, *RCA*, pp. 166–78.

24. *Variety*, September 12, 1956, pp. 23, 44; *Business Week*, February 16, 1957, p. 100; quotation from ibid., p. 105. Not coincidentally, this move from centralized to dispersed management power conforms to the model put forward by Alfred D. Chandler, Jr. (*The Visible Hand* [Cambridge, Mass.: Harvard University Press, 1977]) in his famous description of the mature, modern corporation. NBC provides a microexample of that pattern.

25. *Variety*, November 7, 1956, pp. 35, 38; on Kintner's role at ABC,

see: Sterling Quinlan, *Inside ABC* (New York: Hastings, 1979, pp. 48–66; and Baughman, "Weakest Chain."

26. *Time*, September 17, 1956, pp. 88–89; *Variety*, December 26, 1956, p. 23; *Business Week*, February 16, 1957, p. 90.

27. Quoted in *Newsweek*, April 22, 1957, p. 72.

28. On the allocation plan and its role in assuring network power, see A. Frank Reel, *The Networks* (New York: Scribner's, 1979), pp. 18–26.

29. *Broadcasting*, May 6, 1957, p. 27; ibid., February 24, 1958, p. 162.

30. *Variety*, March 6, 1957, p. 23; *Time*, November 16, 1959, p. 78.

31. *Variety*, March 27, 1957, p. 21; ibid., April 3, 1957, p. 33; Sarnoff quoted in *Broadcasting*, October 27, 1958, p. 66.

32. On NBC and MCA, see Edward T. Thompson, "There's No Business Like MCA's Show Business," *Fortune* 62 (July 1960), pp. 114–17, ff.; the Kintner quotation is from ibid., p. 116. For a fuller discussion of the sort of "option contract" involved in these arrangements, see Barry Litman, *The Vertical Structure of the Television Broadcasting Industry* (East Lansing: Michigan State University Business Studies, 1979), chap. 6.

33. *Variety*, December 25, 1957, p. 23; *Business Week*, February 16, 1957, pp. 92, 96.

34. For an example of harsh critical commentary on Kintner-era programming, see Frank Pierson, "The Dying TV Drama," *The New Republic*, February 2, 1959, p. 22 (e.g.: "The live drama turned to an endless parade of glum kitchen comedies and misunderstood cops. The sponsors went West."). On NBC's ratings and billings gains, see: *Business Week*, February 16, 1957, p. 92; *Time*, April 30, 1965, p. 68; *New York Times*, October 24, 1965, sec. 2, p. 21.

35. On Kintner's background, see Quinlan, *Inside ABC*, p. 21; on his challenge to CBS's news leadership, see *Variety*, October 23, 1957, p. 27.

36. *Broadcasting*, December 13, 1965, p. 33.

37. *Newsweek*, March 13, 1961, pp. 54–56 (Frank quoted on p. 56); ibid., September 23, 1963, p. 65.

38. *Newsweek*, September 23, 1963, p. 62; on the economies of the format, see Edward J. Epstein, *News from Nowhere* (New York: Vintage, 1974), pp. 87–89.

39. Epstein, *News from Nowhere*, pp. 126–27; *Variety*, October 6, 1965, p. 51.

40. On personnel changes during the mid-1960s, see: Bilby, *The General*, pp. 259–61; and Sobel, *RCA*, pp. 184–87.

41. See also Barry R. Litman, "Network Oligopoly Power," chap. 4 in this volume.

SUGGESTIONS FOR FURTHER READING

Barnouw, Erik. *Tube of Plenty: The Evolution of American Television.* New York: Oxford University Press, 1982.

The Sponsor: Notes on a Modern Potentate. New York: Oxford University Press, 1978.

Baughman, James. "Television in the 'Golden Age': An Entrepreneurial Experiment." *The Historian* 47 (1985): 175–95.

Bergreen Laurence. *Look Now, Pay Later: The Rise of Network Television.* New York: Mentor, 1980.

Bilby, Kenneth. *The General: David Sarnoff and the Rise of the Communications Industry.* New York: Harper & Row, 1986.

Castleman, Harry, and Walter J. Podrazik. *Watching TV: Four Decades of American Television.* New York: McGraw-Hill, 1982.

Dreher, Carl. *Sarnoff: An American Success.* New York: Quadrangle, 1977.

Nord, David Paul. "An Economic Perspective on Formula in Popular Culture." *Journal of American Culture* 3 (1980): 17–31.

Sterling, Christopher, and John Kittross. *Stay Tuned: A Concise History of American Broadcasting.* Belmont, Calif.: Wadsworth, 1978.

Chapter 2

Building the World's Largest Advertising Medium: CBS and Television, 1940–60

William Boddy

*T*he Columbia Broadcasting System has always had a privileged place in popular accounts of American broadcasting. The special attention given CBS owes something to Columbia's domination for a half-century by a single individual, William S. Paley, but it also reflects the fact that even in an industry driven by the duel demands of both show-business and government oversight, CBS has been unusually concerned with its own public image. Since the 1950s, Columbia has been a recurring special target for right-wing critics of American media as well as the exemplar of television's "Golden Age" of investigative journalism and quality drama, symbolized by Edward R. Murrow and programs like "Playhouse 90"—so much so that when CBS Inc. became a corporate takeover target in the 1980s, the company's financial maneuverings, executive battles, and newsroom layoffs became front-page news in the nation's quality press and fodder for op-ed commentators.

CBS's place in American television history was cast when the underdog network overthrew the audience leadership of the larger NBC network in 1953 to establish an unprecedented 24-year reign as America's most popular TV network. NBC was CBS's chief industry rival during television's first two decades, and their differing interests and strategies can be traced through five distinct historical phases: the era of network radio that anticipated television; the prolonged battles over color television in the 1940s; CBS's rise to television audience leadership in the early 1950s; Columbia's more defensive posture as industry leader in the late 1950s; and CBS's new profile in the new television industry since the 1960s.

As the dominant actors in the television industry through the 1960s, CBS and NBC had distinct overall corporate identities and goals in the medium. One CBS advantage in its campaign for television audience leadership was the continuity and single-mindedness of its corporate leaders after World War II. Paley's move to CBS chairman and Frank Stanton's to CBS president in 1946 began a remarkable 30 years of management stability at Columbia; in contrast, six NBC presidents served under three different RCA presidents between the mid-1940s and the mid-1960s. Industry observers frequently contrasted the attitude toward television at CBS with that at NBC/RCA. David Sarnoff at RCA was often described as more interested in engineering than programming; in contrast, CBS engineering head Peter C. Goldmark called William S. Paley "an impatient antitechnologist," who by most accounts was interested in broadcasting only as it related to programming. Former CBS executive Mike Dann stated, perhaps hyperbolically, in 1987: "Paley was very lucky in that he had no competition. . . . His biggest competition, NBC, was run by a man who thought that the advertisers and the agencies should really run the programming, should operate stations, and he essentially liked the engineering aspects." Unlike NBC, a broadcast subsidiary of electronic manufacturing giant RCA, nearly all of CBS's revenues came from the sale of airtime to advertisers. The fundamental role of station and network operation at CBS underpinned the network's programming strategies in television and colored its relations with television advertisers, affiliated stations, and the Hollywood film industry. Upon these relations CBS would build its remarkable success in the first decades of commercial television in the United States.[1]

CBS AND RADIO

In 1927, CBS became the first radio network explicitly organized to earn a profit from the sale of advertising time; NBC had been set up a year earlier by RCA as an ancillary and public–service minded service designed to boost sales of RCA radio sets. Furthermore, Columbia reformulated the economic ties between a broadcast network and its affiliated stations. While NBC charged affiliates for sustaining programming (unsponsored programming provided to stations by the network) and paid affiliates a flat fee for airing the network's sponsored programming, CBS shared national advertising revenues with its affiliates and offered them sustaining programming without charge in exchange for network option time—the contractually guaranteed access to affiliate airtime for the network's sponsored programming. Thus, in return for about 30 percent of its revenues from network advertisers, CBS gained effective control of its affiliates' airtime, especially during the lucrative evening hours with the largest audiences. The CBS policy, which NBC adopted by 1935, ensured better affiliate clearances for network advertisers and more efficient network use of expensive AT&T long lines. Network access to affiliate airtime, guaranteed in the option time agreements, was the cornerstone of CBS's radio growth and the key to its power in network television.

CBS's fortunes rose in a radio industry that expanded almost without pause through the 1930s. Although CBS was hampered in the early 1930s by fewer high-power affiliates than NBC, by 1935 CBS had larger advertising billings than either one of NBC's two radio networks, and *Fortune* noted dryly, "to say that CBS has made money is to damn with faint praise." Although CBS was associated with several prestige programs of the classic period of 1930s radio drama, the network's financial success was rooted in the programming philosophy expressed in 1935 by William S. Paley, in what he called the "first axiom in program building: to give the public what it wants to hear." While CBS garnered critical prestige from its association with programs like "Columbia Workshop" and "Mercury Theatre of the Air" and with writers Archibald MacLeish, Norman Corwin, and Orson Welles and radio journalists H. V. Kaltenborn and Edward R. Murrow, the network's advertising growth was fueled by the more routine fare of daytime serials and prime-time musical variety, thrillers, and situation comedies. CBS was also recognized for its emphasis on audience research, including its use of the Frank Stanton-Paul Lazarsfeld "program analyzer," a device that recorded the continuous likes and dislikes of a sample audience to a specific program; and the young Frank Stanton and other CBS executives in the 1930s demonstrated great sensitivity to the "modern" programming concepts of audience demographics, audience flow, and counterprogramming. At the same time, by the mid-1930s neither CBS nor NBC produced much of its prime-time radio programming, which was generally produced or licensed by national sponsors who controlled a specific "time franchise" on a network schedule. This was an industry practice that CBS was determined to challenge when the television era began.[2]

By the end of the 1930s, CBS was a strong second to NBC in total radio program ratings and revenues, but the maturation—some feared saturation—of the radio receiver market by 1940 caused both networks to look to new areas of profitable investment. With little corporate debt and a large amount of cash on hand by the end of the 1930s, CBS spun off some of its AM radio revenues into new investments, including the acquisition of Columbia Records Inc. in 1939; plans for an 18-nation

Latin American commercial network, announced in 1940; and the purchase of major radio talent contracts after World War II. Another major investment target, of course, was commercial television.[3]

At the same time, with 90 percent of its revenues representing the sale of AM advertising time, CBS faced with some anxiety the prospect of technological upheaval in broadcasting at the hands of the new services of television and FM radio. Unlike CBS, NBC's parent RCA saw vast potential patent and manufacturing profits in commercial television, and such nonbroadcast interests were inextricably linked to NBC's activities in television. Columbia's early attitudes toward television were more ambivalent. CBS had operated an experimental television station between 1931 and 1933 (when William S. Paley optimistically announced that commercial television had indeed arrived), but notwithstanding the efforts of CBS's five-person research staff, initiated by engineer Peter C. Goldmark in 1935, CBS's interest in television in the 1930s was primarily defensive, reacting to RCA's moves in the medium, and circumscribed by Columbia's desire to protect its AM radio business. William S. Paley told a 1936 FCC hearing on possible allocations for FM radio and television: "We should do nothing to weaken the structure of aural broadcasting in the present band until experimentation in other bands has yielded us new certainties," and pointed to the "need to go slow in adding to or revising the present commercial broadcast structure." Following RCA's television patent licensing agreements with Philo Farnsworth in 1937, *Business Week* noted Columbia's plans for an experimental television transmitter atop the Chryler Building in New York City, but added that no alliance of RCA rivals could challenge RCA's patent position in television manufacturing. Despite CBS's 1937 appointment of prominent critic Gilbert Seldes as its new director of television and its announcements of the Chrysler Building transmitter and planned television studios in Grand Central Station, CBS leaders remained cautious in their forecasts of the imminence of commercial television.[4]

CBS AND THE COLOR TELEVISION WARS, 1940–53

As a broadcaster and network operator wedded to the fortunes of AM radio, Columbia's television policies between 1940 and 1947 were often viewed skeptically by others in the broadcast industry. RCA and the rest of the industry were surprised by CBS's announcement in August 1940 that it had developed a color television system that it claimed would render obsolete the RCA-developed very-high-frequency (VHF) monochrome system the FCC had already approved for limited commercial use. CBS followed its color television announcement with a publicity campaign designed to delay FCC approval of black-and-white commercial television. However, despite a September 1940 demonstration of CBS color television for the commission, the following summer the FCC approved full commercial service in VHF black-and-white television and postponed commercial color television licensing indefinitely. CBS continued its experimental color broadcasts, warning the public that color television would eventually replace black and white and urging consumers not to invest in monochrome receivers. In any event, by 1942 most television programming and manufacture was suspended for the duration of World War II and the public battle for television frequency allocations was suspended.

With the end of the war in sight, in April 1944 CBS unveiled new color television proposals which were highly controversial in the industry and especially galling to RCA and its plans for immediate postwar VHF television. CBS pressed its proposed standards for ultrahigh frequency (UHF) wide-band color television before the FCC's allocation hearings of 1944–45, and though the commission refused to license UHF for commercial broadcasting, CBS took heart at the curious commission logic in its 1945 decision, which affirmed the constricted VHF frequencies for television while admitting that VHF was inadequate for "a truly nationwide and competitive system." Meanwhile, as network radio boomed in 1945 and 1946, sales of VHF black-and-white sets languished, encouraging Columbia in what it called its "millitant . . . sponsorship of color television in the ultrahigh frequencies." By August 1946 nearly half of the postwar VHF station license applications before the FCC had been withdrawn; Zenith announced that it would not manufacture black-and-white receivers, and RCA scaled back its predictions of annual set sales from one hundred thousand to twenty-five thousand. It was clear that the contradictory logic of the FCC's 1945 allocation decision and the CBS anti-VHF campaign were having an effect on the foundering television industry. A CBS executive told a reporter, "we found ourselves in a barrage of abuse" from the rest of the industry, and CBS leaders responded with a number of public rationales for its color television proposals, arguing that prewar television standards were inadequate and obsolete as a result of wartime research; that black-and-white television would be judged inadequate by a public made sophisticated by motion pictures and radio entertainment; and that low set sales and audiences for monochrome television would present television broadcasters with a long period of unrecouped costs.[5]

Many in the broadcasting industry believed that CBS was less concerned about potential television viewers or broadcasters than about its own formidable investment in AM radio and saw in CBS's color television proposals an attempt to delay commercial television altogether. According to CBS executive Worthington Miner, the entire CBS color television campaign during this period was a "covert policy to cripple television in order to enhance CBS's primacy in radio." On the other hand, RCA, with commanding patent control in VHF television, was committed to the immediate launch of commercial television. Both networks estimated that in the first five to ten years of commercial operation the only profits in the television industry would be from manufacturing, and CBS's color television proposals can therefore be seen either as a good-faith attempt to capture some of the manufacturing and royalty revenues of commercial television or as a disingenuous move to stave off the disruption television would bring to network radio.[6]

Following the lackluster commercial success of VHF black-and-white television immediately following the 1945 FCC decision, CBS executives demonstrated a revised system of color television in 1946 and 1947 and were cautiously optimistic that the commission would approve commercial color television in the UHF band, eventually replacing the existing VHF allocations. A major decision in the long and convoluted history of CBS color television proposals came in the spring of 1947, when the FCC denied the revised CBS UHF color television petition. Six months after its 1947 decision against CBS, FCC Chairman Charles Denny left the commission for a vice-presidency at NBC at three times his commission salary.

After the 1947 FCC defeat, CBS developed a new color system that would operate in the narrower VHF bandwidths, and from 1947 to 1950 Columbia waged a renewed campaign for color television. While the system demonstrated by CBS was praised by critics, it was incompatible with existing receivers. By the time of the FCC's eventual adoption of the CBS color television system in 1950, 9 million black-and-white sets had been sold, and neither viewers nor set manufacturers were much interested in an incompatible system of color television. *Fortune* called CBS's 1950 color television victory at the FCC a disaster for the company, "a championship dive with no water in the pool." In addition to the obstacles of an RCA lawsuit, a million dollar negative ad campaign organized by black-and-white set manufacturers, and the delays of material shortages caused by the Korean War, the CBS color television system was almost certainly already doomed by 1950 merely by the fact of its incompatability. Well before the final turn in the color television story came in 1953, when the FCC rescinded its approval of the stillborn CBS system in favor of an RCA-developed compatible system, it was clear that CBS's fortunes in television were to be won as a broadcaster, not as a manufacturer or patent holder. This was confirmed by an estimated $50 million in accumulated losses from Columbia's subsequent unsuccessful attempts to compete in the television manufacturing industry in the 1950s.[7]

BLEEDING RADIO TO SUPPORT TELEVISION, 1947–51

If TV manufacturing would prove to be disastrous for CBS, the company was much more successful in other sectors of the young industry. Despite the distractions of its color television campaigns and its misadventures in set manufacture, CBS managed to overtake NBC in television audience ratings and advertising revenues within five years of the 1947 FCC decision that served as the starting gun for commercial television.

CBS achieved network leadership in early television despite some substantial initial handicaps. Columbia's color television strategy between 1944 and 1947 had placed the network in an awkward and contradictory position as a television broadcaster; as a champion of UHF color television, CBS repeatedly denigrated VHF black-and-white television standards while it reluctantly pursued commercial television along the only lines approved by federal authorities—that is, black-and-white VHF broadcasting. Arguing against a 1945 FCC proposal to require five hours of daily TV programming, for example, CBS executive Paul W. Kesten told the commission that requiring such VHF programming would be akin to "speaking the lines and rehearsing the parts for a play that will never really open, or will close down almost as soon as it opens." Columbia's ambivalence toward commercial television during the period is underscored by the disclaimer CBS aired at 30-minute intervals during all its VHF broadcasts, warning viewers that its programming could be discontinued at any time and that current TV receivers could be made obsolete. Furthermore, CBS shut down its recently touted Grand Central Station television studios, discouraged its radio affiliates from applying for commercial VHF licenses in favor of experimental UHF licenses, and shelved its own application plans for four large-market VHF stations in order not to undermine the credibility of its UHF petition before the FCC. Columbia's desultory start in black-and-white television not only deprived the network of the burgeoning revenues from large-market station operation, but also forced it to spend an estimated $30 million over the next eight years to acquire a full complement of stations. In contrast, by the end of 1948 NBC, ABC, and DuMont all had acquired their quota of five VHF stations, while CBS owned only one television station until 1951. Finally, both NBC and DuMont could draw upon substantial revenues from television manufacturing to underwrite network expenses in the late 1940s, a source of revenues unavailable to CBS.[8]

Despite continued efforts on behalf of its incompatible color television system, Columbia viewed the FCC's spring of 1947 denial of the CBS UHF petition as the starting gun for VHF commercial television. Moving decisively into VHF television after the FCC decision, CBS organized television conferences for its radio affiliates in the fall of 1947 and the spring of 1948. In February 1948, CBS president Frank Stanton announced plans for a Boston-to-Washington Eastern Seaboard network with programming from the reopened Grand Central television studios. CBS's closing of its New York studios the previous spring had been part of an ill-fated "remote" program strategy of sports, parades, and outside special events which had attracted few sponsors or viewers. *Newsweek* noted that "Stanton's announcement meant that CBS was finally climbing all the way up on the video bandwagon," while pointing out that the network was lagging far behind NBC in television audiences and intercity cable hookups.[9]

Underlying Columbia's moves into the new medium was Paley's postwar programming philosophy, elaborated in his widely reported 1946 speech to the National Association of Broadcasters convention in Chicago:

> First we have an obligation to give most of the people what they want most of the time. Second, our clients, as advertisers, need to reach most of the people most of the time. This is not perverted or inverted cause and effect, as our attackers claim. It is one of the great strengths of our kind of broadcasting that the advertiser's desire to sell his product to the largest cross section of the public coincides with our obligation to serve the largest cross section of our audience.[10]

Paley's strategic collapse of network audience with advertising target and his single-minded determination to serve mass advertisers by attracting maximum network audiences with popular programs became the foundation of CBS's successful postwar strategy in both radio and television, and CBS's attempts to win control of programming and scheduling away from network sponsors was a key element of the strategy.

Despite its initial postwar efforts, Columbia lagged behind NBC in the business of delivering radio listeners to advertisers. The key to Paley's audience leadership strategy was direct CBS control of the most popular broadcast performers through network talent contracts, which exploited a novel financial mechanism Paley credited to "some clever tax lawyers." The famous CBS talent raids of 1948–49 lured top NBC radio performers (who paid personal income tax rates as high as 75 percent) by offering them assistance in setting themselves up as individual corporations that would in turn be licensed to CBS, permitting the performers' incomes to be taxed at a much lower capital gains rate. The strategy brought the two white creators of "Amos 'n' Andy" to CBS in September 1948; Jack Benny, George Burns, Gracie Allen, Red Skelton, and Bing Crosby followed within six months. The success of the talent raids was startling: by 1949, CBS had 12 of the top 15 radio programs, with overall radio ratings 14 percent higher than NBC. CBS revenues jumped $6.6 million over its 1948 revenues of $64 million. A biographer of RCA chairman David Sarnoff called the CBS talent raids "perhaps the single most decisive competitive development" in broadcast history.[11]

The CBS 1949 *Annual Report* began: "The year 1949 was the most significant transition period in the history of your Company," and it noted "the strength and stability of the AM structure, which enabled it to support the necessary TV programming experimentation and development." Network radio revenues continued to increase through 1951 as CBS relentlessly cut sustaining programming and radio production costs in order to subsidize a television deficit amounting to an estimated $9 million by mid-1948. The same year, *Variety* reported deep CBS layoffs in the radio network's educational, science, and documentary production units in order to pay for the network's television efforts.[12]

PACKAGING LIVE TELEVISION AT CBS, 1949–54

While the trade press pointed to CBS's concern with radio revenues, not television, as the motivating factor behind the network's talent raids, the company's *Annual Report* for 1949 noted that "the major new CBS programs . . . such as Amos 'n' Andy, Jack Benny, Bergen and McCarthy, Ozzie and Harriet, Bing Crosby, Red Skelton . . . not only have established value as radio entertainment, but are also particularly well suited to the requirements of television." The radio talent moves were integral to the network's success in television programming, providing the model for what CBS called "packaged programs," defined as shows developed, owned, and scheduled by the network itself. Although in 1948 Frank Stanton said that CBS "has made no hard and fast rule about who shall control the production of commercial television programs," CBS clearly favored the development of its own packaged programs. The network explained that such packaging allowed the network greater flexibility in program scheduling, especially in building popular shows as "anchor points" at strategic points in the daily and weekly schedule.[13]

CBS's battle for control of program development was thus also a battle for control over the network schedule, fueled by a growing network appreciation of the importance of audience flow and program adjacencies in television. This second battle pitted the network against sponsors and advertising agencies committed to their traditional major roles in producing and scheduling network prime-time programming. Despite sponsor resistance and network staff shortages, CBS enjoyed growing success in creating packaged programs. As early as December 1948 a CBS executive reported that Columbia had more number-one rated quarter-hours in television in the New York market than all its competitors combined and that three of the top five shows in New York were CBS packages. "Thus—in less than 9 months—CBS has created the largest reservoir of program-opportunities for the advertiser—programs tested, preferred and ready-to-go," the official boasted. By 1949 CBS maintained the largest program department in the broadcast industry and could point to 22 CBS-created programs sold to sponsors. By the end of 1950 more than half of the prime-time programming on CBS television was owned by the network.[14]

Despite the lack of revenues from television manufacturing and from a full complement of owned-and-operated stations, CBS was able to underwrite its early TV investments from its still-growing radio revenues, a booming postwar record business (in large part fueled by the LP record, developed by Peter Goldmark at CBS in 1948), and from additional debt assumed by the network. As Columbia's financial commitment to television grew, so did its determination to develop network-packaged programs and to control its program schedule. Between 1948 and 1950 CBS borrowed heavily to support its television expansion, including substantial expenditures in talent contracts and other direct program production costs. Columbian bankrolled its growing and still unprofitable television operations from vastly increased revenues from radio and television advertising time sales; CBS income quadrupled between 1946 and 1952. Expanding network revenues seemed linked to the strategy of network program packaging in early television; *Fortune*, in 1951, estimated that CBS packaged 70 to

75 percent of its programs, versus 50 percent at NBC, and in 1952 CBS announced that it had 33 packaged programs on the network, the largest number ever carried at any network.[15]

NBC did not immediately challenge CBS's raid upon its top broadcast comedians in 1948–49; David Sarnoff told an RCA stockholders' meeting: "Leadership built over the years on a foundation of solid service cannot be snatched overnight by buying a few high-priced comedians. Leadership is not a laughing matter." However, NBC soon offered expensive deals to keep Bob Hope and Fred Allen on the network, and later Sarnoff set up a $1.5 million fund for new comic talent for television, without notable success. In 1951 Sarnoff approved a contract with Milton Berle guaranteeing the comedian $100,000 a year for 40 years whether or not Berle appeared on the network, dwarfing Paley's talent raid fees and signaling NBC's willingness to compete for expensive television performers. Both networks continued to bid for high-priced comedy talent in the early years of network television; Berle's long-term contract at NBC was followed by Jackie Gleason's 15-year, $100,000 a year contract at CBS in 1952, and CBS signed Lucille Ball to an $8 million contract the same year, the largest in television history until then.[16]

Like NBC, CBS publicly favored live production over the film format for both its packaged productions and shows supplied by others in the early years of network television. Most of the top CBS shows in the years 1948–52—the variety programs of Ed Sullivan and Arthur Godfrey, the dramatic series "Studio One," "Suspense," "Man Against Crime," and "Ford Theatre," and the majority of the network's situation comedies—were produced live. While both CBS and NBC used film programs in their early TV schedules, for competitive and public relations reasons both networks emphasized what they termed the "magic nationwide live television" that was by definition a network monopoly. More than their counterparts at NBC, however, CBS program executives promoted the situation comedy as a more predictable and durable format than the variety program for its high-priced comedians. And when CBS packaged its own variety show to answer NBC's hyperkinetic Milton Berle, it chose the colorless but enduring Ed Sullivan as host of "Toast of the Town." Sullivan's show premiered two weeks after Berle's in 1948 and quickly became television's number two program, and while Berle eventually wore out his welcome with television audiences, Sullivan's program lasted 23 years on CBS.

In 1948 CBS launched adaptations of two of its popular radio situation comedies, "The Goldbergs" and "I Remember Mama." "The Burns and Allen Show" and "The Jack Benny Program" in 1950 became the first of the radio talent-raid vehicles launched in television; "Amos 'n' Andy" began in the summer of 1951. The premiere of "Amos 'n' Andy" capped a five-year effort at CBS to adapt one of history's most lucrative radio programs to television, including a 40-state, two hundred thousand mile talent hunt, which enlisted the help of General Dwight Eisenhower and President Harry Truman. After unsuccessful attempts to use white performers in blackface and hand puppets for the Harlem-based situation comedy, black actors were eventually cast for the series. The NAACP immediately decried the racial stereotyping of the program and called for a national boycott of its sponsor, Blatz beer. While CBS defended the show, which had landed in the top-25 list, within two seasons it dropped "Amos 'n' Andy" from the network schedule, placing it in syndication until 1966, when renewed civil rights protests caused the network to withdraw the program altogether.[17]

"Amos 'n' Andy" demonstrated CBS's early interest in Hollywood filmmaking as a format for its radio situation-comedy properties; the program was filmed at Hal Roach Studios at a weekly production cost of forty thousand dollars. CBS had expanded its Los Angeles live television production facilities as early as 1949 with "The Ed Wynn Show." Construction of the CBS Television City studios in Los Angeles, announced in 1950 and completed in 1952, was described by Fortune as "a huge gamble" in production facilities for a still-infant medium, reflecting Columbia's commitment to major investment in program production. When the transcontinental coaxial cable was completed in 1951, situation comedies and other live programming from the network's Los Angeles studios became an important part of the CBS prime-time schedule.[18]

Unlike NBC under Pat Weaver, who was associated with the innovations of the "Today" and "Tonight" shows and with the special-event live network spectacular, CBS by the mid-1950s was committed to regularly scheduled, generally 30-minute programs, with an emphasis on situation comedy. Prestige programming at CBS at the time was led by the New York–based live dramatic anthology program "Studio One" (1948). Although in its first two seasons "Studio One" emphasized literary adaptations from Shakespeare, Tolstoy, Hawthorne, Austen, and James, by the 1953 season it was turning increasingly to topical and sometimes controversial original teleplays from a new generation of TV writers, including Rod Serling ("Buffalo Bill Is Dead," November 23, 1953), Gore Vidal ("Dark Possession," February 15, 1954), and Reginald Rose ("The Remarkable Incident at Carson Corners," January 11, 1954; "Thunder on Sycamore Street," March 15, 1954; "12 Angry Men," September 26, 1954). While popular among TV critics, "Studio One" did not enjoy the critical reputation of "The Philco Television Playhouse" or many of Weaver's increasingly frequent network spectaculars on NBC. Another element of CBS's prestige programming in the early and mid-1950s was "See It Now" (1952), a 30-minute public affairs program aired on Tuesday nights at ten o'clock and hosted by veteran journalist Edward R. Murrow. "See It Now" gathered the most attention for its March 9, 1954 report on Senator Joseph McCarthy, which consisted of a careful and deadpan assemblage of the right-wing senator's increasingly reckless and incoherent charges of communist infiltration of the Eisenhower administration.

Despite the high profile of CBS's handful of New York-based live dramas and the enormous publicity generated by Murrow's McCarthy program, by the mid-1950s Columbia's prime-time schedule was dominated by the half-hour light entertainment format. Former CBS programming head Michael Dann told an interviewer in the 1970s: "Historically, Bill's [Paley] program philosophy from the time he stole Jack Benny from NBC was based on the star system. He didn't like gambles; never started any new program concepts." The financial impact of a single broadcast performer could be enormous to the network. In 1950 Arthur Godfrey was on the CBS radio and television networks nine and a half hours a week and had two television shows in the top ten; Godfrey's programs represented 12 percent of the network's total revenues as late as 1954.[19]

One situation comedy in particular, "I Love Lucy," became the most lucrative 30 minutes in CBS history and accelerated the wholesale shift from live to film programming at the network. Radio and film actress Lucille Ball had been approached by CBS to develop a comedy series for the 1951 television season, and when Ball and her sponsor insisted on doing the series on film and using her real-life husband as costar, the network sold back its financial stake in the series to the actress. CBS vice-president Harry Ackerman explained the network's public attitude at the time: "We definitely wanted to shoot 'I Love Lucy' live. But the sponsor made us go to film. You can say that we went into the film business at the whim of the sponsor." Shot on film before a live audience in the three-hundred seat Desilu auditorium and budgeted at between twenty-one and twenty-seven thousand dollars per episode, with a combined cast and crew of 50 to 75 members, "I Love Lucy" became television's number-one program within four months of its launch in 1951 and stayed in the top ten for nine seasons, reaching a record audience share of 70 in 1953. Even New York TV critics otherwise hostile to West Coast film programming praised "Lucy," arguing that the program's filmed-before-a-live-audience format brought the virtues of spontaneity and performance style from legitimate theater and live television drama. The unprecedented audience for the "Lucy" episode featuring the birth of Little Ricky in January 1952 helped push

CBS temporarily ahead of NBC in the season's ratings for the first time. Other West Coast situation comedies, mostly on film, followed the spectacular success of "Lucy" at CBS, including "Life With Luigi," "My Little Margie" (introduced as a summer replacement for "Lucy" and produced by Hal Roach Studios), "Our Miss Brooks," and "My Friend Irma" in 1952.[20]

Columbia's programming successes took place in a television industry that was growing rapidly on the heels of the FCC's 1947 go-ahead. Despite the FCC freeze on new television station construction permits, the period 1948–52 saw the number of stations on the air rise from 14 to 108, the number of television households grow from 1 million to 20 million, and the number of CBS affiliates increase from 11 to 43. By 1953, when the CBS color television system was given its *coup de grace* with the FCC's approval of RCA's compatible system, CBS was passing NBC in television advertising revenues; in that year, RCA earned $32 million on total sales of $690 million while CBS earned twice as much on sales of only $251 million. In May 1953 CBS boasted that the network was taking business leadership in network television, with a three-to-one lead in weekday daytime program revenues over NBC, and six of the top-ten prime-time programs (including "I Love Lucy," in first place by 13 ratings points over its nearest competitor). CBS's *Annual Report* for 1954 pointed to a 50 percent increase in television revenues and announced that CBS Television had become the world's largest single advertising medium.[21]

With the number of television homes climbing to 16 million by the end of the FCC station freeze in 1952, the advertisers' cost per thousand of reaching network television audiences was falling steadily, and the revenues of both NBC and CBS television networks grew enormously. Meanwhile, CBS's emphasis on the situation comedy seemed vindicated. Ratings of the two major NBC comedy-variety programs, Berle's "Texaco Star Theater" and "The Colgate Comedy Hour," weakened steadily after 1952, and by 1954 neither show was in the top ten. While Pat Weaver was launching the high-culture sampler philosophy of "operation frontal lobes" at NBC and promoting lavish all-color spectaculars following the FCC approval of RCA's color television system in 1953, CBS maintained its reputation for popular, less-elevated fare. "The Jackie Gleason Show" on CBS became the number-two show of the 1954 season, and a new crop of situation comedies, "Private Secretary" (1953), "December Bride" (1954), "The Phil Silvers Show" (1955), and "The Danny Thomas Show" (moved from ABC in 1957), were also successful for the network in the mid-1950s. Finally, CBS pioneered a new prime-time genre, the high-stakes quiz program, following the extraordinary ratings success of a 1955 summer replacement program,

"The $64,000 Question," which quickly became TV's number-one show, with a record network audience of 51 million people. CBS responded to the show's popularity with several other high-stakes quiz programs in 1956 and 1957, and the programs' creator, Louis G. Cowan, was named programming chief at the network.[22]

LICENSING FILM PROGRAMMING, 1955–59

Despite the network's success in program packaging in the early 1950s, by the middle of the decade, CBS revised its strategy of prime-time program procurement as the network faced new economic opportunities and regulatory challenges. One of the most striking changes in mid-1950 prime-time television was the shift from live to film program formats, and behind the shift were the changing markets of program production and distribution. The revenue potential from the reuse of film programs grew as television markets expanded in the United States and abroad, and despite CBS's earlier announced fears that film programming would threaten its financial relationship with affiliates on the one hand and with national sponsors on the other, by mid-decade CBS moved to embrace wholeheartedly the film format for prime-time television. The rapid decline in live prime-time programming meant the near extinction of the defining program genre of television's "Golden Age," the New York–based anthology drama. On all three networks, the proportion of live programming in prime time declined from 50 percent in 1955 to 31 percent the following year; the proportion of network prime-time programming originating in Los Angeles jumped in 1957 from 40 percent to 71 percent, and the number of live prime-time dramatic shows declined from 14 in 1955–56 to 7 in 1957–58 and to only 1 by 1959–60. A marker of the change can be found in CBS's long-running live anthology series "Studio One," which moved to Hollywood in 1957; by that season all three of CBS's quality drama series—"Studio One," "Playhouse 90," and "Climax"—originated from Television City in Los Angeles. Only CBS's quiz shows, fringe-time talk shows, and Ed Sullivan's variety show remained in New York by the 1957 season.[23]

The shift to film programming by the networks in the mid-1950s brought the major Hollywood studios into the prime-time programming market to an unprecedented degree. The entrance of the major studios worried CBS leaders, including Frank Stanton, who warned a group of CBS affiliates in 1954: "There are some elements who . . . calculate that if somehow they could destroy the present structure, some more pieces would fall their way. . . . They talk about control by Madison Avenue; yet they seem to feel that control by Hollywood is somehow a blessing. These men are either ignorant or dishonest."[24] CBS especially feared the economic power of the studios' huge libraries of previously released feature films. In contrast to the buyer's market for filmed series programming that the networks had achieved by the mid-1950s, the wholesale television release of thousands of feature films controlled by a handful of studios and the studios' success in trading feature rights for ownership positions in program syndication firms and television stations were deeply disturbing to CBS and NBC executives.

The shift from live to film program formats involved a reconsideration at CBS of its own role in program production, resulting in the network moving away from direct production in favor of licensing telefilms made by independent producers, including the Hollywood studios. Although CBS directly produced 75 percent of its 1951 program schedule, by April 1956 the figure was only 23 percent. Following the pattern pioneered by ABC in its deal with Walt Disney for "Disneyland," CBS began to replace the model of network-packaged programs with one in which the network offered financial contributions to independent producers for series pilots in return for network profit shares and syndication rights to completed series. While CBS did not directly produce the new programming, the network generally insisted upon and gained profit shares and syndication rights to the independently made programs as part of the network licensing agreement. Frustrated independent producers and others in the industry accused the networks of favoring programs in which they had gained financial interests.[25]

As a consequence of the network's aggressive moves into program licensing in the mid-1950s, program producers saw the market for prime-time programming shrink from several national sponsors, each controlling a network time slot to a market consisting of only the three networks. Between 1954 and 1955 the percentage of network-produced prime-time programming on CBS fell from 52 percent to 33 percent and that of outside producers rose from 38 percent to 58 percent. Over the period 1957–68, the percentage of prime-time entertainment programming produced by CBS dropped from 24 percent to 5 percent, while programming in which the network held a financial interest increased from 39 percent to 91 percent. Independently produced programming not licensed by CBS dropped from 36 percent to 3 percent in the same period. Between 1960 and 1964, the three networks provided pilot financing for about half of the programs produced by independent producers and in return received domestic or foreign syndication rights in 38 percent of the programs and profit shares in 81 percent. The customary network rationale for such financial and syndication interests was the risk to the network of unsold advertising time, but in the sellers' market of network advertising, the risk seemed more hypothetical than real to most observers. The decline in original production for syndication left local station nonprime-time schedules increasingly dominated by reruns of off-network programming, displacing local live programming and first-run syndicated programs.[26]

CBS's use of film programming to supply its own network schedule and the syndication market followed the lure of exploding domestic and international markets for film programming. By the time "I Love Lucy" left the network schedule in 1957, CBS was already syndicating its 179 episodes in 29 countries. CBS had started its own telefilm subsidiary, CBS Films, Inc., in the early 1950s to produce as well as distribute film programming. In 1961 the CBS unit halted production of original film programming altogether, "eliminating the need for highly speculative investment in television pilot films and series," as the CBS *Annual Report* explained, in favor of the lucrative and risk-free syndication of proven off-network reruns; CBS Films Inc.'s sales went up 32 percent that year. By 1963 CBS was the world's largest exporter of television programming, and that year, for the first time, it sold more programming abroad than in the United States, selling 80 television series in 70 countries.[27]

In this context of shifting economic structures, CBS programming policies in the late 1950s reveal a combination of lopsided daytime program success (by 1955 CBS's daytime ratings were 57 percent above NBC's), a wholehearted commitment to ABC's telefilm and young-family audience strategies, and an unusual respect for the value of good public and governmental relations. Following the success of a number of ABC Western series produced by Warner Bros. in the 1957–58 season, CBS answered with "Have Gun Will Travel" and "Trackdown" that year and three more Western programs the following season. In the 1958–59 season, seven of the top-ten programs were Westerns. While CBS followed the ABC model of independently produced action-adventure programs, however, Columbia was careful to avoid both an overdependence on the Western and an association with such specific targets of critics of television violence as ABC's "The Untouchables" and "Bus Stop." ABC network chief Oliver Treyz's unsatisfactory performance before an FCC probe of violent programming reportedly cost him his job, and CBS had long been convinced of the importance of public relations and regulatory goodwill.

CBS prime-time ratings leadership in the late 1950s was boosted by several popular filmed variety shows and three lucrative film series created along the new network-licensed program model—"Alfred Hitchcock Presents" and "Gunsmoke" in 1955 and "Perry Mason" in 1957. Hitchcock's move to the television medium in January 1955 was an important marker of network television's new status and financial appeal in the Hollywood community. The TV series followed the launch of "Alfred Hitchcock's Mystery Magazine," a successful spinoff devised by Lew Wasserman, head of MCA, a talent agency that was itself becoming a major producer of network film programming in the mid-1950s. The series was sold to CBS and sponsored by Brystol-Meyers without a pilot, on the strength of Hitchcock's reputation. The show's contract called for Hitchcock to supervise the entire series and to direct an unspecified number of episodes (eventually 16 of 359). The most memorable feature of the program was undoubtedly Hitchcock's brief on-camera prologues and epilogues, where he commented on the episodes and occasionally offered gentle jibes at his sponsor. These sequences were filmed four times a season in three languages, a sign of the recognition of the growing importance of foreign markets for U.S. television programming. The ratings success of "Alfred Hitchcock Presents" led to a number of other filmed-anthology series at CBS in the late 1950s, including "Zane Grey Theater" (1956), "Assignment Foreign Legion" (1957), "Desilu Playhouse" (1958), "Pursuit" (1959), and "Twilight Zone" (1959).

CBS's "Perry Mason" represented a different kind of presold property for television, in this case the lawyer-detective character created by novelist Erle Stanley Gardner in 1933 and sustained across 3,000 episodes of a network radio program from 1943 to 1955. *Variety* commented on the 1957 CBS television debut of "Perry Mason," which the network scheduled against Perry Como's popular variety show on NBC: "In content and format it approximates a junior-size feature meller, and considering the 100G cost of these tv cinematics, that's turning a neat trick." Like Hitchcock's series, "Perry Mason" was typical of the new program procurement and syndication patterns: the show was produced by independent producer Paisano Productions, Inc., but CBS held a 40 percent interest in the property and retained syndication rights. When the program finally left the network in 1966, it was already being shown in 56 countries, and 25 independent stations in the United States immediately licensed the series reruns for $3 million that year alone.[28]

The clout of CBS and NBC in the programming market in the mid-1950s grew despite their retreat from the earlier levels of direct network program production. The second half of the 1950s increasingly witnessed CBS in a defensive public position, beating back not only the potential competitive threat of new film-based networks and subscription television systems controlled by the Hollywood studios, but also battling rising political and regulatory complaints of improper network power in the television industry. Many observers argued that one of the factors encouraging CBS in its new program procurement policy was network fears of the antitrust and regulatory vulnerabilities that accompanied its role as program packager. CBS anxiety at the prospect of regulatory reform in the late 1950s reflected its recognition of the importance of previous regulatory actions (and inaction) in creating the restricted competitive structure in the television industry. Neither the FCC freeze on station construction permits nor its 1952 *Sixth Report and Order*, which opened the financially crippled stations in the UHF band, disturbed the essentially oligopolistic structure of network competition in television. By 1954 CBS and its three owned-and-operated stations captured more than 20 percent of the revenues of the entire television industry and 28 percent of total industry profits. The return of tangible investment at CBS in 1954 was 108 percent from its overall television operations and 370 percent from the network's owned-and-operated stations; profits at CBS's New York station were estimated at 1800 percent. CBS acquired its full complement of five VHF stations by the mid-1950s, and Columbia's owned-and-operated stations provided the network with enormous resources for program acquisition. By 1955 CBS and NBC were responsible for 95 percent of total network revenues in what was nominally a four-network economy, and the shortage of three- and four-station VHF markets under the *Sixth Report and Order* doomed wider network competition. During these years, ABC and DuMont often watched helplessly as a sponsor moved a hit show or performer from their networks to the more powerful CBS or NBC; even when ABC in the late 1950s licensed a series of popular programs from Walt Disney and Warner Bros. and began winning rating nights in markets with network affiliate parity, ABC still lagged far behind CBS and NBC in overall circulation and billings. Meanwhile, CBS profits in 1957 reached a record high for the sixth year in a row, lifted by higher network time sales and the liquidation of CBS's unprofitable set manufacturing division; revenues from CBS's film syndication business also rose substantially that year.[29]

CBS's programming success in the 1950s therefore has to been seen in the context of a federally administered shared network monopoly; not surprisingly, much of the energies of CBS executives in the late 1950s, led by network head Frank Stanton, went into forestalling major changes to industry structure from disruptive Washington action. While the CBS *Annual Report* for 1955 warned of the "cloudy climate" prevailing in Washington, by April 1957 Frank Stanton told a group of CBS affiliates that he detected "some signs of sun and calmer weather" in Washington. CBS anxiety at the prospects of regulatory action quieted after 1957, when it became clear that disruptive federal action was unlikely.[30]

The importance of Columbia's emphasis on good governmental and public relations became evident when CBS's major commitment to the prime-time quiz show collapsed in scandal in 1958, bringing down CBS network head Louis G. Cowan. Following two years of industry rumors and a flurry of tight-lipped program cancellations at CBS and NBC, several prominent contestants from the most popular quiz programs, including "The $64,000 Question," confessed that their performances had been methodically rigged by program producers. Capping years of rising critical disillusionment with program "mediocrity" and the death of live drama, the quiz show scandals sparked television's most serious public relation's crisis, and CBS led the industry's public rehabilitation campaign. Columbia's efforts included lofty public statements by "industry statesman" Frank Stanton and a renewed emphasis on non-violent, escapist situation comedy in prime time. Former CBS executive Fred Friendly painted Stanton's role in the public relations crisis in apocalyptic terms:

> Most of the spokesmen for the other networks were dazed, frightened inarticulate towers of jello whose public statements only seemed to compound the faults that the quiz show scandals had brought to light. In his austere, brutally frank willingness to assume responsibility rather than seek a scapegoat, Stanton may have saved the industry.[31]

In the fallout of the quiz show scandals and President Kennedy's new FCC chairman Newton Minow's 1961 blast at network television's program schedule as a "vast wasteland," news and public affairs programming assumed a greater role in the CBS prime-time schedule, if only briefly. CBS and NBC were much more heavily invested in the quiz show format than ABC, and when CBS canceled every big-stakes quiz show in its prime-time schedule in 1958, it moved even more wholeheartedly to both the 60-minute filmed action-adventure series in the ABC mold and to a new generation of 30-minute situation comedies (starting with "Dennis the Menace" and "The Many Loves of Dobie Gillis" at CBS in 1959), making the break with the era of live anthology drama even more decisive.

CBS SINCE THE 1960S

By the end of the 1950s, the program schedules and executive personnel at all three networks more and more resembled one another, as alumni of ABC were installed as program heads at CBS and NBC. Despite the trauma of television's public scandals at the end of the 1950s, network audiences and advertising revenues continued unabated. The early 1960s brought unprecedented ratings success and financial prosperity to CBS under network president James T. Aubrey, who replaced Louis G. Cowan in the wake of the quiz show scandals. Aubrey had been manager of West Coast programming for CBS in 1955, overseeing the network's early moves into film programming, before moving to ABC, where he developed "77 Sunset Strip," "The Rifleman," "Maverick," "The Real McCoys," and "The Donna Reed Show." Among Aubrey's first acts as CBS network head was to cancel the single remaining prestige drama series on the network, "Playhouse 90." Aubrey launched a string of new situation comedies, often with rural settings, that kept CBS on top of the ratings for nearly a decade, including "The Andy Griffith Show" (1960); "The Dick Van Dyke Show" and "Mr. Ed" (1961); "The Beverly Hillbillies" and "The Lucy Show"' (1962); "Petticoat Junction" and "My Favorite Martian" (1963); "Gomer Pyle, U.S.M.C.," "The Munsters," and "Gilligan's Island" (1964); "Green Acres," "My Three Sons" (moved from ABC), and "Hogan's Heroes" (1965).

The 1960s represented the beginning of a new era at CBS, when record profits from continued daytime- and prime-time ratings leadership propelled the company into new fields of acquisition and operation. Nonnetwork broadcast and record activities flourished at the company, with expanding revenues from owned- and-operated stations, film program syndication, overseas ventures, and the exploding popular music industry. In 1962 CBS Television captured 80 percent of total network profits, and by 1964 the network controlled 10 of television's top 10 daytime programs and 12 of the top 15 prime-time programs. In 1966 CBS could look back at a half-decade of double-digit annual increases in television advertising revenues, reflecting television's share of national advertising, which had grown from 18 to 25 percent between 1961 and 1966. Not surprisingly, CBS stock was a Wall Street favorite in the bullish 1960s; when CBS profits rose 28 percent in 1966, its stock price jumped 55 percent in a single year, reflecting investor contentment at successive 15 percent annual advertising rate hikes imposed by the network. CBS built a new $40 million corporate headquarters in New York City, and the high-flying company followed the 1960s diversification trend of American business, making a series of generally unsuccessful corporate acquisitions during the decade.[32]

In its core business of network television, CBS's success with the rural situation comedy format in the 1960s increasingly collided with its carefully cultivated public image as television's quality network, patron of Edward R. Murrow and "Playhouse 90," both of which in fact had been pushed off the network by 1961. Rising general cynicism about network television programming created a split corporate identity at CBS under the Aubrey-Stanton regime, suggested by CBS News president Fred Friendly's recollection of Aubrey's account of their mutual functions in the CBS structure: "They say to me, 'Take your soiled little hands, get the ratings, and make as much money as you can.' They say to you, 'Take your lily-white hands, do your best, go the high road, and bring us prestige." Another CBS executive recalled a memorandum from Aubrey describing the requirements of a successful CBS show as "broads, bosoms, and fun." CBS producer William Froug told Erik Barnouw that when he was hired as the network's West Coast executive in charge of drama, he was bluntly instructed by a CBS superior: "Your job is to produce shit."[33]

Perhaps ironically, in many respects the prosperity of the 1960s allowed CBS to enforce even more firmly some of its founding programming principles in television. Columbia's growing financial clout in the early 1960s stiffened its resolve to challenge the power of television performers; the network refused Jerry Lewis's demands for artistic control of his program and dropped Jack Benny's option in 1963 when Benny balked at CBS's plan to insert the new "Petticoat Junction" between "The Red Skelton Show" and Benny's program. Tight network control of the prime-time schedule "allows CBS to tinker with shows without interference from anyone," Forbes reported in 1964. James Aubrey explained the CBS programming approach: "The schedule is simply a checkerboard. You look at all the squares and put your winners where they will give you the most." Greater CBS program control gave the network uncontested power to shuffle shows around the schedule to maximize audience flow through adjacent programs and compete against the schedules of other networks.[34]

Growing CBS schedule control also came at the expense of the power of individual sponsors in network television. In 1965 CBS programming vice president Mike Dann proclaimed that "the days of sponsor rule no longer exist." Thus, the programming principles proclaimed at CBS since its earlier television schedule reached full fruition only after the network's successful 1950s battles with television sponsors, program producers, and would-be regulatory reformers. In advancing those programming principles earliest and most forcefully among the networks, CBS ensured that it would prosper and dominate the giant advertising medium that was American television by 1960.[35]

The rise of CBS to leadership of the American television industry through the periods of anticipation, reorganization, and dominance between 1940 and 1960 illustrates several basic historical forces in the medium, from the significance of a single hit show or performer to the importance of network program and schedule control and the complex determinations of federal regulation and public opinion. While these general forces still hold considerable sway in the television industry, the competitive and regulatory contexts facing CBS and the other networks in the 1990s are quite different from those of the previous 40 years. CBS may require a new set of business and programming skills for continued success or survival in the new television environment.

NOTES

1. The author would like to thank Laura Kapnick and her staff at the CBS Reference Library for their assistance. For accounts of David Sarnoff's programming attitudes, see Kenneth Bilby, *The General: David Sarnoff and the Rise of the Communications Industry* (New York: Harper & Row, 1986), p. 249; Judine Mayerle, "The Development of the Television Variety Show as a Major Program Genre at the National Broadcasting Company: 1946–1956" (Ph.D. diss., Northwestern University, 1983), p. 128. At CBS see Peter C. Goldmark, *Maverick Inventor: My Turbulent Years at CBS* (New York: E.P. Dutton, 1973), p. 109. In his autobiography Paley confesses, "I never could learn what made the insides of radio and television work" (*As It Happened* [New York: Doubleday, 1979], p. 201). Dann is quoted in Robert Slater, *This . . . Is CBS* (Englewood Cliffs, N.J.: Prentice-Hall, 1988), p. 151.

2. "And All Because They're Smart," *Fortune*, June 1935, p. 81; William S. Paley, "Radio as a Cultural Force," speech to Federal Communications Commission, October 17, 1934, p. 9 (Collection of the CBS Reference Library, New York).

3. See William A. Nugent, "Columbia Broadcasting's Position: Earnings Growth Shown During Depression Now Slowing Down," *Barrons*, September 29, 1941, p. 13; "Thumbnail Stock Appraisal: Six Stocks with Good Peace Prospects," *Magazine of Wall Street*, December 26, 1942, p. 289.

4. For a discussion of CBS's television activities in the 1930s, see Goldmark, *Maverick Inventor*, p. 46; William S. Paley, "Statement before an Informal Engineering Hearing of the Federal Communications Commission," June 16, 1936, pp. 2, 4; "CBS Moves in on Television, Plans Transmitter on Chrysler Building," *Business Week*, April 10, 1937, pp. 20–21; Columbia Broadcasting System, "Gilbert Seldes Is Selected to Direct CBS Experimental Television Programs," press release, August 20, 1937.

5. For material on CBS's actions during this period, see Paul W Kesten, "Statement of the Columbia Broadcasting System," to Federal Communications Commission, January 15, 1940 (Collection of the CBS Reference Library, New York), pp. 10–12; Bradley Chisholm, "The CBS Color Television Venture: A

Study of Failed Innovation in the Broadcasting Industry" (Ph.D. diss., University of Wisconsin-Madison, 1987), pp. 130, 273–75; Columbia Broadcasting System, "A Statement of Some Television Facts," July 1941 (Collection of the CBS Reference Library, New York); Paul Kesten, *Postwar Shortwave, FM, and Television* (New York: Columbia Broadcasting Service, 1944); Columbia Broadcasting System, *Annual Report* for year ending December 29, 1945 (New York: Columbia Broadcasting System, March 22, 1946), p. 9.

   6. Franklin J. Schaffner, *Worthington Miner* (Metuchen, N.J.: Directors Guild of America and Scarecrow Press, 1985), p. 179; CBS historian Robert Metz cites similar suspicions of CBS motives held by *New York Times* television critic Jack Gould. (*CBS: Reflections in a Bloodshot Eye* [New York: New American Library, 1975], p. 160.)

   7. C.B.S. "Steals the Show," *Fortune*, July 1953, p. 164. The divergent fortunes of CBS in television broadcasting and manufacture were underscored by Columbia's unhappy experience in television manufacturing in the 1950s. In 1951, in exchange for nearly a quarter of Columbia's stock (worth close to twenty million dollars at the time), the network acquired Hytron, Inc., an electronics and television receiver manufacturer that was the nation's fourth largest producer of television sets. The CBS set-making subsidiary lost money steadily until it was terminated in 1956, and the entire Hytron subsidiary was liquidated in 1961, at an estimated cost of fifty million dollars. CBS historian Lewis J. Paper concluded: "The Hytron episode represented the worst corporate financial decision made by CBS, and some Wall Street analysts believed it was one of the worst corporate deals in modern American history." (*Empire: William S. Paley and the Making of CBS* [New York: St. Martin's Press, 1987], p. 155.) For a discussion of the Hytron story, see Chisholm, "CBS Color Television Venture," pp. 424–27; Metz, pp. 161–65; Paley, pp. 182–84, 221–22; "Albatross Lifted," *Forbes*, October 15, 1961, pp. 15–16; *CBS, Empire*, pp. 151–55.

   8. For Kesten's testimony, see "CBS Has Successfully Broadcast High-Frequency Television in Full Color, Paul Kesten, Network Executive Vice President, Reveals at FCC Hearings," press release, October 1945, p. 2. The text of the CBS broadcast disclaimer is contained in "A Statement of Some Television Facts".

   9. Frank Stanton, "CBS Constructs Nation's Largest Television Studio Plant to Serve as New York Program Center for CBS-TV Network," summary of press conference, February 17, 1948. "CBS and Television," *Newsweek*, March 1, 1948, p. 45; Bruce Robertson, "CBS To Build World's Largest Video Plant," *Broadcasting*, February 23, 1948, p. 14.

   10. William S. Paley, "Radio and Its Critics" (speech to the National Association of Broadcasters, Chicago, October 22, 1946), p. 6. For reaction to the speech, see John Crosby, "Mr. Paley and the Critics," *New York Herald Tribune*, October 28, 1946, p. 26.

   11. Paley, *As It Happened*, p. 193; Bilby, p. 249; see also Slater, *This . . . Is CBS*, p. 118.

   12. Columbia Broadcasting System, *Annual Report* for fiscal year ending

January 1, 1949 (New York: Columbia Broadcasting System, March 22, 1949), p. 24; George Rosen, "CBS Swings Axe to Pay for TV," *Variety*, July 14, 1948, pp. 23, 55.

13. Columbia Broadcasting System, *Annual Report* for fiscal year ending January 1, 1949 (New York: Columbia Broadcasting System, March 22, 1949), p. 3; "CBS To Build World's Largest Video Plant," p. 14. The scheduling rationale for program packaging is offered in Columbia Broadcasting System, *Annual Report* for year ending December 30, 1950 (New York: Columbia Broadcasting System, 1951), p. 5. Concerning the place of television in the talent raids and on the development of packaged programs, see "Revolutionizing Radio: CBS Wants to Buy ABC and Hytron," *Business Week*, May 12, 1951, p. 21; "One Round to CBS," *Business Week*, September 3, 1949, p. 24; "CBS Steals the Show," p. 82; Laurence Bergreen, *Look Now, Pay Later: The Rise of Network Broadcasting* (New York: New American Library, 1980), p. 182; Paley, *As It Happened*, p. 193.

14. "TV-FM-FAX," *Sponsor*, November 1947, p. 36; memorandum from William C. Ackerman to L. Hausman, December 30, 1948, p. 1; Columbia Broadcasting System, "Innovations Made by and Other Facts about the Columbia Broadcasting System," press release, 1949, p. 3 (Collection of the CBS Reference Library, New York); 1950 *Annual Report*, p. 16.

15. "Innovations Made by the Columbia Broadcasting System," p. 3 (Collection of CBS Reference Library, New York); J. C. Clifford, "Securities Disturbing Investors," *Magazine of Wall Street*, May 21, 1949, pp. 192–93; Slater, *This . . . Is CBS*, p. 149; "TV's Time of Trouble," *Fortune*, August 1951, p. 134; Columbia Broadcasting System, *Annual Report* for year ending December 29, 1951 (New York: Columbia Broadcasting System, 1952), p. 14.

16. Sarnoff is quoted in Eugene Lyons, *David Sarnoff* (New York: Pyramid Books, 1966), p. 333. For information on television talent contracts during these years, see Bilby, *The General*, p. 249; Mayerle, "Development of the Variety Show," p. 125; Jack Gould, "NBC Leads the Field in Video Funny Men," *New York Times*, September 24, 1950, Sec. 2, p. 11; Metz, *CBS*, p. 195; Slater, *This . . . Is CBS*, p. 145.

17. For accounts of "Amos 'n' Andy," see Harold Brown, "Television: Five-Year Hunt Finds New Amos 'n' Andy," *New York Herald Tribune*, June 24, 1951;' "Amos 'n' Andy Set To Begin on Video," *New York Times*, January 31, 1951; "Negro Thesps Score NAACP on A&A Stand; Set 'Positive Action' Council," *Variety*, August 8, 1951, p. 1.

18. "Television City," *Fortune*, April 1953, p. 141.

19. For Dann's comments, see Metz, *CBS*, p. 332; for similar comments by Dann, see Slater, *This . . . Is CBS*, pp. 150–51. For a discussion of the importance of Godfrey, see Harry Castleman and Walter Podrazik, *Watching TV: Four Decades of American Television* (New York: McGraw-Hill, 1982), p. 47; Metz, *CBS*, p. 176; Bergreen, *Look Now, Pay Later*, p. 179.

20. Ackerman is quoted in Max Wilk, *The Golden Age of Television: Notes From the Survivors* (New York: Delacorte, 1976), p. 251. For critical reaction to "I Love Lucy," see John Crosby, "The Hollywood Drift," *New York Herald Tribune*, March 19, 1952; idem. "The Rush to Hollywood," *New York Herald Tribune*, August 15, 1952.

21. "C.B.S. Steals the Show," pp. 79, 82; Columbia Broadcasting System, "CBS Television Takes Industry Sales Leadership," press release, May 5, 1953, p. 1; Columbia Broadcasting System, *Annual Report* for the year 1954 (New York: Columbia Broadcasting System, 1955).

22. On the falling cost per thousand of CBS prime programming, see "Is Television Pricing Itself Out of the Market?" p. 4; 1950 *Annual Report*, p. 33; 1951 *Annual Report*, p. 14; Columbia Broadcasting System, *Annual Report* for the fiscal year ending December 31, 1952 (New York: Columbia Broadcasting System, 1953).

23. For information on the programming shifts, see Castleman and Podrazik, *Watching TV*, p. 122; "Sponsor Scope," *Sponsor*, April 27, 1957, p. 10; Frank Henry Jakes, "A Study of Standards Imposed by Four Leading Television Critics with Respect to Live Television Drama" (Ph.D. diss., Ohio State University, 1960), p. 9; NBC, "Television Trends," *Research Bulletin*, November 25, 1959, p. 5.

24. Frank Stanton, speech to Second General Conference of CBS Television Affiliates, Chicago, April 13, 1956, pp. 10–11.

25. House Committee on Interstate and Foreign Commerce, *Network Broadcasting, Report* (Washington, D.C.: Government Printing Office, 1958), p. 185.

26. Columbia Broadcasting System, "Network Practices: Memorandum Supplementing Statement of Frank Stanton, President, Columbia Broadcasting System, Inc.," prepared for the Senate Committee on Interstate and Foreign Commerce (New York: Columbia Broadcasting System, Inc., 1956), June 1956, pp. 88, 90; Ashbrook P. Bryant "Historical and Social aspects of Concentration of Program Control in Television," *Law and Contemporary Problems* 34 (Summer 1969): 626–29.

27. Columbia Broadcasting System, *Annual Report* for year ending December 30, 1961 (New York: Columbia Broadcasting System, 1962), p. 6; Columbia Broadcasting System, *Annual Report* for year ending December 28, 1963 (New York: Columbia Broadcasting System, 1964), pp. 4, 19.

28. For CBS's daytime ratings, see its 1955 *Annual Report*, p. 25; for a discussion of the Hitchcock program, see Val Adams, "Hitchcock Signs for Video Series," *New York Times*, January 25, 1955; John McCarty and Brian Kelleher, *Alfred Hitchcock Presents* (New York: St. Martin's Press, 1985). For a discussion of "Perry Mason," see Jack Gould, "TV: 'Perry Mason's' End Really a Rich Beginning," *New York Times*, May 23, 1966, *Variety*, September 25, 1957.

29. U.S., Congress, Senate, Committee on Interstate and Foreign Commerce. *The Network Monopoly, Report* by Senator John W. Bricker (Washington, D.C.: Government Printing Office, 1956), pp. 3, 5, 15. As late as the mid-1970s, WCBS-TV contributed an estimated 11 percent of total CBS earnings. Metz, *CBS*, p. 382. Bernard Schwartz, "Antitrust and the FCC: The Problem of Network Dominance," *University of Pennsylvania Law Review* 107 (April 1959): 773; Bergreen, *Look Now, Pay Later*, p. 230; *Network Broadcasting*, pp. 637–38.

30. Columbia Broadcasting System, *Annual Report* for year ending December 31, 1955 (New York: Columbia Broadcasting System, 1956), p. 13; Frank Stanton, talk to Third General Conference of CBS Television Affiliates,

Chicago, April 6, 1957 (Collection of the CBS Reference Library, New York).

31. Fred Friendly, *Due to Circumstances Beyond Our Control* (New York: Random House, 1968), p. 102.

32. "Doing What Comes Naturally," *Forbes*, May 15, 1962, p. 18; "Showing of TV, Records Brightens CBS Picture," *Barrons*, May 28, 1962, p. 16; "Money Tree of Madison Ave., Special Report," *Forbes*, January 15, 1964, p. 20; Columbia Broadcasting System, *Annual Report* for year ending January 1, 1966 (New York: Columbia Broadcasting System, 1966), pp. 2, 13. For material on Columbia's unsuccessful efforts in major league baseball, educational publishing, and electronic video recording in the 1960s, see "Money Tree of Madison Ave.," p. 25; Metz, *CBS*, pp. 256–58; Goldmark, *Maverick Inventor*, chaps. 10, 11.

33. Friendly, *Due to Circumstances*, pp. xi–xii; the Aubrey memo is quoted in Bergreen, *Look Now, Pay Later*, p. 240. Aubrey denied writing the memorandum. Froug is quoted in Erik Barnouw, *The Image Empire*, vol. 3 of *The History of Broadcasting in the United States* (New York: Oxford University Press, 1970), p. 244.

34. "Money Tree of Madison Ave.," pp. 22, 23.

35. "CBS Story; Special Report: Onward, Ever Onward," *Sponsor*, September 13, 1965, p. 50.

SUGGESTIONS FOR FURTHER READING

Useful secondary accounts of CBS exist in Robert Slater, *This . . . Is CBS* (Englewood Cliffs, N.J.: Prentice-Hall, 1988); Lewis J. Paper, *Empire: William S. Paley and the Making of CBS* (New York: St. Martin's Press, 1987); and Robert Metz, *CBS: Reflections in a Bloodshot Eye* (New York: New American Library, 1975). The sometimes self-serving recollections of CBS executives are also helpful; see William S. Paley, *As It Happened* (New York: Doubleday, 1979); Peter C. Goldmark, *Maverick Inventor: My Turbulent Years at CBS* (New York: E.P. Dutton, 1973); and Fred Friendly, *Due to Circumstances Beyond Our Control* (New York: Random House, 1968). For an illuminating book-length interview with an early Columbia television executive and producer, see Franklin J. Schaffner, *Worthington Miner* (Metuchen, N.J.: Directors Guild of America and Scarecrow Press, 1985). Two *Fortune* profiles of Columbia are also valuable: "And All Because They're Smart," June 1935, p. 81 and "C.B.S. Steals the Show," July 1953, p. 78.

Chapter 3 ————————————————————————

The Weakest Chain and the Strongest Link: The American Broadcasting Company and the Motion Picture Industry, 1952–60

James L. Baughman

————————————————————————

O n a Sunday evening late in 1952, most of America's 17 million television sets were new and likely tuned to programs on one of two networks, the Columbia Broadcasting System or the National Broadcasting Company. Each offered a mix of variety programs, original weekly dramas, and situation comedies. The majority of network programs originated from network facilities in New York City. Although some smaller studios and Hollywood-based independent producers assembled shows for TV, most of the larger, more prestigious film companies had spurned the newest medium.

In the next eight years, television programming underwent a transformation. A motion picture theater chain, United Paramount Theatres (UPT), took control of the struggling third-place network, American Broadcasting Company, early in 1953. After persuading the Disney and Warner Bros. studios to enter program production in the mid-1950s, UPT's network began challenging the NBC-CBS duopoly. The celluloid covering on ABC's success was not lost either on its competition or on the other film factories. By the late 1950s, all of the major motion picture studios produced television programs. The movie colony had become television town.

UPT's network played the decisive role in a struggle between the networks and the film industry. In effect, ABC broke a deadlock between the largest studios and the television networks. A change in ownership at ABC early in 1953 brought a different managerial philosophy toward the Hollywood-made program. This new attitude combined with technological and financial disadvantages that all but compelled ABC to look west. While both NBC and CBS produced their own programming or closely supervised independent production units based in Hollywood and New York, ABC virtually surrendered that responsibility to several major film studios.

THE COMMISSION'S CHILD

A regulatory ideal, and not market forces, had created ABC. The Federal Communications Commission, sharing the antitrust activism of Franklin Roosevelt's Justice Department in the late 1930s, championed diversity. In 1941, a commission majority approved a Chain Broadcasting Report that included a rule forbidding a network from having more than one affiliate in any market. The order, which the Supreme Court upheld in 1943, compelled NBC to sell off its smaller "Blue Network." Edward J. Noble, a wealthy candy manufacturer, purchased NBC's weaker chain and renamed the network ABC. Noble soon realized that the FCC's enthusiasm for a multiplicity of voices had a very shaky economic base. ABC could not keep pace with its established rivals in radio, CBS and NBC, which aired the vast majority of popular programs.

ABC entered television after World War II only to find the costs of entering television even more disheartening. Nobel had to draw on his Life Saver fortune to cover ballooning yearly deficits. And he was only willing to reduce his net worth so much. Citing $3.5 million already lost in television operations in October 1949, Noble canceled programs and laid off personnel. CBS TV picked up one of the programs, "Actor's Studio," and lured away another, "House Party." In the fall of 1950, ABC greatly expanded its evening television offerings and then had to retrench because of heavy losses.[1]

Like Allen DuMont, a TV set manufacturer and owner of the DuMont television network, Noble found himself cast as David facing two Goliaths, and without a slingshot. Although all four networks lost money in their first years of operation, NBC could be sustained by its self-interested parent corporation, RCA, a major electronics concern. CBS, while lacking NBC's resources, had a stronger radio chain from which to derive revenues. Columbia had also successfully "raided" NBC and ABC talent, leaving CBS with the most impressive list of popular radio performers. Many of these in turn entered television as stars of CBS series. If more than two television networks were to survive, DuMont and ABC needed large infusions of cash to sign talent and expand program production. The "little two" chains had two options. The first was to raise money through the offering of stock, a tactic ABC tried in 1946 with disappointing results. The second, more dramatic step was to seek a "friendly" merger—in effect, selling the network under terms favorable to the owners and management of the chain. Unlike Allen DuMont, who stubbornly resisted surrendering control of his small enterprise, Noble and ABC president Robert Kintner sought a buyer. They had already been approached by CBS, which wanted some of ABC's TV stations. They also negotiated with representatives of International Telephone & Telegraph (ITT) and several film companies.[2]

The visible hand of the federal government again came to ABC's assistance by creating a well-to-do suitor for the struggling chain. The five largest motion picture companies, the Justice Department contended, had used their ownership of theaters to the disadvantage of independent theater operators. A Justice Department consent decree required the major studios to sell off as separate companies their exhibition units. Under the divestiture order, the new theater chains, formed in December 1949 as part of the court's ruling, had to liquidate some of their properties. Awash in money, the largest of the new exhibitors, United Paramount Theatres, looked to expand into a related industry. A logical and promising area, UPT president Leonard Goldenson reasoned, would be television. And Kintner, who approached him in the spring of 1950, handed him and UPT the chance to enter the newest medium. After extensive negotiations, Noble agreed in May 1951 to sell ABC in an exchange of UPT stock.[3]

Any transfer of the radio and television stations that ABC owned to UPT required the approval of the Federal Communications Commission. And the FCC and its staff divided sharply over the combination. UPT's infusions of cash—it had pledged some $37 million—to shore up ABC's operations would plainly increase competition among networks. Such new rivalries, some commissioners concluded, would realize a regulatory objective by fostering more diversity in programming; they assumed that three, rather than two, strong networks would mean more types of series and shows. Still, UPT's record of antitrust violations as part of Paramount Pictures prior to the 1948 divestiture order discredited the company in the eyes of the commission staff. Permitting United Paramount to enter television was akin to giving a convicted bootlegger a liquor license after Prohibition's repeal. Moreover, they and others feared that UPT represented an attempt by the film industry itself to take over television. The proposed merger, the chief of the FCC's Broadcast Bureau warned, "is but the first step in the eventual complete unification of the motion picture industry in all its phases, production, distribution and exhibition, with the television and radio industry."[4] FCC staff members also doubted the capacity of film executives without experience in radio to behave "responsibly." Broadcasters, like their counterparts in film, had coveted large audiences; unlike the governors of the movie colony, they had been subject to public service regulations for more than 25 years. Broadcasters could not concern themselves only with majority taste. Those entering television with a background in radio understood the governmental expectation that they provide more than entertainment. UPT officials promised not to impose on the newest mass medium a Hollywood sensibility. With such assurances in mind, and the probability of greater network competition, the FCC approved the union in February 1953.[5]

All of the networks in the early 1950s managed their chains mindful of industry traditions. One, born during the first days of "chain broadcasting" in the 1920s, had been that consumers preferred the live transmission of programs. The simultaneous broadcast had given radio listeners the sensation of "being there"—of hearing, in the modesty of their parlors across the country, a renowned orchestra performing in a fancy New York ballroom. When the networks began airing more "transcriptions" in the mid-1940s, Kintner broke ranks and ordered ABC Radio to increase its live broadcasts; rivals had to reduce their recorded programming. Although the bias against transcribed performances had begun to break down, network officials publicly continued to profess their dedication to live broadcasting. Goldenson himself had told the FCC in March 1952 that "the real vitality in the future of television is in live television." In June 1953, 81.5 percent of all three networks' hours came over live.[7]

None of the networks apparently expected this high live-to-film ratio to be maintained indefinitely. As early as 1949, some at RCA had been urging NBC's chief programmer, Sylvester L. "Pat" Weaver, to consider airing more filmed programming. Weaver himself, while publicly dedicated to live variety and dramatic programs, could not resist trying to interest David O. Selznick, producer of some of Hollywood's "classic" middle-brow efforts in the 1930s and 1940s, in making TV programs for NBC. In 1951, *Fortune* quoted CBS president Frank Stanton predicting that television would, after a period, come to rely on filmed over live presentation.[8] Yet Stanton, like Weaver, wanted the production of programming, whenever possible, to remain within his network's grasp. As the FCC pondered the UPT-ABC merger, CBS had been investing in production facilities in Hollywood. Then, too, as Vance Kepley, Jr. has argued, Weaver's preference for expensive live programs promised to create a demand for television that in time would become a habit that could be satisfied by less costly filmed fare. A year before the UPT-ABC merger's approval, Kintner had indicated that up to 50 percent of ABC's schedule would be on film, three-fourths of which would be produced in Hollywood.[9]

GOLDENSON'S INITIAL STRATEGY AND FRUSTRATION

Entering network television, UPT prepared to play both sides of the street or, in show business parlance, both coasts. With great fanfare, the suddenly cash-rich ABC signed popular performers—some to host live variety programs from New York—as part of a strategy of bringing name players to the network. More quietly, Goldenson and Kintner, in search of sources for program production, began a concerted courtship of the major motion picture studios. Initially, however, only the small Hal Roach company would deal with the third network.

Goldenson appears to have entered television with an excess of optimism. As a theater chain executive, he assumed he was, in effect, filling so many "home" screens. The right mix of shows would create demand for ABC programming. Successful showmanship alone would pull ABC up. But Goldenson did not realize that UPT was entering a decidedly unbalanced competitive environment. In battle with NBC and CBS, the impresario needed an engineer's sensibility. Money and ability could not together overcome an inequitable distribution of TV channels. It was as if UPT sought to build a movie house in a theater district on a small island, only to discover that no land or buildings were available. Established rivals owned all the property.

The technological imbalance in networking became apparent soon after the FCC began awarding TV frequencies in the late 1940s. The commission had granted television licenses on an individual basis. A large city, capable of supporting three or more TV outlets, might have only one station for several years until the commission determined which applicant would receive the second, and then, depending on the size of the market, the third outlet. In addition, the commission limited the number of frequencies per viewing area to prevent inter-ference, especially in the more densely populated sections of the Midwest and Northeast. In a move that strengthened the position of the dominant networks, the FCC in 1948 suspended issuing new TV licenses and prepared a master channel assignment plan; frequencies already allocated to individual parties could go on the air. Columbia and NBC, with the most established records in network radio, easily cajoled those with licenses—many held by owners of local radio outlets with CBS or NBC agreements—to affiliate with them. In all but 12 of the 63 areas with television service before the lifting of the four-year "freeze," CBS and NBC, a DuMont representative later charged, had almost exclusive access.[10]

When the FCC in 1952 issued its *Sixth Report and Order*, ending the station freeze and allocating TV frequencies for the entire nation, the commission in effect reinforced the front-runners' leads. As in regulating radio, federal overseers wanted most to provide all potential viewers with television service; of secondary concern was the opportunity for small communities to have a TV assignment. Allowing for competing services ranked third.[11] In medium and small markets, ABC and DuMont, along with nonprofit, educational broadcasters, would have to rely on stations on an experimental portion of the radio spectrum on the ultrahigh frequency (UHF), channels 14 through 83. The commission "intermixed" allocations in some viewing areas. That is, the FCC set aside one or two VHF outlets; competitors would have to broadcast on UHF. DuMont and his engineers, skeptical of UHF's potential, had ardently argued against intermixture and pleaded for more VHF assignments in the larger cities—in effect, providing all four chains with equal access. The commission, however, contended that the DuMont proposal would have cost some rural areas all television service. And ABC, the technological innocent, had no objections to the FCC's UHF solution. DuMont proved all too prescient; UHF signals could not reach as many homes as those on the very high frequency (VHF), channels 2 through 13. Worse, most TV sets could not receive UHF signals. Although most manufacturers began offering "all-channel" sets, the optional UHF converter cost around $35, an extra charge most consumers resisted. As a result, UHF stations in most markets could not, as DuMont had anticipated, compete with their rivals on VHF. In mid-1954, a majority of ABC's and DuMont's affiliates in the one hundred largest TV viewing areas were in the upper frequency. By then, ABC had joined DuMont in complaining about the inadequacies of UHF; two years later, ABC endorsed DuMont's 1950 proposal to create more four-VHF markets.[12]

The FCC's ill-considered UHF policy combined with the lingering consequencies of the 1948–52 freeze to frustrate ABC further. Overwhelmed with applications for the remaining licenses and its own cumbersome "comparative license" procedures, the commission did not allocate third VHF channels in some markets until the late 1950s. Not until 1958 did the FCC award Pittsburgh's third VHF; until then, ABC had to bargain with another VHF outlet. Most stations that shared their affiliation with ABC and one of the Big Two usually only "accepted" or carried the most popular ABC programs. In the 15 largest markets with only two VHF channels in July 1955, ABC could clear only 11 of 23 shows offered. These other affiliates, splitting their association with ABC and another network, either refused to carry live programs or telecast them on a delayed basis on film or kinescope, a crude precursor to videotape. "We weren't a network," one ABC executive recalled. "We couldn't do the Ed Sullivan type of [live variety] show if we wanted to—there are too many places where we'd be saying 'Merry Christmas' in the middle of January."[13]

ABC's inability to deliver audiences comparable to CBS's or NBC's caused most TV advertisers to ignore the network. For want of sufficient station clearances, ABC lost $2 million in the fall of 1954 broadcasting NCAA football. Not enough stations would accept the games to encourage enough advertisers to sponsor the live telecasts and allow the network to recover its fees and production costs.[14] Lacking a Louisville clearance, ABC lost the critically praised "U.S. Steel Hour" to CBS. The failure of some affiliates to carry ABC programs in 1955, Kintner later told a Senate committee, had cost the network $13 million.[15]

GOING WEST

Securing its own well-produced Hollywood programs, Goldenson determined, would spare his network humiliating episodes like the loss of "The U.S. Steel Hour." ABC would deal directly with the major studios and then give advertisers no choice but to buy time from the third network. ABC's 1953 contract with Hal Roach, William Boddy has noted, served as a prototype. ABC would help to defray production costs and, in return, the Roach Studio turned over to the network the task of selling the program to advertisers.[16]

Goldenson's background in film exhibition thus took on new importance. A graduate of Harvard College and Harvard Law School, Goldenson had been a young attorney with a New York law firm when he first did legal work for Paramount Pictures' New England theaters. Impressed Paramount executives named Goldenson, at the age of 32, head of Paramount's theatrical chain. For the next 11 years Goldenson ran Paramount's theater division and, though based in New York, established numerous contacts in the movie colony. He had played poker with Samuel Goldwyn, Darryl Zanuck, and Selznick. He dined regularly with Jack L. Warner, head of Warner Bros.[17]

Goldenson and Kintner visited a movie colony torn over what to do about the home screen. United Artists, Columbia Pictures, and some smaller studios had produced programs for the newest medium from the virtual beginning of regular telecasts. Other, larger film concerns, including Paramount, had invested in alternative telecasting systems—theatrical television and pay television systems—that would provide them more control over the creation and distribution of the product, and more earnings than any network arrangement. In the late 1940s some within the industry had sought TV licenses, the first step toward the creation of their own networks; ABC had weighed acquisition offers from several studios.

Although he did not operate a major studio, Walt Disney had made America's most popular animated cartoons in the 1930s and 1940s and was willing to enter television. He had produced two successful Christmas specials for CBS, and both that network and NBC approached the cartoonist to do more. They backed off when Disney stated his terms. His compensation charge was high, $2 million for 26 one-hour programs.[18] This was more than the tight-fisted CBS would commit itself to. And neither chain could accept Disney's demand that a television deal include co-investment in a new type of amusement park, which he wanted to build in Orange County, California. However infatuated with Mickey Mouse, NBC and Columbia, like the financial community, deemed "Disneyland" too risky a venture. ABC, in contrast, agreed to buy stock in the corporation formed to build and operate the park; the network ultimately paid $8 million for 35 percent interest in the company. Disney signed an exclusive seven-year contract to produce programming for ABC television.[19]

Kintner, trying to secure a sponsor before the Disney program's September 1954 premiere, found advertisers put off by the high cost ABC had to charge. The network president later claimed that over a hundred companies rejected his sales pitch. Not even Mickey Mouse, they averred, could overcome ABC's weak line-up of affiliates. Eventually Kintner adopted a tactic of Weaver's, the "magazine" concept of program underwriting that in time became the industry norm. Rather than ask one company to sponsor a program, Kintner persuaded three to share the bill.[20]

With so much at stake, ABC selected the time slot for "Disneyland" with care. Research suggested that ABC align the program against one of CBS's most popular live variety programs, "Arthur Godfrey and His Friends." Although Godfrey, the host of several radio and television programs, earned more for CBS than any other performer, ABC audience research suggested that younger viewers wanted an alternative to the egotistical star. In a strategy repeated often by the network, ABC scheduled "Disneyland" in the fall 1954 season one-half hour *ahead* of Godfrey's Wednesday night program. Parents planning to switch channels heard their children scream, and Godfrey saw his Wednesday-night following shrink. "Disneyland," Kintner remarked, "cut Godfrey down to size" and overall finished sixth in the 1954–55

A. C. Nielsen audience ratings. ABC had its first top-rated program. "With a bang that blew Wednesday night to kingdom come for the two major networks," *Time* observed, "Disney burst into television."[21]

Disney's program was unusually self-promotional. Individual episodes fit into four categories—Frontierland, Fantasyland, Tomorrowland, and True Life Adventure—three of which served as themes for different sections of Disneyland. Three programs described the conception and building of the park, which opened in mid-1955, with a wonderment that caused a generation of American children to demand that their parents take them to Disney's "permanent World's Fair." Even Soviet leader Nikita Khrushchev tried to see the park when he visited California in 1959. In a like spirit, the program publicized Disney's feature films. An hour-long preview of his studio's adaptation of *20,000 Leagues Under the Sea*, released soon after the premiere of "Disneyland," greatly stimulated interest in the film. The True Life Adventure episodes constituted TV previews of Disney's feature-length wildlife documentaries. Although much praised at the time, the nature programs only affected to realism. Animals, like some Disney cartoon figures, frolicked innocently. These were nature films for city and suburban children. The Disney studio carefully smoothed the rough edges of the outdoors such that prairie dogs, in one program a critic observed, were depicted "as sharp, alert, quick, brave, cute and cunning." The animal protagonists "assume the status of characters in fables like Donald Duck, who for the sake of sympathetic audiences achieve eternal life by triumphing over all adversity."[22] As part of the Frontierland theme, Disney produced three hour-long programs very loosely based on the life of Davy Crockett. Aired on December 15, 1954, January 15, 1955, and February 23, 1955, the Crockett episodes earned impressive ratings. The unknown "B" movie actor cast in the title role, Fess Parker, became a celebrity. And various entrepreneurs cashed in on the craze among youngsters for coonskin caps and related Crockett paraphernalia.[23]

"Disneyland" offered the first and best evidence of Goldenson's strategy. Showmanship would, perhaps, bring success to ABC. In early 1956, 50 stations that shared their affiliations with CBS and ABC, and 10 that had exclusive agreements with Columbia, carried "Disneyland."[24] Station managers suddenly learned what many parents had discovered at the height of the Crockett craze, to their horror: it was hard to say no to children. ABC, heretofore the chain least likely to enjoy success on Madison Avenue, sold all advertising to a second Disney program, "The Mickey Mouse Club," prior to its October 1955 release.[25] Spotting one typist wearing Mickey Mouse ears at ABC's New York offices, TV critic John Crosby observed in May 1956, "Disney got the place off the ground and nobody is going to laugh at Mickey Mouse ears on that network."[26]

FILLING THE LOT

Goldenson pursued an even greater and more elusive prize, Warner Bros. Like virtually all of the studios, Warner Bros. had seriously considered entering television in the 1940s and had negotiated with Noble about purchasing ABC in 1948. In a change of heart that year, the three brothers then voted 2–1 not to seek TV licenses in Los Angeles, San Francisco, Boston, and Detroit.[27] Soon thereafter, as television sharply reduced box office receipts, Warner and others adopted a public pose of hostility toward the home screen. In the early 1950s, studio head Jack Warner had been one of the most vocal proponents of the colony's TV "boycott." He had banned TV sets from the lot and forbade them from appearing in any Warner films.

By the mid-1950s there was less cause for antagonism, as the film industry had begun to recover from the worst effects of television's capture of the Great Audience. The studios, in response first to rising production costs and then to TV's cut into audience demand, produced fewer films. Warner and other studios all but ended the manufacture of cheap "B" movies for the smaller movie house. The number of features dropped from a postwar high of 425 in 1950 to 283 in 1955. UPT, one of the concerned exhibitors, complained of the new "seller's market." [28] The studios had little choice. Americans went to movies less often; weekly attendance per household had dropped from 2.22 in 1948 to .99 in 1953.[29] In what came to be known as "the blockbuster strategy," the movie colony began investing more heavily in films that would draw Americans away from their home screens or, at the very least, prevent attendance from dropping further. Films had to possess higher production values—especially obvious in the elaborate, often biblical, epics, on wider screens—than anything seen on television. In January 1954 Jack Warner announced that his studio's next 16 features would cost as much to produce as Warner's previous 42. Several months later, Sam Goldwyn declared "a new era where quality is replacing quantity."[30] At the same time, filmmakers, correctly calculating that consumers would pay the added costs of production, boosted ticket prices. The new approach appeared to be working. Until 1953, *Fortune* reported, any film that grossed more than $5 million worldwide was considered a hit. The biggest grosser in 1948,

The Road to Rio, had sold $4.5 million in tickets. In 1953 and 1954, however, 17 features had passed the $5 million mark. And average weekly household attendance in 1954, for the first time since 1946, had risen.[31] Finally, the studios limited their risks while reducing their operating costs by co-producing features with independent companies, often headed by a director or star performer. Independents usually needed studio cash, but, as more entrepreneurial endeavors, proved more cost-efficient than studio productions.

Such fundamental changes in the movie colony made an ABC-Warner marriage possible. As Warner made fewer feature films and shot more on location, the company found itself with an underutilized physical plant. Assembling TV programs would justify maintaining the vast Warner lot. "Disneyland," *Time* claimed, had made the cartoonist's studio "the busiest in Hollywood." Disney himself admitted that 80 percent of his operation involved TV production.[32] Like "Disneyland," a Warner Bros. program could also promote the company's theatrical releases, and the blockbuster strategy made publicity all the more important. Warners could also use the money. Taking longer to produce, blockbusters in production tied up monies. And ABC was not asking Warners to produce films that would, in their production values and featured players, compete with theatrical releases. Rather, Goldenson expected B movies. Common in the 1930s and 1940s, B pictures had been made quickly and inexpensively with relatively unknown players. B movies had been the common staple of the smaller, neighborhood theaters or the second billing of a double feature. As marginal movie houses closed, however, the demand for most types of B pictures fell sharply. Yet they could enjoy, as a model for television programming, a new life. However publicly disdainful of television, Warner had made B pictures. The film executives signed an exclusive agreement with ABC in March 1955.[33]

First aired in September 1955, "Warner Bros. Presents" consisted of three different alternating series based on popular Warner theatrical releases: *King's Row, Casablanca,* and *Cheyenne.* The series' title evoked the majesty of the movie colony, as did the backdrop at the beginning and end of each episode, showing the massive Warners lot. In its visual authority, it could be likened to a Sears catalog at the turn of the century, displaying the gargantuan factory where many of the goods listed had been produced. Mindful of Disney's successful promotion of *20,000 Leagues Under the Sea* Warners devoted six to eight minutes of each hour of "Warner Brothers Presents" to a "Behind-the-Cameras" segment of previews and interviews with actors in forthcoming Warner movies.

Yet the Warners' entry into television almost failed. Critics panned the "Behind-the-Cameras" segment and narration by actor Gig Young. The studio perhaps took Goldenson's intentions too seriously and invested little in the series' first scripts and production values, despite, characteristically for a studio product, going over budget. And viewer interest fell, with the program's audience share dropping from 34 percent for the first week to 21 percent the second and 18 percent the third. Warner executives complained about the program's place on the schedule, 7:30–8:30 (Eastern Time). Youngsters made up a disproportionate share of the TV audience in early evening prime time and made the adult themes on "King's Row" and "Casablanca" problematical.[34] Not surprisingly, given the youthful composition of the viewership, the only one of the three regular series to enjoy audience favor was a Western. Warners eventually dropped the "Kings Row" and "Casablanca" segments in favor of "Cheyenne," starring the young and unknown B movie star Clint Walker.

Once again the network scheduled the studio-made program a half hour ahead of the variety program of a popular TV performer, Milton Berle, thought to be losing his "legs," or audience loyalty. The audience viewing "Cheyenne" would not surrender the set after 30 minutes to those loyal to the medium's first star, "Mr. Television."[35]

Berle was a casualty of more than skillful scheduling. The box office successes of Westerns like *High Noon* (1952) and *Shane* (1953) indicated that a mass market remained for horse operas. Moreover, a Western TV series could be expected to appeal to newer members of the television audience, those consumers in smaller Southern and Western areas, among the last to have television services. These smaller markets had long been a source for the B Westerns, fewer of which were available as the studios reduced their B picture output and one, Monogram, ceased operations altogether. This "marginalized" audience for B films took to the filmed Western on the home screen, which held far more appeal than the boorish New York-oriented routines of Uncle Milty. "Berle's day is no more," cracked an ABC vice-president in February 1957. "Tuesday belongs to ABC."[36] And like "Disneyland," "Cheyenne" enjoyed excellent clearances from ABC affiliates.[37]

Nevertheless, the success of "Cheyenne" and two other Westerns premiering in September 1955, "The Life and Legend of Wyatt Earp" and "Gunsmoke," contradicted conventional wisdom about the evening schedule. Despite the success of Disney's Crockett episodes, Westerns on television had been thought the programming of young boys. TV stations and networks had carried some Westerns from the beginning, but usually telecast them for children earlier in the day. Early TV Westerns, like "Hopalong Cassidy" and "The Lone Ranger," lacked the high production values of "Cheyenne" and were written all but exclusively for the very young. They tended to be simple moral tales of evil vanquished by an avenger and his faithful companion. "Cheyenne" deliberately cultivated a larger audience. Parents as well as children could follow the exploits of Cheyenne Bodie. Casting a younger male in the lead encouraged some female viewers to watch the program (and little effort was spared to reveal Walker's muscled torso). Then, too, "Cheyenne" and subsequent Warners TV horse operas like "Sugarfoot"—mildly influenced by some of the more self-consciously "realistic" Western films of the early 1950s—had protagonists actually dealing with human emotions. Violence was more explicit. The humor and mild sarcasm of the new prime-time Westerns, notably "Maverick", as well as CBS's "Have Gun, Will Travel," appealed to a broad range of viewers. Watch out for those TV cowboys, *Sponsor* observed in November 1956. "They're riding and shooting up the network range. Latest ratings on the filmed westerns are enough to make Madison Avenue swallow its gum."[38] Slowly an audience grew for the evening horse opera. By the fall 1959 season, Westerns had become the dominant program form, with more than two dozen on the three networks' evening schedules. So many had their debut that season that a San Francisco TV critic wrote of "the new hoof-and-mouth offerings".[39]

Other studios initially following Disney's lead did not experience Warners' success. For the 1955–56 season, both MGM and Twentieth Century–Fox produced series resembling "Warner Bros. Presents." Excessive promotion—and an overestimation of the nation's fascination with the movie colony—doomed MGM's effort. On ABC, "MGM Parade" originally offered nothing but studio interviews and coming attractions; MGM then presented adaptations of and excerpts based on classic studio releases. Aired on alternate weeks with "U.S. Steel Hour" on CBS, "The Twentieth Century–Fox Theatre" presented hour-long versions of old Fox films, starring lesser-known actors. The program failed to find an audience.[40]

Despite some acrimony over "Warner Brothers Presents," Warners and ABC cemented their relationship late in 1956 when the studio agreed to produce more series for the network. A change in the ownership of Warner Bros., which left Jack, alone of the brothers, in charge, caused a new commitment to TV production. At the same time, Goldenson secured a loan for ABC that allowed him to offer the studio more money for TV programming. Warner began work on more Westerns and a private detective series, "77 Sunset Strip," for the fall 1957 season.[41]

"77 Sunset Strip" set off another programming trend. The series featured young and handsome Los Angeles private detectives invariably working in glamorous settings. No one would confuse the protagonists,

Stu Bailey and Jeff Spencer, with characters in a novel by Raymond Chandler or Dashiell Hammett. As with the Warner horse operas, the leads' physical attractiveness was meant to appeal to younger female viewers who would otherwise have regarded a detective series as too male a genre. Both the ratings and station clearances proved impressive. Warner soon produced other series modeled closely after "77 Sunset Strip," with the leads working in New Orleans, Honolulu, and Miami, and the private-eye genre became the dominant programming type by the 1959–60 season. A dismayed Terrance O'Flaherty of the *San Francisco Chronicle* dismissed Warner's "Hawaiian Eye" in October 1959 as "77 Waikiki Beach."[42]

Warner and ABC had shamelessly brought the B picture to the home screen. By mid-1959, 23 different TV programs were in production at the Warner studio, but—with most theatrical releases shot on location—no feature films. That fall, Fred Silverman estimated, Warners produced approximately one-third of ABC's evening schedule. The stars invariably were, like Norman "Clint" Walker, young and unknown. They could be paid relatively little, as Walker discovered when he struck for a salary increase. A decade earlier, Walker and others would have appeared in the quickly fashioned B movies. In the late 1950s, they starred in TV series shot in five or six days. "The broad economic base of the movie business had always been the 'B,' or program picture," a writer for *TV Guide* observed in 1959. "Today TV has pre-empted that base."[43] As Goldenson had promised Warner, television could replace the marginal movie house as a source for the film industry's cheapest and most profitable commodity. ABC, Martin Mayer wrote in 1961, "believes the B-picture is the correct television show as once it was the correct show in the neighborhood movie house."[44]

The studio action series also gave ABC advantages over NBC and CBS. The network's own research indicated that filmed series were not only less expensive to produce compared to Weaver's spectaculars but also averaged higher audiences over a four-week period. The weekly Western or other action-adventure programs had an added benefit for ABC in competing against CBS with its impressive and costly roster of established performers like Jack Benny and Jackie Gleason. The ABC action show did not have to have an expensive "star," with years of experience in film or radio, to be a success. The series itself, Silverman observed, "could make the star."[45] Like the film industry in the 1930s and 1940s, ABC could create, at first at low cost given the initial obscurity of such performers as Clint Walker and James Garner, its own star system. "We're making new stars today," Goldenson explained in July 1958. "James Garner is as important in his way as Clark Gable was in his heyday."[46]

ABC's stress on filmed series had clearly worked. In April 1956, TV critic Jack Gould of the *New York Times* described ABC's success against NBC and CBS as "little short of miraculous." The third network "is giving the two titans some anxious moments and seems certain to go much further."[47] In December 1958, four of the top-rated programs were on ABC. And the network claimed the largest increase in viewers and percentage increase in total billings to advertisers. In Columbia's 1960 annual report, CBS TV president James Aubrey spoke of the "evolution of a three network rivalry."[48]

CONTINUED DISCRIMINATION

ABC's programming successes in the late 1950s and early 1960s notwithstanding, access to some markets continued to be a severe problem for the network. Some affiliates still proved fickle; in 1958, one-fourth of all ABC stations refused to clear "Wyatt Earp," one of the network's strongest entries.[49] ABC still lacked "primary," or unshared, affiliates in such viewing areas as Louisville, Jacksonville, Rochester, and Syracuse. Stuck with a disproportionate number of shared affiliates, the third network had to rely on film, a network official explained to the FCC in February 1962. The popular filmed series "Ben Casey" reached about 98 percent of all television homes. But 33 percent, or 62 of ABC's stations, carried the program on a delayed basis. Only 6 percent, or 11 of CBS's affiliates, refused to carry the live variety program hosted by Gary Moore.[50]

Although willing to buy time on the network as a result of the Disney and Warner successes, advertisers continued to discriminate against the network, even after ABC began to draw near or ahead in the ratings during the 1959–60 and 1960–61 seasons. More than ratings, Madison Avenue considered "coverage"—that is, the total number of homes ABC programs reached. Because ABC had fewer "TV homes" than NBC or CBS, sponsors would not pay ABC the rates charged by the Big Two. Normally charges to advertisers covered the expenses of individual programs plus the cost of broadcast time, or what ABC paid to relay a program to affiliates. ABC had to give discounts—and, in effect, take a loss—even for a promising new series like "Warner Brothers Presents."[51] During the 1960–61 season in markets where ABC had comparable affiliates—that is, VHFs, such as in Detroit—and led in the local ratings, advertisers still refused to pay the same charges commanded by NBC and ABC.[52]

Sustained ratings leadership might yet have overcome the coverage problem of the early 1960s. The overall success of ABC's evening schedule in the 1959–60 and 1960–61 seasons caused some stations to switch affiliations from NBC and Columbia to ABC.[53] Had this trend continued in the early 1960s, the network would have approached coverage "parity" with the Big Two. Unfortunately for ABC, the network's ratings collapsed after the 1960–61 season and, with it, for another 15 years, the hope of luring strong affiliates away from CBS and NBC.

Nor could a quick resolution to the problem of UHF television be found. In November 1955, the FCC rejected a revision of the Sixth Report and Order that would have aided ABC by making channel frequency distribution more equitable.[54] The UHF plight worsened as the percentage of sets equipped to receive all channels fell from 9.2 percent in 1957 to 7.3 percent in 1962. That year, the commission persuaded Congress to enact the All-Channel Receiver law, which empowered the FCC to rule that all TV sets sold after April 30, 1964, be able to obtain both VHF and UHF signals. Only after Americans replaced their TV receivers in the late 1960s and early 1970s could they begin to view UHF stations.[55]

FINANCIAL EXPLANATIONS

Another competitive disadvantage helped to explain ABC's emphasis on certain types of studio-made filmed series. Simply put, American lacked the financial reserves of Columbia and NBC. Unlike NBC, ABC had no "parent" to cover for a spendthrift child who had spent one day too many shopping. NBC accounted for between 22.0 and 26.2 percent of RCA's total income between 1954 and 1960. By comparison, ABC-UPT after 1956 derived more than half of its income from radio and television operations. Although broadcast properties constituted CBS's main income source, the strong position of Columbia's radio chain in the 1940s had generously subsidized the network's entry into television and left the network more than able to invest in in-house productions.[56] ABC did have income sources. Through the decade, profits from ABC-owned stations helped to make up for losses from networking. ABC-UPT continually received net capital gains from the sale of marginal film houses, which were then poured into programming costs. But Goldenson insisted that his company's theater division not be stripped for its television network.

Goldenson, and some investors holding ABC-UPT stock, knew

the financial community regarded ABC as a relatively unattractive investment. Wall Street had advised Goldenson against acquiring ABC in 1951. The Disney and Warner deals, Goldenson recalled, failed to warm bankers to the third network. Momentarily discouraged, Goldenson "began to think that perhaps the bankers might have been right and I may have been wrong."[57] In 1956, ABC was able to borrow money from the Metropolitan Insurance Company and five banks, but only after extensive negotiations. The consortium agreed to lend ABC $37.2 million to repay debts and provide for credits of up to $27.8 million. Goldenson resolved to avoid soliciting loans in the future.[58] As a result, ABC-UPT stockholders paid dearly. UPT stock the year before the ABC acquisition earned $1.70 per share, exclusive of capital gains; in 1958, earnings per share from operations had fallen to $1.21. Early in 1964, brokerage houses still actively counseled against purchasing ABC stock.[59]

ABC's troubles raising money may puzzle members of a succeeding generation who assume TV's primacy to society and profitability to investors. By the mid-1950s, most TV stations earned money, with some enjoying a pretax profit rate of up to 40 percent. Stations in larger markets, including the limited number that the commission permitted each network to own, made impressive profits. Network telecasting, however, was far less lucrative in the 1950s; especially in the early years, only the networks' owned-and-operated stations kept them in the black. Through the 1960s, Wall Street normally recommended station "groups"—that is, publicly held companies owning individual stations, rather than CBS and ABC stocks. A shrewd investor with a large and diversified portfolio might have anticipated that ABC stock would, in time, be an excellent property. By the mid-1970s, ABC did indeed become fully competitive with CBS and NBC. And two blue-chip stocks of the fifties, U.S. Steel and General Motors, led deeply troubled industries.[60]

In the 1950s, however, potential financial underwriters had to consider ABC's station allocation problem and the hazards of forecasting earnings in show business. Purchases of TV time could be predicted in the short run; a recession was likely to soften demand for advertising spots. Advertiser interest in an individual network was harder to anticipate. Analysts might be able to project sales for tires or machine tool parts. Who could be so sure about the popularity of a new TV program? Would "Sugarfoot" win viewers to ABC? Would "Bourbon Street Beat" last more than one season? To the careful investor, show business seemed too chancy. "The number of companies that are willing to enter this field is very limited," Kintner had told the FCC in 1952. Broadcasting "is a field in which companies do not enter lightly. It involves tremendous risks. . . . Programs on radio and television literally involve guarantees and possible losses of millions of dollars."[61]

ABC compromised and in effect became a video movie house. Going to Disney and Warner spared Goldenson the expenses CBS and NBC incurred producing their own programming. Although neither Disney nor Warner came cheap, the costs of both deals paled when compared to what the network would have had to pay for the equivalents of Weaver's spectaculars and the Big Two's in-house production facilities. Goldenson, trained in film exhibition and in a cash squeeze, thus surrendered his network's sovereignty. According to the FCC's Office of Network Study, independent companies like Disney and Warner produced 62.2 percent of ABC's regular evening weekly schedule in 1957, compared to 45.6 percent of NBC's and 26.5 percent of CBS's.[62] And in making deals with Disney and Warners, the network, despite contributing 50 percent or more to the costs of production, became the junior partner to each. ABC did not insist that Disney and Warner Bros. produce a pilot for "Disneyland," "Zorro," and "Warner Bros. Presents." The network similarly had no significant role in the production of series. Warner Bros., Silverman wrote, "maintained the final decision on all matters of the program itself—casting, writers, producers, directors were all under the control of the studio."[63] ABC's "production work," Martin Mayer observed in 1961, "has been done almost entirely by the movie studios, and though ABC usually pays half the cost of program development, Goldenson's small New York programming staff sits down with Hollywood mostly to talk about buttons and bows, to give the kind of guidance the retailer gives the dress manufacturer."[64]

ABC AND THE HOLLYWOODIZATION OF THE HOME SCREEN

Partly as a consequence of ABC's programming triumphs, both Columbia and NBC aired more filmed programming, produced by nonnetwork, usually Hollywood-based, production companies. Live programming fell from 81.5 percent of all network telecasts in June 1953 to 26.5 percent eight years later.[65] And the enthusiasm that CBS and NBC displayed for program types upon which ABC had first relied, notably the Western and private detective series, caused ABC TV president Oliver Treyz in April 1961 to accuse the Big Two of copying his network's programming approach.[66]

Treyz, in fact, overstated ABC's influence on one of the networks.

CBS had been moving toward a greater emphasis on filmed series even before ABC's successes had become clear. Columbia's adult Western "Gunsmoke," had premiered the same season as "Wyatt Earp" and "Cheyenne," and gradually developed a large following. Its success, together with the unexpected popularity of reruns of "I Love Lucy" aired in December 1955, encouraged Columbia to emphasize still more filmed programs. Their rebroadcast provided added revenues live series could not. Then, too, as CBS increased its ratio of filmed to live programming, the network, unlike ABC, refused to relinquish its authority over the selection of series. Although James T. Aubrey, CBS TV president between 1959 and 1965, had worked at ABC, he insisted on viewing a series pilot before signing any production deals.

Unlike CBS, NBC mimicked the third network. Weaver, who had largely resisted the California temptation, was forced to leave the network in September 1956. After several months, NBC hired Robert Kintner, whom Goldenson had fired in October 1956, to become NBC's chief programmer. Kintner turned to MCA, the major talent agency that had begun TV program production on a vast scale, much as he and Goldenson had gone to Disney and Warner. *Fortune* in July 1960 reported that Kintner, in effect, handed over to MCA prime-time slots to fill as its TV producers saw fit.[67]

By the late 1950s, all of the major studios had joined MCA, Disney, and Warners in cutting deals with TV networks and stations. Industry hopes for theater TV or pay television systems, which would give them more control over production and greater profits, had been frustrated. Studios and independent companies, seeking to make maximum use of their physical plants and contract talent, had little choice but to manufacture programs for the networks; they soon became the senior partners, and the Aubrey system of pilot approval, the industry norm. The studios also began to sell the telecasting rights to recent theatrical films. Originally stations bought the rights to telecast motion pictures. By 1965, however, all three networks regularly scheduled recent features; theatrical releases absorbed 11 percent of the three-network evening schedules (7:00–11:00 Eastern Time) by the 1965–66 season.[68]

Network television's reliance on Hollywood had two other explanations. Many of Weaver's more expensive programming ventures had not proven cost effective or especially popular. The special "Mayerling" had cost five hundred thousand dollars but had been bested in the ratings by "I Love Lucy." Both CBS and ABC had upset the conventional wisdom that audiences preferred live to filmed programming. Moreover, once robust annual growth rates in network sales of time to advertisers, which reflected the rush of sponsors to the medium, began to level off after 1956, a condition briefly worsened by the 1957–58 recession. No longer could the costs of extravagant live programming, which Weaver had championed, be passed along to pliant advertisers. Underwriters started to insist on the less risky filmed series, many of which, despite their studio imprint, actually cost less per episode than some of Weaver's ventures. Weaver had paid five hundred thousand dollars to air the British film, *The Constant Husband*, before its theatrical release in 1955; two hour-long episodes of "Disneyland" that season cost ABC one hundred twenty thousand dollars.[69] A Kintner-selected Western on NBC three years later, "Cimarron City," cost one hundred thousand dollars per episode and could be aired at least twice in evening prime time before being sold as a rerun to stations.[70]

The significance of ABC to TV's westward migration, then, should not be underestimated. Goldenson and Kintner not only opened the door to studio production of television programming, but played the usher at the old movie "palaces," moving things along. The 48 million American homes with television in 1961 were much more likely to view ABC programs and programming on CBS and NBC affected by ABC's rise. Following American's West Coast offensive, New York, once "Television City," had become the host to a few police series (their scripts written in Hollywood), quiz programs, and the network news divisions and corporate headquarters. All but absent from the schedule were the live New York–based shows, including Weaver's spectaculars, live original weekly dramas, and most of the old variety programs. Television, Weaver remarked in 1960, "has gone from a dozen forms to just two—news shows and Hollywood stories."[71]

NOTES

The author wishes to thank R. Christopher Anderson; the author, however, bears sole responsibility for the arguments in this chapter.

1. *Variety*, November 2, 1949, pp. 29, 40; ibid., November 16, 1949, p. 35; Docket 10031, vol. 10, *Proc.*, vol. 35, pp. 5412–13, vol. 41, pp. 6117, 6128, FCC Records, National Archives, Washington, D.C.

2. Docket 10031, vol. 10, *Proc.*, vol. 35, pp. 5443–46, FCC Records; *Variety*, December 1, 1949, p. 2; *Business Week*, March 14, 1953, p. 84.

3. Docket 10031, vol. 11, *Proc.*, vol. 40, p. 6051, vol. 12, *Proc.*, vol. 43, 6608–09, FCC Records.

4. Docket 10031, vol. 12, *Proc.*, vol. 45, p. 7011; proposed findings of fact and conclusions of law, chief, Broadcast Bureau, pp. 164 ff.; author interview with Frederick W. Ford, June 19, 1978.

5. FCC, *Reports* 17 (1953): 264, 350. The commission voted 5–2 in favor of the ABC-UPT combination.

6. Docket 10031, vol. 10, *Proc.*, col. 35, p. 5377 (Kintner), vol. 12, *Proc.*, vol. 44, p. 6866 (Goldenson).

7. *Broadcasting Yearbook 1964* (Washington, D.C.: *Broadcasting Magazine*, 1964), p. 26.

8. *Fortune*, August 1951, p. 131.

9. Milton MacKaye, "The Big Brawl: Hollywood vs. Television," *Saturday Evening Post*, February 2, 1952, p. 102; Vance Kepley, "From 'Frontal Lobes' to the 'Bob-and-Bob' Show: NBC Management and Programming Strategies, 1949–1965."

10. Senate Committee on Commerce, *Status of UHF and Multiple Ownership of TV Stations*, hearings, 83rd Cong., 2d. sess., 1954, p. 1018.

11. FCC, *Reports* 41 (1952): 148, 167; George E. Sterling, address, June 13, 1952, Box 122, DuMont Laboratories Records, Library of Congress, Washington, D.C.

12. Senate Committee on Commerce, *Status of UHF*, hearings, pp. 140, 251, 950, 952; idem., *Television Inquiry*, 84th Cong., 2d sess., 1956, pp. 764, 2468, 2498, 2507–09. DuMont suspended network operations in 1955.

13. Martin Mayer, "ABC: Portrait of a Network," *Show* 1 (October 1961): 60.

14. "What's Left for the Small Networks," *Business Week*, November 27, 1954, p. 114.

15. Senate Committee on Commerce, *Television Inquiry*, p. 2469; *Broadcasting*, October 10, 1955, p. 29; Mayer, "ABC," p. 60.

16. William Boddy, "The Studios Move Into Prime Time: Hollywood and the Television Industry in the 1950," *Cinema Journal* 24 (Summer 1985): 31; Richard S. Tedlow and Henry Feingold, "Interview with Leonard Goldenson," *Amercian Jewish History* 72 (September 1982): 119.

17. Tedlow and Feingold, "Leonard Goldenson," pp. 109–10, 112–16; Docket 10031, vol. 9, *Proc.*, vol. 33, pp. 4980–85.

18. Michele Hilmes, "Hollywood and Broadcasting: A History of Economic and Structural Interaction from Radio to Cable" (Ph.D. diss., New York University, 1986), p. 207.

19. Richard Schickel, *The Disney Version* (New York: Avon Books, 1968), pp. 266–67; "The abc of ABC," *Forbes*, June 15, 1959, p. 17; "ABC Crowds the Other TV Networks," *Business Week*, May 9, 1959, p. 46.

20. Notes of interview with Kintner, n.d., Box 68, Martin Mayer Papers, Columbia University, New York; Spencer Klaw, "ABC-Paramount Moves In," *Fortune* 56 (August 1957): 242.

21. *Time*, December 27, 1954, p. 42; Fred Silverman, "An Analysis of ABC Television Network Programming from February 1953 to October 1959" (Master's thesis, The Ohio State University, 1959), pp. 98–99; Tim Brooks and Earle Marsh, *The Complete Directory to Prime Time Network TV Shows, 1946–present* (New York: Ballantine, 1979), p. 803; *Sponsor*, October 17, 1955, p. 33.

22. George Bluestone, "Life, Death, and 'Nature' in Children's TV," in *TV as Art: Some Essays in Criticism*, ed. Patrick D. Hazard (Champaign, Ill.: National Council of Teachers of English, 1966), pp. 161, 162.

23. "U.S. Again Is Subdued by Davy," *Life*, April 25, 1955, pp. 27, 31.

24. Columbia Broadcasting System, *Network Practices: Memorandum Supplementing the Statement of Frank Stanton, President* (New York: CBS, 1956), p. 98.

25. ABC-UPT, *Annual Report* (1955), p. 16; *Broadcasting*, October 3, 1955, p. 94.

26. *New York Herald Tribune*, May 18, 1956.

27. John Carmody, "The TV Column," *Washington Post*, September 13, 1978, p. B12.

28. *Variety*, January 4, 1961, p. 45; ABC-UPT, *Annual Report 1954*, p. 11, *Annual Report 1955*, p. 11.

29. Garth Jowett, *Film: The Democratic Art* (Boston: Little, Brown, 1976), p. 475.

30. Interview with Goldwyn, *U.S. News and World Report*, March 5, 1954, p. 38; R. Christopher Anderson, "Hollywood TV: The Emergence of Television Production at Warner Bros. Pictures and David O. Selznick Productions" (Ph.D. diss., University of Texas, 1988), pp. 212–13.

31. Freeman Lincoln, "The Comeback of the Movies," *Fortune* 51 February 1955: 127; Anderson, "Hollywood TV," p. 212; Jowett, *Film*, p. 475.

32. *Time*, December 27, 1954, p. 43; Thomas R. Pryor, "Hollywood Tie-Up," *New York Times*, April 17, 1955, sec. 2, p. 5.

33. Tedlow and Feingold, "Leonard Goldenson," p. 117; *New York Times*, April 12, 1955, p. 55; ABC-UPT, *Annual Report* (1955), p. 15.

34. Anderson, "Hollywood TV," pp. 293–98, 302–303, 321–23.

35. Silverman, "ABC Television," p. 146.

36. *Broadcasting*, February 18, 1957, p. 66. See also Arthur Frank Wertheim, "The Rise and Fall of Milton Berle," in *American History/American Television: Interpreting the Video Past*, ed. John E. O'Connor (New York: Frederick Ungar, 1983), pp. 69–70, 74–76.

37. Silverman, "ABC Television," p. 374.

38. *Sponsor*, November, 3, 1956, p. 11; *Time*, March 30, 1959, p. 60. "Maverick," too, had been scheduled one-half hour ahead of the competition. See Silverman, "'ABC Television," p. 231.

39. Terrence O'Flaherty, *San Francisco Chronicle*, September 18, 1959, p. 31. See also *Time* cover story, March 30, 1959, pp. 52–53, 60.

40. Thomas Schatz, *The Genius of the System: Hollywood Filmmaking in the Studio Era* (New York: Pantheon, 1988), p. 477; Brooks and Marsh, *Complete Directory*, pp. 368, 646.

41. Anderson, "Hollywood TV," pp. 366–71.

42. *San Francisco Chronicle*, October 9, 1959, p. 39; *Variety*, September 30, 1959, p. 29; Robert Larka, "Television's Private Eye: An Examination of Twenty Years of a Particular Genre, 1949–1969," Ph.D. diss., Ohio University, 1973, pp. 130, 137.

43. Dwight Whitney, "The Producer Assembles His Products," *TV Guide*, October 31, 1959, pp. 21–22; Silverman, "ABC Television," p. 153.

44. Mayer, "ABC," pp. 61, 62.

45. Silverman, "ABC Television," pp. 89, 143; *Broadcasting*, June 2, 1958, p. 5.

46. *Broadcasting*, July 14, 1958, p. 86.

47. *New York Times*, April 8, 1956, sec. 2, p. 13.

48. CBS, *Annual Report* (1960); ABC-UPT, *Annual Report* (1958), p. 3.

49. Donald Fred Ungurait, "An Historical Analysis of Regularly Scheduled, Prime Time, Network Television Programming Costs (1948–49 to 1967–68)" (Ph.D. diss., University of Wisconsin), 1968, pp. 216–19.

50. Docket 12782, vol. 21, *Proc.*, vol. 61, pp. 9537, 9384–85, FCC Records, Commission Dockets Room.

51. Silverman, "ABC Television," p. 152; "The abc of ABC," p. 17; "ABC Crowds," p. 44.

52. Mayer, "ABC," pp. 60–61.

53. *Television Digest*, February 27, 1961, p. 4; *Wall Street Journal*, May 12, 1961, p. 14.

54. FCC, *Reports* 41 (1955): 739; *Broadcasting*, October 10, 1955, pp. 27–28: ibid., November 14, 1955, pp. 27 ff.

55. James L. Baughman, *Television's Guardians: The Federal Communications Commission and the Politics of Programming* (Knoxville: University of Tennessee Press, 1985), pp. 37–38, 92–100.

56. These data are derived from RCA, CBS, and ABC-UPT annual reports, 1954–60.

57. *Broadcasting*, January 10, 1977, p. 60.

58. ABC-UPT, *Annual Report* (1956), p. 8; Albert R. Kroeger, "Miracle Worker of West 66th Street," *Television Magazine* 18 (February 1961): 64; "abc of ABC," pp. 17–18.

59. *Financial World*, February 5, 1964, p. 13; "The abc of ABC," p. 16.

60. Compare "The Golden Chains," *Forbes*, May 1, 1965, pp. 30–31, with "Analysts Rate ABC-TV Highly," *Business Week*, December 11, 1978, pp. 110–12.

61. Docket 10031, vol. 10, *Proc.*, vol. 35, p. 5445.

62. Percentages of total hours of programming regularly scheduled between 6:00–11:00 P.M. Eastern Time. By comparison, CBS produced 38.8 percent of its own programming and NBC 15.2 percent. The balance was produced by sponsors. See FCC, *Second Interim Report by the Office of Network Study*, pt. 2: *Television Network Program Procurement* (Washington, D.C.: Government Printing Office, 1965), p. 727.

63. Silverman, "ABC Television," pp. 150–52, 186 ff., 238. See also Goldenson interview, *Broadcasting*, July 14, 1958, p. 83.

64. Mayer, "ABC," p. 59. See also Silverman, "ABC Television," pp. 186 ff., 238; Boddy, p. 31; *Variety*, July 27, 1955, p. 20.

65. *Broadcasting Yearbooks 1963*, p. 20. The development of videotape explains only some of the decline of live programming.

66. *Broadcasting*, April 17, 1961, p. 46; Jack Gould, *New York Times*, April 23, 1961, sec. 2, p. 17.

67. "There Is No Show Business Like MCA Business," *Fortune* 62 (July

1960: esp. p. 116. NBC chairman Robert Sarnoff denied *Fortune*'s assertion. See Docket 12782, vol. 19, *Proc.*, pp. 8775 ff.

68. Morris J. Gelman, "The Winning Ways of Movies," *Television Magazine* 22 (April 1965): 46–47, 50–51, 73–80.

69. Gilbert Seldes, "The Lesson of 'Mayerling,'" *Saturday Reviews*, March 2, 1957, p. 27; "Sarnoff Drives to Put NBC Out Front in TV," *Business Week*, February 16, 1957, p. 90; *New York Times*, June 1, 1955; Hilmes, "Hollywood and Broadcasting," p. 207; "TV Programmers Play It Safe," *Business Week*, June 29, 1957, p. 108.

70. Unabridged notes of interview with NBC executives, October 28–29, 1958, FCC Office of Network Study, FCC Records, General Services Administration.

71. Quoted in John Crosby, "What You Can Do to Make Poor TV Better," *Ladies Home Journal* 77 (November 1960): 74.

SUGGESTIONS FOR FURTHER READING

On ABC, Sterling Quinlan, *Inside ABC* (New York: Hastings House, 1979), written by a former ABC station manager, is poor company history, full of errors and exaggerated tributes. Far more helpful are contemporary magazine stories on the network, the best of which is Martin Mayer, "ABC: Portrait of a Network," *Show* 1 (October 1961): 58–63. James Lewis Baughman, "ABC and the Destruction of American Television, 1953–1961," Business History Conference, *Proceedings*, 2d ser., no. 12 (1983), pp. 56–73, is a harsh assessment of the network. On ABC, the FCC, and the station allocation problem, see Baughman, *Television's Guardians: The Federal Communications Commission and the Politics of Programming 1958–1967* (Knoxville: University of Tennessee Press, 1985).

On Goldenson, see Richard S. Tedlow and Henry Feingold, "Interview with Leonard Goldenson," *American Jewish History* 72 (September 1982): 108–21; Albert R. Kroeger, "Miracle Worker of West 66th Street," *Television Magazine* 18 (February 1961): 60–62, 64, 66, 68–70; and two interviews in *Broadcasting*, July 14, 1958 and January 10, 1977.

On Warner Bros. and ABC, see R. Christopher Anderson's forthcoming monograph (on Hollywood TV, to be published by The University of Texas Press), which makes excellent use of Warner Bros. records. See also Dwight Whitney, "The Producer Assembles His Products," *TV Guide*, October 31, 1959, pp. 20–23, a profile of Warner's TV producer William T. Orr.

Chapter 4

Network Oligopoly Power: An Economic Analysis

P arelleling the record speed at which television technology penetrated American households during the 1950s was that at which the commercial TV networks transferred their successful radio model to the emerging industry. They were able to acquire and exert strategic market power during this era and thereafter, aided by a compliant regulatory agency that seemed more content to protect the industry members than the public. After the initial period of confrontation between the major motion picture distributors and the nascent television networks was replaced by the era of rapprochement, the oft-quoted saying, "Know thy enemy," never rang truer. To understand the complexities of negotiation between these parties, one must gain insight into the evolving structure of the commercial television networks.

This chapter will first define the nature of market power and explain its roots in the framework of the economics of cost efficiencies, product differentiation, and vertical integration. Each of these economic concepts will be directly applied to the historical development of network oligopoly control, first as it surfaced in radio and later when transferred over to television. Finally, the points of intersection between the motion picture and television network industries will be explained within the context of bargaining strengths of each side.

OLIGOPOLY POWER

In its simplest terms, market power refers to the ability to dominate the marketplace for a particular product. Such market position usually is derived from creating an inelastic demand (loyal following of customers) for the product. With no close substitutes, the product is indispensable to consumers, thereby enabling such firms to charge high prices and earn excessive profits. When one firm positions itself in this manner, it is referred to as a monopolist; when several large firms collectively encompass the vast majority of industry sales, they are known as oligopolists. While oligopolies are inherently less stable than monopolies, over time rival firms eventually come to realize the economic dividends that accrue to those firms that engage in joint industry action rather than individual firm "grandstanding." The end result is usually a "spirit of cooperation," featuring common industry-wide pricing, with rivalry and individual firm success limited to how well one does in the nonpricing areas of product differentiation (that is, differences in product quality, advertising, and packaging).

One historic example of such industry discipline has been the automobile industry, where prices and standard equipment for comparably sized autos were strictly controlled among the Big 3, while rivalry (primarily through TV advertising) accentuated stylistic differences. Similar examples could be given for product differentiation via advertising and brand proliferation for such products as cigarettes, breakfast cereals, toothpaste, and laundry detergents.

The interesting aspect of this process is that no direct, or open, consultation (for example, illegal price fixing) with competitors over prices, output, territorial exclusivity, or the like is required. As the oligopoly matures and the firms come to know and trust each other, a "meeting of minds" can occur, and each competitor acquires the ability to predict with near certainty the behavior of its rivals under differing economic conditions. Certain common cooperative practices, such as the establishment of standard price margins over wholesale costs and pricing differentials between different quality grades of the same product or compared to unbranded products, become routinized and regularized in the industry, and no open consultation need occur for the rivals to communicate the beneficial policy for the entire industry.[1] When the meeting of minds between industry rivals becomes suspect, tacit means of coordinating behavior, such as price leadership and issuing press releases, become important devices for "signaling" competitors without triggering action from the antitrust authorities.[2]

The television networks have maintained a position somewhere between the extremes of rivalry and "shared monopoly."[3] There is a wide variety of areas in which the networks can choose to compete or cooperate. Cooperation would be expected in those areas that are so visible that cheating is easily detected and retaliation can be quick. These would include advertising prices, commercial minutes per hour, station affiliation payments, and the percentage of original versus repeat programming. There is evidence supporting a spirit of cooperation in these areas of interaction.[4] The networks follow similar policies in setting and changing advertising prices, with the industry leader initiating changes in the price level (price per thousand viewers) while the internal structure of prices remains constant.

The same cooperative behavior is followed in the affiliation area. Network compensation for "clearing" time will be pretty much the same for all affiliated stations in comparably sized markets. With respect to the amount of commercialization per hour, the three networks historically have followed the standards set forth in the National Association of Broadcasters Code. The code permitted different amounts of time for commercialization for different dayparts. By agreeing to this commercialization limit, the networks could restrict the amount of advertising minutes available, raise overall prices, and narrow their range of competition. Even with the formal abandonment of the code in 1982 as part of an antitrust consent agreement,[5] the networks, nonetheless, continue to adhere to the same code limits.[6]

In contrast to these profit areas, it is very difficult for the networks to cooperate on the "quality" of programming, since the ingredients of a successful program are both unpredictable and unstable, and furthermore, cheating could not be effectively policed. Thus, the competitive impulse will probably surface in the program acquisition process for all types of television fare, including theatrical and made-for-television movies.[7] But rivalry over ratings need not drain away all network profits. As long as the networks limit rivalry to the programming sphere while cooperating in the other revenue-generating areas, they can place a floor below which profits will not fall.

CONCENTRATION OF MARKET CONTROL

Concentration of market power in the hands of a relatively small group of firms is usually operationalized by focusing attention on the collective market shares of the industry leaders. The simplest measure for representing such an abstract concept is the four-firm Concentration Ratio (CR_4), which equals the aggregate market share (of industry sales) of the top four firms. While no definitive standard exists for labeling CR indexes, it would be reasonable to label an industry with a CR_4 equaling or exceeding 50 percent as "highly concentrated." Similarly, a CR_4 between 33 percent and 50 percent would indicate a "moderately concentrated" distribution of power. Applied broadly to the U.S. economy, such industries as automobiles, breakfast cereals, and computers would be highly concentrated, while clothes, paper supplies, and calculators would be unconcentrated. Both the television networks and motion picture distributors would easily meet the highly concentrated threshold.

Defining market dominance is only part of the question; understanding the source and duration of such power are equally important. The mechanical forces by which firms expand their assets and output levels emanate from either internal expansion (that is, building from scratch) or merger (acquiring preexisting assets of another firm). More important are the reasons underlying the desire to expand.

Efficiencies

The easiest explanation for seeking large size is to solidify one's hold over an appreciable share of the market, create a brand preference for one's product, and earn excess profits over the long run. While such an expansionist policy within or without industries (for example, conglomerateness) may work temporarily, inevitably it must be based on cost efficiencies in production, distribution, management, or the like, or its vitality and stability will be less secure. A type of managerial malaise occurs where extra layers of bureaucracy are added to control the burgeoning enterprise, and the firm seeks to protect the status quo rather than investing in research and development. Inevitably, these once powerful firms will see their market shares eroded by new high technology entrants and foreign imports, or else they will become takeover targets when their stock prices decline to reflect their poor financial performance. Often, the sum of the parts of such a conglomerate are worth more than the corporation taken as a whole.

The associated cost efficiencies—often known as "economies of scale"—refer to the shape of the long-run average (unit) cost curve for the firm. This curve is the locus of minimum average production and distribution costs associated with different-sized plants and different volumes of output. If one could picture a long-run average cost curve as it declines over a wide expanse of output, efficient-sized firms would produce at output levels corresponding to the lowest cost point, often known as the minimum efficient scale. Firms producing at outputs below this minimum scale will have significantly higher average costs and place themselves in jeopardy of being noncompetitive. For such inefficient-sized firms to coexist, they must be willing to accept compressed profit margins or else compete in a specialty component of he market, with loyal customers who do not mind paying the higher prices needed to cover the higher average costs. Hence, the tendency will be for large firms to populate such an industry.

The further out the minimum efficient output level lies relative to the total industry output, the higher the probability the industry will be an oligopoly and the greater its propensity for remaining one in the future. Only a few large firms will have the wherewithal to survive over the long run, and potential entrants will find it difficult to obtain the heavy capital financing needed to establish a cost competitive enterprise and then capture the requisite market share needed to fully utilize this capacity and compete on an equal footing with existing firms. Of course, the flatter the slope of the long-run average cost curve, the smaller the cost disadvantage of being less than optimally sized and the lower the barrier to entry.

For the commercial television networks (as well as major motion picture distributors), significant economies of scale exist. Because of the unique property of the mass media that program content can be consumed (for example, reused) by a large number of people without diminishing the utility to any individual, there is an economic incentive to "network"—to simultaneously transmit the program to many markets.[8] Given the enormous fixed costs that are associated with creating the "first copy," the greater the potential reach of the broadcast and the greater the actual number of viewers, the lower will be the average cost per household or per viewer. Broadcasters, taken as a group, thus have the incentive to design a content that appeals to the largest common denominator audience, thereby driving down their unit costs. This incentive is intricately interwoven with the advertiser-sponsored financing mechanism in which revenues to the broadcasting system as a whole are enhanced by garnering the largest possible audience. Hence, the concept of networking helps broadcasters maximize profits from both the revenue and cost sides of the equation. For the major movie distributors, the same basic distribution principle exists; the more far flung the distribution network and the greater the access to the best theaters in the major markets, the lower will be unit costs per household and greater financial returns will accrue to the distributor.

A second type of efficiency for networks arises from handling a large number of programs simultaneously, thereby spreading the costs of running a large distribution network across a multiple number of shows. If a network can broker a line-up of daytime, nighttime, and fringe time programs at the same time, their sales force can be fully utilized and achieve maximum efficiency. There will be additional quantity discount savings from fully utilizing the satellite distribution process (or the older terrestrial system) rather than operating as a part time user. The same principle applies to the major movie distributors. I their decentralized offices can simultaneously release several pictures while negotiating access for forthcoming features, they can achieve steadier peak-level economies rather than alternating between peak and off-peak periods.

Finally, because of the large number of broadcast stations, national advertisers, and program producers, a network saves transaction costs by representing a large list of affiliates in the common sale of national advertising time and a substantial number of programmers in the supply of programming to the affiliates. In essence, it is a crucial middleman bringing together those who have air time to sell with those who wish to purchase such time and those who wish to program such time The absence of this crucial intermediary (as we find in the syndication industry)[9] would significantly multiply the number of individual transactions and introduce much higher production, distribution, and advertising costs to the system as a whole.

In terms of motion pictures, there are 20 times as many movie theaters as television broadcast stations, and the motion picture distributors must play the same intermediary role that the networks play in brokering programs. Of course, a major difference between these two industries involves the source of revenues. First, for motion pictures, there is direct consumer sovereignty via the box office while for broadcasting the advertising sector is interposed between consumers and producers. Second, for network affiliates, they need rely only on the exclusive line-up of programs offered from their parent network for roughly two-thirds of the broadcast day while theaters rely on the entire group of distributors to fill their schedule of play dates and often do not have exclusive rights to the movies in their territory.

These multidimensional scale economies foretold the emergence of "networking" in broadcasting and all the mass media and create the propensity for oligopoly in the distribution stage of each of these industries. Fox Broadcasting, the only new entrant into commercial broadcasting since 1955, has not been able to achieve a comparable affiliation line-up of stations (access) nor broker more than three nights of prime-time programming; as a result, it is somewhat less cost efficient than its well-established brethren.

The same fate holds for many small-time motion picture distributors who cannot justify maintaining a full-fledged distribution network (system of regional offices) to obtain truly national exposure for their mere handful of releases each year. Hence, they must handle each film specially by subcontracting out distribution rights to small regional

:ompanies who proceed city by city within their region seeking appropriate access to theaters. Yet, the barriers to entry are lower for movie
distributors as evidenced by the greater number of major players, the
more equal distribution of market power, and the significant entry of
several new (or rejuvenated) majors or mini-majors in recent years
such as Tri–Star, Cannon, and Disney).

Product Differentiation

Once the major television networks have fully exhausted the cost
efficiencies associated with optimal size, they must work on build-
ng a sufficient level of demand to justify their investment. Here
s where product ideas, differentiation, and managerial skill play
such an important role. In terms of content, this means achieving
a precarious balance between finding a product niche, on the one
hand, and yet retaining those common creative elements that appeal to
he vast audience needed to generate sufficient ratings and advertising
revenues to cover their production and distribution costs. In short, they
must do new and different things but not so new or revolutionary that
they will lose the vast middle ground of audience.

This strategy frequently boils down to spinning off one's own
hits, imitating the content of what is currently successful on rival
networks, and updating or resurrecting program forms that were successful at some time in the past. The creative programming process
is accomplished by maintaining a large staff of executives experienced
in measuring and predicting the changing tastes and whims of the
American viewing public.

A similar set of circumstances faces the motion picture programming executives who must consistently make the correct decisions
concerning their product composition. This is not like a modern
industrial enterprise, where automobiles or steel are turned out in
large quantities over long manufacturing runs; rather, each film is
handcrafted, with a very short product life and only occasional
opportunities for reuse of the creative inputs. In fact, the motion
picture differs from episodic television series in this key creative
dimension. The successful studio needs to have a continual stream
of new ideas, since product and consumers' tastes change so often;
this process of matching tastes and product is made more complicated
by the nearly two-year lead time required to produce and release a
new film. Therefore, it should not be surprising that one witnesses a
revolving-door policy for studio production chiefs.

For both of these industries, the expenses involved in maintaining

large programming departments, bankrolling new scripts and pilots
and either covering the production loan for new movies or guaranteeing
the bank loan, act as an additional barrier to full-fledged entry of new
television networks and motion picture distributors.

VERTICAL INTEGRATION

The issue of "vertical integration" is a key concept in understanding centralization of power in both the commercial broadcasting and
motion picture industries. Each product that reaches consumers has
already traveled through several stages of production. These stages are
generally represented in a vertical picture to emphasize the progression
from the lowest (simplest) raw material level to manufacturing and
distribution and then to the final retail stage, where the consumer
ultimately becomes involved. As the product progresses forward
toward the retail area, each stage adds additional value to the final
price at which the product is transacted. For example, in the VCR
industry, the actual production of a "how-to" video may cost $5 per
cassette, duplication then adds another $7, distribution/wholesaling
another $10, and finally retailing an additional $8, yielding a final
retail price of $30 to the consumer (just equal to the sum of value
added from each stage). The amount of "value added" within a stage
depends upon the product transformation or new services that are
rendered as well as the market power of firms in setting prices.
Vertical integration refers to the situation whereby various firms in
an industry simultaneously operate at more than one stage of production. While such vertical integration normally occurs between adjacent
stages, it need not to fulfill the definition. Firms become integrated
to achieve greater coordination and efficiencies across the produc-
tion/distribution process or to avoid having to deal with outside firms
that are undependable suppliers/customers, have poor reputations
for quality, or are unstable or unreliable in some other dimension. On
the other hand, vertical integration is much costlier and even riskier
than operating at a single stage, since a greater total investment must
be made and, furthermore, the managerial skills needed to produce or
manufacture certain products often are different from those needed
to successfully distribute or retail the finished product. Often, the
economies of scale do not coincide between adjacent stages, thus
necessitating producing/distributing at suboptimal levels in one or
more of the stages.

Vertical integration can take several different forms, the most stable of which is direct ownership and operation by the firm (either fully by one company or as part of a joint venture between several companies). Slightly less control accompanies vertical integration by long-term exclusive agreement; here the firm doesn't actually own, but may be able to partially or fully control through restrictive contract provisions, often focusing on quality control. Typical of such arrangements are franchise agreements between manufacturers and retailers in such industries as automobiles, fast foods, and home appliances.

Vertical integration may be transformed into a predatory conduct tactic as a means of strengthening oligopolistic control at one or more stages. Suppose there is a significant but *unbalanced* degree of vertical integration in an industry, combined with a strong degree of market power. For example, assume firms A and B are industry leaders in both the production and distribution stages of an industry; not only are they vertically integrated, but also assume that they are the major suppliers of product (input) to firm C, with whom they compete at the distribution level. Firm C does not have its own production subsidiary but must rely primarily on A and B (and a few independents) for its supply of product.

Should A and B wish to reprimand C for violating industry discipline or drive it from the industry, they could slow down, halt, or temporarily disrupt the supply of product to the company, thereby making it appear to be an unreliable distributor to its customers. This is known as a supply squeeze. Alternately, they could raise the general level of production prices while keeping distribution prices constant. Produce price increases represent real input costs increases to firm C and hence compress its profit margin, yet only represent an accounting transfer to firms A and B because of their vertical structure.[10] Should firms A and B now lower distribution prices, this form of predatory pricing would simultaneously squeeze profit margins for the nonintegrated firms from above and below.[11]

Similar results occur when the imbalance of vertical integration is reversed between the stages. Suppose nonintegrated firm C were now only in the production stage and had to rely on A and B for access to distribution. Firms A and B may decide to deny distribution rights or only partially handle the products of C (an access squeeze) or else lower the overall distribution prices they will pay to all firms, including their own subsidiaries. Once again, this represents a real price squeeze to firm C but only accounting sheet transfers for A and B.

Each example demonstrates the flexibility that vertical integration can give large powerful firms in determining which stage should extract the excess profits. It also teaches the nonintegrated "independent" firm or a potential entrant to avoid dependency on these large companies Counterstrategies for such firms include seeking additional indepen dent sources of input supply, seeking foreign sources, or else vertically integrating themselves. Should the latter scenario occur, this heightens barriers to entry by necessitating two-stage entry and eventually may lead to enhanced concentration of power across several stages.

VERTICAL INTEGRATION IN BROADCASTING

Each of the television networks has followed a deliberate pattern of vertical integration throughout its corporate life. In the station broadcasting stage, each network has significant ownership holdings of television stations in the major markets. To prevent private monopo lization of the airwaves, multiple ownership of broadcast stations is restricted by specific FCC rules. The most recent version of these rules limits group ownership to a maximum of 12 TV stations (VHF or UHF), but not to exceed a penetration of 25 percent of all U.S. television households.[12]

Ownership of broadcast stations facilitates the clearance process for network programming, since the owned-and-operated stations sel dom will hurt their parent organization's national ratings by substituting programming from alternative sources.[13] Furthermore, the networks each have established vertical contractual ties through long-term affil iation agreements with stations owned by nonnetwork entities. These affiliates function much like franchised retail outlets of any manufac tured product, although they have won the freedom to now reject network programs and substitute offerings from other sources.[14]

History of Vertical Integration

Such was not the case in the early days of radio, when CBS and NBC sought to cement their vertical ties with affiliates through restric tive contract provisions. Limited by ownership rules, these networks sought another method to assure preferential clearance of the vast majority of their programs. Such assurances were necessary to induce advertisers into the radio market and allow radio to become competitive with the other mass media. CBS and NBC insisted on five-year exclusive contracts that required automatic clearance, known as "option time," whereby they retained an option on the entire broadcast day. With only

8 days' notice, the network could preempt any local program with a network show, and the station was required to make the substitution. Without actually owning the station, the network nevertheless controlled the station's time. Stations were only too eager to make such a concession if it meant obtaining the valuable affiliation. The networks rationalized such a policy of vertical integration by contract as the only logical method of doing business in this industry. Each of these leading networks had superior affiliate line-ups, since they had cornered the market on high-powered "clear channel" and regional radio stations. By tying up these key stations and refusing access (for example, an access squeeze) to other rival networks, such as Mutual, these industry giants had monopoly control over radio networking.[15]

Chain Broadcasting Rules

Against a rising tide of network control and complaints from independent program producers and Mutual, the FCC launched a three-year investigation and in 1941 issued a *Report on Chain Broadcasting* that condemned the anticompetitive practices highlighted above.[16] In part, the report noted that

> the radio spectrum is essentially public domain. In the delegating to this Commission the power to license, Congress was moved by a fear that otherwise, control would gravitate into few hands. . . . In short, the joint effect of the various practices mentioned is to place the licensee to a considerable degree at the mercy of the network with which he is affiliated, but to leave the network free to pursue interests which may be very different from those of the licensees affiliated with it. . . . *Thus the doorway into the network field is both locked and bolted.*[17] (emphasis added)

The new rules prohibited any station from signing an affiliation agreement (1) containing an exclusivity clause or an option-time clause; (2) for a period longer than one year; or (3) with a network organization that maintained more than one network or that tried to fix advertising rates other than its own rates. The station also retained broad rights to reject any network program already contracted for which it considered contrary to the public interest.[18] The local station was licensed as the arbiter of what programming best served the needs and interests of the local community (the public trusteeship concept of broadcasting). It was held responsible for programming over the local airwaves, regardless of its source; hence, to exercise this fiduciary responsibility, the station needed freedom of choice in all matters regarding programming. They were not to be tied to one network or another for unreasonable lengths of time and required the freedom to reject network programs deemed not to serve the local public interest.[19]

The networks protested that these rules would take radio from known, good service to an unknown anarchy; that it was the end of competitive broadcasting and the destruction of the American system of broadcasting. Because of an unsuccessful appeal to the Supreme Court,[20] the modified Chain Broadcasting Rules did not take effect until 1945. One significant result of these legal proceedings was that the proscription against stations affiliating with any corporation owning two radio networks caused NBC to divest the weaker of its two networks, the so-called "Blue Network," in 1943.[21] This blue network eventually became the American Broadcasting Company.

Therefore, in this early ruling, the FCC not only extended its jurisdiction to the activities of networks, but sought to create new competition as well as evening out the unequal bargaining power between networks and affiliates. Underlying these rules was the FCC belief that "networking" was inherently concentrating in nature, and that the FCC should take an active procompetitive posture in seeking to modify the manifestations of network power. Nevertheless, the fundamental economic lesson taught during this era and thereafter was that networking is the most efficient means of distributing programming, and that even without mandatory pressure to accept network programming, the affiliates would voluntarily continue this practice (for financial reasons), since it meant higher-quality/lower-cost programming than they could procure themselves. As subservient a position as the affiliates had to play relative to the networks, to paraphrase Milton, "It is better to serve in Hell as an affiliate than reign in Heaven as an independent."

Evaluation of Television

The television broadcasting industry had a period of dynamic growth during the mid-forties and fifties. The owners of radio stations were granted licenses to build television stations, and once a new nationwide terrestrial telephone network was established to interconnect the stations, CBS, NBC, and, to a minor extent, ABC and DuMont, entered the television network business and soon had positions of power paralleling those in radio.[22] According to Stewart Long, "Almost every indicator of network concentration examined for the period of 1949–52 shows an already large and in some cases increasing share of the market in the hands of the network oligopoly."[23] Because the commission failed to take any substantive reform policy on the various allocations problems during the 1948–52 "freeze," most observers felt that the fate of the two small networks, ABC and DuMont, was sealed. In order to save at least one of these networks and to provide an additional source of capital funding, the FCC, with the tacit approval of the Justice Department, allowed ABC to merge with Paramount Theaters in 1953. With the ascendancy of ABC and the failure of his revolutionary proposal to reallocate the television spectrum, DuMont folded up operations in 1955, and the present three-network structure was established.

Three separate investigations were launched in the mid-fifties to study economic concentration in the television industry—by the FCC, the Senate Commerce Committee, and the House Committee on Interstate and Foreign Commerce. While voluminous testimony was taken and many critical reports were written, no new legislation concerning television was enacted. During the proceedings, Senator John Bricker commented, "The networks . . . have an unprecedented economic stranglehold on the Nation's television industry. Effective competition is stifled under this yoke of economic dominance. The result is private monopoly."[24] Using their experience and business relationships in radio, the television networks lined up the best VHF stations to be their affiliates, often dealing with the same owners in television as in radio. The much stronger CBS and NBC networks entered television networking first and with a big splash, gaining effective control of the industry.

While the Chain Broadcasting Rules had been passed to restrict some of the abuses of the radio networks, they also applied to television broadcasting. Despite the loud protestations of the radio networks, these rules proved to be only minor inconveniences in both the radio and expanding television industries. In television, the networks combined a modified option-time policy with a "must-buy" advertiser purchase plan to enhance their position and forestall and foreclose effective competition.[25]

Option-Time Controversy

As in the radio industry, the television networks used option-time clauses in their affiliation agreements as a means of quickly assembling a national network in times of emergency and assuring advertisers contemplating the sponsorship of a network show that a sufficient number of affiliates automatically would clear the program. The networks again claimed that without option time they would be emasculated through a checkerboarding of nonclearances throughout the system for the entire broadcast day. The uncertainty thus created would cause hesitancy on the part of both networks and advertisers to commit huge sums of money to create new types of programming.

The Celler and Barrow reports described the abuses of option time in the same terms outlined by the *Report on Chain Broadcasting* 15 years earlier: option time permitted a network to substitute its own programming decisions for the licensee's duty to select programs in the best public interest of the local community.[26] By simply "patching" into the network, the affiliate has abrogated its responsibility to the public. Furthermore, option time allowed networks the power to prevent competing networks and especially syndicated shows from obtaining access to the affiliates during the prime evening hours. While the producers of syndicated programs obviously have access to the fourth station in many markets, some of which are very attractive, they are nevertheless foreclosed from those markets with three affiliated stations, without which the former markets are not sufficient to cover costs.[27] Hence, program quality will suffer from a lack of competition, since the networks essentially are saying, either sell your program through us or forget about access to national time. As with must-buy, option time was also seen as a form of a tied good; the network wanted to protect its inferior programs from competition, so naturally it tied them to the better programs and offered only the entire service. Not only was this practice alleged to be the equivalent of block-booking but also of blind selling, since stations were committed to accept a program without having seen it and, at times, without its having even been completed. Finally, option time was alleged to injure nonnetwork advertisers by denying them access to prime-time television and/or forcing them to operate with the threat of network preemption of the time period.[28]

In terms of the vertical integration issue, option-time clauses when fully exercised and enforced were the equivalent of a fully integrated network system. Since the commission earlier had limited network ownership of stations to five VHF and two UHF, option time was a clever mechanism for circumventing the intent of such a rule and concentrating among the networks control of what is viewed during a large portion of the day. The *Cellar Report* concluded that option time was anticompetitive and inimical to the concept of freedom of choice by each station to choose the best programs available for each time period, letting each program be judged by its own merits and not through an artificial tying restraint.[29]

With all the controversy surrounding the option-time clauses, the FCC decided to take another look, but after noting the restraining effect of this practice on the station licensee's freedom to select programs and its adverse effect on other segments of the industry, the commission concluded that "the optioning of time by affiliated stations to their networks is *reasonably necessary for network operations and is in the public interest*."[30] A hearing on option time followed this finding, and slight alterations were instituted to calm the critics of the FCC's policy. Nevertheless, the commission reaffirmed its findings that option time was a reasonable restraint and necessary to the public interest.

Thoroughly disgusted with the FCC ruling, the independent licensee of KTTV in Los Angeles appealed the decision to the U.S. Court of Appeals, citing the antitrust abuses of option time. Fearing that its decision would be overturned, the commission petitioned the court for a chance to reconsider its decision. This time it concluded: "Upon review of the record herein, and in light of the data and arguments, *we are not convinced that the option time is essential to successful network operations but rather are of the view that it is not*."[31] It dismissed the network argument that option time was essential to planning by citing the success of some of the best network programs during station time. The simultaneity argument was not convincing, since most programs were not live but actually were shown from videotape. The commission also noted that the limited assurance that option time provided would easily be replaced by the automatic clearance of the network owned-and-operated stations (covering nearly 25 percent of all television households). Furthermore, the FCC cited the competitive abuses outlined in the *Barrow Report*, the *Celler Report*, and its original *Report on Chain Broadcasting*. Particularly obnoxious was the limitation on the licensee's freedom to choose programs in the public interest.[32] The final text of the commission's ruling stated:

> No license shall be granted to a television broadcast station having any contract, arrangement, or understanding, express or implied, with any network organization which provides for optioning of the station's time to the network organization, *or which has the same restraining effect as time optioning*.[33] (emphasis added)

The "same effect" provision was challenged by CBS (as applied to its Incentive Compensation Plan) as being so vague as to imperil network-affiliate negotiations and amounting to rate regulation. The commission responded that the language was at least as specific as that of the antitrust laws, and that without the "same effect" provision another anticompetitive practice would merely be substituted for the outlawed practice.[34]

In conclusion, while the option-time clauses were clearly anticompetitive and did result in a somewhat higher rate of clearance during option hours than during station time, the networks never really pressed this issue upon the stations. Perhaps fearing the interference of the Justice Department or simply wanting its affiliates also to carry network programs during station time, there were never any lawsuits instigated against recalcitrant stations. While option time was clearly a factor in inducing clearances, the networks had at their disposal the full range of financial penalties, such as the amount of free time the affiliate must carry, the remittance percentage, and, of course, the threat of disaffiliation if the station failed to clear a large percentage of programs. The most important question left unanswered by the networks was why they needed option time if their programming was so superior.

Prime-Time Access Rules

In the mid-sixties the FCC also noticed an unhealthy condition in the syndication market. It had hoped that the abolishment of option time would give first-run syndication program producers the shot in the arm they desired, and they could then effectively compete against networks in prime time. But the evidence indicated a decline in first-run syndicated fare and an upsurge in network reruns. To restore the health of independent producers, an affirmative action program guaranteeing their access to the top 50 markets during prime time had to be instituted. The adopted rule limited network service to an affiliate to three prime-time hours between 7:00 P.M.–11:00 P.M. in the top 50 markets in the country, and these affiliates were not allowed to substitute network reruns for the lost network service.[35]

With networks joint-venturing series with independent producers and demanding subsidiary rights while simultaneously increasing their share of the syndication market, the commission became concerned with the potential leverage that this created. Being in a position to sell programs to independent stations in competition with their own affiliates and especially their owned-and-operated stations created the possibility for conflicts of interest, squeezes, and denial of supplies. In short, power in the syndication market not only would coalesce the networks' control over what the American public could view on television, but would also allow them to fix the price of a major substitute to their network fare. While only limited evidence of this theory was presented in the hearings, the potentiality for abuse was recognized, and the FCC forced the networks out of the syndication business (with the only exception being that they could distribute programs, of which they are the sole producer, in foreign markets).[36]

Therefore, the removal of the option-time clauses and the opening up of the prime-time access hours were supposed to restore the balance of power in the industry, allow the stations more discretion in their programming selections, and encourage the entry of new networks and truly independent sources of programming.

THE SCARCITY OF TV NETWORKS

Central to visualizing the power of the networks is understanding the fundamental factors underlying the scarcity of television networks. As explained above, the basic reason revolves around the need for obtaining scale economies by gaining access to as many households as possible through affiliation contracts. While some of the largest markets do indeed have "unaffiliated" stations, the vast majority of the top one hundred markets have three or fewer "acceptable" (VHF) TV stations, thus leaving room for only three fully comparable national networks. In fact, the DuMont network left the scene in 1955 primarily because of its inferior affiliate line-up compared to the Big Three. This strengthened ABC and permitted it to become a major player with CBS and NBC. The history of these events demonstrates the culpability of the FCC in establishing such impenetrable barriers to entry into networking.

From the very beginning, the commission has favored a goal of localism in the allocation of television licenses.[37] Consequently, every local community should be able to control what is broadcast over the air to its local citizens. Early in the history of television broadcasting, the question of how to implement such a worthy goal arose, and the FCC had a difficult decision over which band of the spectrum would be most technologically adaptable to television. While the UHF band (ultrahigh frequency) was much larger and could accommodate more frequencies, it had transmission problems that made its development less certain and lengthier. The commission, desiring that television obtain a quick start from the blocks, chose the much narrower VHF band (very high frequency) as the prime instrument for implementing its policy of providing television for all the people with as much speed as possible. Development of the UHF band would be continued, with the hope that it would eventually help to satisfy the important priority of providing a television station to as many local communities as possible. This mixed bag of large, powerful VHF stations intermixed with smaller, less-developed UHF stations would continue until the time that UHF technology caught up with VHF; then all frequencies would be in the UHF band and compete on an equal footing. While the FCC talked about this long-run situation, it nonetheless created a powerful lobbying concern that would not want its power diminished at a later and more convenient hour.

Problems with UHF TV

With these wheels set in motion, it soon became apparent that the UHF system was much weaker than VHF, and only an affirmative action program in favor of UHF would lead to an eventual balance between similarly situated stations in the two systems. VHF had greater appeal because of greater network affiliation and thus higher quality programs. The VHF stations were generally purchased by business-men who owned radio stations already affiliated with the two major radio networks—CBS and NBC. When these two networks moved into television, the VHF owners naturally followed the path of least resistance and business convenience and hence affiliated with them. In this way, CBS and NBC gained a powerful leverage into television through their existing power in radio. This points up another lack of foresight by the FCC and the Congress. While the prospect of each local station freely selecting the appropriate programming for its local public is indeed a worthy goal, the practical economics of broadcasting lends itself to the formation of networks, with the consequent surrender of local autonomy over program selection to those not required by law to act in the public interest. The commission knew that powerful networks were inevitable in television; yet, it chose policies creating a limited number of powerful stations, which would eventually mean a few very powerful networks. Hence, the commission wanted both localism and diversity, but it failed to understand that these two goals were antagonistic rather than complementary and required a tradeoff of sorts.

VHF had technical superiority, since it could cover a wider area with a clearer signal as compared to a similar UHF station. But most importantly, the public had overwhelmingly purchased VHF-only receivers, which would get clearer signals and better programming, rather than UHF-only receivers or the more expensive all-channel receivers. "It was a vicious circle for the UHF independents. They cannot develop all channel set circulation because they are unable to present sufficiently attractive programs and cannot obtain first rate programs because they lack sufficient set circulation to attract high priced advertisers."[38]

The Freeze on TV Stations

From 1948–52, a "freeze" on further television station allocations was instituted by the commission so that it could consider some of its most pressing problems. This four-year period was a crucial turning point in the development of television.[39] VHF stations were affiliated with networks and had a much higher survival rate, while UHF stations were in clear and present danger of foundering; yet television was not so developed that once-and-for-all-time change at this juncture would have markedly retarded its future development. Nevertheless, the commission took the familiar regulatory protectionist policy of not wishing to upset the apple cart, not wanting to change the status quo and disrupt the service to the public. Why move from a system of known good service to one of uncertainty and confusion? What the FCC really meant was, why hurt your friends?

The FCC decided to continue its mixed allocation policy rather than move to an all-UHF system. It rejected out of hand a proposal by Allen B. DuMont that would have created powerful regional VHF stations to facilitate the formation of more competitive networks and hence more quality viewing options for the public. Finally, it postponed the requests of some small communities to "deintermix" their markets—to convert their markets to all UHF rather than retain the mixed bag that so favored the local VHF stations. While failing to act affirmatively on these pressing allocation questions, it enhanced the competitive advantage of VHF by authorizing increases in the permissible antenna heights and maximum power, which only VHF was in a technical position to achieve. Even the "freeze" itself, which dragged on for four years rather than the planned three to six months, is seen by Stewart Long as entrenching a proven VHF technology at the expense of a much younger UHF technology at a critical point in the latter's evolution.[40] It allowed a coalescing of power for the VHF system, while UHF was halted in the midstream of its development. It assured CBS and NBC of an almost impregnable position in television—much like the one they had achieved in radio.

In summary, the FCC laid down a clear perspective for a nationwide and competitive service that would utilize the vast UHF portion of the spectrum. It allowed the quick exploitation of the VHF band only as an expedient, fast interim mechanism to achieve national coverage. Yet, when the opportune time arrived to switch to its long-run game plan, it balked at the thought of disrupting the nationwide service that had been achieved, dreading the confusion and financial losses that would result when VHF licenses were switched or not renewed. It chose a nonneutral policy of promoting the status quo and hence its friends. The net result of its policy was to cement a two-tiered structure in the broadcasting industry, consisting of the haves (the networks and the VHF affiliates) and the have-nots (the independent VHFs and most of the UHF stations). The former would thrive while the latter would live a marginal existence—never fully able to compete and often dependent on the networks for their livelihood.

Therefore, the light network triopoly position was affected by both widespread economies of scale, product differentiation, and technical constraints associated with the scarce number of television frequencies available in most local markets. Together, these factors created an impenetrable barrier to the entrance of new networks for some 30 years.

Emergence of Fox Broadcasting

In 1986, by utilizing the newly purchased group of Metromedia major market stations as a foundation and combining the programming acumen of a giant diversified motion picture–television studio, Rupert Murdock of Twentieth Century–Fox launched a "fourth" television network. By the mid 1980s, the entrance of new UHF independent, stations in middle-sized markets plus the additional coverage offered such stations through cable made such a venture a reasonable gamble. While Fox Broadcasting obtained access to most of the top one hundred markets, its part-time status and overall mediocre ratings will still prove to be an insurmountable stumbling block. In contrast, these obstacles are clearly higher than those facing potential entrants into motion picture distribution. In motion pictures, standardization of theater status (for example, nearly all are now considered first run) and the trend toward a rising number of multiscreen auditoriums have opened up comparable access for independents as well as the more established major and mini-major distributors.

It may be recalled that this lack of access to exhibition outlets was precisely the problem facing the independent motion picture distributors during the pre-*Paramount* days. Since the majors ("Big 5") and minors ("Little 3") had exclusive access to the preponderance of high-quality first-run theaters in the largest markets and were self-sufficient in films, there was a denial of access to other distributors seeking to compete on an equal footing. Similarly, where independent first-run theaters did exist, they were denied the "A" quality films of the aligned distributors or relegated to second-run status (that is, a supply squeeze existed).[41]

MONOPSONY POWER

As mentioned earlier, the networks are caught in a competition/cooperation dilemma. A most fruitful area for cooperation has been the financial side of programming. During the early years of television, the networks simply sold time and access to their audiences; national advertisers (acting through their agency representatives) were responsible for acquiring and overseeing program production by independent production houses. However, production costs soared and soon exceeded the budgets of all but the largest national advertisers, and the networks came to realize the value of planning an entire line-up of compatible programs rather than selling unrelated time spots. Furthermore, with the embarrassment surrounding the Quiz Scandals in 1958, the networks felt that if they were ultimately to be held responsible for programming, regardless of its source, they needed to be more actively involved with selecting and supervising production. For these reasons, the networks eventually assumed responsibility for programming decisions in the 1950s and began selling "participations" to advertisers in units of 60 seconds and later in smaller units. The advertisers insisted that the networks made the change for themselves, to reap the rewards associated with taking greater programming risks. Regardless of who instituted the policy, the net result was a drastic decrease in the number of buyers of prime-time pilots from between 50 and 100 national advertisers to the three networks. Program producers and licensers of theatrical movies were now forced to pass through the narrow network bottleneck or face the prospect of not being on the air.

In this market for regularly scheduled programs, the networks understood that their bargaining advantage was greatest in the initial developmental stages of a television show, when the quality of the scripts and pilot is of unknown value and the future success of the program is uncertain. At this stage, venture capital is scarce because the investment is so risky. Once a show becomes a hit, however, it can command a high price on the open market because its network cannot risk its being bid away by another network. To prevent such competitive bidding, such as in major league sports, the networks have developed a series of parallel steps in the buying process which, if commonly followed, will foster uncertainty of product quality, maintain the networks' bargaining advantage vis à vis their suppliers, and thereby enhance their bottom line. Should competition rather than cooperation break out in this key area, it could drive up programming costs and cause significant financial repercussions.

The Step Process of Program Acquisition

After looking over the story idea, but before funding the script, the networks and program producers sign a "pilot and series" contract that stipulates not only what share of the costs the network will pay for the pilot, but also gives the network the renewal option at a set fee for each year up through the fifth year or longer.[42] This is, effectively, vertical integration through long-term contract. In the past there was normally a price escalation of about 5 percent per year built into the options, but in recent years the more typical procedure has been to set out the exact dollar prices for the entire length of the contract. Therefore, the networks have locked the producers into a set price even before the pilot is shot or the series is accepted and at least a year before the season begins. This practice effectively eliminates competitive bidding for hit shows.

In supplying the scarce venture capital and taking the risks of programming, the networks incur the losses associated with flop shows but reap the bonanzas accompanying hit programs. In the strong bull market for network advertising during the 1970s, the profits from hits greatly exceeded the losses from flops. It may be argued that this step process of program acquisition is necessary for the networks to conduct business, and that this practice was thrust upon them through advertiser reluctance to provide development funds. But the central question is how long must the contract be for a network to recover its developmental expenditures and whether the five- to seven-year contracts cause *unreasonable* restraints on trade.

To further enhance this spirit of cooperation, the networks also have had a common understanding that once any network becomes seriously involved in the consideration of an idea, as evidenced through the financing of a script or pilot, it achieves a virtual lifetime monopoly to the rights for the series or spin-offs, even if it never purchases the show or cancels the show during the lifetime of the contract.[43] If the program does last beyond the contract expiration date, the program producers can negotiate with the other networks, but the original network retains the right of first refusal, which means it can match any offer and retain the series. In practice there have been relatively few pilots and a dozen or so series that have transferred from one network to another. Again, the effect of this practice is to eliminate any competition for ideas (even rejected ones) by binding the program producer to the original network. Producers are also bound by other network practices, in the areas of deficit financing, surrender of syndication, subsidiary rights, and mandatory use of network facilities.

For example, a program producer desiring to obtain network access would discover that network program payments only cover direct outlay costs but not contributions to overhead or normal entrepreneurial profits. This practice, known as deficit financing, in essence means that producers have to work for free or go into debt to meet their personal financial obligations. To "make themselves whole," they depend on future streams of revenues arising from selling syndicated reruns to local stations. Yet, as a quid pro quo for access to the prime-time schedule (necessary to build their stockpile of episodes), they are forced to accept the networks as the actual syndicator of their programs (at a 30 percent rate of commission) and/or permit them to become profit participants in this lucrative market. In short, the networks have used their scarcity and monopoly access to the American people to take full advantage of their program suppliers. These practices were severely restricted under the Financial Interest and Syndication Rules described above and modified to accommodate the arrival of new competitive services in the 1980s.

Vertical Integration into Theatrical Movies

As noted in the previous section, the networks have worked out very elaborate cooperative devices to achieve a virtual monopsony in regular prime-time programming. The essence of their cartel lies in eliminating the monopoly power that rebounds to successful television programs and adversely impacts on their bottom line. But theatrical movies represented a different species of network programming. Their attractiveness derived from knowledge concerning their value in the theatrical premarket. Hence, the risk and uncertainty were significantly lowered for all parties concerned (networks, advertisers, and movie producers), since they were delaying with a known quantity. Because of this, unexpected price wars occurred as each network sought to outbid its rivals for the best pictures. The networks were of course concerned with the collapse of their buying cartel in this increasingly important area, because they understood that cracks in a collusive front in one area foretell its demise all the way down the line. But how could they achieve the same market dominance in this area, which seemed to so favor theatrical movie suppliers? The hypothesis will be advanced that vertical integration into theatrical features and made-for-TV movies enabled the networks to eliminate the only form of price competition that remained—that it solidified their cartel and further stabilized the industry.

Motion Picture Distributor Advantages

In contrast to their role as regular series suppliers (where they have no economic advantage),[44] the movie distributors seemed to have the upper hand because of their strategic position in the film industry and the fact that the supply of movies does not respond quickly to new demand. Long lead periods exist between the planning of a theatrical motion picture and its eventual broadcast. For example, there is significant time spent in obtaining appropriate properties; signing talent and producers; filming the picture; waiting for the appropriate season to release it; allowing it to play for several years in different runs, both here and abroad; negotiating the television license; and finally broadcasting it.

For financial success, a theatrical movie depends primarily on rentals earned in domestic and foreign theaters. The sale of television rights is only a secondary consideration. This is in stark contrast to the extreme financial dependence TV program producers face in obtaining network development financing, making the network sale, and then remaining on the network long enough to create value for the series in the syndication market.[45] In short, the movie companies have greater independence in their financing and more potential profit centers. This flexibility should translate into greater bargaining strength with the networks over theatrical movie rights.

The prices for theatrical movies have always been two to three times higher than the prices of regularly scheduled programs of comparable quality, offering further evidence that movie producers have greater bargaining leverage than series producers. Movie prices started to rise because of increasing network demand and internetwork rivalry for movies. The average price of a theatrical movie rose from one hundred thousand dollars for two network runs in 1961 to around eight hundred thousand dollars by the end of 1967. During this period the number of hours of prime-time movies increased from 2 in 1961 to 14 in 1968.[46]

Network Counterstrategies

In late 1966 and 1967, the networks attempted to stabilize theatrical movie prices by producing their own theatrical movies and made-for-television movies. This vertical integration into the production sphere resulted in some 80 theatrical movies during 1967–71 and 40 to 50 percent of their yearly requirements of made-for-television movies. The effect of such a large foreclosure of product was devastating and sent a clear message to the movie producers that hereafter prices would be stabilized. Private and public antitrust litigation,[47] as well as an inferior product, caused the networks to leave the production industry in 1972.

Therefore, vertical integration by the television networks into theatrical and made-for-television movies was a major catalyst to the spreading of the network strategic control into the last two remaining areas of supply industry competition. The cartel was now complete; program cost inflation was constrained, all sectors of the supply industry were controlled, and, in addition, the networks had through their in-house production arms a better feel for production costs in the industry. Having achieved their informal cartel across all stages of production from storyline through exhibition, they could now sit back and lead the easy life that accrues to those possessing significant monopoly power. It was truly a game they could not lose. While admittedly the possibility exists that short-run profits were not maximized through the plan to enter the production sphere, it seems reasonably clear that a longer-term strategy was contemplated and executed whereby the networks would have power and leverage over the entire industry from top to bottom. Vertical integration allowed the networks to enhance their power and eliminate the uncertainty that competition usually creates.

Unfortunately, this stabilization over prices proved to be short-lived. In the mid-seventies, the price once again skyrocketed due to a shortage of acceptable movies for television. This shortage resulted from the fact that the four-year stockpile of network features amassed during the late sixties ran out around 1972 or 1973; the trend in the seventies toward more R- and X-rated pictures resulted in a smaller percentage of acceptable features. In addition, the major movie studios cut back their production significantly and concentrated their efforts on fewer, high-budget films.[48] This shortage of acceptable theatrical features for TV is further demonstrated by the decrease in the time elapsed between theatrical release and first network telecast.[49] During the remaining 1970s, competition for the limited quantity of available theatrical movies again caused prices to increase. To counteract this problem, the networks increased their requirements for made-for-television movies to all-time record levels and began to blind bid for theatrical films prior to completion of the production process. While the increased demand for these features has increased their prices, they still cost less than half the rental fee for a theatrical movie.

To continue the preceding parallel, the major film distributors, like their television counterparts, have been able to use vertical integration into the production sector as a strategy for maintaining a strong collective buying position. After the divestiture, the major distributors reduced their overwhelming dependence on in-house productions (that is, executed through the studio system).[50] With excess studio capacity and their need to maintain scale economies in distributing a significant number of features each year, they began to court the favor of the independent production sector—the same group of people they had sought to eliminate only a few years before. Yet, the fact that the *Paramount* conspirators now had to rely on this formerly estranged group did not severely diminish their bargaining power. They simply shifted their emphasis.

Independents needed the expertise of the major companies for a first-class release of their movies (just like program suppliers needed the networks). Furthermore, the majors themselves were a source of scarce financing for the production budget, a guarantor of bank loans, and even if not directly involved in the financing, banks were hesitant to loan money without a major distributor "pickup." With this new-found role as the "crucial bottleneck," the majors achieved a spirit of cooperation by standardizing their distribution fees and the net profit shares they required as a quid pro quo for help with financing. In this way, they were able to obtain equity participation (partial vertical integration) in motion pictures without bearing all the financial risks themselves. Distribution would soon replace exhibition as the strategic center of control in the motion picture industry,[51] just as networking came to dominate the television broadcasting industry. And while the breakup had a certain shock value to industry participants, in retrospect, market power simply became redistributed to another stage of production.

CONCLUSION

The history surrounding the acquisition and maintenance of economic power for the television networks is remarkably similar to that of the major motion picture distributors. Distributors in both industries sought to cement their power by taking advantage of economies of scale in combination with their prowess and experience in product differentiation. Furthermore, power, once rooted in distribution, could be extended through vertical integration into the adjacent production and exhibition dimensions. The net effect was to create impenetrable barriers to entry throughout the vertical chain of control. This was especially true in networking where misguided FCC allocation policies fortified existing networks' power structure.

It is in this context that firms in these powerful industries clashed in the 1950s and eventually formed a pattern of stability, mutual inter-dependence, and economic symbiosis—a pattern that would remain until the disrupting forces of new telecommunication technologies like cable and VCRs could once again be harnessed and a new equilibrium established.

NOTES

1. Cooperative practices may be unique to each industry. For example, the historic timing of the introduction of new automobile models or new television seasons are not incidental matters to these industries any more than the peak releasing periods of motion pictures during the summer months and at Christmas.

2. Price leadership occurs where the dominant firm (e.g., General Motors, IBM) or a firm with a charismatic leader determines what the new equilibrium price should be and announces this change. All other industry participants are then expected to follow suit or face economic retaliation of one sort or another.

3. Bruce M. Owen, Jack H. Beebe, and Willard G. Manning, Jr., *Television Economics* (Lexington, Mass.: D.C. Heath, 1974), chap. 4.

4. Ibid.; also, Barry R. Litman, "The Economics of the Television Market for Theatrical Movies," *Journal of Communication* 29 (Autumn 1979: 21–25.

5. *United States vs. National Association of Broadcasters*, 536 F. Supp. 149 (1982).

6. Barry R. Litman and Jan LeBlanc-Wicks, "The Changing Advertising Marketplace for the Commercial Television Networks," *1988 Proceedings of the American Academy of Advertising*, pp. 27–33.

7. Owen, Beebe, and Manning, *Television Economics*.

8. Bruce M. Owen, *Economics and Freedom of Expression* (Cambridge, Mass.: Ballinger, 1975), chap. 1.

9. The syndication industry offers nonnetwork program alternatives to independent stations and to affiliates (at times when the networks are not

offering program choices). These programs range from (a) "off-network reruns" of prime-time shows that formerly were part of the prime-time network schedule; (b) first-run syndicated shows that are new episodes, usually quiz or talk shows, produced specifically for showing five days a week; and (c) old classic motion pictures.

10. For A and B, their production subsidiary raises prices to everyone including their captive distribution subsidiary. Corporation profits from distribution now fall, but profits from production correspondingly rise. In fact, the total corporate profits may actually increase, depending on the magnitude of the higher revenues now received from C.

11. This double squeeze also affects integrated firms A and B by lowering their profit margin, but presumably they have deeper pockets and greater staying power and can outwait their smaller rivals.

12. Sydney W. Head and Christopher H. Sterling, *Broadcasting in America*, 5th ed. (Boston: Houghton-Mifflin, 1987), chap. 17.

13. Barry R. Litman, "Is Network Ownership in the Public Interest?" *Journal of Communication* 28 (Spring 1978): 51–59.

14. Barry R. Litman, "The Affiliation Agreement: The Tie That Binds," *Telecommunication Policy* 3 (June 1979): pp. 116–25.

15. Mutual Broadcasting System was formed in 1934 as a cooperative of the remaining powerful (clear channel) stations that were not directly owned by CBS or NBC or affiliated with them. Eventually this cooperative expanded to include other affiliated stations, but Mutual, having arrived late on the scene, could never match the powerful affiliate line-ups of CBS or NBC and remained at a competitive disadvantage.

16. FCC, *Report on Chain Broadcasting*, Commission Order No. 37, Docket 5060 (May 1941).

17. Ibid., pp. 76–77.

18. Ibid., p. 92.

19. The Chain Broadcasting Rules were modified in late 1941 to permit partial restoration of option time as a means of *guaranteeing* national advertisers full clearance for their spots. For greater details, see FCC, *Supplemental Report on Chain Broadcasting*, October 11, 1941, pp. 10–14.

20. NBC vs. *United States*, 319 U.S. 190 (1943).

21. The NBC networks were originally color-coded red and blue to facilitate AT&T's interconnection of telephone lines.

22. Allen B. DuMont, TV set manufacturer and station owner, formed a television network shortly after the end of World War II in order to compete with the major radio networks (save Mutual), which had entered television.

23. Stewart L. Long, "The Development of the Television Network Oligopoly" (Ph.D. diss., University of Illinois-Champaign, 1974), p. 91.

24. Senate Committee on Interstate and Foreign Commerce, *The Network Monopoly*, report prepared by Senator John Bricker, 84th Cong., 2d sess., 1957, p. 1.

25. Certain small television markets that advertisers might have overlooked were considered mandatory for any national advertising purchase.

26. House Antitrust Subcommittee on the Judiciary, *The Television Broadcast Industry*, 85th Cong., 1st sess., 1957 (known as the *Celler Report*). Also, House Committee on Interstate and Foreign Commerce, *Network Broadcasting*, 85th Cong., 2d sess., 1958 (known as the *Barrow Report*).

27. *Barrow Report*, chaps. 5. 7, and 8.

28. Ibid.

29. *Celler Report*, pp. 92–93.

30. FCC, "Option Time Report and Order," Docket 12859 (June 5, 1963) in Pike and Fisher, 25 *Radio Regulation*, p. 1654.

31. Ibid., p. 1675.

32. Ibid.

33. Amendment 3.658d to Communications Act of 1934, in Pike and Fisher, *Radio Regulation*, current series.

34. "Option Time Order," p. 1686.

35. FCC, "Prime Time Access Report and Order," 23 FCC Reports 2d, 387 (1970).

36. Ibid.

37. In general, see Long, "Development of the Television Network Oligopoly," p. 91; *Celler Report*; and Christopher H. Sterling and John M. Kittross, *Stay Tuned: A Concise History of American Broadcasting* (Belmont, Calif: Wadsworth, 1978), chap. 8.

38. *Celler Report*, p. 9.

39. Long, "Development of the Television Network Oligopoly," p. 91.

40. Ibid.

41. A similar case also existed in the telephone industry prior to the AT&T divestiture in 1982. The Local Bell Operating Companies were tied exclusively in a vertical chain to the Western Electric and Bell Labs subsidiaries of AT&T. Since AT&T was totally self-sufficient and accounted for some 85–90 percent of industry output (General Telephone had a similar vertical structure and accounted for roughly a 10 percent market share), independent equipment manufacturers were thus denied meaningful access to all but the interstices of the industry.

42. For background information, see FCC, *Television Network Program Procurement, Part II: Second Interim Report* by Office of Network Studies, 1965.

43. Ibid., chap. 13.

44. As Owen has noted, the major movie companies have no economic advantage in this latter area, since the supply industry is fairly competitive due to a well-developed rental market for inputs, minimal economies of scale, and easy entry. Their only possible advantage is the minor leverage they could exert by tying movie sales to acceptance of television series.

45. For example, local stations like to "strip" off-network reruns five days a week to create habitual viewing patterns. Such a series would thus need 260 showings a year. Assuming two plays per episode per year, this translates to roughly 130 different episodes. At the rate of about 26 new episodes produced per year during this era, this meant a series had to remain in production for five years on the network to build up value in syndication. The more successful

the series (in terms of ratings) during its network run, the higher the asking price in syndication sales.

46. *Variety*, new season annual editions.

47. *Columbia Pictures, Inc.* v. *ABC and CBS*, complaint filed in U.S. District Court, Southern District of New York, 1972; and *United States* v. *CBS, NBC and ABC*, complaint and brief filed in U.S. District Court, Central District of California, 1974.

48. Ibid.

49. For example, in 1972 the mean number of elapsed years was nearly six; by 1979, it had decreased to less than four.

50. Michael Conant, "The Impact of the *Paramount* Decrees," in Tino Balio, ed., *The American Film Industry* (Madison: University of Wisconsin Press, 1976), chap. 16.

51. Robert W. Crandall, "The Postwar Performance of the Motion Picture Industry," *The Antitrust Bulletin* 20 (Spring 1975): pp. 49–87.

SUGGESTIONS FOR FURTHER READING

Barnouw, Erik. *The Image Empire: A History of Broadcasting in the United States since 1953*. New York: Oxford University Press, 1970.

Brown, Les. *Television: The Business Behind the Box*. New York: Harcourt Brace Jovanovich, 1971.

Gomery, Douglas. "Economic Change in the US Television Industry." *Screen* 25 (March–April 1984): 62–57.

Guback, Thomas H. and Dennis J. Dombkowski. "Television and Hollywood: Economic Relations in the 1970s." *Journal of Broadcasting* 20 (Fall 1976): 511–27.

Litman, Barry Russell. *The Vertical Structure of the Television Broadcasting Industry: The Coalescence of Power*. East Lansing: Michigan State University Press, 1979.

Noam, Eli M. *Video Media Competition: Regulation, Economics, and Technology*. New York: Columbia University Press, 1985.

Owen, Bruce M., Jack H. Beebe, and Willard G. Manning, Jr. *Television Economics*. Lexington, Mass., D.C. Heath, 1974.

Vianello, Robert. "The Rise of the Telefilm and the Networks' Hegemony Over the Motion Picture Industry." *Quarterly Review of Film Studies* 9 (Summer 1984): 204–18.

Vogel, Harold L. *Entertainment Industry Economics: A Guide for Financial Analysis*. Cambridge: Cambridge University Press, 1986.

Chapter 5

Hollywood's Attempt at Appropriating Television: The Case of Paramount Pictures

Timothy R. White

C ontrary to accounts given in the standard textbooks on film history, the major motion picture studios not only were fully aware of the threat posed by television, they actually sought to compete with the broadcasters on their home turf—the small screen. However, broadcast television was not the only target of the studios; they attempted to alter the very form of the new medium, offering an alternative to the commercial, 30- to 60-minute drama and situation comedy format of broadcast television. This attempt to offer alternatives took two forms: theater television and subscription television.

The most aggressive of the studios in this effort was Paramount Pictures. A studio that had established early ties to other media (especially radio), Paramount, more so than the other studios, was prepared to move into the new medium of television as early as the late 1920s. What it was not prepared for, however, was the interference of the Federal Communications Commission in every facet of its television plans. This chapter will present a case study of Paramount Pictures' efforts to enter the television industry, with comparisons to the efforts of the other major studios and some of the reasons these efforts were unsuccessful.

BROADCAST TELEVISION AND TELEVISION NETWORKS

Historians of the film industry traditionally have made the assumption that Hollywood ignored television until the mid-1950s, when, with a philosophy of "If you can't beat 'em, join 'em," the studios plunged into the new medium by producing filmed series for television. In fact, the film industry had begun much earlier to explore the possibilities of television. Before the 1950s, each of the "Big Five" studios at least planned to enter the business of television broadcasting and/or television network operation.

The failure of the studios to establish themselves as forces in television broadcasting was a result of FCC policy, not Hollywood incompetence. Although the commission had never been receptive to the film companies entering the television industry, the FCC's 1940 hearing on technical standards for television marked the beginning of open hostilities between the studios on one side and the FCC, along with the major radio networks, NBC and CBS, on the other. At this hearing, Allen B. DuMont Laboratories, a television company in which Paramount Pictures had a significant investment, challenged the standards offered by RCA. The fact that DuMont, with the backing of a major Hollywood studio, was making a move into the field of television was not overlooked by RCA (parent company of NBC), which suggested that DuMont's proposed standards were inadequate, and that DuMont was purposely trying to keep television inferior to motion pictures, under orders from Paramount:

> The motion picture interests which are financing DuMont Laboratories have a much greater financial stake in the movie industry than they have in television. Their recent interest in television is primarily for the purpose of 'protecting' their larger interest in the movie and theatre industry and not to develop the new art of television. Therefore, they desire the adoption of systems and methods that would make television inferior rather than superior to motion pictures.[1]

The implication that the film industry wished to usurp television for crass commercial gains, as opposed to the radio networks, which were concerned with the "public interest," stuck with the FCC for decades. After the 1949 decision in the *Paramount* case, in which the Supreme Court found the Hollywood studios guilty of antitrust violations, the commission and the radio interests found the perfect weapon with which to keep the film industry out of broadcasting. Because the studios were required to separate production and distribution from exhibition, the FCC argued that the ownership of television stations ("exhibition outlets") by the studios would restore such a relationship. As early as 1946, the antitrust issue affected the efforts of the studios to enter the television industry, when the FCC temporarily approved

Paramount's television station license for KTLA in Los Angeles but refused to make a determination on the studio's eligibility to own and operate a television station.

The commission's policy on applicants (especially those from outside broadcasting who sought to enter the industry) who had been found guilty of antitrust violations was vague; in fact, there was no specific policy. In 1951, the FCC declared that it would establish no blanket policy covering antitrust violators, but would consider them on a case-by-case basis. However, it is clear from statements made by the commission that the Hollywood studios were the target of the FCC's use of antitrust violations as a barrier to entering the television field:

> It is important that only those persons should be licensed who can be relied upon to operate in the public interest, and not engage in monopolistic practices. . . . It is obvious . . . that violation of the antitrust laws by the motion picture companies is a matter that the Commission must consider carefully in determining the qualifications of these companies to operate in the public interest.[2]

> In all such cases, a strong presumption of ineligibility is raised and a heavy burden of proof is imposed on the applicant to show he is qualified to operate a broadcast station in the public interest.[3]

The FCC's antitrust policy, because it was so vague, proved helpful in preventing motion picture interests from entering the television industry. For example, Warner Bros. abandoned plans to buy radio and television properties (KLAC-TV in Los Angeles) when the FCC held off action on the transfer application for over a year, unable or unwilling to make a decision. In July 1948, Tri-States Meredith Broadcasting Co., 25 percent owned by Paramount, sought to purchase station KSO in Des Moines. The FCC declined to authorize the transfer without an investigation of the antitrust status of Paramount, but seemed to be in no hurry to undertake such an investigation.

Despite these obstacles, the studios continued their efforts to enter the television business. In 1948, Twentieth Century–Fox established two subsidiaries to build and operate television stations; by February 1949, the studio had applications for five stations pending before the FCC. Loew's/MGM, also in 1948, already owned two radio stations and had applied for several television station licenses, but withdrew the applications. The studio was still interested in broadcasting, however, and in 1952, hoped to build its first television station in New York

City. When this fell through, Loew's remained determined to enter broadcasting, and in 1956, announced plans to acquire interests in several TV stations. Even RKO, despite its financial difficulties, in 1945 established the RKO Television Corporation to investigate the possibilities of television, including station ownership.

The most ambitious of the studios, however, was Paramount. In 1938, Paramount began its relationship with the DuMont Television Network, one which lasted until the end of the 1950s. Through a relatively small investment of $164,000 in DuMont's stock, Paramount obtained a great deal of power over the television company, which not only operated a network but eventually owned three television stations: WABD (later WNEW) in New York, WTTG in Washington, D.C., and WDTV in Pittsburgh. With these and Paramount's own television stations—KTLA in Los Angeles and WBKB in Chicago—the studio owned or had an interest in five television stations in some of the biggest markets in the United States.

In 1948, the studio, through its wholly owned subsidiary Paramount Television Productions, Inc., started the Paramount Television Network, a service that supplied filmed television programs to broadcasters. These programs were produced at the studio's Los Angeles television station, KTLA, and booked out of the network's New York office. According to an executive of the network, by 1950 the network's films were seen nationwide: "The Paramount TV Network is transcontinental in scope, numbering its affiliates from Philadelphia to San Diego, from Chicago to Houston."[4] But this was not a true broadcast network—one that both supplies programming and sells advertising on a national basis—as were ABC, NBC, and CBS, and its revenues were much less than those that could be generated by a true broadcast network.

Paramount never entered the broadcast television network business, either with its own network or through its interest in DuMont. In fact, Paramount's involvement with DuMont helped to ensure the network's demise; the studio provided neither funds nor programming for the network, which ceased operations in 1955. Because its interest in DuMont was not sufficient for it to completely control the company, Paramount sought to enter the network business on its own and used its influence at DuMont to limit the company to the more profitable areas of television station operation and the manufacturing of television sets, equipment for broadcasters, and other electronic equipment.

Although the studio fully intended to begin the Paramount Television Network as a true broadcast network, it was stifled in this attempt by the Federal Communications Commission. Network operations are not profitable without owned-and-operated television stations, and

Paramount faced opposition from the FCC in its efforts to obtain those stations. In 1949, Paramount was blocked by the FCC from receiving licenses for applications for television stations in San Francisco, Detroit, and Boston. These applications were rejected due to the FCC's limit of five television stations controlled by any one party; including DuMont's three stations, Paramount had reached this limit (the FCC ruled that Paramount's minority interest in DuMont was sufficient to constitute control, which, according to the FCC, was "not limited to majority stockownership, but includes actual working control in whatever manner exercised").[5]

The Supreme Court's 1949 finding that Paramount and the other studios were guilty of antitrust violations resulted in a divorcement decree, which split Paramount into two separate companies—Paramount Pictures Corporation (the film production and distribution company, which received television station KTLA) and United Paramount Theatres (the theater company, which received WBKB, and later merged with ABC). Although this left Paramount with only one television station and interests in only three others, the FCC still refused to grant licenses to either Paramount or DuMont. The commission further damaged the studio's television plans by placing KTLA's license on a temporary status, again using Paramount's involvement in antitrust violations as a weapon against the studio. This tended to create a lack of confidence in the station on the part of sponsors, who took their business to the more stable and established stations.

The effect of all this on Paramount was a decision to drop its plans for ownership of a chain of television stations and a television network. Through the mid- and late 1950s, Paramount's efforts to establish itself as a force in the television industry were concentrated primarily on nonbroadcast uses of television.

THEATER TELEVISION

Although all of the majors took an interest in station ownership and network operation, they also sought ways to combat broadcast television in ways that would allow them to have more control over the distribution of their own television product, and would differentiate their product from that of broadcast television. Although these efforts have been ignored for years by film historians, they were well reported in not only the trade press, but also mass market publications such as *The American Mercury* as early as 1944:

[A] group which approaches television from a box office rather than advertising point of view are the movie interests, several of which have invested considerable money in the industry. Most movie men have pretty well gotten over the fear that television may squeeze them out of business. Instead, they see that it may provide an additional and very lucrative source of revenue.[6]

The earliest of these schemes was theater television, the projection of large-screen television images (through a variety of technologies) in theaters to paying customers. This form of television had been demonstrated as early as 1930, when RCA presented theater television on a 6-by-8-foot screen at RKO-Proctor's 58th Street Theater in New York City. In 1938, the film industry expressed an interest in the medium when its Academy of Motion Picture Arts and Sciences established a committee to investigate ways in which the Hollywood studios could control the profits from the new medium of television; the committee recommended that the industry counter broadcast television with theater television.

There were several practical reasons for the film industry's promotion of theater television. Some of these reasons involves product differentiation; in order to compete with broadcast television, the movie companies needed to offer a product that was clearly different from (and, if possible, superior to) the "free" television available at home. Large-screen theater television offered the viewer an image that could not be matched, in size at least, by that of the largest home television screen.

The type of programming planned for theater television also would differentiate the medium from broadcast television. Because it would be supported by theater admissions, theater television would be able to present programming unavailable, because of costs, to broadcasters—including prize fights and other live sporting events (of national and/or local interest) and live Broadway shows. Theater television also would make the theaters competitive with the networks in offering news events; instead of the outdated newsreels theaters had shown in the past, theater television enabled them to bring to the audience live speeches, inaugurations, and other events on a large screen, coincidentally saving the studios the cost of printing and distributing the newsreels. Likewise, a savings could be realized on the presentation of live acts (such as singers and comedians), who could appear live in one theater and on large-screen theater television in many others at the same time. As with sporting events, the price of admission (in theory, at least) would allow the studios to offer a superior product;

instead of the little-known vaudevillians and local performers seen on broadcast television between poorly staged and static commercials, theater television would present well-known acts that were out of the price range of the networks and free of commercial interruptions.

World War II put a temporary end to theater television plans; but in 1944, when both the end of the war and the proliferation of broadcast television seemed inevitable, Hollywood renewed its interest in theater television. The first attempt by the motion picture industry to obtain radio frequencies for theater television came in 1944, when the Society of Motion Picture Engineers sent Paul J. Larsen to FCC allocation hearings to request the authorization of radio frequencies, feeling that coaxial and wire facilities were not sufficient to supply major metropolitan areas such as New York City with theater television. The use of radio frequencies for theater television required the FCC first to allocate frequency bands for this purpose, then establish rules governing the use of the bands, and finally to assign frequencies to licensees.

In 1945, the FCC made some bands of the electromagnetic spectrum available for experimentation of all sorts, including theater television. By 1947, these experimental frequencies were deleted, and no other bands were set aside for testing theater television or any other sort of experimentation; those frequencies that were used for these purposes were from the UHF band. However, from late 1947 to 1949, the FCC made available frequencies allocated to other services for experimentation with theater television. These frequencies, which were offered on a strictly temporary basis, were awarded to Paramount (five allocations) and Twentieth Century–Fox (one allocation).

In July 1947, Twentieth Century–Fox and Warner Bros. collaborated with RCA to develop theater television. The three sponsored a private showing of the system (with an image measuring 15-by-20 feet) at Warner's Burbank studio in May 1948; in June 1948, they exhibited it publicly at the Fox-Philadelphia Theater, and in June 1949, at the Society of Motion Picture Engineers convention in New York City. In September 1948, Fox was granted a temporary authorization to experiment with theater television on a UHF frequency in the New York area.

The relationship among the three companies did not last long, however. Although Warner abandoned the idea of theater television, Twentieth Century–Fox's president, Spyros P. Skouras, unhappy with his company's relationship with RCA, made a deal in 1951 with the Swiss company Eidophor to exploit its theater television system worldwide. Later that year, Fox acquired the rights to use the Columbia Broadcasting System's color TV process with its large-screen television system and announced that it would begin the manufacture of theater television equipment. Also in 1951, Fox and General Electric made a deal by which GE would produce high-definition color television studio equipment to be used in conjunction with the Eidophor system.

Despite Twentieth Century–Fox's efforts, its theater television system could not compete with that of RCA, especially in cost; in 1953, RCA cut the cost of its units to fifteen thousand dollars each, compared to Fox's twenty-five thousand dollars. However, even as late as 1959, Fox retained the rights to, and had some hope for, the Eidophor theater television system.

Warner and Fox were not the only motion picture companies interested in theater television; in the late 1940s , Loew's/MGM announced plans to develop theater television to provide "live" acts in its theaters, and RKO felt that its best bet to establish itself in television was in theater television. However, none of the film studios were involved as deeply in the development and exploitation of theater television as Paramount.

As early as 1938, Paramount expressed great interest in the possibilities of theater television, especially as a medium for the presentation of Broadway plays and sporting events. It was, in part, this interest that led Paramount to become involved with Allen B. DuMont Laboratories, for DuMont had a reputation for innovative research in television; the company had developed the cathode-ray tube for successful commercial use; had worked on the development of radar and similar technologies; and, perhaps of most interest to Paramount, DuMont was committed to finding ways to increase the size of the then-tiny video image.

Although DuMont was willing to cooperate in the development of large-screen theater television, and agreed to Paramount's plan to transmit news events and motion picture features from local transmitters to local theaters, Paramount used only a small amount of DuMont's equipment, and none of its facilities, for theater television. Instead, in 1942, with Twentieth Century–Fox, the studio's subsidiary Paramount Television Productions invested in Scophony Corporation of America, a firm that had been developing theater television. This relationship was short-lived, due in part to an antitrust suit brought against Paramount and other investors in Scophony by the Justice Department in 1945. Paramount then invested in the Paramount Intermediate Film System, an expensive process by which televised images were filmed and developed in 66 seconds. This system, although expensive, resulted in a reusable 35mm print that could be edited and shown at any point during a theater's program.

There is no doubt that Paramount wished to control television and saw theater television as a way to fight the broadcasters. In 1944, Paramount's Paul Raibourn addressed the Theater Panel Meeting at the First

Annual Conference of the Television Broadcasters Association, making clear that his company had no special allegiance to television as it was envisaged by the networks: "If the broadcasters are economically unable or don't want to further television, I assure you that within a few years the theaters will have it and the broadcasters will be far behind, which all present would be very happy about."[7] Paramount did indeed have television on theater screens within a few years; in November 1947, Paramount was granted temporary authorization to experiment with theater television on two UHF frequencies in the New York area and was granted two more temporary authorizations in May 1948.

Paramount officially premiered its theater television system in April 1948 at the Paramount Theater in New York City with a prize fight; between 1948 and 1951, the Paramount Theater used theater television to present, among other diverse fare, presidential speeches; UN meetings; election returns; political conventions; the Kefauver Senate Crime hearings; and especially, sporting events. These features ran from five minutes to one hour, and, according to contemporary accounts, were shown to capacity crowds. Later in 1948, Paramount launched theater television in Chicago at its Chicago Theater to a capacity crowd; the studio hoped to make Chicago a theater television success story and soon installed equipment in more of its theaters in that city. The following year, Paramount installed theater television equipment in some of its theaters in Los Angeles.

This was as successful as Paramount's Intermediate Film System would become. Although Paramount had 2 color systems for use in large-screen television before color was available on broadcast television, exhibitors were not interested. By 1950, Paramount had the system installed in a few of its own theaters, with only 4 more installations ordered; by the end of 1951, 6 were installed, with 6 more on order. At the same time, RCA, Paramount's chief competitor in the theater television business, had 50 theater television units installed in theaters nationwide. Even so, Paramount announced that it was increasing production of its system to 10 units per month.

However, the studio remained unable to attract customers for the Intermediate Film System. And, after the separation of production and distribution from exhibition, the studio no longer had guaranteed customers for theater television. Its former theater chain, United Paramount Theatres, had shown some early interest in theater television, but when United Paramount decided to expand its theater television operations in 1951, it ordered additional units from RCA, not Paramount. When United Paramount decided that theater television was not profitable, it concentrated instead on broadcast television, merging with the American Broadcasting Company in 1953.

In 1953, Paramount Television's president, Paul Raibourn, threatened to halt production if the company didn't receive at least one thousand orders for installations, the figure he felt was necessary to provide a profit for Paramount and bring the price down to twenty-five thousand dollars per unit. Exhibitors did not rally to Raibourn's call to action, and later that year, after more than a decade of efforts to establish theater television as an alternative to network broadcast television, Paramount abandoned theater television, having lost money at most of the theaters that had been equipped for the medium.

There are a number of factors that led to the failure of Paramount's Intermediate Film System as a commercial operation, some of which are specific to that process. The system had the advantage of creating a reusable product; after they were viewed in the original theaters, the films were sent by cab to other theaters for projection, then sold to TV stations for one thousand dollars each. However, RCA's system had the advantage of being easier to operate, and could be operated by only one projectionist; Paramount's system was more expensive to operate and required the use of several unionized technicians. In one case, a speech by President Truman was not shown in Chicago because the theater's technicians had already gone home. Both Fox's Eidophor and RCA had a big advantage over Paramount in initial cost, also; the Intermediate Film System carried a price tag of thirty-five thousand dollars for installation in a theater, compared to Eidophor's twenty-five thousand and RCA's fifteen thousand.

There were other factors that contributed to the failure of theater television as a medium, regardless of the system used or the company promoting the process. Although the Paramount system required the use of numerous union members to operate its equipment, motion picture unions demanded additional workers to operate the equipment of other systems as well, and there were jurisdictional disputes among other involved unions, thus increasing the costs of operation.

Another major drawback of theater television involves the two methods of delivery possible to the medium. The use of radio frequencies to transmit the signals to theaters was both cheaper and technically and aesthetically superior. Because the FCC refused to allocate separate frequencies beyond the temporary, experimental allocations of 1949, theater television was forced to use more expensive telephone lines to transmit programs to theaters. This method of transmission also affected the quality of the theater television image; denied the wide-frequency channels it required, the medium was forced to use AT&T relays. This limited theater television to a six-megacycle channel that could not provide sufficient detail for large-screen, theater exhibition. More expensive than broadcast television, and lacking the

quality of the motion picture image, theater television could compete
with neither.

PARAMOUNT AND PAY TELEVISION

With the failure of theater television, the best strategy for the
motion picture studios to offer an alternative to broadcast television
seemed to be pay (or toll or subscription) television, which could
offer a higher quality image, could be offered commercial-free, and
f transmitted via cable, could avoid the jurisdiction of the Federal
Communications Commission. Although there was speculation that
the possibility of pay television was an important factor in the retention
of film libraries by the major studios, only one of the Hollywood studios
made a significant effort to exploit pay television in the 1950s. That
studio is Paramount. Throughout the 1950s and the early 1960s, pay
television was Paramount's most important interest in the exploitation
of television.

However, as with broadcast and theater television, the studio's
plans had begun far earlier than the 1950s. Paramount had planned to
exploit pay television as well as theater television through Scophony
when it bought into the company in 1942. When its relationship with
Scophony ended, Paramount made plans to continue its efforts through
DuMont. In 1944, Paramount announced plans for an elaborate video
subscription network, which could also function as a transmission
service to theaters. Mobile transmitter stations installed in vans would
be used to connect two groups of cities, one through the north and one
through the south. DuMont's equipment would be used to transmit the
broadcasts, which would utilize the lower portion of the electromagnetic spectrum. This plan proved too cumbersome, however, and was
dropped before actually being put into practice. Instead, Paramount
bought the controlling interest in International Telemeter, a subscription television service that transmitted scrambled television signals over
telephone lines—a technology first tested in 1951. Telemeter remained
Paramount's most ambitious bid for a piece of the video action during
the 1950s.

Paramount's Telemeter system of pay television was unique in
that it used a coinbox; when customers placed the proper amount
of coins in the coinbox, a decoder unscrambled the transmission. To
accomplish this, Paramount provided customers with a unit called
a "Telemeter," which supplied three channels of programming plus

a "barker" channel that gave customers information about available programs and times. Inside the unit was the coinbox, in which the coins were deposited for the programs desired, and a magnetic tape, on which was recorded the amount of money spent on each show. The unit was replaced every two months, when the "Telemeter Man" picked up the unit along with the coins deposited in it.

The Telemeter system had several attractions for Paramount. In addition to its hope to avoid the FCC by using telephone lines rather than radio waves, Paramount's executives believed that pay television appealed to a fundamental aspect of human nature; explaining Paramount's preference for pay television, and particularly the coinbox variety, Paramount's president Barney Balaban said,

> [T]he reason for this is that 'going to the theatre' is an emotional urge, and it's especially true of 'going to the movies.' We're conditioned to put money on the till. So what's more natural than, as the urge moves us to see which ever attraction is proffered some night, to put money-in-the-coinbox and that is that.[8]

Another important attraction of Telemeter, however, was the possibility of usurping television technology, taking it from the broadcasting industry and adapting it to the motion picture industry. Not only did Telemeter's form of pay TV bypass broadcasters, it offered a clearly differentiated product in both form and content; through its coinbox approach, it provided a pay-as-you-watch commercial-free medium presenting recent and current Hollywood movies unavailable to the networks, films that otherwise could be seen only in theaters at higher prices. Through its coinbox, Telemeter also differentiated itself from other forms of subscription television, more closely resembling the traditional "payment up-front" format of theater exhibition. In an era of declining movie attendance, pay television was seen as a way of bringing the theater to the customer, since the customer seemed reluctant to go to the theater.

Paramount's first commercial test of the Telemeter system came in 1953 in Palm Springs, California. Using closed-circuit lines to transmit its films (therefore requiring no FCC approval), Paramount wired 274 homes to receive its scrambled signals. The installation fee was $150 to $450, depending on the location of the home; there were additional charges of $60.00 per year for use of the cable, $21.75 for the Telemeter coinbox, and a minimum of $3.00 per month in program charges. Paramount initiated the service by showing a USC–Notre

Dame football game to its Telemeter subscribers for $1.00, followed by the first-run film *Forever Female* for $1.35.

Ironically, the movies were transmitted from the projection booth of the El Rancho Theater, which had never been completed; construction had been begun in the late 1940s, and when movie box office receipts fell off nationally, work on the theater was halted. The parts of the building that had been completed, other than the projection booth, were converted to a bank, grocery store, and farmers' market. However, there were still some operating movie theaters in the Palm Springs area. Because the first-run films shown on the Telemeter system were playing at the same time in local theaters, these first-run films would be shown on pay television only once, in an effort to alleviate some of the fears of local theater owners that the showing of first-run films on television would destroy their box office. Along with these films, Telemeter offered sporting events and some "live" shows, which could not be seen in local theaters.

Although the test proved reasonably successful, with the average wired home paying ten dollars per month for programming, Telemeter ceased operations in Palm Springs in 1955. The test ended, Paramount claimed, because no other studio would supply first-run films. However, there was another factor contributing to the end of the Palm Springs experiment. The owner of a Palm Springs drive-in theater, the Sun Air Drive-in, sued Paramount, charging violations of the studio's recent antitrust divorcement decree. Having suffered at the hands of both the Justice Department and the FCC for antitrust violations, real and alleged, Paramount wished to avoid further punishment.

Adding to the studio's difficulties in exploiting subscription television was the uncertainty surrounding the issues of the legal status of pay television, and whether or not the FCC actually had jurisdiction (and if so, how much) over pay television, especially that which used cable instead of the airwaves. These issues became more complicated after Paramount's Palm Springs experiment, which resulted in a massive anti-pay television movement in the United States. This movement was led primarily by the established television networks and theater owners, who succeeded in creating a fear among the American population that "free" TV would be doomed if "fee" TV were allowed to compete with it. This public outcry influenced both the FCC, which was reluctant to authorize tests for pay-TV that used the airwaves instead of cable, and members of the U.S. Congress, who were concerned not only about public opinion, but also about the investments many of them had in television broadcasting stations, and seemed opposed to pay television in any form. When the House Committee on Interstate and Foreign Commerce held public hearings on pay TV in 1956, five bills were introduced in Congress that would have banned pay television altogether, and Chair Emanuel Celler of the House Judiciary Committee introduced a bill imposing a fine of ten thousand dollars or a five-year prison term or both on anyone attempting to charge a fee to home television viewers.

In 1956, Paramount's Paul Raibourn and the studio's legal counsel, Paul Porter (a former FCC chair), testified before the Senate Interstate and Foreign Commerce Committee's hearings on toll television. Using language purposely close to charges of antitrust violations, Raibourn squared off specifically against the networks; according to Raibourn, the networks "resist change and progress," while "their restrictive covenants and exclusive arrangements with their affiliates" allowed the networks alone to determine what the American public could and could not see. Paramount and Telemeter, on the other hand, were making a "fundamental and American appeal for the doctrine of competition."[9] RCA's president Robert W. Sarnoff, seeking to create a sense of panic and impending doom at the prospect of pay television, announced that if subscription television were authorized and began to pay off, RCA and NBC would have "no choice but to follow the pay tide," and soon the United States would be left without any "free" television at all.[10]

This sort of threat by the broadcasting industry increased Congressional hostility toward pay television, which in turn tended to halt even the slow progress being made by the FCC. In 1957, the FCC announced that it would accept applications for a temporary subscription television trial; although the commission then authorized very restrictive trials for pay television (trials were limited to major markets with at least four television stations, no company could conduct trials in more than three markets, and the trials were limited to three years), the Senate asked the commission to delay these trials while they held hearings on the television industry in 1958. Also in 1958, the House Interstate and Foreign Commerce Committee, influenced by the television broadcast networks and theater owners, considered bills concerning pay TV, and ordered the FCC to halt testing of subscription television services.

Paramount optimistically gambled that in the long run the House and Senate Interstate and Foreign Commerce committees would rule in favor of pay television and also would decide that the FCC did not have jurisdiction over subscription services. Paramount's pay television interest also helps to explain why it waited so long to sell its inventory of pre-1948 films. Although the studio had received attractive offers, it held on to its films long after the other studios had sold theirs to television interests. Paramount was holding on to the films in case they were needed for its toll television subsidiary. Even after the films supposedly had been put up for sale, Barney Balaban announced that they would possibly be leased to its Telemeter franchise operators instead. Paramount could then collect not only franchise fees, but film rentals as well.

Despite the obstacles, Paramount persisted in its faith in subscription television. In both 1955 and 1957, Barney Balaban attempted unsuccessfully to sway theater owners to the Paramount cause by offering them first chance at Telemeter franchises. Even without this support, Paramount remained confident enough to increase its interest in International Telemeter from 50 percent to 88 percent in 1958, and 100 percent in 1959. The studio then planned to begin operations in three markets: the New York area, the West Coast, and Canada. The only one of these markets in which Telemeter actually operated, however, was Canada.

Paramount had considered establishing its Telemeter pay television service in Canada as early as 1955; through its affiliate Famous Players, Ltd. of Canada, Paramount planned to use Canadian television stations near the U.S. border to transmit Telemeter programming to U.S. homes, using radio frequencies but avoiding the jurisdiction of the FCC. Instead, in 1959, Trans Canada Telemeter, a subsidiary of Paramount and Famous Players of Canada, began operation of the Telemeter system in Etobicoke, Ontario, a Toronto suburb. Starting with a thousand subscribers, by May 1960 the subscription television service had its Telemeters installed in five thousand homes, near the point at which the studio felt it could break even.

By 1960, when only Paramount and the electronics company Zenith remained in the pay TV fight, proponents of subscription television felt that the recent television game show scandals, which had shocked the nation, had left the broadcast television networks particularly vulnerable; with the image and influence of the networks at a low point, it seemed that the time for pay television was at hand. In that year, three-year trials were finally authorized by the FCC. With a promising start in Canada, Paramount planned for Little Rock, Arkansas, to became its first U.S. market. However, because of legal actions taken by opponents of pay TV, trials did not actually begin until 1962, when Zenith, working with RKO General, began operations in Hartford, Connecticut.

By this time, conditions had changed for Paramount. Not only had the outlook for motion pictures brightened, with movie attendance on the rise and profit margins increasing, but the Etobicoke experiment was faltering badly. Although by the end of its operation Telemeter reached six thousand subscribers, or about half of the families in the wired area of Etobicoke, Telemeter was not particularly popular with its subscribers; weekly revenues averaged less than one dollar per week per subscriber, and the operation folded in 1965 after losing $3 million. Paramount's efforts to exploit subscription television through the Telemeter system had come to an end.

Although the Zenith/RKO experiment in Hartford was not a commercial success, it did lead to the FCC's decision in 1968 to allow pay television over the airwaves as a commercial enterprise nationwide. This brought renewed interest in subscription television from the Hollywood studios; the industry did not wish to see a repeat of the situation that existed in broadcast television, in which the networks controlled the means of distribution (the source of the bulk of the profits), reducing the studios to mere suppliers of product.

However, it was not over-the-air pay television services which proved to be the salvation for subscription television in its struggle against commercial broadcasting. The vehicle for the eventual emergence of pay television, albeit in a rather different form from that envisioned by Paramount and the other subscription television proponents, was cable, which proliferated in the United States in the mid-1970s and 1980s. As Michele Hilmes points out,

> Certainly one odd result of the early pay television debate is that the networks and theater interests, in attacking the immediate threat of pay TV, paved the way for greater cable penetration, which now poses an arguably greater threat and one much more likely to succeed. The growth of satellite-distributed cable networks, and film industry involvement in them, promises to provide in the 1980s the first real challenge to the supremacy of the three-network system.[11]

Cable television, as it has evolved over the past decade, indeed has presented a strong challenge to the network dominance of television, and it has done this in large part by offering Hollywood films, uncut and uninterrupted by commercials. Although cable is similar to the sort of subscription medium planned by such firms as Paramount's Telemeter, it differs in that it is usually the service itself that the viewer purchases, not individual programs or films. Cable also differs from the earlier schemes in that it is supplied by a relatively inexpensive, national system of distribution: satellite transmission, which, since its introduction in the late 1970s, has stimulated the explosive growth of pay television services.

Relying on cable and satellite transmission instead of the airwaves, the studios have made their presence felt in this new form of subscription television. Warner Bros., now part of the conglomerate Time Warner Inc., was the first of the studios to become involved in subscription television after 1968. In 1973, Warner Communications began Warner Cable (which later became The Movie Channel), one of the first pay services (and the first to be offered 24 hours a day) after the FCC's authorization of subscription television. Also now included in Warner's cable television interests are Showtime, MTV (Music Television), VH-1, and Nickelodeon.

In 1977, along with MCA and Time Inc., Paramount (which in 1967 had become part of the Gulf+Western conglomerate, now known as Paramount Communications) launched the USA cable channel, which was not primarily a subscription television service, but planned to offer occasional pay-per-view programs. In 1979, with MCA, Columbia, and Twentieth Century–Fox, Paramount attempted to create a new pay television channel called Premiere. The studios planned to use the service to show their own films; they felt that HBO, the most powerful of the pay services, had too much of an advantage in negotiations over the sale of television rights to their films. This venture was not allowed by the Justice Department, which felt it was both anticompetitive and illegal. For the same reason, and with the same results, Paramount and MCA tried to buy into Showtime/The Movie Channel with Warner Communications in 1983.

Today, the Hollywood studios still seek to increase their share of the American consumer's entertainment dollar, regardless of the medium. The recent struggle between Warner Communications and Paramount Communications, the giants of the industry, for Time Inc. and its pay television service HBO (the most successful of such services) involved not only billions of dollars, but also control over a form of television that has caused the end of the dominance of both the networks and commercial broadcast television.

CONCLUSION

All of the major Hollywood studios attempted to enter the television industry in the early years of the new medium; they sought both to exploit broadcast television through the ownership and operation of television stations and networks and to offer alternatives to broadcast television. These alternatives—theater television and subscription television—offered ways in which the studios could differentiate their products from those of broadcast television. They also fit in with the ways in which the motion picture companies had been doing business for decades and allowed them to retain control over distribution of their products and over the profits that resulted from that control. The initial failure of all of these schemes is due to a variety of factors, not the least of which is the intervention of the Federal Communications Commission and the U.S. Congress, who, through both their actions and inaction, ensured that the broadcasters would retain control of television for more than three decades. This control now has been challenged, and in fact ended; with the products of the Hollywood studios, and the financial clout of the conglomerates that now own the studios, cable and satellite transmission have altered the medium of television.

NOTES

1. *Broadcasting*, May 15, 1940, p. 15.
2. *Broadcasting*, April 2, 1951, p. 25.
3. *Variety*, April 4, 1951, p. 26.
4. George T. Shubert, "Paramount's TV Network Plan," *Film Daily Yearbook*, 1950, p. 844.
5. *Variety*, February 23, 1949, p. 26.
6. Robert Conly, "The Promise of Television," *The American Mercury* (July 1944): 63.
7. "Proceedings of the First Annual Conference of the Television Broadcasters Association" (December 11–12, 1944, New York), p. 108, Allen B. DuMont Papers, Division of Electricity and Modern Physics, National Museum of American History, Smithsonian Institution, Washington, D.C.
8. Barney Balaban, quoted in Abel Green, "Barney Balaban Slants on Fee-TV," *Variety*, November 27, 1957, p. 32.
9. *Broadcasting*, April 30, 1956, p. 63.
10. *Broadcasting*, October 28, 1957, p. 31.
11. Michele Hilmes, "Film Industry Alternatives to the Networks: Subscription Television, 1949–1962," *Quarterly Review of Film Studies* 10, no. 3 (Summer 1985): 222.

SUGGESTIONS FOR FURTHER READING

Austrian, Ralph B. "Some Economic Aspects of Theater Television." *Journal of the Society of Motion Picture Engineers* 44, no. 5 (May 1945): 377–85.

Gomery, Douglas "Failed Opportunities: The Integration of the U.S. Motion Picture and Television Industries." *Quarterly Review of Film Studies* 9, no. 3 (Summer 1984): 219–28.

"Theater Television: The Missing Link of Technological Change in the U.S. Motion Picture Industry. *The Velvet Light Trap* 21 (Summer 1985): 54–61.

Hilmes, Michele, "Film Industry Alternatives to the Networks: Subscription Television, 1949–1962." *Quarterly Review of Film Studies* 10, no. 3 (Summer 1985): 213–23.

Howe, Hartley E. "Will You Pay for TV Shows?" *Popular Science* (April 1952): 126–27.

McCoy, John E. and Harry P. Warner. "Theatre Television Today," pts. 1 and 2. *The Hollywood Quarterly* 4 (1949–50): 161–77 and 262–78.

Quigley, Martin Jr. "Telemeter in Action." *Motion Picture Herald*, June 18, 1960, pp. 18–20.

Waltz, George H., Jr. "Theatre Vision Presents the Big Fight Transmitted Direct From Ringside." *Popular Science* (July 1949): 109–13.

White, Timothy R. "Life After Divorce: The Corporate Strategy of Paramount Pictures Corp. in the 1950s." *Film History* 2, no. 2 (1988): 99–119.

Chapter 6

New Producers for Old:
United Artists and the Shift
to Independent Production

Tino Balio

*B*y the 1960s, Hollywood had rebounded from the effects of the *Paramount* decrees, changing audience tastes, and the growth of television. CinemaScope, 3-D color, location shooting, and all the ingredients that went into the "big picture" revived the ailing industry. But the public did not resume the old ways; it became selective. As *Variety* quipped in 1959, "People no longer consider every film exciting because it moves on the screen."[1] Motion pictures became special events, which had the effect of widening the gap between commercial winners and losers. Where middling films may have scraped along before, they now did dismal business. On the other hand, pictures striking the public's fancy acted like magnets for the consumer dollar. Hollywood, as a result, concentrated its production efforts on fewer and more expensive pictures in its quest for profits.

In adjusting to the new market conditions, the majors opted for independent production over the studio system. After televison, the mass production of motion pictures ceased, and it was no longer practical for studios to keep large numbers of actors, directors, screenwriters, and other production personnel under long-term contract. To secure quality product, it made more economic sense to tailor-make individual pictures. An expedient way to accomplish this was to finance independent producers who had assembled "packages" of talent especially suited to a project. By 1960, over 50 percent of the pictures distributed by the majors were made by independents.

When independent production took off after World War II, observers of the industry hailed it as "a kind of cure-all for what [ailed] Hollywood, both artistically and commercially" and as "a source of new freedom, new talent, and new ideas."[2] For example, when

165

Frank Capra and partners William Wyler and George Stevens formed their independent production company Liberty Films in 1946, Capra announced that independent productions would be different—they would have individuality. Of his company, he said,

> Each one of these producers and directors has his own particular style of film-making, his own individual ideas on subject matter and material, and the manner in which it should be treated. And each one, on his own and responsible only to himself, will as an independent producer have the freedom and liberty to carry out these ideas in the manner he feels they should be executed.[3]

Behind Capra's statement lay a deep dissatisfaction with the studio system. During the heyday of Hollywood, motion pictures achieved technical perfection, he believed, but in the process they lost their individuality. Producer-director Otto Preminger described his experience at Twentieth Century–Fox by saying, "I was turning out a string of films following rules and obeying orders, not unlike a foreman in a sausage factory."[4] Capra did not blame the mass production methods of the studios per se, but rather the hierarchical chain of command that required each picture to meet the approval of the studio chief. As he put it,

> The creative side of film-making, from the selection of the story, the writers who would put it into script form, the casting of the players, the designing of their costumes and the sets which provided their backgrounds, the direction, the cutting and editing of the final film was tailored (consciously or unconsciously) to the tastes of the studio's head man.[5]

Thus it would be no exaggeration to say that during the thirties and forties, five or six men decided what was to be shown on the nation's screens.

But when the independent movement was firmly in place, Richard Dyer MacCann assessed the situation by saying, "the departure from the old studio system is more apparent than real. . . . Producers are still only as free as their production-distribution deals let them be."[6] The balance of power did not favor the independent producer during the age of television, simply because the *Paramount* decrees failed to break the power of the major companies. Although shorn of their theaters, the *Paramount* defendants have continued to dominate business through the 1950s and 1960s and even to this day. As explained in the introduction to Part I of this book, distribution presents high barriers to entry. Since the market absorbed less and less product during the spread of television, it could support only a limited number of distributors—about the same as existed at the time of the decrees. But because production financing became riskier than ever, the majors were not about to venture far afield from the tried and true, or, as I will explain later, to relinquish important controls over production to independents.

Who were the new independent producers? Just how independent were they? And what was the bargaining relationship between independents and the major film companies? We can gain some insights into these questions by examining United Artists (UA) in the decades after 1951 when the company changed ownership and became the prototype of today's motion picture corporation.

TAKING THE OFFENSIVE

From its inception in 1919, United Artists had functioned exclusively as a distributor for independent producers: it never owned a studio nor had it ever held actors under contract.[7] The founders of the company—Mary Pickford, Charlie Chaplin, Douglas Fairbanks, and D. W. Griffith—secured production financing on their own and used the company as a service organization to market their pictures. During the twenties, UA's best-remembered pictures were Mary Pickford's *Pollyanna* (1920), *Tess of the Storm Country* (1922), and *Rosita* (1923); Chaplin's *The Gold Rush* (1925); Fairbank's *The Three Musketeers* (1921) and *Robin Hood* (1923); and Griffith's *Broken Blossoms* (1919), *Way Down East* (1921), and *Orphans of the Storm* (1922). During the thirties, UA's roster included popular hits by such filmmakers as Sam Goldwyn, Alexander Korda, David O. Selznick, and Walt Disney.

Although UA's prestigious releases during the days of the studio system earned it a reputation as the Tiffany's of the industry, it was the smallest of the eight majors. After the war, UA went downhill as a result of incessant wrangling on the part of its owners, mismanagement, and lack of capital. The threat of bankruptcy in 1951 convinced Mary Pickford and Charlie Chaplin, the two remaining stockholders, to turn over operating control to a management team headed by two young lawyers, Arthur B. Krim and Robert S. Benjamin.

In devising a plan of action, Krim and Benjamin took the offensive. As Hollywood retrenched in the face of television, UA turned the situation to its advantage by differentiating itself from the old-line majors. This was the plan: in return for distribution rights, UA would offer independent producers complete production financing, creative control over their work, and a share of the profits. The strategy turned the company around. UA went public in 1957 and ten years later, had become the largest producer-distributor in the world.

Although the other majors shifted to unit production and shared the profits with independents, UA's brand of independent production gave it an edge over its competitors. *Fortune* published an article on UA in 1958 entitled "The Derring-Doers of the Movie Business" that spotlighted Krim and Benjamin's achievements in revolutionizing the industry.[8] The first point was that, unlike the other majors, UA was strictly a motion picture distribution company. UA neither owned a studio nor produced motion pictures under its own name. UA financed motion pictures simply to guarantee a steady supply of product. Much of what was distinctive about UA followed from this different operation.

Second, UA offered independent producers automony, once the basic ingredients (story, cast, director, and budget) had been approved by all parties. As Otto Preminger said,

> Only United Artists has a system of true independent production. They recognized that the independent has his own personality. After they agree on the basic property and are consulted on the cast, they leave everything to the producer's discrimination. Most of the time when the others make an independent contract, they want to be able to approve the shooting and the final cut.[9]

Preminger exaggerated somewhat, but the point is that UA gave a producer complete autonomy over the making of his picture, including the final cut. As UA liked to say, a producer had the right "to visualize the picture as he saw fit." Company executives never asked to see rushes or asked a director to justify creative decisions. Working at another company, an independent operated under the eye of the studio head, whose staff viewed rushes every day whether the producer liked it or not, simply because the rushes would be screened in the studio's theater. A prominent director under contract with UA was quoted as saying, "When I was at _____ ,they looked at my rushes every day. That's like a novelist having to send in his daily few pages to his publisher as he writes them. What kind of talent can work that way?"[10] Krim and Benjamin realized they might die by the sword, granting autonomy to filmmakers, but they decided to adopt the policy from the start.

Third, UA gave an independent producer ownership in his picture, which offered tax savings in addition to profit participation. Moreover, the producer made his picture under his own name. Concerning screen credits, the director quoted above said,

> Don't let anyone kid you that they're not important. If you're an independent with other major studios, you won't get top credit on the opening title. With UA I get top credit and somewhere down at the bottom there'll be a modest line, "Released by United Artists." Benjamin and Krim stick to their roles; they don't make believe they're producers and they don't compete with us for kudos."[11]

Fourth, UA allowed a producer to set up his production any place in the world to suit the needs of the story or the economics of the venture. UA's producers regularly took advantage of foreign subsidies, frozen funds—that is, funds that could not be removed from foreign jurisdiction—and tax benefits from incorporating abroad. But the other majors could not give independents this leeway. These companies had large amounts of money tied up in their studios and naturally wanted to rent their facilities to the filmmakers they were backing. But the day of the big studio-pictures could be made anywhere. *Variety* said, "It is generally believed that the entire theatrical output of Hollywood can now (1958) be made in one studio, such as Metro's or Warner's."[12] Nonetheless, until the majors dismantled or sold off some of their studios, they would continue to tack on a standard overhead fee to the budgets of independent productions that inflated costs by as much as 40 percent. Steven Bach has said that the overhead charge was viewed by producers as "at best an override and at worst legalized larceny."[13] UA, by contrast, owned no studio and charged no overhead fee. Working for UA, a producer rented only what he needed and when he needed it. This situation lowered production costs and made the venture potentially more profitable.

In short, UA tried to create what Krim called "the psychological climate" to nurture long-term relationships with independent producers. Since the other majors had produced and distributed pictures under their own logos from the start, they found it difficult to provide the same treatment to independents. But as the years went on, said

Krim, "the other majors came closer and closer to UA's way of doing things. They did so because they had no alternative."[14]

UA'S METHOD OF OPERATION

UA's operation generated two sources of profits—one from distribution and another from production. The former was generated by the distribution fee for the benefit of the company; the latter for the benefit of both the company and the producer. In handling a picture, UA charged the producer a schedule of fees ranging from 30 to 45 percent of the gross receipts, depending on the market. These fees went to meet the company's fixed expenses on a worldwide network of 90 sales offices that employed over two thousand people and cost $15 million a year to maintain. Thus, the company had to do a sizable volume of business each year just to break even. But the distribution fee not only paid for housekeeping bills, it also generated profits. Since the marketing costs of a picture remained relatively fixed regardless of its box office performance, a hit could generate revenues well in excess of distribution expenses. Distribution profits rewarded the company, to be sure, but they were also used to offset losses on production loans and to contribute to a pool for the financing of new projects.

For those pictures that earned back their investments, UA also enjoyed production profits. Since the distribution fee offset UA's risk as financier, the company could afford to be generous with the production profits. UA typically divided the profits with a producer 50-50, but in special cases, such as for Otto Preminger and Burt Lancaster, UA gave away 75 percent. These were the rewards for a producer's efforts. But UA as financier took the greater risk and earned first call on the revenues.

To illustrate the risks of production financing, we can examine UA's efforts from the time of the Krim-Benjamin takeover in 1951 to when the company went public in 1957. Of the hundred plus pictures UA financed in this period, practically all failed to earn back their production costs in the theatrical market. As a group, they generated only around $25,000 in profits. If UA's producers took it on the chin, the company went unscathed. These pictures generated distribution fees during this period that increased from $20 million a year to more than $60 million; correspondingly, UA's earnings jumped from $350,000 to over $6 million. The obvious conclusion is that a distribution company like UA could operate profitably even if it earned nothing from its participation in production profits. Another indicator of the distribution fee's importance is that UA in only a few instances failed to recover, through its distributor's share of the film rentals, the loans it advanced for production.

Although UA's brand of independent production accorded talent more freedom than it ever enjoyed during the days of the studio system, the company retained ultimate discretionary power by exercising approval rights over the basic ingredients of a production and by establishing tight fiscal controls. Approval rights permitted UA to judge the commercial potential of each creative component in a package; fiscal controls ensured that the producer lived up to his part of the bargain once shooting began.

In evaluating a project, UA did not measure the potential profits, but, rather, the potential loss. The company might lose some big ones in the process, but that was worth the risk. As Krim put it, "We are determined to avoid disaster in individual pictures. That means we must constantly weigh and gauge how many pictures we can profitably handle, and we must make sure that we don't take undue risks. Our policy here is to consider every picture a failure from the start. That's the way we figure it. Then, if it's a success, well that means the hard work has paid off and we're agreeably surprised." Some pictures are a safer investment at $12 million than others are at $3 million. The classic example was the James Bond series. "For *Dr. No* we allowed a budget of a million-two and we wouldn't let them go over one dollar," said Krim, "*Dr. No* grossed six million and was a mild success. We then allowed *From Russia with Love* to go to two million. *Russia* did better so we let *Goldfinger* go to three. By the end we were permitting budgets to go to sixteen million, but still the investment was safe."[15] Cost per se, then, was not the issue; it was cost against the potential return. That was the key. And that was a management judgment.

Types of Independent Producers

As the ranks of independent producers swelled during the sixties, UA's roster contained a mix of creative producers, packagers, talent, and combinations thereof. The creative producer typically had experience in most phases of the production process and had earned his stripes in the studio system. In going independent, this type of producer acquired properties, oversaw the development of the screenplay, hired the talent, controlled the budget, and worked closely with the director. In other words, he was involved in all facets of production and the picture bore his stamp.

Perhaps the best example of a creative producer is the team of Harry Saltzman and Albert "Cubby" Broccoli, producers of the James Bond series. Saltzman and Broccoli did not merely pull down successive titles from the Ian Fleming bookshelf and order up new pictures. The producers devised a formula of their own inspired by the novels and that accounted for the enduring popularity of the series. Unlike the novels, the James Bond films were laced with humor, ranging from subtle tongue-in-cheek in the early efforts to broad farce in the later ones. The films, in addition, differed in plot details, ranging from only slight changes, as in *From Russia with Love*, to the total departure from the Fleming story in *You Only Live Twice*.

What Broccoli and Saltzman served to the public was the Bond formula. Containing a series of "Bondian effects," the formula was the handiwork not only of Broccoli and Saltzman but also of their production staff. The formula consisted of the famous gun-barrel logo that introduced each picture, followed by the distinctive "James Bond theme," the precredits sequence, and then the main titles, the latter typically accompanied by a title tune. The plot consisted of a series of what Broccoli called "bumps"—that is, a series of self-contained action sequences strung together as set pieces. For each picture, the producers introduced a new exotic locale, a new James Bond woman, and fantastic gadgets to enliven the formula. The formula proved to be durable because it continued, with minor variations, to captivate the mass audience for over two decades.

The star and/or director as independent producer was also creatively involved in production and, like the creative producer, had a support staff that might consist of a production manager, story editor, accountant, lawyer, and agent. Theoretically, the staff concerned itself with business affairs and the logistics of production while the star or director pondered creative matters.

Producer-director Stanley Kramer is a good example of such an independent. Like every top-ranked independent, Kramer had to devise a strategy to carve a niche in the market, which is to say he had to create a distinct identity for himself and his pictures. Upon signing a multiple-picture contract with UA in 1955, Kramer took the tack of making "forceful films on vital themes," in the words of *New York Times* film critic Bosley Crowther.[16] Kramer's *The Defiant Ones* (1958, for example, dealt with race prejudice. In it, two convicts, "an arrogant white man" (Tony Curtis) and "an intelligent Negro" (Sidney Poitier), chained together, make their break for freedom from a Southern chain gang. As the posse hunts them down, they learn to respect one another. Generally regarded as one of Kramer's best efforts, the picture won the New York Film Critics Best Picture Award.

On the Beach (1959) aroused "the ire of civil defense and military authorities" by suggesting "that everyone in the world would be killed by fall-out from an atomic war," said Crowther.[17] Starring Gregory Peck and Ava Gardner, the picture was based on Nevil Shute's best-seller set in southern Australia, the last safe spot on earth, whose inhabitants await the poisonous fallout from a nuclear war.

Judgment at Nuremberg (1961) probed Germany's war guilt. Adapted from an original teleplay by Abby Mann, which was presented on CBS's "Playhouse 90" in 1959, the picture dramatized the Nuremberg war-crime trials of 1948. Kramer did not focus on the notorious Nazi leaders but on members of the German judiciary who went along with the infamous legal mandates of the Nazis that resulted in the deaths of 6 million innocent people. *Judgment at Nuremberg* was produced at a timely moment and was perhaps even suggested by the publication of William L. Shirer's tremendously popular book, *The Rise and Fall of the Third Reich* (1960), and by the impending trial of Adolph Eichmann in Israel.

The packager was the most typical type of independent producer. A packager assembled the ingredients of a picture but, unlike the creative producer or star, took a secondary position in the production. More often than not, packagers were former talent agents. During the breakdown of the studio system, agencies such as William Morris and MCA assumed the traditional production function of the Hollywood studios by searching out appropriate properties for their clients, by formulating production projects, and by creating production units. After the Department of Justice investigated MCA for possible antitrust violations in 1962, MCA chose to get out of the talent agency business, and many of its former employees established their own agencies, joined others, or went into independent production.

By far the most successful packager connected with United Artists was the Mirisch company. The brainchild of Harold Mirisch and his two brothers, Walter and Marvin, the Mirisch company operated as an "umbrella" organization that provided business and legal services to independents. The objective was to allow filmmakers to concentrate on production while the company managed the logistics of production, arranged the financing and distribution, and supervised the marketing.

The Mirisches entered into joint ventures with talent and in return received a management fee and a share of the profits from the productions. The Mirisches decided from the start to concentrate on directors, on the assumption that directors would attract the stars. To produce its top-of-the-line product, Mirisch gave multiple-picture contracts to such ranking directors as Billy Wilder, John Sturges,

Robert Wise, and George Roy Hill, among others. These directors originated projects, worked with screenwriters to develop scripts, and regularly received the right of final cut. Mirisch gave promising younger directors like Blake Edwards and Norman Jewison freedom to develop and when they proved themselves, they too were given long-term contracts with all the perquisites. To produce the remainder of the Mirisch pictures, the company hired free-lance directors. As experienced craftsmen, directors such as Joseph Newman, Michael Curtiz, Daniel M. Petrie, Walter Grauman, Gordon Douglas, and a host of others could get the job done. They worked at a straight salary and typically were assigned to projects after the scripts had been prepared.

The Mirisches produced 67 pictures for UA over 15 years. They were in every size and style and consistently took Hollywood's top honors. Three pictures won Oscars for Best Picture: Billy Wilder's *The Apartment* (1960), Robert Wise's and Jerome Robbins's *West Side Story* (1961), and Norman Jewison's *In the Heat of the Night* (1967). Among the other acclaimed pictures were Wilder's *Some Like It Hot* (1959), John Sturges's *The Magnificent Seven* (1960), Blake Edwards's *Pink Panther* (1964), and Norman Jewison's *The Russians Are Coming, the Russians Are Coming* (1966).

During the sixties, the Mirisch operation became the ideal structure for independent production. Other production units exhibited many weaknesses as businesses, but the most significant had to do with product differentation. By placing his eggs in a single basket, like Kramer, an independent placed himself at a disadvantage if his brand of pictures had limited appeal. The Mirisch brothers understood this drawback and devised a structure that enabled the company to tap all segments of the market.

ANATOMY OF THE DEAL

Projects typically took the form of a "package" consisting of a story, property, director, and/or star. Nearly all projects emanated from outside the company. As Benjamin said, UA strove "to have as many minds working for us as possible. After all, there is a limit to one man's ingenuity. It's better to have fifty men looking for the unusual, and striving to achieve it, than to have two or three. The trick is to attract the right people."[18] The package was the seed of the motion picture deal. If it interested UA, the company drew up

a production-financing agreement and a distribution contract setting
forth the conditions of the deal. The project progressed in steps. The
first, which the industry called research and development, involved
writing and/or revising the screenplay, preparing the budget and production schedule, and securing the director and cast. These are the
basic ingredients of a project, designated as the "above-the-line" costs
in a budget. UA had the right of approval over these ingredients.

In this era of blockbusters, launching a big-budget project was
sometimes a long, drawn-out process. An example is Kirk Douglas's
The Vikings. The production history of this picture "would make an
ordinary businessman blanch," said *Fortune*, which focused on *The
Vikings* in a feature story on UA. The following excerpt illustrates
Douglas's step deal:

- February 1955: After a couple of months spent by U.A. and Bryna
  (Douglas's production company) executives searching for and reading
  material about the Vikings, Douglas found a book he liked. It was *The
  Viking*, by Edison Marshall. Douglas sent it to Krim. Krim thought it
  would take too much money to turn the book into a good screenplay.
  But he sent it on anyway to U.A. Vice President Max E. Youngstein, who
  was vacationing in Haiti. Youngstein recommended that it be bought
  "if the price is reasonable." The asking price was about $75,000, plus
  a large percentage of the movie's net profits, which Krim didn't think
  was "reasonable."
- October 1955: Continued reading of plays, books, stories, and even
  juveniles having failed to turn up a better vehicle, U.A. bought movie
  and TV rights to Marshall's book for $30,000 plus 6 percent of the net
  and transferred ownership to Bryna.
- May 1956: Douglas got an OK from Krim and Robert Benjamin, U.A.'s
  board chairman, to hire Richard Fleischer to direct *The Vikings*. Fleischer
  was to get $50,000 cash, a deferred payment of an additional $50,000,
  and 5 percent of the net.
- June 1956: Bryna hired Noel Langley to write the screenplay. Another
  $50,000 was thus committed by U.A., making a total of $180,000
  so far; and 11 percent of the movie's take had been surrendered.
  There was still no formal agreement between Byrna and U.A. on *The
  Vikings*.
- Summer 1956: Bryna representatives in Europe went looking for a
  location in Norway, studio space in Germany, a castle in France,
  and a shipwright who could build tenth-century longboats.
- October 1956: U.A. had by now advanced Byrna $75,000 in pre-
  production costs, was committed for $105,000 more. Douglas estimated
  he would need another $100,000 for pre-production costs in the next
  few months. Benjamin and Krim told him to go ahead.

- January 1957: The screenplay was completed and read at U.A. Max Youngstein's verdict:" I think this can now be a very big money picture." Three longboats were under construction ($16,000).
- February 1957: U.A.'s total advance on *The Vikings* was up to $250,000. (U.A. had also, meanwhile, loaned Bryna $108,000 for three other movies in the planning stage.) U.A. had security for its money—Bryna's interest in *The Indian Fighter*, then being shown, plus *The Vikings* script—but there was still no final Bryna-U.A. contract on *The Vikings*.
- March 1957: Douglas and Krim got together in Hollywood to draw up a contract. U.A. agreed to loan $2,500,000 for *The Vikings* if Douglas were the sole star, $3,250,000 if he enlisted a co-star (which he subsequently did). If costs went above these figures, U.A. would provide the additional money but would receive additional "protection"; i.e., for each $250,000 in excess, Douglas agreed to make another picture for U.A. and himself assume a quarter of a million initial costs. U.A. was to get 25 percent of *The Vikings'* net profit plus its standard distribution fee: 30 percent of the gross in the U.S., Canada, and England, 40 percent elsewhere. (As Kirk Douglas said recently, "They make tough deals, but they talk my language."
- Krim sent his partner Benjamin—both of them are lawyers—a memo that reflected neither the devotion a lawyer is supposed to have for hard and fast agreements, nor the distrust that is traditional in Hollywood. "I realize," Krim wrote, "there are many loopholes, but Kirk said we could rely on the kind of people we are dealing with. We are therefore going forward in large measure based on moral considerations as well as the legal document."[19]

Everything in the budget was negotiable, theoretically, but in general UA required the principal creative participants of an independent production to function in varying degrees as coventurers with the company by deferring most of their salaries until the cash costs of the picture had been recouped. UA paid a producer's fee up front to the producer for multiple-picture deals. The company also paid the producer an overhead fee to maintain continuity of his administrative staff. Creative personnel receiving profit shares, such as the screenwriter, star, and director, were known collectively as "third-party participants." Profits paid to them came from the producer's share or, on occasion, from UA's and the producer's on a formula basis—for example, if a star was to receive 10 percent of the profits, UA might contribute 40 percent and the producer 60 percent. Top stars might demand, in addition to their fees, a percentage of the gross in lieu of profit participation, in which case the cost would be borne equally by the producer and the company. The first time

UA agreed to a percentage deal was to get Gary Cooper to costar with Burt Lancaster in *Vera Cruz* in 1954. At the time this type of deal was rare, but by the seventies, percentage deals became "almost the starting point for negotiation with important talent."[20] Participation could begin after break-even, or at a negotiated dollar point, or "off the top"—that is, from the very start of distribution, among other variations.

If UA and the producer could not agree on any of the basic ingredients, the producer had the right to "turnaround"—that is, to set up the project elsewhere to get the picture made. In picking up a project, a company had to reimburse UA for its research and development (R&D) expenses. The turnaround provision was particularly important in multiple-picture deals. In attempting to establish long-term relationships with talent, UA emphasised its policy of nonexclusivity. UA wanted first approval rights from its producers, but if mutually satisfactory terms could not be worked out, the producer was free to take his project elsewhere. If the project found no takers it was abandoned and the development costs either written off or charged to the producer's next picture.

When UA gave the go-ahead, the project entered the preproduction period, during which a start date was set and the department heads and other "below-the-line" personnel were hired for the production and postproduction periods to make the picture. At this point, UA arranged for the complete financing, usually by guaranteeing a bank loan—and when the picture was to be produced abroad, by securing frozen funds and/or foreign subsidies. To finance Kirk Douglas's *The Vikings* (1958), for example, UA guaranteed a $1.5 million loan from a New York bank. French and German banks agreed to lend $500,000 each in francs and marks. A loan of $263,000 in kroner came from Norway; $393,000 in sterling was borrowed in England. Foreign loans, which financed the location shooting, were guaranteed in part from UA funds in blocked accounts. Banks did not evaluate the commercial value of the picture; their primary consideration in making the loan was UA's financial situation. As a UA executive said,

Banks naturally want to know about the picture and they like to see a script, but the loan commitment is probably already made by the time they receive one. They like to know—maybe it would impress their loan committee to know who's in it or who's directing it. But I don't think they really are concerned [about the financial possibilities of the picture] because they are looking to the credit of UA and not to the picture for repayment.[21]

Although a producer had creative control while shooting a picture, UA kept tabs on its investment. As the person responsible for watching the money, the line producer had to submit to UA daily call sheets, production reports, and a running account of the cash flow. On location, UA assigned a disbursing agent to cosign the checks. UA, in other words, did not just turn over the money to the producer outright.

UA assumed a producer would be frugal, since an escalation of the budget would jeopardize his profits. Nonetheless, UA built into the financing arrangements safeguards to keep the picture on track. Natural disasters and other catastrophes such as the death of the star were covered by insurance. But even in the best of circumstances, many unforeseen things could delay shooting. Since these were also unavoidable, the company might build in a 10 percent contingency to the budget. Delays caused by producer negligence or by an excessively slow director were more serious, so UA did one of several things. A first-time producer might be required to furnish a completion bond guaranteeing that extra money would be forthcoming to finish the picture no matter what. The producer had to secure completion money on his own, typically from a bonding company, which asked for a share of his profits and sometimes a fee as conditions for the loan.

UA placed different constraints on an established producer. Once he exceeded the 10 percent cushion, he might begin losing profit points—that is, a portion of his percentage of the profits—or his profit participation might be delayed until the company recouped the overage plus a penalty. Penalizing the producer involved only a finite amount of money; if the production got out of hand, UA protected itself by retaining the right of takeover. This was the ultimate remedy, but also the most radical and perilous course to take. The company preferred to apply pressure. As one UA producer said, "All of a sudden we would start getting phone calls when we hadn't got phone calls before. We would feel pressure, the director would feel pressure."[22] Too much pressure or renegotiating the contract might cause the director to rebel and lose even more time. But closing down the production while a replacement director was found could be even more costly for a whole different set of reasons.

In reality, there wasn't much UA could do to keep producers within budget except to deal with the right people. In giving the green light to a producer, UA executive William Bernstein said,

You're taking the risk that you've made the right choice. What ultimately it always comes down to is have we bet on the right people? They are the ones who are executing the film and if you guess wrong, if you're dealing with a fiscally irresponsible producer or director, they can hurt you terribly.[23]

In return for financing the picture, UA received worldwide distribution rights in all media, film gauges, and languages. The company also received worldwide soundtrack album rights and music-publishing rights. Concerning remakes and sequels and ancillary rights to the underlying literary material, UA might share joint control with the producer.

The term of UA's distribution contracts was only five years at the time of the Krim-Benjamin takeover, but after the company started the financing program, it was able to increase the term first to ten years and then to perpetuity. Obviously, the longer UA could distribute a picture, the more revenue it could collect from ancillary markets. UA's library of current feature films therefore consisted of pictures for which UA had limited-term distribution rights, pictures for which it had perpetual rights, and pictures that the company owned outright as a result of a buyout. A producer normally did not sell his interest in a picture, since the point of going into independent production was to benefit from the annuity provided by long-term distribution. But, at times, producers wanted out for tax purposes or simply because they needed cash. The price UA offered was negotiable, like everything else in the relationship, and was based on the residual value of the picture. In a buyout, UA purchased a producer's participation in the picture. Partnership with a producer required a range of distribution matters to be handled by mutual consent; a buyout gave UA more flexibility over marketing. In confronting new technologies, UA wanted all the freedom of movement it could muster.

To make certain the picture got through the distribution pipeline, UA demanded that the finished picture conform to a designated theatrical running time and receive a seal of approval from the Production Code Administration and an "A" or "B" certificate from the Legion of Decency. If not, UA retained the right to ask for the appropriate cuts. If the picture encountered censorship problems during release, UA could require the producer to cut any scene, to shoot additional scenes, or to do retakes—whatever was necessary to ensure that the picture reached the market.

In devising distribution strategies and promotion campaigns, UA sometimes granted the producer consultation rights, but only for the domestic market. UA did not tell a producer how to shoot his picture and in return did not want to be told how to handle the marketing—even though the costs of prints and advertising were ultimately billed to the producer. Distribution, after all, was UA's stock-in-trade. Each year, the company released a minimum of 20 to 30 pictures in all budget levels and popular genres—Westerns, mythological and biblical epics, teenage exploitation pictures, and even French New Wave art films. A producer might know something about the U.S. market, but not necessarily much about Italy, Japan, Australia, or South Africa.

After the picture was released, revenues were allocated to the participants in accordance with the degree of risk they had taken. Rentals from theatrical exhibition are known in total as the "distribution gross." From every dollar collected, UA deducted its distribution fee. The remainder, called the "producer's share," went first to reimburse UA for print and advertising costs; second, to pay off the production loan and completion money; and third, to pay the deferred salaries. Thereafter, the revenues (with the distribution fee still being deducted) constituted profits and were divided among the participants in the agreed-upon proportions.

In multiple-picture deals, profits were typically cross-collateralized. Essentially, cross-collaterization treated the pictures of a producer as a group, with the profits and losses averaged. Producers considered the provision onerous, but UA wanted protection against a situation whereby a producer enjoyed windfall profits on one film while the company absorbed substantial losses on his other pictures. UA sometimes refined the condition by crossing pictures in groups of two or three or limiting the producer's liability to 25 to 100 percent of his profits, depending on his track record. Stanley Kramer, for example, produced five pictures for UA from 1955 to 1960. The pictures were crossed in groups of two and three. In the first group, *Not as a Stranger* (1955) and *The Pride and the Passion* (1957) were produced at negative costs of $1.5 and $3.7 million, respectively. *Stranger* had a worldwide distribution gross of over $8 million and earned a profit of $1.8 million, a substantial amount based on the investment. *Passion*, however, grossed only $6.7 million worldwide and lost $2.5 million, also a substantial amount. UA's total exposure came to over $5 million. Because the two pictures were cross-collateralized, UA lost $700,000. Correspondingly, Kramer earned no profits instead of $1.8 million for *Stranger*. The pictures in the second group all lost money, which UA had to absorb on its own.

This analysis is a simplified version of a complex process, but it typifies the relationship between an independent producer and UA. It would be simplistic to think of this relationship simply as a struggle between the creative artist on the one hand and business people on the other. Both parties were interested in profit maximization by creating commercially successful motion pictures.

Negotiations between the distributor-financier and independent producer focused on two questions: can the picture earn back its cost? And, to what degree is each party to share the risks? The former involved mainly a marketing decision. Given a company's limited financial resources, it had to select projects to attract the largest audiences. However, the company could not always play it safe; its share of the market would most likely decrease if it regularly followed trends. Taking a calculated risk with a controversial or offbeat picture—with Otto Preminger's *The Moon Is Blue* (1953), Hecht-Lancaster's *Marty* (1955), or Stanley Kubrick's *Paths of Glory* (1958)—was necessary to revitalize and attract audience interest. UA never risked its money foolishly for art's sake. As a condition for backing an experimental venture, the company insisted that production costs be cut to the bare bones to minimize risks. The cash outlay for *Marty* and *The Moon Is Blue*, for example, amounted to less than four hundred thousand dollars each, making them small-budget pictures compared to the blockbusters being turned out by the industry.

Which brings up the second issue. Although UA competed for talent and fresh ideas, the company put up the money and established the parameters—the rules, if you will, of the game. An independent producer might have the clout to negotiate a hefty salary and producer's fee up front in addition to a healthy share of the profits, but for UA and most likely for other majors, one thing was not negotiable—the distribution fee. The distributor, as a result, had first call on the rentals and the producer the leavings. To place this ranking in perspective, we can look to the apportionment of box office receipts. For every dollar taken in by theaters in 1960, the distributor collected as rental about forty cents, on the average. After deducting the distribution fee and print and advertising costs, less than twenty cents remained to cover negative costs.[24] Spiraling print and advertising expenses after 1960, the result of saturation booking and an increased use of television advertising, left even a smaller share for protection. But given the uncertainties of the market, UA and the other majors would have it no other way.

NOTES

1. Fred Hift, "Decades of Success Propel Films Down Now-Impractical Paths?" *Variety*, January 21, 1959, p. 19.

2. Richard Dyer MacCann, "Independence with a Vengeance," *Film Quarterly* 15 (Summer 1962): 14, 19.

3. Frank Capra, "Breaking Hollywood's 'Pattern of Sameness,'" *New York Times Magazine*, May 5, 1946, p. 18.

4. Otto Preminger, *Preminger: An Autobiography* (Garden City, N.Y.: Doubleday, 1977), pp. 99–100.

5. Ibid., p. 18.

6. Richard Dyer MacCann, "Independence with a Vengeance," *Film Quarterly* 15 (Summer 1962): 19.

7. See Tino Balio, *United Artists: The Company Built by the Stars* (Madison: University of Wisconsin Press, 1976).

8. Quoted in the "The Derring-Doers of the Movie Business," *Fortune* 57 (May 1958): 137–41 ff.

9. Ibid., p. 141.

10. Murray Teigh Bloom, "What Two Lawyers Are Doing to Hollywood," *Harper's Magazine* 216 (February 1958): 43.

11. Ibid.

12. "Studio O Head: What to Do?" *Variety*, March 12, 1958, p. 5.

13. Steven Bach, *Final Cut: Dreams and Disaster in the Making of "Heaven's Gate"* (New York: William Morrow, 1985), p. 48.

14. Interview with Arthur B. Krim, March 20, 1985.

15. Interview with Arthur B. Krim, August 3, 1983.

16. Bosley Crowther, "Hollywood's Producer of Controversy," *New York Times Magazine*, December 10, 1961, p. 76.

17. Ibid., p. 82.

18. "The Company of Independents," *Variety*, June 24, 1959, p. 13.

19. "The Derring-Doers of the Movie Business," 137–40.

20. Interview with Herbert T. Schottenfeld, March 19, 1985.

21. Interview with Alan Wilson, February 3, 1976.

22. Interview with Larry DeWaay, November 14, 1975.

23. Interview with William Bernstein, October 19, 1983.

24. I have extrapolated this apportionment from data contained in Robert A. Crandall, "The Postwar Performance of the Motion Picture Industry," *Antitrust Bulletin* 20 (Spring 1975): 49–88.

SUGGESTIONS FOR FURTHER READING

Bach, Steven. *Final Cut: Dreams and Disasters in the Making of "Heaven's Gate."* New York: William Morrow, 1985.

Balio, Tino. *United Artists: The Company that Changed the Film Industry.* Madison: University of Wisconsin Press, 1987.

Donahue, Suzanne Mary. *American Film Distribution: The Changing Market-
ﬂace*. Ann Arbor: UMI Research Press, 1987.

"Hollywood Independents." *The Velvet Light Trap*, no. 22 (1986): entire issue.

Lazarus, Paul, N. III. *The Movie Producer*. New York: Barnes & Noble, 1985.

Litwak, Mark. *Reel Power: The Struggle for Influence and Success in the New
ﬂollywood*. New York: William Morrow, 1986.

Pirie, David, ed. *Anatomy of the Movies*. New York: MacMillan, 1981.

Squire, Janson, ed. *The Movie Business Book*. Englewood Cliffs, N.J.:
ﬂentice-Hall, 1983.

Staiger, Janet. "Individualism Versus Collectivism." *Screen* 24 (July–Octo-
ﬂer): 68–79.

Chapter 7

Glorious Technicolor, Breathtaking CinemaScope, and Stereophonic Sound

John Belton

*T*he first Cinerama feature, *This Is Cinerama* (1952), begins with a roller coaster ride. Filmed with the Cinerama camera mounted on the front of an actual Coney Island roller coaster, the sequence effectively lifts the audience out of their seats in the movie theater and plunges them headlong into the thrill-packed world of the amusement park. The opening credits of *The Robe* (1953), the first CinemaScope film, appear over an enormous red velvet theater curtain, which slowly parts to reveal an ever-expanding wide-screen vista of ancient Rome. Here, the customary space of the movie theater, symbolized by the curtain, opens up, breaking down the narrow confines of the standard motion picture screen. The almost-square image of earlier cinema gives way to the panoramic space of spectacle, into which the audience is slowly drawn.

Both Cinerama and CinemaScope directly engage audiences in a new kind of motion picture experience, an experience characterized, in part, by a rejection (in the case of Cinerama) or a redefinition (in the case of CinemaScope) of the traditional pre-wide-screen motion picture experience. Before Cinerama and CinemaScope, the movies entertained their audiences, holding them entranced in front of a screen whose dimensions averaged 20 feet by 16 feet. With Cinerama and CinemaScope, the movies *engulfed* their audiences, wrapping images as great as 64 by 24 feet around them. At the same time, the movies began to engage their audiences more actively, creating for them a compelling illusion of participation in the action depicted on the screen, an illusion that proved far greater than that achieved by previous, narrower exhibition formats. With *This Is Cinerama*, going to the movies became similar to going to an amusement park, a theme park like Disneyland (which opened in July 1955 but had been in preparation for over three years), or a World's Fair. With *The Robe*, the audience was invited to cross over the barriers of the footlights and pass beyond the theater curtain, which separate the spectacle from the spectator, and to "enter" into the space of the spectacle.

FROM ENTERTAINMENT TO RECREATION

The wide-screen revolution that took place during the early 1950s clearly involved more than a change in the size and shape of motion picture theater screens. It represented a dramatic shift in the film industry's notion of the product that it was supplying to the public. During this period, the industry redefined, in part, what a motion picture was or should be, shifting its primary function of providing entertainment to the public to include another function as well—that of recreation. Motion picture audiences were no longer conceived of as passive spectators but as active participants in a film experience—at least, this is how the industry described the new relationship it sought to establish with its patrons.

Though movies continued to be shown in the same theaters that they had played in for decades and, for the most part, the same sorts of stories were being told on the screen, there was something decidedly different about movie-going in the early 1950s. In contrast to the routine distribution treatment of typical motion picture productions of the past, wide-screen films were treated as special theatrical events. Road show exhibition—launched with *Queen Elizabeth* (1912), *Quo Vadis* (1913), and *The Birth of a Nation* (1915), and periodically revived for certain one-of-a-kind, highly touted releases—became the dominant release pattern for every Cinerama and Todd-AO film (roadshowing, as a regular practice however, was not used in the case of CinemaScope). In other words, virtually every wide-screen film was treated as a potential blockbuster booked in exclusive engagements into a small number of large, first-run theaters.

The theaters, especially the large, first-run, downtown movie palaces, underwent an expensive facelift; old procenniums were torn down and replaced with wall-to-wall curved screens. These old movie palaces finally found, with wide-screen films, an image size commensurate with the overall proportions of their auditoriums

With the installation of multitrack stereo sound systems, theaters not only looked but also sounded different than they had in the past. And, if the same old stories were still being told, there were now fewer of them being told and they were being told more expensively and at greater length. Production budgets increased to accommodate filming in color, wide-screen, and stereo sound. The greater the production values, the industry reasoned, the greater the potential profits. Or, as Cole Porter noted in 1954, "if you want to get the crowds to come around, you've got to have glorious Technicolor, breathtaking CinemaScope, and stereophonic sound."[1]

The reasons for change were obvious; box office statistics, detailing a sharp decline in average weekly admissions from a postwar high of 90 million in 1948 to an all-time low of 46 million in 1953, told much of the story.[2] Behind the statistics lay a dramatic change in the postwar U.S. economy, which the motion picture industry suddenly discovered it had to address. During the 1930s and 1940s (except for the war years), the average workweek had dropped from 60 to 40 hours.[3] At the same time, disposable personal income had doubled between 1940 and 1949, soaring from just under $80 billion to $190 billion.[4] Given greater leisure time and greater disposable income, more and more money was spent for recreation; from just under $4 billion in 1940, recreational expenditure rose to $10 billion in 1948.[5] With more money to spend on recreation and more time to spend it in, Americans could now afford more expensive forms of recreation than they had in the past. They could afford to spend more on entertainment than the relatively inexpensive cost of a movie ticket. They also had not only more time but larger blocks of it. A brief evening at the movies gave way to a day (or even a weekend) of golfing, fishing, or gardening.

In other words, the redefinition of the motion picture as a form of participatory recreation (as opposed to passive entertainment) took place against the background of its competition for audiences with other leisure-time activities. The motion picture sought a middle ground between the notion of passive consumption associated with at-home television viewing and that of active pariticipation involved in outdoor recreational activities. The model chosen by Hollywood for purposes of redefining its product, however, was less that of the amusement park, which retained certain vulgar associations as a cheap form of mass entertainment, than that of the legitimate theater.[6] The theater emerged as the one traditional form of entertainment that possessed the participatory effect of recreational activities and, at the same time, retained a strong identification with the narrative tradition within which the cinema remained steadfastly rooted. In aligning itself with the experimental quality of the theater, wide-screen cinema sought to erase the long-standing distinction between spectatorship in the theater and in the cinema, which viewed the former as active and the latter as passive.

THEATER AND CINEMA

In comparing the theater and the cinema, Andre Bazin argued that the theater, featuring a live performance presented in a space shared by both performers and audience, elicited the participation of the audience in a much more direct and intense way than did the cinema, which separated the space of the performance (that is, the space depicted on screen) from that of the audience (the space of the movie theater). Bazin wrote that

> the theater is based on the reciprocal awareness of audience and actor. ... The theater acts on us by virtue of our participation in a theatrical action across the footlights and as it were under the protection of their censorship. The opposite is true in cinema. Alone, hidden in a dark room, we watch through half-open blinds a spectacle that is unaware of our existence.[7]

The cinema, as Jean Cocteau observed, was an event seen through a keyhole.[8] Wide-screen cinema expanded the keyhole to a point where, though it did not quite disappear, it provided spectators with a spectacle that possessed an increased sense of presence, especially in theaters with curved screens in which the image engulfed the audience. Participation was no longer a matter of absolute distinctions drawn between the theater and the cinema in terms of active as opposed to passive spectatorship. Wide-screen cinema had created an entirely new category of participation. What wide-screen cinema created was a greater illusion of participation, at least in comparison with the narrow, 1.33:1 aspect ratio of pre-wide-screen cinema, in which that illusion, if it existed at all, was weaker.

Advertisements for CinemaScope films even told the audiences that they would be drawn into the space of the picture much as if they were attending a play in the theater. Publicists compared the panoramic CinemaScope image to the oblong "skene" (or stage) of the ancient Greek theater and insisted that "due to the immensity of the screen, few entire scenes can be taken in at a glance, enabling the spectator to view them . . . as one would watch a play where actors are working from opposite ends of the stage," the wide-screen format enhancing the sensation of the actors' presence and giving spectators the illusion that they could reach out and touch the performers.[9]

The wide-screen revolution proved to be more of a revolution in the nature of the movie-going experience than it was in the narrative content of motion picture films. Shooting in large-screen formats transformed the psychology of both filmmaking and film viewing. Wide-screen filmmakers treated every project as if it were a special, big-budget production. Fewer films were being made (the total dropping from 391 domestic releases in 1951 to 253 in 1954) and greater care was lavished on them in production (with negative costs rising from $1 million to $2 million during this same period). The new formats provided even fairly conventional stories with an appeal, as film spectacle, that the narrow 1.33:1 format could not exploit as fully or as successfully as the panoramic vistas of CinemaScope, VistaVision, and Todd-AO did. Film audiences, as well as filmmakers, fell under the spell of the new era of the wide-screen blockbuster, regarding films made in any of the new wide-screen formats as special events well worth the increased admission price that first-run exhibitors charged to see these pictures on a big screen and to hear them in stereo sound.[10] As the average weekly attendance declined, audiences became more and more selective in terms of what they chose to see, demanding more bang for their buck—a demand that the over-produced, wide-screen blockbusters sought to satisfy.

While Hollywood insisted that bigger was also better, audiences, though not necessarily equating bigger with better, definitely perceived bigger as, at the very least, different. Though the industry continued to tell the same old familiar stories, the larger canvas on which they were presented transformed old into new. The new format obscured the fact that wide-screen extravaganzas retained a good deal in common, especially in terms of the sorts of subjects deemed suitable for spectacularization, with prewide-screen spectacles. Biblical epics, for example, remain a staple of prewide-screen and wide-screen cinema. *Samson and Delilah* (1949), *Quo Vadis* (1951), and *David and Bathsheba* (1951) were answered by *The Robe* (CinemaScope, 1953), *The Ten Commandments* (VistaVision 1957), and *Ben-Hur* (MGM Camera 65, 1959). Wide-screen cinema also drew heavily on other traditional genres that rely upon spectacle, such as the period costumer and the musical. Even the low-budget, nonspectacular genre of the Western was called upon to provide story material, which, through big-screen treatment, helped transform that genre, capitalizing upon its postwar renaissance as adult movie fare and solidifying its elevation from "B" to "A" picture status.

Screenwriters joked that they would have to learn to write differently for the new screen dimensions, adapting their craft to fit the new format. Fox's Nunnally Johnson reportedly quipped that now he would have "to put the paper in the typewriter sideways when writing for CinemaScope."[11] But, in fact, the wide-screen revolution had little or no immediate impact upon the craft of the screenwriter. Indeed, all of the scripts for Twentieth Century-Fox's first batch of CinemaScope spectacles were completed long before the studio acquired the CinemaScope process. What distinguished *The Robe* from Fox's earlier *David and Bathsheba* was not so much story or cast but presentation and perception. The wide-screen format produced a radically different perception of generically similar material: biblical spectacle remained biblical spectacle, but became, for the spectator, markedly more spectacular.

CINERAMA: A NEW ERA IN CINEMA

The wide-screen revolution began in earnest with the opening of *This Is Cinerama* at the Broadway Theatre in New York City on September 30, 1952. Cinerama had been developed independently, outside traditional industry channels, by a jack-of-all-trades inventor, Fred Waller, who had earlier invented water skis, a still camera that took a 360-degree picture, and a PhotoMetric camera that could measure a man for a suit of clothes in a fiftieth of a second.[12] Waller perfected the Cinerama camera and projection system in the late 1940s, basing it, in part, on his prior invention of the multiple-camera/projector Vitarama system, which was developed for (but never actually exhibited at) the New York World's Fair in 1939, and on the five-camera, five-screen Flexible Gunnery Trainer, which was used by the Air Force in World War II to train gunners. Though Waller repeatedly tried to interest the majors in his new process, inviting studio heads to demonstrations staged at a converted tennis court on Long Island, the industry rejected Cinerama because of the expense involved in its installation, which necessarily excluded its wide-spread deployment in the nation's movie theaters and because of its technical flaws, which ranged from the visibility of the joints or seams where its multiple images overlapped to the optical distortion produced by its wide-angle lenses. To some extent subsequent history vindicated the reservations of the majors. At the height of its success, Cinerama, which cost from $75,000 to $140,000 to install, played in only a handful of theaters—there were only 22 Cinerama sites in 1959.[13] By comparison, CinemaScope, which cost from $5,000 to $25,000 to install, was available in over 41,000 theaters worldwide by the end of 1956. However, although *This Is Cinerama* (which cost only $1 million to produce) played, on its initial run, in only 17 theaters, it earned over $20 million, becoming the third largest grossing picture of all time.[14] Subsequent reissues of *This Is Cinerama* increased its total earnings to over $32 million, and though the first five Cinerama features could be seen in only a handful of theaters, they grossed more than $82 million.[15]

Cinerama discovered what the industry had not yet realized—there was a growing market for a new kind of motion picture entertainment, and, given the sort of specialized distribution and exhibition that the industry as a whole, geared for traditional mass market practices, was not capable of providing, this new product could return substantial profits.

Cinerama was a wide-screen process involving the use of three interlocked cameras (rather than one), which recorded an extremely wide field of view on three separate strips of 35mm film, and which were, in turn, projected by three projectors (in three separate booths) onto a 25-foot high by 51-foot wide, deeply curved screen, resulting in an aspect ratio of roughly 2.6 to 2.77:1. Stereo sound was recorded magnetically on seven separate channels (on a sound system pioneered by Hazard Reeves), which were combined on a separate strip of 35mm film and played back in the theater on five speakers behind the screen and two surround speakers. In collaboration with the technical talents of Waller and Reeves were the creative contributions of radio commentator and globe-trotting journalist Lowell Thomas, Hollywood producer Merian C. Cooper, and Broadway showman Mike Todd, who collectively produced *This Is Cinerama*.

Cinerama as Event

Cinerama transformed the nature of the movie-going experience, which had gradually become unconsciously automatic, habitual, and routinized over the years. Cinerama defamiliarized the cinema, restoring to it an affective power that, as pure experience, it had lost long ago. In his review of *This Is Cinerama*, *New York Times* critic Bosley Crowther compared Cinerama to the first large-screen projection of motion picture at Koster and Bial's Music Hall in 1896, when shots of sea waves rolling in on a beach supposedly sent naive viewers running for cover. Cinerama recaptured the *experience* of those early films. During Cinerama's aerial sequences, audiences are said to have "leaned sharply in their seats to compensate for the steep banks of the airplane. Others became nauseated by their vicarious ride in a roller-coaster. Still other ducked to avoid the spray when a motor boat cut across the path of the canoe in which they were apparently riding."[16] Even veteran airmen reacted to Cinerama's illusion of reality. Lowell Thomas reports that war ace Gen. James Doolittle clutched his chair when stunt pilot Paul Mantz flew through the Grand Canyon. Drugstores near the Cinerama theater in New York did a land-office business during intermission, selling Dramamine to spectators who either became airsick in the first half or wanted to prepare themselves for the film's finale.[17]

Like early cinema, Cinerama was more than cinema; it was a special phenomenon. People went to it the way they went bowling or golfing. Unlike conventional narrative cinema, Cinerama was not so much "consumed" as it was "experienced." Cinerama was as much "recreation" as "entertainment." As a social phenomenon, it both reflected and generated popular culture as a whole; in fact, it serves as a remarkable index of postwar leisure-time activities. For example, Cinerama's travelogue format not only takes advantage of the increased interest by Americans in domestic sightseeing and travel abroad but functions itself to stimulate tourism.

> Almost immediately after the New York premiere, transcontinental air-lines began to report requests for flights that "go over those canyons" seen in Cinerama. The British Travel Bureau was flooded with inquiries about the date of the Rally of Pipers, which is featured in the film. . . . Closer to home, the roller coaster at Rockaways' Playland, which provides the first sensation in the film, did a record-breaking business all last winter, when amusement parks are generally deserted. . . . Cypress Gardens in Florida . . . reported that the number of visitors jumped to 40 per cent after Cinerama was released.[18]

Like the sights seen within its films, Cinerama itself became a tourist attraction, becoming something that visitors from out of town had to see.

Cinerama advertising capitalized on its own status as one of the seven wonders of the modern world, suggesting to the midwestern populace that "when you visit Detroit, Cinerama is a must stop." One Texas columnist even commented that "it was particularly worth a trip to New York to see Cinerama."[19] Going to see Cinerama became a special event in itself, like a trip to the World's Fair. Cinerama theaters were situated in cities with the largest populations, and the theaters themselves were frequently the largest theaters in those cities. Unlike the rest of the film industry, which distributed films as widely and in as many theaters as possible, Cinerama was not an everyday experience for its audiences—only eight films were ever made in the three-strip Cinerama process, each playing only in Cinerama theaters for runs that (like those of successful Broadway plays) lasted from one to two years. Since only a few spectators could enjoy these films at any one time, there was tremendous demand for tickets, which were old on a reserved-seat basis weeks, and even months, in advance.

Like the first films, Cinerama presented "life as it is," rather than narratives. The initial advertising campaign for *This Is Cinerama*, devised by the McCann-Erickson agency, promoted the film as an incomparable motion picture experience. Unlike 3-D and CinemaScope, which stressed the dramatic content of their story material and the radical new means of technology employed in production, Cinerama used a saturation advertising campaign in the newspapers and on radio to promote the "excitement aspects" of the new medium. Cinerama sold itself through appeals to neither content nor form but to audience involvement. Though it failed to duplicate the experience of the theater in terms of telling a story, Cinerama did attempt to mimic the theater in terms of its sense of participation. Ad copy promised that with Cinerama, "you won't be gazing at a movie screen—you'll find yourself swept right *into* the picture, surrounded with sight and sound."[20] Publicity photos literalized this promise, superimposing images of delighted spectators in their theater seats onto scenes from the film. And while 3-D slowly alienated its audiences by throwing things at them, Cinerama drew them into the screen—and the movie theater—in droves. Despite the absence of story or characters, Cinerama enthralled its customers.

The first five Cinerama features were travelogues.[21] Though Cinerama distinguished itself from traditional Hollywood fare by choosing the travelogue as its major format, its basic technology gave it little choice in the matter. Cinerama initially had difficulty telling stories. Traditional close-ups were impossible, given its lens technology. Cinerama relied on three 27mm lenses, mounted at angles to one another. The use of extreme wide-angle lenses resulted in noticeable distortion, which was magnified in close-up cinematography. Unlike the single focal length required by Cinerma, traditional motion pictures employ a variety of different lenses. The optical restriction in the focal length of Cinerama lenses further reduced the medium's options, denying it what Bosley Crowther referred to as the basis of narrative cinema— "flexibility of the images and the facility of varying the shots."[22] Without close-up, which has become the linchpin of film narrative, the medium was reduced to the nonnarrative, presentational techniques of early cinema and virtually forced to choose the travelogue as the format for its first five features. Ten years after the opening of *This Is Cinerama*, the Cinerama system was used by MGM to film two narrative features, *How the West Was Won* and *The Wonderful World of the Brothers Grimm* (both 1962), but until that time, Cinerama found the travelogue to be the best format for exploiting the Cinerama effect. Unlike traditional cinema, Cinerama established itself as pure experience, unadulterated by the Original Sin of storytelling. In discarding narrative, Cinerama, during the first ten years of its independence from traditional Hollywood production, distribution, and exhibition practices, cut itself off from mainstream narrative cinema and became itself something of a non-traditional, leisure-time activity.

ERSATZ WIDE-SCREEN

The success of Cinerama changed the level of expectations for film audiences; from Cinerama on, motion pictures had to be least projected in, if not made in, wide-screen. Its success made obsolete traditional film formats (that is, the 1.33:1 aspect ratio, which was now identified with television). The advent of Cinerama, which threatened to "dilute the value of millions of dollars worth of 'flat' films in circulation and in Hollywood vaults," startled the majors into frenetic activity.[23]

The immediate response on the part of a number of studios was to produce an ersatz wide-screen image by cropping films shot in the standard 1.33:1 format to an aspect ratio of from 1.66:1 to 1.85:1 and enlarging the image on the screen by using a wide-angle projection lens. In the spring of 1953, Paramount released *Shane*, suggesting that it be projected 1.66:1.[24] Shortly thereafter, Universal promoted *Thunder Bay* as a wide-screen film, encouraging exhibitors to project it on a slightly curved screen, which was an obvious imitation of the Cinerama screen.[25] *Time* magazine, noting that cropping provided only a bargain-basement solution to the challenge posed by Cinerama, dryly observed that "the wide-screen revolution was looking more and more like an inventory sale."[26]

What distinguished Cinerama from these ersatz wide-screen proc-essess was Cinerama's radically new perception of events based not only on a deeply curved screen that wrapped around the audience, engulfing it, but also on its dramatically increased angle of view, which multiplied the participation effect suggested by the curved screen, creating an illusion not only of engulfment but of depth as well.

According to Waller, Cinerama owes its sense of audience participation to the phenomenon of peripheral vision. Waller's own experiments with depth perception led him to the conclusion that the successful illusion of three-dimensionality derived as much from peripheral as from binocular vision. The three lenses of the Cinerama camera, set at angles of 48 degrees to one another, encompass a composite angle of view of 146 degrees by 55 degrees, nearly approximating the angle of view of human vision, which is 165 degrees by 60 degrees. When projected on a deeply curved screen, this view tends to envelop the spectator sitting in the center of the theater. Stereo sound, broadcast from five speakers behind the screen and from one to three surround horns, reinforces the illusion of three-dimensionality.

In order to duplicate the effect of Cinerama, rival systems had to duplicate its angle of view as well as its peripheral field. Cinerama's first and most successful rival, CinemaScope, played, in the largest theaters, on slightly curved screens as large as 64 feet wide by 24 feet high; in similar sites, VistaVision, developed by Paramount in early 1954, could reach a screen dimension of 55 by 27 feet, while Todd-AO, the last successful, Cinerama-inspired, wide-screen system to reach the theaters (in 1955), filled a deeply curved 60-by-25-foot screen. Unlike the ersatz wide-screen "processes," CinemaScope used an optical system that actually doubled the angle of view of traditional lenses; VistaVision and Todd-AO both achieved an improvement in angle of view by using wide film, necessitating a wider camera aperture, which automatically increased angle of view. As a result of both this and the use of wide-angle lenses, VistaVision achieved a horizontal angle of view roughly one and two-thirds that of standard lenses. Todd-AO, led by optics expert Dr. Brian O'Brien, developed a bug-eye lens, possessing an angle of view of 128 degrees, bringing it remarkably close to Cinerama's 146 degrees, but Todd-AO, inspired by Mike Todd's experiences filming the European footage for *This Is Cinerama*, achieved this angle of view using only one lens rather than three.

CINEMASCOPE: A POOR MAN'S CINERAMA

The CinemaScope process employed cylindrical lenses that take in an angle of view twice that of normal lenses and that anamorphically distort the image in the horizontal plane, squeezing it (by a compression factor of 2) in order to fit it onto a single strip of 35mm film. In projection, an anamorphic lens unsqueezes the compressed image, expanding it to an aspect ratio of 2.66:1 (which was subsequently reduced to 2.55:1, then 2.35:1 when soundtracks were added to the film strip). Stereo sound was recorded and played back on four magnetic tracks that, shortly after the opening of *The Robe* in September 1953, were fixed to the same strip of 35mm film that bore the anamorphic image. In effect, CinemaScope provided the industry with a simplified version of Cinerama, approximating its 2.77:1 aspect ratio and its seven-track stereo sound system but using one strip of 35mm film (instead of Cinerama's four) to do so.

CinemaScope optics are based on the "Hypergonar" anamorphic lens invented in the late 1920s by French scientist Henri Chretien. Engineers at Twentieth Century–Fox, the studio that innovated CinemaScope, adapted Chretien's invention to suit the demands of the contemporary motion picture production and exhibition marketplace. Chretien's lens permitted Fox to obtain a wide-screen image without the expense of wide-film or multifilm production and exhibition processes, thus maintaining the 35mm standard observed by the industry as a whole. In this way, Fox sought to satisfy the demands of the industry for innovative formats while keeping to a minimum the expenditure for new production and exhibition technology.[27] In other words, unlike Cinerama, which sought to exploit a new, specialized market for wide-screen entertainment, CinemaScope offered itself as a compromise between traditional, mass-market production and exhibition practices and the new redefinition of the motion picture experience introduced by Cinerama.

Unlike the early Cinerama features, which foregrounded the participation effect through the use of attention-grabbing, forward-tracking movements with the camera mounted on the front end of a roller coaster, CinemaScope feature films sought to achieve a balance between narrative and spectacle, using the format to expand the range of the narrative. As Fox executive Darryl Zanuck suggested, implicitly comparing CinemaScope with rival systems (like Cinerama) that indulged in gimmickry, "CinimaScope is not a substitute for a story nor for good actors. But it does give us more octaves in which to tell our story and gives our actors greater range for their talents."[28] Unlike Cinerama, which was left free by the travelogue format to exploit the effect of engulfment and to present itself as pure spectacle, CinemaScope's participation effect remained regulated by the conventions of narrative, which sought to hold the wide-screen format's spectacular qualities in check. CinemaScope enhanced the

movie-going experience but carefully avoided foregrounding itself as
a process, as did Cinema and 3-D.

Mise-en-Scène in Cinemascope

In *The Robe*, Cinemascope expands the scope of the drama, inten-
sifying the emotional mood or atmosphere of individual scenes while
also—somewhat paradoxically—effacing itself before the demands of
the narrative. It spectacularizes action while, at the same time, it
naturalizes the spectacle. For example, when Diana (Jean Simmons)
bids Marcellus (Richard Burton) farewell as he departs for the Near
East, the space between them gradually expands as his boat pulls
away, until each stands at the opposite end of the CinemaScope
frame—the spatial dynamics echoing the emotional drama of their
separation. Their moment of separation has been drawn out, expanded
in both time and space, yet the camera movement and wide-screen
framing in no way call attention to themselves as effects. The sequence
exists as an experience unique to CinemaScope, yet that experience
is not foregrounded as an experience of technology or technique; it
has been regulated, integrated into the fabric of the film through its
narrativization.

The Robe, though celebrated for introducing a new quasi-theatrical
style of filmmaking that permitted filming in long takes and staging action in a way that eliminated the need for shot/reverse shot
and/or cause/effect editing, remains something of a conventional film.
Cinematographer Leon Shamroy, referring to a scene in which a Roman
archer on extreme screen left hits a leader of the Christians (played by
Dean Jagger) with an arrow on extreme screen right, proclaimed that
"no longer must the cinematographer cut from one bit of action, showing cause, to another bit of action showing effect. In one big scene, the
CinemaScope camera shows both."[29] But moments later, in the same
scene, when the hero, Marcellus (Richard Burton), challenges a Roman
centurion to do battle, the film intercuts their hand-to-hand sword fight
with reaction shots of those looking on. Though the CinemaScope *River
of No Return* (1954) composes Marilyn Monroe's gold-camp rendition
of a song to include Robert Mitchum's intransigent response (within
the same frame) as he circles the barroom in search of his son, the
film regularly peppers Monroe's songs with reaction shots of groups
of beer-guzzling miners lasciviously eyeing her performance. Though
CinemaScope's expansive width offered filmmakers new options for
staging sequences and audiences new perspectives for viewing them,

it relied, at times, on fairly conventional techniques for telling its stories.

Unlike Cinerama, which engaged its viewers in the experience provided by the new technology, quite often grabbing them by the scruff of the neck and dragging them into it, CinemaScope explored that new experience in familiar ways, often relying upon conventions of the theater to achieve its effect. CinemaScope, rather than exploiting the Cinerama-effect achieved by camera movement into the screen, relied more often upon character movement than camera movement for its dramatic impact. Aware of the way in which excessive camera movement in CinemaScope called attention to itself, Zanuck cautioned Fox directors to move the actors more and the camera less.[30]

In this respect, CinemaScope mise-en-scene looked back to that found in the theater, but it did so in a way that introduced greater complexity into the traditional approach to motion picture composition. As a result, the theatrical nature of the staging of events in CinemaScope was not a reversion to the filmed theater of the *film d'art*, in which the camera merely recorded a performance designed for the stage. Rather, CinemaScope marked a dramatic step forward in the evolution of *cinematic* mise-en-scene. The introduction of deep-focus cinematography in the late 1930s and early 1940s "converted the screen into a dramatic checkerboard," as Andre Bazin once put it.[31] But the narrow 1.33:1 frame limited the development of that checkerboard to staging in depth, which reached its limit in the work of Welles and Wyler, or to staging spread successively across a surface (through reframing and lateral camera movement), a practice that culminated in Hitchcock's *Rope*. CinemaScope permitted a staging in width, in which adjacent actions could be seen simultaneously rather than successively. With the wide-screen format, filmmakers could stage action in width as well as in depth, doubling their options for compositional strategies and enabling mise-en-scene to evolve as a means of expression on two different axes. Given the larger canvas of wide-screen, filmmakers found new ways of staging action and of directing the spectator's attention through it. Though they continued to rely on camera movement and upon analytical editing to "read" the action, they also discovered ways to articulate space by working within the expanded borders of the frame. Filmmakers were forced to rethink their craft from the different vantage point of the wide-screen frame, and audiences were forced to adjust to conditions of spectatorship in which traditional ways of reading the image gave way to new, less-familiar practices. CinemaScope, like other wide-screen techniques adopted by narrative cinema, emerged as an amalgam of new and old, combining the new methods of organizing compositions made possible by the wide-screen with the old practices of conventional storytelling. The advent of the wide-screen format disturbed, if only momentarily, the smooth surface of classical cinema's equilibrium profile, causing the whole system to change slightly in order to readjust itself.

VISTAVISION

In contrast, Paramount's VistaVision, with its 1.66:1 aspect ratio, marked less of a departure from prewide-screen cinema than Cinerama or CinemaScope did. Its chief virtues, according to Paramount president Barney Balaban, lay in its "compatibility" with traditional modes of production and exhibition and in its "flexibility"—that is, in its adaptability to a variety of different theater situations.[32] The VistaVision camera used 35mm film but exposed it horizontally (like 35mm still camera film), producing an image that occupied the space of two traditional 35mm frames (that is, eight perforations in width). This two-frame exposure generated a wide-area negative without the use of wide film. When this large image was rotated 90 degrees and reduced to standard 35mm, it produced an image that possessed tremendous sharpness and depth of field. VistaVision thus solved many of the problems inherent in ersatz wide-screen, providing greater image resolution and a better angle of view for wide-screen projection, without committing itself to the radical redefinition called for by the more extreme wide-screen processes cited above. The conservative nature of VistaVision, in contrast to the radical difference of Cinerama, might be understood in terms of a major studio's—Paramount's—conformity to traditional production and exhibition practices versus the non-Hollywood independent's—Cinerama's—deliberate violation of those same practices.

Paramount publicly criticized Fox for the excessiveness of the CinemaScope aspect ratio, which they argued produced a wider image than any theaters could possibly accommodate. They also refused, as a matter of principle, to pay a rival studio for the use of its technology (especially since that technology was, as Fox freely admitted, in the public domain), thus becoming the only major studio to refuse to make films in CinemaScope. Paramount saw VistaVision less as a wide-screen process than as a big-screen process. The VistaVision image could be blown up to fill an enormous 62-by-35-foot screen without the loss in clarity or sharpness that plagued ersatz wide-screen (and without the blurring or fuzziness that occasionally appeared at the extreme edges of CinemaScope films). As one Paramount executive put it, "height was equally important as width."[33] Knowing that they could not compare with CinemaScope in terms of width, Paramount sought to capitalize on the height of the VistaVision image, and the first few VistaVision films, such as *White Christmas* and *Strategic Air Command*, did not so much stress width in their compositions as height.[34] While actors in CinemaScope films reclined (like Marilyn Monroe in *How to Marry a Millionaire* [1953]) or sprawled across the full width of the frame (like James Dean in the credit sequence of *Rebel Without a Cause* [1955]), actors in VistaVision films were shown erect, their full figures visible within the frame (like Bing Crosby and Danny Kaye in *White Christmas*).

Though Paramount converted its own production schedule to VistaVision, releasing over 65 films in that format during the next ten years, only a handful of VistaVision films were ever made by other studios (though several major works by major directors, including John Ford's *The Searchers* [Warner Bros. 1956], and Alfred Hitchcock's *North by Northwest* [MGM, 1959], number among them). Fox, on the other hand, quickly succeeded in a matter of months in selling CinemaScope to the rest of the industry, licensing it in 1953 to MGM (March), United Artists (June), Disney (June), Columbia (October), and Warners (November). In February, Fox had announced that all of its future films (which amounted to roughly 15 to 18 pictures a year) would be made in CinemaScope. These films, together with the CinemaScope productions of the other studios, assured theaters a steady supply of CinemaScope product, encouraging them to convert to CinemaScope. Indeed, more than six hundred CinemaScope features were released over the next 12 years—not to mention the more than two thousand anamorphic films made in compatible processes (such as Panavision, Technicscope, Tohoscope, Dyaliscope), which have been and continue to be released since 1953.[35]

TODD-AO

If CinemaScope could be seen as an answer to Cinerama, it was only a partial answer; to its critics, it was only a "poor man's Cinerama." Todd-AO, introduced with the premiere of *Oklahoma* at the Rivoli Theatre in New York on October 10, 1955, answered Cinerama in full, even surpassing it in several respects. Like Cinerama, Todd-AO was developed by independents working outside of the film industry. Mike Todd, dissatisfied with the cumbersome Cinerama process that he had worked with in producing the European sequences of *This Is Cinerama*, secured the assistance of Dr. Brian O'Brien, formerly professor of optics at the University of Rochester and currently serving as vice-president of research and development at the American Optical Company, in designing a single lens that could duplicate the combined angle of view of Cinerama's three 27mm lenses. With Todd-AO, Todd sought to re-create the experience of Cinerama for spectators in the theater by using a single film and projector rather than the three strips of film and projectors required by Cinerama. As Todd himself put it, he wanted a projection system "where everything comes out of one hole."[36]

Todd-AO emerged—in comparison with the industry's best wide-screen system, CinemaScope—as a process associated with product that was even more exclusive, since it was used, as was Cinerama, to make only one lavishly produced film a year instead of a studio's entire output for the year, as was the case with CinemaScope at Fox. In fact, Todd-AO was used in the production of only 15 films over a period of 16 years.[37] Todd-AO not only duplicated the "Cinerama effect," but it did so at about half the cost. Todd-AO's 128 degree, "bug-eye" lens provided an angle of view that closely approximated that of Cinerama, which was 146 degrees. The opening shots of Passepartout (Cantinflas) bicycling through the narrow streets of London in *Around the World in 80 Days*, for example, use this lens to exploit the "Cinerama effect," engulfing the spectator within the tight confines of the stone walls of buildings on either side and plunging the viewer into the midst of the diverse movements of surrounding traffic.

American Optical also designed three other lenses for the Todd-AO system, whose angles of view were 64, 48, and 37 degrees, thus introducing a greater optical variety into the system than Cinerama possessed and permitting the full range of expression traditionally found in 35mm production, which relied on a variety of lenses each possessing different focal lengths. This facilitated producers' use of the system for narrative films. Indeed, the first seven Todd-AO features—*Oklahoma, Around the World in 80 Days, South Pacific, Porgy and Bess, The Alamo, Can-Can*, and *Cleopatra*—fared quite well in competition with other narrative films of the period, winning a total of 11 Academy Awards.

Todd-AO's film speed of 30 frames per second matched and surpassed Cinerama's 26 frames per second, providing a more detailed and more steady image in projection. The higher film speed and the use of a larger filming and projection aperture produced an image that was not only sharper but brighter. Brian O'Brien anecdotally recalls that the woman with whom he attended the premiere of *Oklahoma* put sunglasses on to watch the picture because the image was so bright.[38]

Similarly, Todd-AO's six-track stereo magnetic sound system closely approximated Cinerama's seven-track stereo system, and its use of 65mm film and of a five-perforation frame resulted in an image quality that approached the three-strip, six-perforation frame of Cinerama. Robert Surtees, director of photography on *Oklahoma*, argued that Todd-AO's use of a 65mm negative made it, "from the standpoint of optics alone, a superior picture process" to all other 35mm wide-screen processes.[39]

Cinerama introduced the curved screen—which served to amplify the sense of audience participation by surrounding spectators with the image—to motion picture exhibition. However, deeply curved screens also introduced distortion into the image. Anytime that a flat image is projected upon a curved screen the horizontal lines of the image are necessarily distorted. CinemaScope minimized distortion by opting for a slightly curved screen—a screen that curved at the approximate rate of 1 inch per foot, resulting, in the case of a 62-foot-wide screen, in a 5-foot curve. Todd-AO used a screen that curved to a depth of 13 feet over a width of 52 feet, compensating for distortion by means of an "optical correcting printing process."[40]

Like Cinerama, Todd-AO was conceived of a specialized form of entertainment that would be restricted to a finite number of theaters. Like Cinerama, Todd-AO was based on the notion of the creation of a supercircuit in theatrical exhibition—that is, on the existence of a small number of large first-run urban theaters that could afford the forty thousand dollar conversion cost and that would be rewarded, in turn, with an exclusive product that would be guaranteed, as a result of the 70mm, multitrack stereo technology, not to play in non–Todd-AO houses until the first-run market had been virtually exhausted. In this way, Todd-AO reinstituted, in a legal way, the system of runs and clearances that had been outlawed as a result of the 1948 Consent Decree (also known as the *Paramount* Case). Indeed, *Oklahoma* ran for over a year in Todd-AO in several cities, rivaling the two-year run of *This Is Cinerama*, before it was released in its 35mm CinemaScope format. Unlike Cinerama, however, Todd-AO succeeded in converting a good number of the best theaters in the country to show their product, securing more than 60 new installations in its first two years of operation.[41] Todd's partnership with the United Artists Theater Circuit served to assure the success of the process by providing him with a built-in market (of over 100 theaters located in 50 major cities) for Todd-AO productions.

Again, like Cinerama, Todd-AO exhibition relied on a "theatrical," roadshow pattern, scheduling only two or three screenings a day and making tickets available on an advance sale, reserved-seat basis.

Todd's copartners and creators of *Oklahoma* for the Broadway stage, Richard Rodgers and Oscar Hammerstein, insisted, as well, that the integrity of the original stage musical be respected and forbade the inclusion of any sensational "audience participation type of screen action," such as the roller coaster ride used in Cinerama.[42] This did not, however, prevent Todd and Fred Zinnemann from indulging in a modified "Cinerama effect" when the camera dollies forward through an enveloping field of corn "as high as an elephant's eye" during the opening, "Oh, What a Beautiful Morning" song sequence or to introduce a roller coaster-like thrill with a sequence filmed on a runaway carriage. The "theatrical" quality of the presentation of Todd-AO even extended, in the case of *Oklahoma*, to a ban on the sale of popcorn in the theater.[43]

Todd-AO drew on the theater in other ways as well. Todd, a Broadway producer, launched Todd-AO in collaboration with the Broadway playwright and composer team of Rodgers and Hammerstein, whose theatrical properties provided the basic dramatic material (*Oklahoma*, *South Pacific*) to be filmed in the system. Even though *Around the World in 80 Days* superficially resembles a Cinerama travelogue, it, too, has theatrical origins, deriving from Mike Todd's collaboration with Orson Welles on a Broadway version of the Jules Verne novel in the early 1940s. Todd-AO producers continued to ransack Broadway for material, adapting *Porgy and Bess, Can-Can*, and *The Sound of Music* for the screen and spearheading a trend in which producers began to draw more and more regularly upon Broadway for material for their big-budget, wide-screen spectacles.

As a result of the creation of a theatrical-style supercircuit, producers of Todd-AO (or other special-format films) gained a control over exhibition that recent government antitrust lawsuits had attempted to deny them. And since more than half of a film's total income during this period came from first-run exhibition in only a handful of theaters (that is, from approximately 700 first-run theaters in 92 cities), Todd-AO producers realized fantastic profits, as did the stockholders of Todd-AO and of Magna Theatres, who received a combined royalty of 5 percent of the admission price for each spectator who saw the film in Todd-AO but who received no royalty for the 35mm CinemaScope release.

The ultimate success of the Todd-AO process can be measured, in part, by its triumph over rival wide-film systems and its emergence as the premier system for filming big-budget blockbusters. Aware of the limitations of 35mm film as a format and of the potential challenge posed by Todd-AO, shortly after early demonstrations of Todd-AO, Fox began development of its own wide-film process, dubbing it CinemaScope 55.

Though Todd had signed Rodgers and Hammerstein, two of their Broadway musicals, *Carousel* and *The King and I*, had already been optioned to Fox, giving the studio two extravaganzas to film in CinemaScope 55. Though Fox had been experimenting with wide-film processes for 25 years (since their 70mm Grandeur system in 1929), CinemaScope 55 emerged less as an innovative than as a derivative process—an apparent attempt to answer Todd-AO's success with *Oklahoma*, which played in theaters a year before.

Fox shortly thereafter abandoned CinemaScope 55 and capitulated to Todd-AO. Fox even privately acknowledged that by 1958, when *Around the World in 80 Days* was experiencing record profits at the box office, "CinemaScope had lost much of its novelty and that customers were no longer drawn to theatres solely because the picture was in the CinemaScope process."[44] In 1958, Fox made an investment of six hundred thousand dollars in the Todd-AO company, securing the right to make pictures in that process, and eventually, after Mike Todd's death in an airplane crash in 1958, secured control of the Todd-AO Corporation.

CASUALTIES OF THE WIDE-SCREEN WARS

By the end of the 1950s, CinemaScope had been eclipsed as a special-event process by Todd-AO and other wide-film processes, such as Ultra Panavision (which was used to film single-strip Cinerama features) and Super Panavision 70, both of which provided sharper and brighter big-screen images. CinemaScope had, in effect, been destroyed by its own success. By the mid-1950s, CinemaScope had become a new motion picture standard; it was used in the production of all kinds of films, ranging from color spectacles to black-and-white Elvis Presley movies. Its initial technology had also been seriously compromised. The refusal of small, independent exhibitors to install stereo sound systems had forced Fox, in the spring of 1954, to announce that it would alter its stereo-only policy, making monaural prints available to theaters. Though first-run theaters continued to present CinemaScope films in four-track magnetic stereo sound, the majority of theaters did not, tarnishing somewhat the image of CinemaScope as a high-quality process seen (and heard) in only high-quality theaters. CinemaScope's widespread adoption weakened its initial association with exclusive, lavishly made, big-budget productions—which were now linked in the industry's and the public's minds with Todd-AO, MGM Camera 65, Technirama, Super Technirama 70, Ultra Panavision and Super Panavision 70, which continued to be seen in only a handful of first-run theaters and which continued to provide audiences with stereo sound. Even within the 35mm wide-screen market, CinemaScope had given way, as an anamorphic standard, to Panavision, which producers preferred for its superior close-up lenses.

During the 1960s, Cinerama joined the 70mm bandwagon. In 1963, for the filming of *It's a Mad, Mad, Mad, Mad World*, Cinerama abandoned its three-strip process for Ultra Panavision 70, a 70mm system that employed anamorphic optics to squeeze a wide angle of view onto a single film strip and that, when unsqueezed in projection, produced a Cinerama-like image with an aspect ratio of 2.76:1. Throughout the 1960s Cinerama continued to compete, though with varying degrees of success, with other wide-film systems, faring well with *The Battle of the Bulge, Grand Prix*, and *2001: A Space Odyssey* and not so well with *The Greatest Story Ever Told* and *Ice Station Zebra*. With the collapse of the Cinerama theater chain (with its deeply curved screens) in the early 1970s, Cinerama became indistinguishable as a presentational process from other wide-film systems and disappeared (though its assets were not finally liquidated until 1978).

During the 1960s, many first-tier theaters around the country screened films exclusively in 70mm, a practice that continues today in the more than nine hundred theaters equipped to show 70mm films.[45] However, the motion picture marketplace has taken its toll on 70mm production as well. The expense of filming in 65/70mm has, since the early 1960s, resulted in the gradual elimination of original production in 70mm. In 1963, Panavision's Robert Gottschalk introduced an optical system that enabled producers to blow 35mm film up to 70mm for purposes of theatrical, roadshow exhibition, virtually pulling the rug out from under wide-film production.[46] Now any 35mm film could be blown up to 70mm for roadshow presentation without the expense involved in wide-film production. Since then, less than 30 films have been shot on wide film and more than 230 have been shot in 35mm and blown up to 70mm for first-run exhibition.[47] And the films that have been blown up range from 35mm anamorphic productions (*The Cardinal, Dr. Zhivago, Close Encounters of the Third Kind, Star Wars, Apocalypse Now*, and *The Untouchables*) to 35mm, flat, 1.85:1 productions (*E.T., the Extra-Terrestrial, Gremlins, Back to the Future, The Color of Money*, and *The Last Temptation of Christ*), resulting in blow-ups that crop the edges of the former and necessitate the addition of black masking along the sides of the latter.[48]

TV TAKES ITS TOLL

Though the trade name "CinemaScope" disappeared from the cinema in 1962, tacitly acknowledging defeat at the hands of Panavision's similar anamorphic optical system, the shape of CinemaScope—its 2.35:1 aspect ratio—remained, having become, along with the wide-screen aspect ratio of 1.85:1, which was achieved by simple masking in the theater, an industrywide standard. In other words, by the end of the decade CinemaScope was no longer revolutionary; it was the norm against which new wide-screen technologies differentiated themselves. At around the same time, CinemaScope and other wide-screen systems, in response to new economic demands, began to subtly alter themselves from within, defusing the very qualities that made them radically different from prewide-screen cinema in the first place. Wide-screen cinema started to "think thin," denying its own width. Wide-screen began to pull in its expansiveness, to restrict the extremity of its compositions in order to accommodate itself to a new subsidiary market—the sale of motion pictures to television. In 1962, the American Society of Cinematographers issued a series of recommendations to its members, advising them to compose their wide-screen images for TV's "safe action area." Camera manufacturers began to produce viewfinders that indicated this area with a dotted line, and cinematographers began to protect their compositions for TV by keeping essential narrative and/or aesthetic elements within this frame-within-a-frame. Cinematographer Nestor Almendros explains (in conversations with the author, spring 1987) that today compositions that exploit the extreme edges of the frame are generally avoided.

Though it would be an oversimplification to write the story of wide-screen cinema solely in terms of a competition in the marketplace for viewers with television, any account of the history of wide-screen cinema must, in some way, acknowledge the rule that television has played in its demise. In an attempt to protect themselves from the ravages of panning and scanning, contemporary filmmakers have tended to avoid filming in extreme wide-screen ratios or, when shooting in 'Scope, have tended to compromise their compositions. The extreme wide-screen compositions of the "high" CinemaScope era of the 1950s, which exploited the full width of the frame, often placing figures at either edge of it, has given way to conservative compositions characterized by "dead" space on either side of the central area of interest in the frame. The wide-screen revolution has been betrayed by the counterrevolution, inspired by dreams of sales to television.

What is at risk in today's motion picture marketplace is the very ense of the cinema *as experience*, a sense that was dramatically heightened by the advent of wide-screen cinema in the 1950s. As theaters increase the number of their screens through multiplexing, he screens themselves grow smaller, slowly reverting to the pre-wide-screen average width of 20 feet. As the difference between he experience of viewing films in the home on video tape and n the theater on mini-screens diminishes, so do the prospects of recovering the excitement of the early Cinerama and CinemaScope experience.

The motion picture experience is rapidly becoming, for many spectators, the video experience. A recent study conducted by Wilkofsky Gruen Associates for Merrill Lynch predicts that by 1995 the sale of prerecorded videocassettes will reach the 700 million per year mark, accounting for over $14 billion in revenues. In addition to this, another $6 billion will be realized in video rentals, adding up to a total of $20 billion. At the same time, they predict that motion picture box offices will take in revenues of only $8 billion.[49] In other words, they foresee that the video revenues of a motion picture will more than double its box office gross.[50] The only force within the marketplace that might reasonably retard this process, bringing audiences back into movie theaters in the same numbers as they did in the 1950s and 1960s, is the experience of wide-screen cinema in large first-run theaters. Coupled with stereo magnetic sound, 70mm remains an experience that can never be fully duplicated in the home. The recent development by Arriflex of a new state-of-the-art 65mm production camera may signal the beginning of a new trend in the use of 65mm as a production medium, restoring to big-screen motion picture entertainment something that has been missing for the last 20 years. In 1953, Andre Bazin wrote an essay on wide-screen cinema entitled "Will CinemaScope Save the Cinema?"[51] His answer then was a tentative "perhaps." With hindsight we can see that yes, CinemaScope did save the cinema, but only for a few years. The question remains whether it, or processes like it, can save the cinema again.

NOTES

The chapter title is taken from the 1954 lyrics by Cole Porter for the "Stereophonic Sound" number in *Silk Stockings*. The complete text runs as follows: "Today to get the public to attend a picture show / It's not enough

to advertise a famous star they know / If you want to get the crowds to come
around / You've got to have / Glorious Technicolor / Breathtaking CinemaScope
and / Stereophonic sound."

1. See note above.
2. Cobbett Steinberg, *Reel Facts: The Movie Book of Records* (New York,
Random House, 1978), p. 371.
3. Paul Lazersfeld and Robert Merton, "Mass Communication, Popular
Taste and Organized Social Action," in *Mass Culture: The Popular Arts in America*,
ed. Bernard Rosenberg and David Manning White (Glencoe, Ill.: The Free
Press, 1957), p. 460.
4. Leo A. Handel, *Hollywood Looks at Its Audience* (Urbana: University o
Illinois Press, 1950), p. 97, chart 5.
5. Handel, *Hollywood Looks*, p. 97, chart 5.
6. Comparison of the participation effect produced by wide-screen
cinema to the theatrical experience constitutes a major thread of the
industry discourse surrounding CinemaScope, as James Spellerberg points
out in "CinemaScope and Ideology," *The Velvet Light Trap*, no. 21 (Summer
1985): 30–31.
7. Andre Bazin, "Theater and Cinema—Part Two," in *What Is Cinema?* vol
1, trans. Hugh Gray (Berkeley: University of California Press, 1967), p. 102.
8. Cited by Andre Bazin, "Theater and Cinema—Part One," in *What Is
Cinema?* vol. 1, trans. Hugh Gray (Berkeley: University of California Press,
1967), p. 92.
9. Spellerberg, "CinemaScope and Ideology", p. 30. See also Thomas
Pryor, "Fox Films Embark on 3-Dimension Era," *New York Times*, February
2, 1953.
10. David Cook writes that "the blockbuster craze" started in 1956 with
King Vidor's *War and Peace* (VistaVision), Michael Anderson's *Around the
World in 80 Days* (Todd-AO), and Cecil B. DeMille's *The Ten Commandments*
(VistaVision), all of which had running times of more than three and one-half
hours. *A History of Narrative Film* (New York: Norton, 1981), p. 424. However,
blockbusters existed long before the wide-screen era; *The Birth of a Nation* and
Gone With the Wind, for example, both satisfy Cook's criteria for expensively
made and unusually long film spectacles. As for the wide-screen blockbuster
craze, it surely begins with *The Robe* (1953), which was lavishly produced and,
at 135 minutes, somewhat longer than other films of 1953. If the blockbuster
is defined, in part, by box office revenues, then the year 1954, in which seven
of the top-grossing ten films were made in either CinemaScope or VistaVision,
certainly qualifies as the beginning of the wide-screen blockbuster era.
11. *The Letters of Nunnally Johnson*, ed. Dorris Johnson and Ellen Leventhal
(New York: Knopf, 1981), p. 103. Director Jean Negulescu also claims author-
ship for this wisecrack. See "New Medium—New Methods," in *New Screen
Techniques*, ed. Martin Quigley (New York: Quigley Publishing, 1953), p. 174.
12. For more information on Waller and Cinerama, see my "Cinerama:
A New Era in the Cinema," *The Perfect Vision* 1, no. 4 (Spring/Summer
1988): 78–90.

13. *Film Daily,* January 21, 1963, p. 26.

14. Michael Todd, Jr. and Susan McCarthy Todd, *A Valuable Property: The Life Story of Michael Todd* (New York: Arbor House, 1983), p. 244.

15. *Film Daily,* January 21, 1963.

16. *Fortnight,* October 13, 1952.

17. *Magazine Digest* (September 1953): 40.

18. *New York Herald-Tribune,* September 27, 1953.

19. Clifford M. Sage in the *Dallas Times Herald,* November 4, 1952.

20. Lynn Farnol, "Finding Customers for a Product," in *New Screen Techniques,* ed. Martin Quigley, p. 143.

21. They were *This Is Cinerama* (1952), *Cinerama Holiday (1955), Seven Wonders of the World* (1956), *Search for Paradise* (1957), and *Cinerama South Seas Adventure* (1958). *Windjammer* (1958), filmed in the CineMiracle process (a three-camera system similar to Cinerama), was also a documentary and properly belongs on this list as well.

22. *New York Times,* October 5, 1952. As late as May 1960, *American Cinematographer* noted that "closeups of people shot with Cinerama cameras show typical wide-angle closeup distortion. Noses appear very long and foreheads slant back. Ears are very small in proportion and chins recede" (p. 304). Early CinemaScope, which employed an anamorphic lens that was unable to focus clearly at distances under four feet from the camera, faced a somewhat different problem involving not distortion but sharpness of focus. However, though extreme close-ups remained difficult to achieve in CinemaScope, standard close-ups were easily accomplished. Three-strip Cinerama was ultimately used to film narratives, such as *The Wonderful World of the Brothers Grimm* and *How the West Was Won,* but narrative information was conveyed in these films without the use of close-ups, relying on narrative techniques borrowed from the theater (and which CinemaScope had earlier drawn upon).

23. "Cinerama—The Broad Picture," *Fortune* (January 1953): 146.

24. *Daily Variety,* April 6, 1953. Two months later, they attempted to extend the life of their 1952 hit, *The Greatest Show on Earth,* by rereleasing it "in 1.66:1" (*Daily Variety,* June 11, 1953).

25. *Daily Variety,* May 20, 1953, p. 1.

26. *Time,* (June 8, 1953) p. 70.

27. See my "CinemaScope: The Economics of Technology," *The Velvet Light Trap,* no. 21 (Summer 1985): 35–36.

28. Darryl Zanuck, "CinemaScope in Production," in *New Screen Techniques,* ed. Quigley, p. 156.

29. Leon Shamroy, "Filming *The Robe,*" *New Screen Techniques,* ed. Quigley, p. 178.

30. Zanuck memo, CinemaScope: General Information, August 12, 1954, Sponable Collection, Columbia University Libraries.

31. Andre Bazin, "The Evolution of the Language of Cinema," in *What Is Cinema?* Vol. 1, p. 34.

32. *Daily Variety,* March 3, 1954, p. 14.

33. Thomas Pryor, "Hollywood Expands," *New York Times*, March 7, 1954.

34. In the first public demonstration of VistaVision, Paramount compared it with CinemaScope, projecting CinemaScope at the same width as VistaVision, thus diminishing CinemaScope's wide-screen edge over VistaVision along with its apparent height. Fox, of course, objected to this manipulation. See Leonard Spinrad, *Motion Picture Newsletter*, May 3, 1954.

35. See the list of anamorphic titles in Robert E. Carr and R. M. Hayes, *Wide Screen Movies: A History and Filmography of Wide Gauge Filmmaking* (Jefferson, N.C.: McFarland, 1988), pp. 91–143.

36. Todd, *Valuable Property*, p. 245.

37. Carr and Hayes, *Wide Screen Movies*, pp. 187–88.

38. Dr. Brian O'Brien, in telephone conversation with the author, November 1988.

39. Arthur Rowan, "Todd-AO—Newest Wide-screen System," *American Cinematographer* (October 1954): 495.

40. *Film Daily*, May 2, 1956.

41. Todd-AO/TCFF Corp. folder, Box 120, Sponable Collection, Columbia University Libraries.

42. *Film Daily*, May 2, 1956.

43. Reported by James Limbacher in his *Four Aspects of the Film* (New York: Brussell and Brussell, 1968).

44. Internal Fox memo by Donald A. Henderson on The Todd-AO Matter, September 16, 1963, Box 120, Sponable Collection.

45. Statistics courtesy of Dolby Laboratories, Inc., as of March 24, 1988.

46. Douglas Turnbull, in conversation, October 14, 1988.

47. Carr and Hayes, *Wide Screen Movies*, pp. 187–89, 200–206.

48. The anamorphic image, which has an aspect ratio of 2.35:1, does not quite fit on a 70mm frame, which is roughly 2.21:1, thus requiring cropping. A 1.85:1 image doesn't quite fill the 70mm frame, which must then be masked. For an excellent discussion of blow-ups, see Carr and Hayes, *Wide Screen Movies*, pp. 196–206.

49. For admissions and VCR statistics, see the Motion Picture Association of America's "1987 U.S. Economic Review," pp. 2, 8.

50. Bob Brewin, "VCR's: Bigger Than Box-Office," *The Village Voice*, March 11, 1986, p. 45.

51. *Esprit*, no. 207–208 (October–November 1953): 672–83.

SUGGESTIONS FOR FURTHER READING

Barr, Charles. "CinemaScope: Before and After." *Film Quarterly* 16, no. 4 (Summer 1963): 4–24.

Belton, John. "CinemaScope and Historical Methodology." *Cinema Journal* 28, no. 1 (Fall 1988): 22-24.

——"The Age of Cinerama: A New Era in the Cinema." *The Perfect Vision* 1, no. 4 (Spring/Summer 1988): 78–90.

Bernstein, Matthew, ed. "American Widescreen" issue of *The Velvet Light Trap* 21 (Summer 1985), which includes essays by Andre Bazin, David Bordwell, James Spellerberg, John Belton, and Richard Hincha.

Bordwell, David, Janet Staiger, and Kristin Thompson. "Wide-screen Processes and Stereophonic Sound" in *The Classical Hollywood Cinema: Film Style & Mode of Production to 1960*, pp. 358–64. New York: Columbia University Press, 1985.

Carr, Robert E. and R. M Hayes. *Wide Screen Movies: A History and Filmography of Wide Gauge Filmmaking*. Jefferson, N.C.: McFarland, 1988.

Limbacher, James L. *Four Aspects of the Film*. New York: Brussel and Brussel, 1969.

Macgowan, Kenneth. *Behind the Screen: The History and Techniques of the Motion Picture*. New York: Delacorte, 1965.

Quigley, Martin Jr., ed. *New Screen Techniques*. New York: Quigley Publishing, 1953.

Chapter 8

Red, Blue, and Lots of Green: The Impact of Color Television on Feature Film Production

Brad Chisholm

*F*or many years the primary colors of the photographic arts were black, white, and gray, not red, blue, or green. The film and television industries had particularly large investments in black and white and were not about to convert to color before that became the financially prudent thing to do. Color became commonplace in photography, motion pictures, and television only after extended periods in which black and white was the norm. There are technological reasons for color's later start, but there are business reasons for black and white's long dominance. Joseph Niepce, W.K.L. Dickson, and Vladimir Zworykin, camera inventors for the respective media, all found it easier to render shades of light and dark than to capture the hues we see in nature. Eventual scientific breakthroughs made color rendition possible, but these did not prompt the photographic, film, or television industries to scale back their monochrome product in favor of color. In the histories of each medium, years passed during which color technology was patiently refined while black and white technology was allowed to proliferate. Then, only when key corporations determined the market was ready did the industries act to encourage color's widespread use at the expense of black and white.[1]

The shift from black and white to color was made in the photo, film, and video industries between the end of World War II and the end of the 1960s. Photographic color had become technically possible in each medium much earlier: photography first (by Maxwell in 1861), cinema second (Isensee, in 1897), then television (Ives, in 1929). Yet in 1945 color-print film was unavailable to most consumers, black and white motion picture releases outnumbered color releases ten to one, and color television was still in the laboratories. By 1970, however,

213

color-print film was readily available to consumers, color motion picture releases now held a ten-to-one advantage over monochrome, and nearly half of America's 60 million TV households had color receivers.[2] Eastman Kodak, the major Hollywood studios, and the broadcasting networks separately determined at different points during this 25-year period that the time had come to supersede black and white with color. Yet each industry's leaders did not initiate the "big shift" in isolation from the other industries. The motion picture and television businesses were especially conscious of one another's activities. Photography was related to the other media but did not compete in the same consumer market, while television and the movies were thought to be rivals for the same entertainment dollar. Many film studio executives viewed television as a threat and felt obliged to respond to every successful maneuver made by the younger industry. Color got caught up in this competitive relationship and the long-delayed profusion of color film and video was hastened as a result of it.

The near-complete conversion to color by both the television networks and the studios resulted from a series of reactions by the motion picture companies to the moves of the broadcasting firms. The broadcasters reacted in turn to the moves of one another as each responded to the progress of black and white TV set sales. At five juncture between the mid-1940s and the late 1960s, certain reactions and responses constituted business decisions that greatly influenced the prospects of color in both media. The first two involved the selection of the types of color technologies that would be made available to the film and television industries. These decisions, made in 1950 and 1953, effectively determined who was to control, utilize, and profit from color. The third key decision occurred just after these, when Hollywood studio chiefs appropriated color as a weapon in a self-styled war to win back their thinning audiences. When color proved ineffective, the fourth decision came in 1956 when Hollywood reversed itself by cutting back on color releases and increasing its black and white output. Finally, the fate of monochrome was sealed with the fifth decision—that of Hollywood's virtual abandonment of black and white in the wake of NBC's announced plan to go "full color" in 1965.[3]

COLOR FOR MOTION PICTURES

No name is repeated more frequently in the history of color motion pictures than that of the Technicolor Corporation. From the

1930s to well into the 1950s, Technicolor set the quality standard for color film photography, processing, and printing. During its heyday, Technicolor held a monopoly over color filmmaking in Hollywood, but it struggled for decades before it attained that advantageous position. When it was incorporated in 1915 by Herbert Kalmus, Daniel Comstock, and Barton Prescott, there were already numerous companies in the United States and Europe busy developing and promoting methods for color motion photography. Among them were Gaumont Studios' Chronochrome, Charles Urban's Kinemacolor system, and a process by Prizma, Incorporated.[4]

Neither the European nor American film industries had adopted any of these processes, for they were cumbersome, expensive, and gave less-than-perfect results. The color processes that were acceptable to the film industry in these early years were those that used non-photographic methods to achieve color. These processes applied color to a film after it had been shot, either by stenciling, tinting, or toning. Stenciling was a painstaking, frame-by-frame application of color to individual positive prints. Tinting was the immersion of black and white film stock into dyes of red, blue, green, violet, or sepia that would result in footage of a uniform color. Toning achieved color gradation through the application of chemicals to film stock, which colored black and gray portions of each image while they left white sections untouched. By several accounts, the number of films which used these nonphotographic processes outnumbered black and white films for a portion of the 1920s.[5] The founders of Technicolor, however, believed that film studio chiefs could become interested in a photographic or "natural" method of rendering color once somebody came up with a reliable system that was easy to integrate.

Technicolor persevered where its early rivals failed partly because of its development of a subtractive color process. Kinemacolor, Chronochrome, an early version of Prizma, as well as Technicolor's first color process were additive systems. This meant that color was not attained until the moment of projection. These systems used color filters inside their cameras to split each photographed image onto separate negatives or alternate frames and then required corresponding color filters in their projectors to recombine the images in their original colors on the screen. One could not look at a piece of exposed Kinemacolor, Chronochrome, or Prizma film stock and see images in their true colors, because additive systems require the recombination step to complete the process. Technicolor's additive entry fared no better than its competitors at overcoming the inherent weakness of such processes: accurate registrations, or the proper alignment of the two or three overlaying images coming from the projector. The subtractive process created by Technicolor researchers in 1922 used cameras and color filters, which, like some of the additive methods, resulted in two separate positives—one red, one green. Unlike its predecessors, the new process eliminated the necessity of recombination at the projection stage by adding a step in the lab printing process. This new step involved cementing together the red and green positives, back to back. From this cemented positive a second negative was made with which to print new positives that contained all the colors of each image.[6]

Hollywood did not immediately embrace Technicolor's subtractive process, nor its improved version, called "imbibition," that became available in 1928. Imbibition created the second-step negative through two separate passes of the red and green positives on a contact printer, thereby eliminating the somewhat awkward cementing of the two positives. Despite Technicolor's refinement, the film industry was more interested in the conversion to sound at that time than it was in improving color. Studios were even willing to abandon their widespread use of tinting and toning in favor of black and white when those practices appeared to interfere with sound playback. Technicolor's subtractive system added significantly to any movie's production costs, and while a number of feature films were shot using the process during a brief color boom in 1929–31, it was more often utilized for sequences that emphasized spectacle in films that were primarily black and white. The color quality of the red/green process was considered unsuitable for films that did not contain spectacle or fantasy of some sort. A red and green negative could not quite render the full color spectrum, and while images shot in it were striking, they were also garish and unreal. Because blues were noticeably absent, a competitor, Cinecolor, made a point to offer a red/blue alternative. Technicolor did likewise, but black and white remained the format of choice for Hollywood in the 1930s.[7]

Technicolor's period of dominance began with the perfection of a three-color subtractive process. In 1932 a large new camera was designed in order to house three separate negatives: one red, one green, one blue. When combined in the laboratory via imbibition, images from the three negatives ultimately resulted in a positive that contained the truest as well as the most complete rendering of color the cinema had yet seen. The process made its commercial debut in Disney's animated short *Flowers and Trees* later that year, and with 1935's *Becky Sharp*, it broke into full-length features.[8] For the next 15 years the major Hollywood studios would turn exclusively to Technicolor for their photographic color needs. This did not mean, however, that color films became the rule. Ninety percent of the films released in the United States during that time were still black and white. Color, ven three-color Technicolor, continued to be reserved for spectacles, antasies, and big-budget musicals. Expense was a major factor, but so vas the widely held belief that color detracted from dramatic realism. 'et a few dozen films per year was enough to enable the Technicolor Corporation to flourish.[9]

No competitor's process approached the quality of the three-color mbibition technique. Moreover, Kalmus refused to sell "Trip-Pak" ameras or processing equipment; instead, his firm leased them to he studios to be used under the close supervision of Technicolor ersonnel. Technicolor provided the camera operator and handled ll film processing at its labs, where the company's patented methods vere closely guarded. Kalmus also imposed a strict code governing set lesign, costume, and lighting techniques over the studios to ensure that he process would always retain a certain pleasing "look." Any studio vishing to make a Technicolor motion picture not only got a Tri-Pak amera and a Technicolor camera operator, but also a representative rom the Technicolor consulting service who advised cinematogra- hers, costume designers, and art directors on their use of color. The est known of these color consultants was Kalmus's wife, Natalie. he and her fellow "advisors" enforced a consistent set of aesthetic ralues that favored the harmonious use of complementary colors. While Natalie claimed to have drawn up a specific color scheme to reflect he mood of each particular scene, the following three principles seem o have always been observed. First, backgrounds should not contain rivid colors that would distract the viewer's eye from foregrounds. n other words, scenery in Technicolor films was usually in muted hades while costumes or foreground objects were in brighter, more aturated colors. Second, colors in a scene should complement one nother rather than clash. The one exception was if the scene called or discordance of some kind. Third, color should be subordinate to he story and therefore ought not to attract undue attention on its own vithout proper narrative motivation.[10]

Not until after World War II did Technicolor's control over film ndustry color begin to wear thin. There were a limited number of [ri-Pak cameras and these were sufficiently expensive for Techni- olor's management to refrain from letting a single camera sit idle or any period of time. This meant that there was always a backlog f orders for Technicolor cameras—the demand was slightly higher han the supply. During World War II, shortages of equipment and film tock were accepted by all concerned as unavoidable consequences f waging war. Studio executives grew impatient when Technicolor's ndersupply of cameras persisted after the war. Impatience turned to enuine frustration by the end of the 1940s after Technicolor's rates had risen sharply, relative to the stable costs of black and white. These seeds of dissatisfaction sparked the renewal of competition in the area of color technology.[11]

In 1950 Technicolor was forced to revise its manner of doing business, thanks to a government antitrust suit and a new color process available from Eastman Kodak. The U.S. Department of Justice initiated the suit three years earlier because it felt Technicolor had a monopolistic stranglehold over the film industry. The court ruled against Kalmus's firm and forced Technicolor to make key patents available to competitors who wished to enter the three-strip color market. Worse yet for Kalmus and company, the Eastman Kodak process required no special cameras at all and cost sufficiently less than Technicolor's process. Eastman color was derived from the principles of Agfacolor, a German process that rendered red, green and blue on a single strip of negative film. Eastman Kodak sold the studios Eastman Color negative stock and gave them the option of either having Eastman process and print the films or having it processed and printed by other companies. Clients were not even required to call the process Eastman Color, and WarnerColor, TruColor, De Luxe, and other names were used depending upon what lab was involved or whether a studio wished to advertise its color as unique. The Tri-Pak system continued to be used, but Eastman Kodak's "Mono-Pak" made inroads on Technicolor's territory. Eastman Color images were less dazzling than those of Technicolor, although many observers felt the new process rendered more natural-looking colors.[12]

The film studios' color activity after the break-up of Technicolor's monopoly amounted to a 2 percent rise in new color film releases over a three-year stretch. The ratio was 70 color to 338 monochrome in 1948 and 81 color to 346 monochrome in 1951. The film studios were no longer dependent on the availability of Technicolor cameras, but the demand for color did not appear to be drastically greater than what Kalmus's company had always met in the past. Film industry executives saw no tremendous need to convert to color, and their decision to keep things much as they had been was to indirectly affect the fledgling television industry.[13]

COLOR FOR TELEVISION

The growth of the as yet small television audience slowed markedly between 1948 and 1951 because of a government-imposed freeze on he licensing of new TV stations. During this delay, numerous technical standards were reevaluated in light of recent developments in video technology. Color television was among these developments, but its advocates found little support for their claims that the United States needed color television right away. Neither the photography nor film industries had as yet forsaken black and white in favor of color, and there was no precedent for suspending the spread of monochrome simply to permit color technology to catch up. The freeze was lifted in 1952 without the establishment of a successful color television system.[14] The first of the crucial decisions to affect the eventual shift away from black and white was made when the Hollywood studio heads elected not to make a mad dash for color despite the increased availability of proven color processes. The second key decision would now determine which system of color television technology was to be used by U.S. broadcasters, and more important, which company would be in a position to control that system's implementation.

The nature of television is such that governments often find it necessary to sanction technological monopolies in order for the medium to proliferate. If a nation is to have an organized television system, both broadcasters and consumers need equipment that is mutually compatible. The alternative is to have a laissez-faire market, which allows the sale of multiple incompatible video formats to broadcast stations and consumers alike. Market growth might then be stymied as potential buyers avoid purchasing any equipment for fear of getting stuck with obsolete or limited systems. Many other industries, including the motion picture business, reach agreement on certain technical standards without the government's prodding. In the late 1930s, however, feuding broadcasting manufacturers were on the verge of selling the public TV sets that would not pick up one another's signals. The Federal Communications Commission (FCC) intervened and forced a compromise that in 1941 resulted in the black and white television system that remains in place today. Later, that busy regulatory agency did the same for color.[15]

The first attempt to introduce a viable system of color television was instigated by CBS in 1940. At the FCC's behest, interested electronics firms had that year formed a committee of over 60 scientists and engineers to evaluate the competing proposals for video pick-up, transmission, and reception systems. This group called itself the National Television Systems Committee (NTSC), and its task was to forge a consensus among its members. CBS engineers demonstrated to the committee a video system which rendered color images via a spinning color filter disc inside its cameras and receivers. However, the NTSC was primarily occupied with the study of several black and white systems, many of which seemed closer to being market-ready than CBS's color process. In 1941 the NTSC's consensus was that a television system based primarily on patents held by the Radio Corporation of America, along with some modifications based on Philco's system, should be made the national standard. The FCC accepted this recommendation. The resulting system, named after the NTSC, transmitted monochrome only. The matter of color was tabled, over the objections of CBS and two other companies that felt RCA's technology had been favored by the NTSC from the start.[16]

CBS's system was called "field sequential," because it created full color images by rapidly filling the screen with first a red, then a green then a blue picture. This sequence of three color fields was repeated 40 times each second. Observers found the color to be both striking and true, but the system's large color wheels could be heard spinning inside the bulky CBS receivers. Critics also considered the system a throwback to earlier mechanical television systems that required moving parts.[17]

The onset of World War II gave CBS engineers an opportunity to refine their color system while the commercialization of black and white was put on hold. The spinning color wheel was retained, but the noise and some of the size problems were remedied. Furthermore the picture resolution was vastly improved by the use of a transmission channel that was three times as wide as a channel for NTSC monochrome. When the war came to an end CBS called upon the FCC to scrap the already approved black and white system that RCA, Philco and other firms were about to put on the market. The network argued that if NTSC monochrome were permitted to go ahead, there soon would be no channel space for its improved field-sequential color system. In 1946 the FCC allowed manufacturers to proceed with black and white, but it also conducted its own hearings to consider the matter of color television.[18]

The preeminent technological innovator in the broadcasting field was RCA, the owner of NBC. RCA had a huge investment in black and white technology, and its management had been waiting to market television since 1939. The corporation expected CBS's call for new postwar video standards and in anticipation developed a color television system of its own. RCA's "simultaneous" color system required no spinning wheel; rather, it overlaid the images from red, green, and blue picture tubes to render color. Like the early additive color film processes, this system's weakness was in its recombination stage—proper registration of the three color images was difficult to achieve. In 1946 and 1947 the FCC evaluated the color systems of CBS, RCA, and a partial system from DuMont Labs. All three required channels of triple width, and all three could have stood further refinement. As the deliberations continued the number of television stations in the country rose sharply, and there was soon no room left in the VHF band for wide color channels. The FCC elected not to authorize any of the color systems at that time and to wait until a future date, after specifications could be worked out for the as yet experimental UHF band.[19]

The FCC's 1947 rejection of all color petitions was a blow to CBS and a victory for RCA. Executives at the latter company privately admitted that they were in no position to market simultaneous color. They used their entry in the color derby to counter CBS's claims that the field-sequential method was the most desirable. With their own system before the FCC, RCA's representatives were allowed to cross-examine CBS engineeers, counter CBS's claims point by point, and generally complicate and prolong the hearings. After the decision, RCA's managers relegated the simultaneous system to the company cellar and got on with the more profitable business of promoting its line of monochrome cameras, transmitters, and TV sets.[20]

The late 1940s was a time when monopolies were under siege in the entertainment industry. Not only had Technicolor been slapped with an antitrust suit, in 1948 Hollywood's biggest studios were ordered by the Supreme Court to divest themselves of their theater chains. Several months later Senator Edwin Johnson of Colorado directed the government's antimonopoly ire at the television industry and accused the FCC of sanctioning a restraint of trade. Angered that the recent allocations freeze had left his home state with a single TV station, Johnson lambasted the FCC commissioners for making no progress on the matters of UHF transmission and color. The senator's highly publicized tirade prompted the commission to reopen the color television case.[21]

CBS presented the commissioners with a version of its field-sequential system that could operate on channels of normal width. The industry's unshakable acceptance of NTSC monochrome now determined all norms. RCA countered with a "dot-sequential" system that used red, green, and blue electron "guns" to stimulate color dots on the interior surface of a single picture tube. CBS color transmissions could not be received even in black and white by monochrome TV sets without the installation of an adaptor. RCA color transmissions could be seen in black and white on monochrome receivers without adaptors and was therefore compatible with the country's existing television system. For this reason most manufacturers expected the FCC to choose RCA's system as the national standard. However, the dot-sequential system had been rushed prematurely out of RCA's Princeton, New Jersey, labs in time for the FCC hearings, and it still had alignment difficulties and inconsistent color. In addition, several commissioners felt that free competition in the television industry was not best served by decisions that always seemed to favor RCA's technology. In 1950 the FCC stunned the industry with the selection of CBS's system as the national color television standard.[22]

The new ruling was a hollow victory to CBS. Equipment manufacturers refused to cooperate. CBS broadcast hours of color programming in 1951, but the network could entice no company to make or sell field-sequential color receivers to the public. Without any urging from the government, the industry reconvened the NTSC the following year to reach a consensus on color. That came about when, in 1953, the committee recommended that a compatible dot-sequential system based mostly on RCA patents be made the national standard. Then, after a half-hearted attempt to promote color video production and receiver sales, RCA resumed its role as the nation's leading proponent of monochrome. Color television became a token project for the remainder of the 1950s.[23]

HOLLYWOOD'S NEW INTEREST IN COLOR

The decisions that determined the availability of color technology for motion pictures in 1950 and for television in 1953 left black and white quite intact. The emergence of Eastman Color did not trigger a serious run on color, and the failure of CBS's color television advocacy left color in the hands of monochrome magnate RCA. Years would pass before either industry converted to color, but the motion picture business experienced a temporary surge in color production between 1953 and 1956. The prospect of color television was not responsible for scaring Hollywood executives into going color at that time. The surge actually had its inception in 1952, when studios were making production decisions that would affect the following year's movie output. Color television was dead in the water that year—the reformation of the NTSC received minimal attention even in the trade journals. Not until July 1953 did RCA ballyhoo its color system's endorsement, nearly a year after color film production had begun a sharp climb.[24]

Hollywood was prompted to try more color in films because it had embarked on a strategy designed to differentiate its product from that of television. An essential component of this plan was an emphasis on those qualities motion pictures could provide that television could not match. Color was one such quality. Color showed off the splendor of ancient Rome in *The Robe* (1953), it captured the breathtaking beauty of the North American West in *The River of No Return* (1954), and it enlivened the music and dancing in big-screen musicals such as *Carousel* (1956). However, color was not the most prominently promoted feature of these films, nor of many of the color films of 1953–56. Instead, expanded screen size, improved image resolution, and stereophonic sound were the aspects most loudly heralded as qualities that television lacked. Unlike color, these three modifications involved major changes in exhibition equipment and mechanics. The studio chiefs were interested in making audiences feel swept up by motion pictures in ways the small video screen could never equal. Wider vistas, larger and sharper images, and soundtracks that seemed to surround their audiences contributed to a scene of "really being there." Studio heads, such as Spyros Skouras of Twentieth Century–Fox felt that monochrome images would undermine that sensation of being there. Color therefore became a critical part of Hollywood's strategy to win over viewers. The increase in wide, high-resolution, and stereophonic films (as well as 3-D pictures, which would not have achieved their stereoscopic effect in black and white) fueled the increase in color production.[25]

Drastic measures were deemed necessary because movie attendance had dropped steadily since 1946 and the growth of the television market promised to give even more Americans a reason to stay home. The spectacular three-screen Cinerama process premiered in 1952, followed over the next two years by CinemaScope and VistaVision. Why did the film studios wait until after more than five years of declining attendance to adopt this strategy of product differentiation? Not because of color television, but because of a new growth spurt in the sale of black and white television sets. The FCC's freeze was lifted in 1952, and new stations popped up across the United States. AT&T had just completed laying television transmission lines across key portions of the country, which made live national broadcasts possible. Monochrome television had begun a vigorous period of expansion that would not level off until 90 percent of American homes had TV.[26]

Technicolor's president, Herbert Kalmus, once told of how "in the year 1952, Merian Cooper, representing Cinerama, appealed to Technicolor for technical cooperation and help." *This Is Cinerama* had just been photographed on Eastman Color stock, but no lab was able to process the complicated three-camera/three-projector negative and get the colors of the side-by-side images to match up. Kalmus characterized Cinerama's backers as "desperate," and he described how Technicolor's lab solved their problems and helped make Cinerama a hit. He credited his company with similar rescues of Twentieth Century–Fox's initial CinemaScope effort, *The Robe*, as well as Paramount's first VistaVision features. Kalmus's self-laudatory account underscores the fact that the advocates of the big- and wide-screen processes considered color essential. Fox was willing to make CinemaScope available to competitors, but in these early years the studio would not permit 'Scope films to be shot in black and white. The promotional logic behind all these systems, as well as 3-D and such large-negative formats as Todd-AO and Camera 65 that followed, was that they made the movies spectacular. Monochrome was not considered spectacular.[27]

As the major studios used these new technologies to wage war against television for the attention of the viewing audience, other film industry factions began working with the television companies. Technicolor itself was a prime collaborator. In 1954, the first year more new color films were released than new black and white films, Technicolor's labs began processing monochrome stock for both motion picture and television producers. The company developed a special color stock expressly for television use that year, and soon firms such as Ziv-TV were shooting in color, even though their programs aired in black and white. Prescient executives anticipated a second life for programs shot in color in the far-off future, at such time as color really came to television. In addition, cinematographers and other craftspeople from the film industry turned to television for employment opportunities in a steady stream beginning in the mid-1950s.[28]

Hollywood's new interest in color led to a cutback in black and white film releases, while the number of new color films rose until the two were roughly at equal levels. After monochrome maintained an edge of 246 to 115 over color in 1952, the ratio changed to 252 to 163 in 1953, 160 to 169 in 1954, 166 to 173 in 1955, and 199 to 170 in 1956. Many color productions were in some wide format during these years; indeed, 90 percent of all Fox and Paramount pictures were shot in color at this time. Nevertheless, attendance at movie theaters continued to decline. The third important decision that affected the course of color in the moving image industries had been to make more color films at a time when television seemed content with black and white. This proved expensive, and when after four years there was no clear evidence that color made a broad difference at the box office, Hollywood returned both color and black and white production to their 1951 levels.[29]

BLACK AND WHITE BOUNCES BACK

While preparing to film his 1957 feature, *The Wrong Man*, Alfred Hitchcock told his director of photography, "I wouldn't want the stark, colorless documentary treatment I expect to reflect on your reputation as a cinematographer." Many directors felt color detracted from good drama and that black and white looked more serious and true to life. Such highly respected monochrome films as *12 Angry Men* (1957) and *The Three Faces of Eve* (1957) could hardly have been improved by color. Hitchcock is thought to have begun shooting his masterpiece, *Psycho* (1960), in color, but judged that to be a mistake and switched to black and white.[30] Yet many members of the American Society of Cinematographers remained enamored of the technical and aesthetic challenges of color shooting. Through late 1950s and early 1960s, the Academy of Motion Picture Arts and Sciences acknowledged this divided opinion by offering two Oscars for camera work: one for best color cinematography, the other for best black and white cinematography. Hollywood continued to make lavish color spectaculars with showy technology that combined wide-screen and large-negative processes with stereophonic sound, but after 1956, each studio resumed the practice of making the majority of its films in monochrome. Big-budget releases shot in color and wide formats, such as *Around the World in 80 Days* (1956), *Gigi* (1958), and *Ben-Hur* (1959) captured audiences and accolades, but while they were capable of breaking box office records, they were also tremendous financial risks. Color and spectacle did not ensure success, so, to the pleasure of many directors, monochrome films once again became the studios' staple.[31]

The television industry showed no signs that it was in a hurry to switch to color during this period, a fact that was not lost on Hollywood. NBC had declared 1954 "The Year of Color" and kicked off a schedule of color broadcasts with the Rose Bowl festivities. In the years that followed, specials like "Peter Pan" (1956) received the color treatment from the network, but these were few and far between. Throughout the 1950s the press was prompted to ask whatever happened to color television. "The Year of Color" and NBC's subsequent color promotions were perceived as premature. The film industry expressed its confidence that color was no immediate threat by boosting black and white releases by 70 percent in 1957 over the previous year. It was clear to Hollywood's executives and everyone else that consumers were not going to buy color television sets until there was a steady amount of color programming. The networks were not anxious to undertake the expensive conversion necessary to do regular color broadcasting at a time when many households still remained without even a black and white TV set. Affiliates would also have to invest in color transmission equipment before any network could broadcast color to every city.[32]

In the late 1950s Technicolor and other film processing and equipment firms began to take into consideration the way motion pictures would look when aired on television. The studios had earlier made their pre-1948 film libraries available for TV, and as the young medium became more entrenched, it was apparent that all films would someday play on television. The major studios had been gradually increasing their business connections with the video industry through the decade, so it was not surprising that as a part of a sales pitch to the studios, certain labs promoted the way their film stock looked on television. As late as 1961, Panavision, Inc. bragged that color films shot in its process looked better on black and white television than did other films. This was a sign that Panavision's management did not expect most Americans to have color TV for many years, whether or not the networks elected to increase color programming. Television was gaining Hollywood's acceptance as a site of exhibition for motion pictures, yet film producers did not withdraw their support for monochrome because color television still did not seem to be at hand.[33]

The increase in color film production from 1953 to 1956 was not a simple reaction to a challenge from the black and white video medium; rather it was tied to a marketing strategy that sought to keep television from compounding the problem of declining theater attendance. Likewise, the fourth key decision that affected the course of color—to return monochrome and color production in 1957 to the old 2-to-1 ratio —was not simply a direct response to the absence of color television. Hollywood studio executives weighed production decisions against corporate balance sheets. They factored in earning potential for color versus monochrome films, relative production costs, and changes in theatrical exhibition. They seem to have concluded after their experiment with more color that audiences would not stay away from a film just because it was in black and white. The popularity of black and white television and the lack of a public outcry for color video no doubt reinforced this. The studios' collective decision to discontinue the four-year color surge was a response to a multitude of conditions, of which the lack of color television was one. Because the television industry was not forcing the color issue, however, Hollywood had no qualms about staving off a conversion to color for several more years.[34]

THE CONVERSION TO COLOR

In the early 1960s the sales of black and white television sets neared the peak of an extraordinary climb. In 1950 less than 10 percent of American homes had TV, but by 1962 the figure had risen to 90 percent. This was close to market saturation, a point at which shrewd companies traditionally introduce new products. RCA officials had been planning for the moment of saturation for some time, and the product they hoped would pick up where monochrome television set left off was the color set. In the ten years since the FCC approved the company's color system, RCA had sold over a million color sets. These were high-end luxury items for most Americans and color set sales still represented less than 3 percent of all U.S. households. As part of the RCA plan, NBC began broadcasting five hours of color per week in 1959. At first these colorcasts were special movies, variety programs, or weekend sporting events that could be broadcast in color with less disruption than colorcasting would have been for any regular prime-time series. Later, Jack Paar's "Tonight Show," a live series produced by the network, went color. Live programs required new cameras and transmitters, but they did not have the additional expense of film processing, as did most series. The network took that costly step shortly thereafter when it approved the higher budget necessary for shooting on color film for the popular Western, "Bonanza." In 1961 NBC acquired "Walt Disney Presents" from ABC, a program with a backlog of color episodes that ABC had aired in black and white. NBC renamed the show "Walt Disney's Wonderful World of Color" and committed to airing both old and new episodes in color.[35]

For six years the network gradually increased its hours of color broadcasting, until by the fall of 1965 NBC committed to a complete prime-time line-up in color. At that time the network unleashed the kind of wholehearted promotional campaign that had been missing from its "Year of Color" in 1954. NBC replaced its chimes and letters logo with that of a peacock with red, green and blue tail feathers. The peacock appeared in not only the network's televised promotions, but in numerous color magazine ads and promotional brochures. The word "color" figured prominently in every half-hour of NBC programming, as announcers mentioned it before each station break and in the voice-over introduction to every program. No viewer could miss the fact that the peacock network had color. NBC billed itself as the first full-color network, although once aware of its rival's plan, CBS also committed itself to a complete prime-time color schedule. ABC followed their leads a year later. Consumers responded cautiously at first, but by 1967 color television set sales had begun an even more rapid growth than black and white had ever experienced.[36]

Hollywood was quite aware of the increased RCA-NBC color activity in the early 1960s. When the film industry stepped up black and white production in 1957, it reduced but did not abandon color. Color film releases remained steadily near one hundred per year between 1958 and 1963. Black and white releases subsequently began dropping until 1962, when monochrome and color starts were nearly equal. That year the number of features produced hit a record low. In 1963 production perked up, and for two years the number of black and white films available to theater audiences remained the same as the number of color films. Then, in 1965, faced with full-color network television, the major Hollywood studios cut black and white production to its lowest levels yet. Within three years black and white had become so rare that the only new monochrome films to appear in American theaters were infrequent documentaries. At the same time, color releases hit an all-time high of 240 and were still climbing. Television's phasing-out of black and white was incremental as far as viewers were concerned. Even after 1965 most TV stations continued to produce their local programs in black and white for several years. By contrast, Hollywood's abandonment of monochrome was especially abrupt.[37]

Somehow, in the midst of this changeover, color came to be regarded as suitable for serious dramatic productions. This may have come about in part because of an increased use of color film for television news. Ansco's 16mm color film process was relatively inexpensive, and its visual quality was acceptable for broadcasting. In addition, the prettier-than-life colors of Tri-Pak Technicolor were no longer in evidence. In order to compete with the less costly and more versatile Eastman Color derivations, Kalmus's company had phased out the process that made Technicolor famous in favor of its own Mono-Pak system. By the 1970s, Technicolor's name on new releases meant only that its labs processed the negative and possibly manufactured the prints. The difference between each lab's color processes could no longer be discerned by the casual observer.[38]

The film industry did not convert to color in order to distinguish its productions from those of television; rather, Hollywood went color to avoid such a distinction. Faced with the prospect of full-color networks and a color TV sales curve that would pass the 50 percent mark in the early 1970s en route to saturation, studio executives had no desire for motion pictures to become disparagingly known as a colorless medium. After the highly rated color broadcasts of such films as *Bridge on the River Kwai* (1957) in the early 1960s, sales of films to television figured prominently in each studio's earnings plan.

Hollywood could not afford to make its productions less valuable to the full-color networks by shooting in black and white. Abrupt though it was, any other response that the film industry might have made to television's color conversion would likely have been bad for business.[39]

CONCLUSION

The engineer who designed CBS's first color video system in 1940 claimed to have been inspired by *Gone With the Wind* (1939), the most popular film ever shot in Technicolor. Whether accurate or not, it is safe to say Hollywood's success with occasional color motion pictures paved the way for attempts by CBS and several television companies to introduce color to their medium. It is also reasonable to believe that had broadcasting manufacturers rallied around either CBS's system or color television in general as early as 1941 or 1946, before black and white sales took off, the networks might have been prompted to go full-color much sooner than they did. Since this never occurred, it was not until the mid-1960s that television reciprocated by "inspiring" the film industry to convert to color. Had any of the first four key decisions mentioned above gone differently, the fifth—Hollywood's decision to drop black and white—would have transpired at a time earlier or later than it did.[40]

Hollywood's conversion to color was part of a series of changes in film industry production practice designed to accommodate television broadcasts of theatrical motion pictures. Cinematographers soon found themselves instructed to keep in mind the somewhat square television aspect ratio when composing shots for wide-screen motion pictures. Actors were frequently asked to retake profanity-laden movie scenes with dialogue sanitized expressly for the television prints of that film. This same accommodation plan today includes the controversial practice of nonphotographic colorization that makes black and white films appear to be in color. Yet it is no longer surprising to anyone that film and television companies should be interested in trying to broaden the appeal of monochrome films for audiences of color television. Colorization is but the latest product of Hollywood's dependent relationship with the television industry that was first publicly acknowledged when the motion picture studios themselves went full color in 1965.[41]

NOTES

1. Beaumont Newhall, *The History of Photography: From 1839 to the Present Day* (New York: MOMA, 1978), pp. 12–16, 191–94, Gordon Hendricks, *The Kinetoscope* (New York: Beginnings of the American Film, 1966), pp. 14–15, Brian Coe, *The History of Movie Photography* (Westfield, N.J: Eastview Editions, 1981), p. 62; V. K. Zworkyin, "Television with Cathode-Ray Tube for Receiver," *Radio Engineering* 9 (December 1929): 38, reprinted in George Shiers, ed., *Technical Development of Television* (New York: Arno, 1977).

2. Brian Coe, *Colour Photography, The First 100 Years 1840-1940* (London: Ash & Grant, 1978), pp. 28–30; Maxwell is sometimes called Clerk-Maxwell, as in Helmut and Alison Gersheim's *The History of Photography* (New York: McGraw-Hill, 1969), p. 521; Steve Neale, *Cinema and Technology* (Bloomington. Indiana University Press, 1985), p. 114; Herbert E. Ives, "Television in Colors," *Bell Lab Record* (July 1929): 439–44; Ian Jeffrey, *Photography: A Concise History* (New York: Oxford University Press, 1981), p. 245; Charles S. Aaronson, ed. "Pictures," in *International Motion Picture Almanac (IMPA)* (New York: Quigley, 1970), pp. 337–476; Colbert Steinberg, ed., "The Number of TV Households in America" and "Viewers with Color TV," in *TV Facts* (New York: Facts on File, 1985) pp. 85–88.

3. For the histories of color motion pictures and color television, see respectively Roderick T. Ryan, *A History of Motion Picture Color Technology* (New York: Focal, 1977); Thomas H. Smith, "Description and Analysis of the Early Diffusion of Color Television in the United States" (Ph.D. diss., Ohio State University, 1970).

4. Neale, *Cinema and Technology*, p. 129; D. B. Thomas, *The First Colour Motion Pictures* (London: HMSO, 1969), pp. 14–38.

5. Thomas, *The First Color Motion Pictures*, pp. 2–4; James Limbacher, *Four Aspects of the Film* (New York: Brussell and Brussell, 1969), p. 12; Roger Manvell, ed., *The International Encyclopedia of Film* (London: Michael Joseph, 1972), p. 29; Ryan, *History of Motion Picture Color*, p. 16.

6. For the history of Technicolor, Inc. see Fred E. Basten, *Glorious Technicolor* (London: A. S. Barnes, 1980); Coe, *The History of Movie Photography* p. 132; Thomas, *The First Color Motion Pictures*, pp. 16–22.

7. Ryan, pp. 16–18; Coe, *The History of Movie Photography*, pp. 128–30; David Bordwell, Janet Staiger, and Kristin Thompson, *The Classical Hollywood Cinema: Film Style and Mode of Production to 1960* (New York: Columbia University Press, 1985), p. 353.

8. Gorham A. Kindem, "Hollywood's Conversion to Color: The Technological, Economic and Aesthetic Factors," *Journal of the University Film and Video Association* 31 (Spring 1979): 32–34; Herbert T. Kalmus, "Technicolor Adventures in Cinemaland," in Raymond Fielding, ed., *A Technological History of Motion Pictures and Television* (Berkeley: University of California Press, 1967), p. 56.

9. "Color Film Increase," *Business Week*, May 22, 1947, p. 47; Robert

Surtees, "Color Is Different," *American Cinematographer* (January 1948), pp. 10–11, 31; figure compiled from *IMPA* 1944–45, pp. 827–906, and 1952–53, pp. 619–705.

10. Natalie Kalmus, "Color," in Stephen Watts, ed., *Behind the Screen: How Films are Made* (New York: Dodge, 1938), pp. 116-23 Neale *Cinema of Technology* pp. 140-42 Basten *Glorious Technicolor* p. 66.

11. "Scramble for Color Film," *Variety*, January 1, 1945, p. 3; Kindem, Hollywood's Conversion," pp. 34–35.

12. J. Dudley Andrew, "The Post-War Struggle for Color," *Cinema Journal* 18 (Spring 1979): pp. 41–52. A Belgian licensee of Agfa had already begun to promote the system in Europe under the name GevaColor, and in 1949 it surfaced in the United States under the name Ansco Color. Coe, *The History of Movie Photography*, pp. 136–37. Technicolor developed a Mono-pak three-color camera that was used in the early 1940s with limited success.

13. *IMPA*, pp. 337–476. In 1948, 17 percent of new releases were color film; in 1951, 19 percent were color. The color/monchrome ratio for the years in between was 63:318 in 1949 and 71:348 in 1950.

14. The most complete study of the 1948–52 allocations freeze can be found in John M. Kittross's *Television Frequency Allocation Policy in the United States* (New York: Arno Press, 1979).

15. Alex E. Alden, "The Role of Standardization in Technological Progress," *Journal of the Society for Motion Picture and Television Engineers* (JSMPTE) 75 (October 1966): 1019; "General Hearing on Television to Be Held This Spring," *Broadcasting*, March 1, 1939, p. 72; "Drive to Promote Video Sales Started by RCA," *Broadcasting*, March 15, 1940, p. 86; "FCC Reopens Television Hearings April 8: RCA Called to Task for Video Activity," *Broadcasting*, April 1, 1940, p. 102; "Color Television: 1941–1953," *Broadcasting*, December 21, 1953, p. 31.

16. Columbia Broadcasting System, "Description of CBS Color Television System," confidential report submitted to the NTSC, September 17, 1940; U.S. FCC, "Television Report, Order, Rules and Regulations," *Journal of the Society for Motion Picture Engineers* (JSMPE) (July 1941), pp. 87–97. CBS's two allies were Stromberg-Carlson and Zenith.

17. Peter Goldmark, J. N. Dyer, E. R. Piore, John M. Hollywood, "Color Television," *Journal of Applied Physics* (November 1942):13 666–77.

18. Memo from NBC chief engineer O. B. Hanson to NBC administrator Frank E. Mullen, December 2, 1943, (NBC Papers, Box 104, folder 26, State Historical Society of Wisconsin, "Delay Pending Better Video Is Endorsed by CBS Affiliates," *Broadcasting*, May 15, 1944, p. 28; Robert W. Erlich, "Color Television," *Radio News* (July 1945), pp. 32–34, 130–38; "CBS's Battle for Color Television Rages On," *Televiser* (March–April 1946), pp. 24–26.

19. "Green Light to Black-and-White," *Newsweek*, March 31, 1947, p. 70; Frank Stanton, CBS president, "The Public and Color Television" speech presented at March 1, 1946 color television press demonstration, pp. 1–9.

20. "Report of the Commission," FCC Docket No 7896, (March 18, 1947); Harriet Van Horne, "Television in Color: Royal of NBC Declares Programs More

Important Than Medium," *New York World-Telegram*, January 17, 1946, interview with CBS engineer Robert Castrignano, June 14, 1985, Stamford, Conn.

21. Jack Levy, "Senator Johnson's 'Sooner the Better' Stand on Color TV; Bares Video Soul," *Variety* November 9, 1949, p. 24.

22. FCC "Second [Color] Report of the Commission," (October 11, 1950), pp. 2–6; Wayne Coy, "Color Television Standardization," *Journal of the Television Society* 6 (July–September 1951): 264–65; J. L. Van Volkenburg, CBS administrator, "CBS Television: The Year-End Review," CBS stockholders report, December 27, 1951.

23. This section is based on the author's Ph.D. dissertation, "The CBS Color Television Venture: A Study of Failed Innovation in the Broadcasting Industry" (University of Wisconsin, 1987).

24. J. Dudley Andrew states that the French film companies were prompted by 1953 U.S. color television developments to increase their own color film output in "Post-War Struggle," p. 51, but it seems more likely the French studios wished to compete with the growing number of American color releases; "Technicolor in France," *American Cinematographer* (November 1954), p. 542; "Hollywood Studio Production," *American Cinematographer* (August 1954), p. 402; "At Last: Color TV," *Time*, July 17, 1953, p. 66.

25. Coe, *The History of Movie Photography*, pp. 158–59; John Belton, "CinemaScope: The Economics of Technology," *The Velvet Light Trap*, 21 (Summer 1985): pp. 40–41.

26. Les Brown, *Encyclopedia of Television* (New York: Zoetrope, 1982), p. 492; Kenneth MacGowan, "The Wide Screen of Yesterday and Today," *Quarterly Review of Film, Radio and Television* 11 (Spring 1957): 218; William Weaver, "Paramount Enters the Lists with VistaVision," *Motion Picture Herald*, March 6, 1954, p. 12.

27. Herbert T. Kalmus, "The Adventure of Technicolor," *JSMPTE* 67 (December 1958): 830; Belton, pp. 35–36 "VistaVision Moves Forward," *American Cinematographer* (November 1954), p. 552; "Summary of Current Wide-Screen Systems of Photography," *American Cinematographer* (November 1955), pp. 654–55.

28. Fred Foster, "The Big Switch Is to TV," *American Cinematographer* (January 1955), pp. 26, 38; "Color By Technicolor," *American Cinematographer* (October 1954), p. 488; "Industry News," *American Cinematographer* (September 1954), p. 426.

29. *IMPA*, pp. 338–476.

30. Frederick Foster, "'Hitch' Didn't Want It Arty," *American Cinematographer* (February 1957), p. 85; Robert A. Harris and Michael S. Lasky, *The Films of Alfred Hitchcock* (Secaucus, N.J.: Citadel, 1976), p. 219.

31. "Nominees Announced for Cinematography 'Oscars'," *American Cinematographer* (March 1960), pp. 171, 190; "1960 'Oscar Nominees,' *American Cinematographer* (April 1961), pp. 228–31; Limbacher, *Four Aspects* p. 133; Lloyd Thompson, "Progress Committee Report for 1959," *JSMPTE* 69 (May 1960): 311; *IMPA*, pp. 338–476.

32. Francis Bello, "Color TV: Who'll Buy a Triumph?" *Fortune* (November

1955), pp. 202–204; "Rainbow Still Elusive," *TV Age*, February 23, 1959, pp. 28–33, 76–77; Oliver Read, "For the Record: Color Needs More Exposure," *Radio & TV News* 55 (September 1956): 8; "Must Have Been Great in Color," *Life*, April 4, 1956, pp. 97-100; *IMPA*, 338–476.

33. Technicolor Advertisements in *American Cinematographer* (March 1957), p. 137; Allan D. Larson, "Integration and Attempted Integration Between the Motion Picture and Television Industries Through 1956" (Ph.D. diss., Ohio University, 1979), pp. 240–41; "Industry News," *American Cinematographer*, (November 1961), p. 638.

34. "Color Audience," *TV Age*, June 29, 1959, pp. 28–29, 119; Douglas Gomery, "Failed Opportunities: The Integration of the U.S. Motion Picture and Television Industries," *Quarterly Review of Film Studies* 9 (Summer 1984): 219-28.

35. "*Television Age* Network Programming Chart—Nighttime," *TV Age*, November 28, 1960, pp. 47–50; "Color Climb," *TV Age*, February 22, 1960, pp. 33–37, 63; Tim Brooks and Earle Marsh, *The Complete Directory to Prime Time Network TV Shows: 1946–Present* (New York: Ballantine, 1981), pp. 100, 806; "RCA Pushing Color TV Via NBC Programming," *Broadcasting*, August 21, 1961, p. 36.

36. *TV Facts*, pp. 85–88, "Want a Color Set?" *TV Age*, August 8, 1960, pp. 34–35, 72; "Growth of Color," *TV Age*, December 5, 1966, pp. 33–35.

37. *IMPA*, pp. 338–476.

38. Neale, *Cinema and Technology*, pp. 145–51; Nadine Pizzo, "The Drama of Color in Cinematography," *American Cinematographer* (February 1956), pp. 100, 110-13, 116; and from the same issue, "Industry News," p. 82.

39. "Growth of Color," *TV Age*, December 5, 1966, pp. 33–35; *TV Facts*, "Viewers with Color TV," pp. 85–88.

40. Peter Goldmark with Lee Edson, *Maverick Inventor: My Turbulent Years at CBS* (New York: E.P. Dutton, 1973), pp. 54–55.

41. Karl Freund, "Improved Television Viewfinder for Motion-Picture Production," *JSMPTE* 67 (November 1958): 745–46; Hap Kindem, "Theories of Film Technology: The Case of Color Film" (paper presented at the joint meeting of the Society for Cinema Studios & University Film and Video Association, Bozeman, Mont. July 1, 1988).

SUGGESTIONS FOR FURTHER READING

Bello, Francis, "Color TV: Who'll Buy a Triumph?" *Fortune* (November 1955): 136–37 ff.

Coe, Brian. *The History of Movie Photography*. Westfield, N.J.: Eastview Editions, 1981.

Fielding Raymond, ed. *A Technological History of Motion Pictures and Television*. Berkeley: University of California Press, 1967.

Goldmark, Peter, with Lee Edson. *Maverick Inventor: My Turbulent Years at CBS.* New York: E.P. Dutton, 1973.

Kindem, Gorham A. "Hollywood's Conversion to Color: The Technological, Economic, and Aesthetic Factors." *Journal of the University Film and Video Association* 31 (Spring 1979): 29–36.

Neale, Steve. *Cinema and Technology: Image, Sound, Color.* Bloomington: University of Indiana Press, 1985.

Ryan, Roderick T. *A History of Motion Picture Color Technology.* New York: Focal Press, 1977.

Shiers, George, ed. *Technological Development of Television.* New York: Arno, 1977.

Chapter 9

Feature Films on Prime-Time Television

William Lafferty

F eature films, defined here as productions of around 75 minutes or more in running time and intended originally for theatrical distribution and exhibition, have been a staple of television programming in the United States since well before the beginning of commercial telecasting in 1940. Generally, features produced by the major studios did not appear on television until the mid-1950s and not in network prime time until the next decade, an absence often attributed to an intense, adversarial relationship between Hollywood and television in their struggle to maintain and increase their respective audiences, with the studios' film libraries as a pawn in that struggle. However, the obvious antipathy that Hollywood held toward television was not the result of an implacable opposition to television bordering on the irrational, as described in many conventional accounts of the relations between the two media. The Hollywood film industry has always acted to protect its own economic self-interest while maximizing the revenue potential of its primary product, feature films, despite the threat or opportunity. Rather than springing from some fit of pique over the apparent ascendancy of television as the nation's most popular entertainment medium, the film industry's policies and attitudes concerning the broadcast potential of its feature film libraries arose from the most pragmatic factors, determined by shifting economic patterns within the film and television industries, the evolving programming policies of the networks and, ultimately, the challenge presented by new communication technologies such as videocassettes and cable television.

THE STATUS OF FEATURE FILMS IN EARLY
TELEVISION PROGRAMMING

The role feature film programming would play within a mature U.S. television industry remained unclear during the formative years of the medium following World War II. Many within broadcasting believed that television's "immediacy," anchored in live programming, was its aesthetic essence. As a result of this attitude, the networks and even individual stations focused their energies into developing formats and genres compatible with live-origination, particularly variety, sports, audience participation, and dramatic programming, both daytime "soap operas" and evening "serious" drama. Although filmed programming may have been devalued during the early 1950s, both local and, to a limited extent, network programming did include feature films, mainly as an efficient means to fill lengthening broadcast schedules. During these early years of postwar television, though, only those films produced outside the established Hollywood industry by independent or foreign producers, or by studios on the margins of mainstream Hollywood, reached the nation's television.[1] The conspicuous absence from the small screen of feature films produced by the major studios (Paramount, MGM, Twentieth Century–Fox, Warner Bros., Columbia, RKO, and Universal) led many to assume that the Hollywood industry had closed ranks against television in denying its competitor the potential programming bonanza the studios' film libraries represented.

Actually, the established Hollywood motion picture industry had sufficient economic and legal reasons not to release its vast film libraries to television, be it network or nonnetwork. First, the issue of the assignability of television rights of the major studios' films posed a contentious question. Since by far the majority of the studios' films had been produced before television became commercially viable, express broadcasting rights had not been an initial consideration in the talent and craft labor contracts governing studio production. Legal speculation ensued after the war, concerning a studio's or producer's implied right to license a film for television without compensating the various production personnel involved in the film's creation, an issue that would not be clarified until a 1954 court decision ruled that studios did hold implied television rights to their films. Until the court's clarification, legal absolution in granting television rights required the arduous task of negotiating television payments with all the craft and creative personnel involved in a film's production. For the major Hollywood studios—members of the Association of Motion

Picture Producers, which negotiated master contracts with the craft and talent guilds on the studios' behalf—failure to negotiate would mean union reprisals if the unions were not recognized in licensing agreements. Meanwhile, those talent and craft unions themselves, led by the American Federation of Musicians (AFM), recognized both the potential revenue and the future bargaining power their lease of the majors' feature films to television held for their memberships. The musicians, in their 1946 agreement with the studios, prohibited the release to television of films containing AFM-produced soundtracks made after that year, unless the films were rescored using AFM musicians.

Over the next five years, the Screen Actors Guild, the Screen Directors Guild, and the Writers Guild of America followed the musicians' lead, demanding in new contracts with the major studios additional payments to their memberships on the television release of films made after August 1, 1948. If a studio failed to negotiate, the guilds could strike the studio, an economically disastrous possibility for an industry just recovering from major postwar labor disputes. The studios, though, had no incentive to negotiate with the unions for the release of pre-1948 films, as the late 1940s and early 1950s saw Hollywood begin to explore avenues by which the film industry could exploit their libraries through alternatives to television release, including pay-television schemes and theater television. Rather than dilute the films' audience potential for these alternatives through "free" broadcast television, the union demands, representing a not inconsequential amount of money, provided a convenient excuse for Hollywood to withhold its films from television while deflecting Department of Justice scrutiny over possible restraint-of-trade violations of the Sherman Act, a sensitive issue to an industry already undergoing federally mandated divestiture of its theater holdings for precisely such violations.

Those theaters themselves presented a compelling reason, as well, for the major studios to refrain from vending their film libraries to television. Well into the 1950s, the major studios' biggest customers remained theatrical exhibitors—exhibitors faced during that decade with continually shrinking audiences because of shifts in the leisure-time activities of Americans, particularly toward television viewing. Between 1946, the year of Hollywood's peak revenue, and 1953, motion picture audiences declined by 50 percent, while between 1946 and 1952, the presence of television sets in American homes rose from 0.2 percent of all households to over 34 percent. Independent theater owners and chains soundly admonished the studios not to cooperate with television, especially in the release of feature films to the electronic medium, threatening, as did the various production unions and guilds, to boycott the studios that did. Meanwhile, although exhibition had been ordered divorced from the studio structure by the Paramount consent decree of 1948, the actual process of divorcement would not be completed by the major Hollywood studios until 1959. With these studios still involved in exhibition to varying degrees throughout the 1950s and with independent theater owners presenting a united front in protesting any accommodation with the exhibitors' chief competitor, television, the Hollywood film industry refrained from actively seeking television placement of their film libraries.

One factor, though, during the early 1950s far overshadowed all others in explaining the studios' reluctance to release features to television: the studios' film libraries were simply worth much more than early television could afford to pay. In testimony before the Federal Communications Commission in 1952, a Paramount executive justified the studio's withholding features from television by pointing out that even in theatrical re-release, a film could earn $215,000 to $750,000, while national telecasting rights to top-quality features, given the current economics of television advertising and programming, could realistically bring no more than $55,000. Even by 1954, the weekly cost of network television's most expensive dramatic program, the live "Studio One" sponsored by Westinghouse, amounted to only $40,000. With the additional time charges needed to fit a feature film of well over an hour into a network time slot, coupled with the film's potential earning capability in theatrical re-release, during the 1950s no individual sponsor could afford to pay what feature films were realistically worth in revenue for the major studios, while an industry study predicted that, should the studios release their quality features to television, the film industry would lose $68 million in theatrical exhibition revenue as a result of decreased theater attendance.

Although the postwar decade saw no real interest on the part of the networks to program feature films nor any desire by the major studios to release to television, this does not mean that feature film, even in prime time, had not become a major aspect of television programming. By the late 1940s, those feature films available for telecasting proved unexpectedly popular with audiences. As a result, in a large market like Chicago, with four stations, 60 features were telecast weekly, with the city's lone independent, WGN-TV, accounting for a third of that total. Network affiliates used features to fill nonnetwork time, particularly late-night "fringe" hours, and as replacements for network programs on summer hiatus. By 1953, CBS's New York flagship station used 30 hours of feature film a week. Independent stations, forced to program their entire broadcast day, found feature films indispensable, particularly in prime time, to counter network programming; by 1958, independent stations devoted over 45 percent of their programming hours exclusively to feature film.

The unexpected ratings potential of feature film posed a distinct problem. As early as 1950, markets ranging in size from New York to Cincinnati had exhausted the supply of features, around fifteen hundred, then available to television, prompting a scramble by stations for any and all features. With the vast film libraries of the major Hollywood studios not in television distribution, these stations relied upon what one trade publication characterized in 1950 as "a motley collection of Westerns, grade B comedies and melodramas, . . . a small supply of grade A features, and some foreign films."[2]

This "motley collection" was assembled from three primary sources: Hollywood's "Poverty Row" studios, the likes of Eagle-Lion, PRC, and Monogram; foreign, particularly British, producers and studios, including J. Arthur Rank and Ealing; and independent Hollywood producers like Edward Small and Sol Lesser. These producers and studios, not signatories to master labor agreements like the Hollywood majors, could offer their films to television without fear of union or exhibitor reprisal. Throughout the early 1950s, program distributors scoured the available output of these producers, attempting to find features for which television rights could be cleared. Since the "Poverty Row" studios often specialized in Western features and serials, examples of this genre comprised an inordinate share of the films telecast—venerable Westerns coming to denote early television film. With court decisions handed down during the early 1950s clarifying producers' television rights and acknowledging the rights of the studios to withhold their features from television until economically feasible, the proliferation of new television stations desperate for feature film programming, and the decline of theatrical exhibition during the 1950s, the major studios' reluctance to release film to television began to diminish quickly.

THE HOLLYWOOD MAJORS RELEASE TO TELEVISION

With more stations hitting the air and advertisers willing to spend more money on proven feature film programming, cracks began to form in Hollywood's resistance to television release. Faced with a rapidly declining market for the "B" films, which had been their source of income, smaller studios like Eagle-Lion, Republic, and Monogram had already either negotiated with the various talent guilds to release their features to television, or released and then dropped out of production altogether or entered television film production, avoiding union retaliation. By 1955, the majors finally took interest in the tremendous potential of releasing to television, with Twentieth Century-Fox selling a group of Charlie Chan features, Warner Bros. a block of cartoons, and Paramount 30 features to television distributors. Since the properties had been independently produced, the studios did not have to deal with the guilds for their release. Aside from their relations with the major Hollywood studios, which persisted in their reluctance to release their own product to television, there was the issue of the price these films, and other features offered to television at the same time, could command. While the studios had earlier cited the reissue value of their older films versus what television could pay for them as a primary factor against the films' release to television, the declining exhibition market rendered reissues economically infeasible for the studios: There simply was no longer a viable reissue market. The independently produced features released to television by Paramount brought fifty-two thousand dollars apiece, far above what each film could realistically bring in theatrical re-release. Meanwhile, independent producer David Selznick realized a hundred thousand dollars for each of ten of his films sold into television release. Apparently, at last, television could afford to outbid theatrical exhibitors for use of the studios' backlog of features. Faced with virtually no reissue market and a television industry able to pay attractive prices, the reluctance of the major Hollywood studios to release their own films to television quickly dissipated by mid-decade, prompted by the fiscal problems of one of their own.

The Radio Corporation of America formed Radio-Keith-Orpheum (RKO) in 1928 as a means of establishing a beachhead in its fight with Western Electric for dominance in the then-evolving American sound film equipment market. Although notable for aesthetic contributions to the medium, ranging from the Astaire-Rogers musicals to *Citizen Kane*, RKO never truly gained prominence among the major Hollywood studios. In 1955 General Teleradio, a subsidiary of the General Tire & Rubber Company, assumed control of RKO. General anticipated the conglomerates of the 1960s and 1970s, which would assume control of major Hollywood studios. General Tire had diversified into broadcasting, forming General Teleradio in 1952 to manage its extensive broadcasting properties, including five television stations, among which was WOR-TV, a major New York independent that had built its success, as had many other major market independents, upon televising feature films. General intended to appropriate the vast cash potential of RKO by liquidating its assets, paramount of which was its film library. In December 1955, General Teleradio sold the RKO film library, encompassing over seven hundred features, for $15.2 million to C & C Television Corporation.[3] Excluding markets where General had television properties and planned to use the RKO films itself, C & C obtained rights to sell the films in perpetuity to one station in each remaining television market. Pre-1948 features represented the bulk of the sale, but many post-1948 films, forbidden from television release by various guild contracts, were also included. The RKO contract with C & C stipulated that the distributor negotiate with the guilds for release of the post-1948 product: after a negotiated payment of over seven hundred thousand dollars to the Screen Actors Guild, C & C included over 80 post-1948 features in its distribution packages.[4] To make the packages affordable for stations in all markets, C & C pioneered the use of "barter" arrangements, an important aspect of today's syndication market, where a station would provide C & C with cash but also airtime during the films' presentation, which C & C would then sell to national advertisers. By July 1956, the RKO features began to broadcast in 58 markets; a year later, through cash and barter deals with these stations, C & C had grossed over $25 million.

The success of C & C demonstrated conclusively that television could pay substantial prices for the industry's features, but the sudden deluge of RKO films threatened to flood the market, depressing the potential worth of the other major studios' features in television release. Soon after the announced sale of the RKO library, other studios followed, releasing blocks of mostly pre-1948 films free of guild claims. Columbia's video arm, Screen Gems, announced a month after the RKO sale that it would begin distributing pre-1948 features to television, becoming the first major studio to do so; by the next year, 1957, the studio's three packages of almost two hundred films had grossed close to $10 million. Over the next five months, Republic, Warner Bros., and Universal released huge numbers of pre-1948 features to television syndicators. In contracts executed in May and November 1956, Twentieth Century-Fox struck a major deal wit National Telefilm Associates (NTA), releasing almost 450 features for over $30 million and receiving a 50 percent interest in NTA. National Telefilm modified the standard barter scheme and anticipated a current programming practice by forming an ad hoc network comprised primarily of independent stations. In exchange for a guaranteed 90 commercial minutes of airtime a week to be sold by NTA to national advertisers, NTA would supply affiliates of the NTA Film Network with NTA's Fox features. By the summer of 1956 Metro-Goldwyn-Mayer, previously tentative about the potential of television, began leasing 750 features, and by the end of the year had secured partial ownership of televison stations in Los

Angeles, Denver, and Minneapolis in exchange for licenses to broad-cast MGM features. Meanwhile Paramount, the studio that, ironically had evinced the earliest and most extensive participation in television postponed releasing its features to television unti early 1958, apparently to protect its pay-TV schemes. The Music Corporation of America (MCA), already a major producer of filmed television programming purchased outright 750 Paramount features for $50 million; the films rentals resulted in enough cash for MCA to purchase both Universal and Decca Records, allowing MCA to become not only a Hollywood rival of Paramount but a leader in the American entertainment industry as well.

In 1956 alone, as a direct result of the major studios finally releasing product to television, almost three thousand features entered television distribution—two-thirds of the number released in all previous years Aside from several RKO features cleared through the guilds for release by C & C Television Corporation and the independent product handled by United Artists, virtually only pre-1948 releases accounted for this flood of feature film reaching the air by 1956. Blanket contracts between the major studios and the Hollywood craft and talent guilds prohibited the release, in most cases, of features made after 1948 unless the guilds reached an agreement with the studios. With Hollywood's most recent and desirable features still withheld from television distribution, the networks had little faith in programming pre-1948 films in prime time, aside from "specials" like CBS's 1956 acquisition of *The Wizard of Oz* to counterprogram NBC's color "spectaculars" or NBC's occasional telecasting of recent British films as part of its "Omnibus" program. Feature films, particularly in prime time, found their way to television almost totally through syndication to individual stations, especially independents, throughout the 1950s. By the end of the decade, though, profound changes in the nature of network television broadcasting would finally precipitate the release of recent Hollywood features for network, prime-time telecasting.

FEATURE FILM IN NETWORK PRIME TIME: NBC'S "SATURDAY NIGHT AT THE MOVIES"

During the 1950s, network television became defined no longer by the model established by network radio but rather by shifts in the national marketing and advertising trends of the decade, which directly affected the structure of network telecasting—trends that would, by the early 1960s, produce a favorable climate for the prime-time network programming of recent Hollywood feature films, led by the National Broadcasting Company. During the 1950s, under the leadership of former advertising executive Pat Weaver, NBC embarked upon a restructuring of the network. Weaver championed what he termed the "magazine concept" of broadcasting, wherein the network would control the development and production of programming, as a publisher would determine the editorial content of a magazine; the network would then sell advertising throughout that programming to sponsors, just as a publisher would sell advertising space within the magazine. Weaver tirelessly promoted this approach to network advertising and programming, claiming it encouraged innovative programming freed from the parochial self-interests of advertisers and prevented large advertisers from monopolizing significant blocks of prime time, as had been the case with single-sponsorship in network radio, allowing more advertisers to exploit the tremendous advertising potential of television.

Weaver's belief in the "magazine concept," however, did not spring solely from an altruistic desire to democratize television advertising and improve programming quality. By deemphasizing single-sponsorship and making all network commercial minutes available to any and all advertisers, NBC achieved three significant goals. First, with more advertisers competing for a finite amount of commercial airtime, the network's advertising revenue would increase; second, with single sponsorship eliminated and program production removed from the sponsors and their advertising agencies, the network could participate in the lucrative potential of program creation and production, selling programs for initial network play and eventually for syndication; and third, the network could determine its own prime-time schedule, no longer beholden to any single advertiser's time "franchise" as in radio, and therefore able to organize programming to achieve maximum viewership and to counterprogram the other networks. As the 1950s drew to a close, NBC had redefined network broadcasting.

By 1960, already participating in the creation of its programming and in control of its schedule, NBC would spur the programming of post-1948 Hollywood features in network prime time. The Radio Corporation of America (RCA), parent of NBC, used the network to promote a market for RCA color television by steadily increasing the amount of color programming offered, with 35 hours telecast by 1956 (compared to a half-hour at CBS). To showcase color and to counterprogram CBS, Pat Weaver conceived the "spectacular," an often flamboyantly staged special broadcast devised to generate audience interest in color programming and to lure viewers away from CBS's series programming;

however, such spectaculars were exorbitantly costly to produce, as demonstrated by the half-million dollar price tag on NBC's 1957 production of "Mayerling," forcing NBC to contemplate cheaper, but effective, color programming. Meanwhile, in 1956, a change in the NBC management occurred when Robert Kintner replaced Weaver as head of NBC Television. Kintner, as president of ABC Television, had consolidated that network's position as a worthy rival to NBC and CBS by embracing filmed programming, mostly produced by Hollywood's Disney and Warner Bros., which generated significant ratings. Whereas Robert Sarnoff that year had admonished that television would "ride a toboggan of decline"[5] should filmed television gain ascendancy in network programming, NBC nevertheless chose a man with a strong commitment to filmed programming to lead the network.

As Kintner took over at NBC, a shift in its advertising philosophy began to take hold. The attitude existed in both radio and television advertising, until around 1960, that the aggregate number of listeners or viewers tuned to a program, as represented by the program's rating measured that program's efficiency as an advertising vehicle. However, by the end of the 1950s, faced with the high costs of television advertising and the proliferation of television watching through all strata of American society, advertisers began to emphasize reaching selected audiences—those groups most likely to use an advertiser's product—as the most efficient use of advertising dollars. Pat Weaver recognized this trend also in 1956, when he remarked that the television industry was "moving from indiscriminate masses of potential buyers to the screening and delivery of selected audiences."[6] NBC embraced the turn toward demographic research, in part as a strategy to lure advertisers from ratings leader CBS, claiming that even if a program drew the most viewers in a time slot, as did many CBS shows, a lower-rated program might still be a more effective selling tool depending upon the demographic groups it reached. ABC had scored impressive ratings among the key 18–49 age group with its filmed television series during the late 1950s, while NBC studies showed that this group comprised the most frequent theatrical film-goers. Recent features made programming sense at NBC, since they represented, in many instances, ready-made color programming with proven appeal that could occupy large segments of prime time and attract quality audiences, and that advertisers would be keen to sponsor. And, with their relative box office success as a barometer indicating their ratings potential, features could be a formidable weapon with which to counterprogram the competing networks.

The release of post-1948 features to television made economic sense within certain quarters of the Hollywood industry, as well. In 1960

Forbes estimated that the release of post-1948 features to television would mean in excess of $300 million to the studios at a time when at least two studios, Twentieth Century–Fox and Columbia, were experiencing losses despite the sales of most of their pre-1948 features to television. The cash potential of the post-1948 films, especially at the prices the networks could conceivably then pay, proved an irresistible lure to all sectors of the Hollywood industry. In 1960, after protracted negotiations and a month-and-a-half-long strike by the Screen Actors, the studios and the guilds reached a collective-bargaining agreement guaranteeing residual payments to guild members for the release to television of post-1948 features. Of the three thousand post-1948 features held in 1960 by United Artists, Allied Artists, Disney, and the major studios, over a quarter of them had been released to television by July the following year. The studios had learned from their experiences of the previous several years concerning the release of their pre-1948 films: rather than relying upon deals with independent distributors or syndicators, who had reaped fantastic profits from syndicating the studios' older films, the studios struck their own licensing agreements with the networks and syndication deals with individual stations, cutting out the middleman and making network release exceptionally lucrative.

NBC ushered in the era of prime-time, network feature film when it debuted "NBC's Saturday Night at the Movies" on September 21, 1961. For the program's first season, NBC obtained 31 post-1950 features, 15 in color, from Twentieth Century–Fox, with the initial offering *How to Marry a Millionaire*—a 1951 release that had been shot in color and CinemaScope—originally intended to draw viewers away from their television sets and back to the theaters. Reflecting its emphasis upon demographics and drawing a bead upon CBS's ratings dominance, NBC placed the program opposite two popular CBS Westerns that had their origins in radio, "Gunsmoke" and "Have Gun, Will Travel," and ABC's popular "Lawrence Welk Show," all programs that catered to older (and demographically less desirable) audiences. Although "Saturday Night at the Movies" would not make the Nielsen "Top Twenty" until the 1966 season, its delivery of a young, urban audience gratified advertisers and served to siphon viewers from CBS's "Gunsmoke," which, during the first three years of "Saturday Night at the Movies," dropped off the Top Twenty ratings leader list entirely, from third place. The success of "Saturday Night at the Movies" led to a deluge of feature film programming flooding the networks during the next decade, making feature film (and made-for-TV film) an ascendant aspect of network schedules throughout the 1960s, with a maximum of 14 network hours a week devoted to feature film, comprising eight different programs on all three networks, by the end of the decade.

THE RISE, FALL, AND RISE OF FEATURE FILMS
IN PRIME-TIME

Aside from the most recent releases, virtually all of Hollywood's feature films became available to television following the 1960 agreement between the film industry and the Screen Actors and other guilds. With less than three hundred features available for telecasting in 1951, ten years later, following the guild agreements, more than seven thousand were available to the networks and individual stations, and by 1964, over ten thousand. Following NBC's lead, ABC began scheduling prime-time feature film showcases in 1964 and CBS in 1965. The tardiness of ABC and CBS to take immediate advantage of the availability of post-1948 features apparently stemmed from the networks' reluctance to tamper with their current and successful programming orientation— ABC toward filmed action-adventure shows and CBS toward situation comedies. Nevertheless, prime-time feature films became the programming phenomenon of the 1960s and would remain an integral aspect of network programming into the 1980s. In the decade following the premiere of "NBC's Saturday Night at the Movies," total prime-time programming hours devoted by the networks to features increased from 2 hours to over 16 with feature film accounting for over a quarter of all prime-time programming by the 1971–72 season.

As expected, feature films provided the networks with a highly flexible weapon in their programming arsenals. As the ratings performance of prime-time network feature showcases quickly proved during the 1960s, huge television audiences existed for films with established box office appeal, and even recent features of limited success. The networks found the ratings of feature film series to be on average somewhat higher than that of other series programming, although the range of any given feature film series' rating fluctuated widely, depending upon the individual appeal of the titles aired. Network programmers could more easily gauge the probable audience share of a feature film with proven popularity than that of a new, unproven series program. Therefore, the networks used features as potent and convenient counterprogramming against their rivals, as NBC had originally done with "NBC's Saturday Night at the Movies." As a result, the number of "movie nights" increased dramatically over the 1960s. By 1968, at least two hours of prime time were occupied by feature film series every night of the week, with each network staking out at least two nights a week for itself to counterprogram competing networks' series programs; by the 1969 season, the networks began counterprogramming feature films with feature films.

By telecasting features with the most potential audience appeal at the beginning of the fall television season, a network film series could effectively keep viewers from either sampling another network's competing new programs or returning to another network's established programs, diminishing the audience share of each. Popular features could also be telecast elsewhere during the season in the important "sweeps" periods, when affiliates' local ratings are determined, as a means to maximize viewership during that month. Certain "blockbuster" titles could be used as "specials" outside of the scheduled feature film series, to be used as necessary to counter other networks' programming. During the 1970s, two-part presentations of films over different evenings, occasionally padded with material not seen in the films' theatrical releases, became increasingly common. From a programming standpoint, two-parters helped sustain one night's ratings potential into another, while from an economic standpoint, twice as much advertising time could be sold per title, an efficient means to defray the wildly escalating costs for proven films charged by the studios throughout the 1960s.

While features proved valuable and versatile programming, their popularity also posed a vexing problem for the networks. As early as 1961, when NBC began televising its Fox features, an industry trade magazine predicted that, based upon that year's licensing rate, in three years television would consume over 90 percent of all the sound films ever made by Hollywood. Throughout the 1960s and well into the 1970s, the rate at which the networks telecast first-run feature films far outstripped Hollywood's capacity to replenish that supply. While television consumption of feature films, both by networks and in syndication, had increased dramatically following the release of post-1948 films, feature film production in Hollywood had declined steadily since after World War II. With the theatrical market diminished, Hollywood devoted itself more and more to producing filmed television programming.

As a result, the networks found themselves in a seller's market when attempting to acquire feature film properties for telecast. With fewer features available, the licensing fee for a desirable title or per film package escalated annually. While in 1961 NBC paid Twentieth Century-Fox an average of $180,000 per feature, by the end of the decade the average price per film industrywide had reached around $800,000, and this at a time when the network schedules were becoming saturated with feature series. In the ten years between 1969 and 1978, the three networks alone spent almost $1.5 billion on securing the rights to telecast theatrical features, from over $126 million in 1969 to over $230 million in 1979. Prices paid for individual films, as well as packages, contributed toward this total: In 1966 ABC paid Columbia $2 million to present *Bridge on the River Kwai*; 12 years later, CBS paid MGM $35 million for the right to televise *Gone With the Wind* 20 times over a 20-year period, even though it had already been televised by NBC 2 years earlier. With the income generated soley from vending features and filmed programming to television, the Hollywood studios, as well as major independent producers, could subsidize their feature film production. As had occurred with RKO, by the late 1960s the cash potential of the studios' film libraries lured corporate conglomerates—Warners was absorbed by Kinney National, Paramount by Gulf+Western, and United Artists by Transamerica.

Within ten years of the release of post-1948 Holywood features to television, another factor would also contribute to the scarcity of available features for telecasting. After World War II the influence of the motion picture industry's self-censoring body, the Production Code Administration, eroded considerably, and by the 1960s a substantial number of feature films appeared that were far more politically and particularly sexually adventurous, as well as violent, than anything previously seen on the nation's screens. Broadcast television stations, not having the First Amendment protection films had enjoyed since 1952, were beholden to the FCC to "operate in the public interest," meaning that broadcasting material that could be potentially offensive to segments of their audiences could result in loss of license, as well as drawing the enmity of those segments. By 1970, both the networks and individual stations began shunning recent releases in increasing numbers because of the films' content, signaling the beginning of a steadily declining percentage of theatrical releases reaching television. By the mid-1980s, with around 70 percent of Hollywood production devoted to "R" films or films unrated by the Motion Picture Association of America, the pool of suitable features for telecasting had become precariously small.

During the 1960s, aware of the impending shortage of feature film programming, the networks explored alternatives to relying upon Hollywood's steadily decreasing feature film production to assure themselves a supply of adequate films to fulfill their programming needs. The first, and ultimately most fruitful, alternative lay in producing "made-for-television" features. As it had with telecasting Hollywood films, NBC again took the lead in premiering its first telefeature in 1964, a coproduction between the network and Universal. Approximating the production values of feature films but produced on smaller budgets and tailored expressly for the programming needs of the networks, made-for TV features became the programming phenomenon of the 1970s; by the 1971–72 season, made-for-TV films outnumbered theatrical features on the networks, while by decade's end, made-for-TV features accounted for 70 percent of network feature film presentations. Not only did made-for-TV films make economic sense for the networks, but, able to explore topical issues in narratives geared to the flow of television, they often produced remarkable ratings, as demonstrated by the awesome success of ABC's multipart "Roots" in 1977 or the 1979 premiere of the made-for-TV film "Elvis," which beat both *Gone With the Wind* on CBS and recent Oscar-winner *One Flew over the Cuckoo's Nest* on NBC. After their initial showings and a repeat, these made-for-TV films could earn additional revenue for their producers and the networks through foreign theatrical and television release, and, by the 1980s, through cable television and videocassette release.

Less than six years after post-1948 features began to appear in prime time, the looming shortage of features for television programming forced the networks to enter theatrical feature production themselves. The networks had good reasons to pursue such production. With youthful, burgeoning audiences during the 1960s, the feature film experienced a renaissance of popularity, with box office grosses equaling those of the pretelevision era, making film production an attractive investment, while production ensured the networks a supply of theatrically proven feature films for eventual television presentation. By 1967 both ABC and CBS had established theatrical feature units, Circle Films at ABC and Cinema Center at CBS, while NBC appeared content to devote its production energies to its successful made-for-TV films. Both Circle and Cinema Center produced some noteworthy films during the units' relatively short-lived existences, including CBS's *Little Big Man* and ABC's *Charlie*, but the combined effects of a Federal Communications Commission inquiry into the networks' control of programming production, an antitrust suit brought by the Motion Picture Association of America against ABC and CBS in 1970 over their entry into theatrical production, and a national recession that particularly affected the television industry's earnings prompted the networks to close down their theatrical film divisions by 1972.[7] For the remainder of the decade and into the 1980s, the networks limited their participation in feature film production to investing in promising properties in return for first-run broadcast rights and, generally, a say in script development so that the film would be suitable for broadcasting, or easily adaptable to broadcasting.

However, by 1975 the overall importance of theatrical feature film programming on the networks had begun a steady decline, with that year seeing the networks' first major production of "movie nights" in their program schedules. The increasing costs charged by Hollywood for television release of its films, the dwindling supply of suitable television releases, the ratings success of made-for-TV films, and a renewed emphasis upon creating series programming to build viewer loyalty and more consistent ratings all contributed to this decline, but the primary reason was the feature film's loss of audience. The networks had always used feature films as important programming tools, with popular features virtually guaranteeing a strong rating, but in the eight seasons between 1975 and 1983, the overall ratings performance of feature films fell off markedly. During the last week of the February 1984 "sweeps" period, three recent and relatively successful box office draws—*Taps, Blue Lagoon,* and *Urban Cowboy*—finished in the bottom seven of the Nielson ratings, hardly the performance expected of the networks' traditionally most effective ratings weapon. Exorbitantly expensive to purchase but no longer delivering the audience they once had, feature films would become increasingly peripheral in the networks' programming plans during the 1980s.

The decline of the feature film in network prime time corresponded with the decline of the networks' previously unchallenged supremacy in the television industry. Beginning in 1976, and continuing to today, the networks' overall share of the television-viewing public has continually shrunk. The reasons for the networks' diminished audience, and for the network ratings decline of the feature film, have been the dramatic growth of new program delivery technologies, especially videocassette recorders and cable television, whose success has been based, in large measure, upon offering very recent theatrical releases, uncut, before they receive network exposure. During the glory days of network television, the standard domestic commercial life of a feature film included original theatrical release, sale to the networks, and ultimately syndication to individual stations. By the mid-1980s, with cable penetration at almost 50 percent of all television households and VCRs almost as ubiquitous as television sets, videocassette release, cable pay-per-view release, and cable premium channel release came between a film's appearance at theaters and its appearance on the networks. As early as 1980, cable movie channels like HBO began drawing a greater share of audience from among their subscribers than network television, a trend that continues.

With these films' wide previous exposure, the audience for feature films had shrunk considerably by the time the films reached the networks. While during the 1960s and into the 1970s first-run features in prime time still held an aura of specialness within the television audience, the foundation of their ratings success, by the mid-1980s, had been eroded. As one CBS executive explained, "Not only have the films been seen before, they've been seen before on television."[8] When CBS telecast the first network run of the phenomenally successful *Star Wars* in 1984 and it was beaten in the ratings by the first episode of an ABC made-for-TV miniseries, "Lace," forcing CBS to reimburse advertisers for viewers guaranteed but not delivered, the direction of film programming on the networks was cast. The emphasis shifted to made-for-TV films, particularly miniseries, which cost nearly the same to produce as Hollywood theatrical features cost to license for television play; and concomitantly Hollywood features nearly disappeared on the networks.

The dismal ratings performance of features of the networks during the 1980s did not mean in the least that theatrical films had been banished from prime time. As network interest in programming features declined precipitously throughout the 1980s, many features experienced no network exposure at all, going directly into syndication for broadcast release. The features that no longer interested the three networks proved an invaluable source of programming for independent stations, with which to counterprogram competing network affiliate stations. This decade has seen the emergence of the recent feature film, as well as, to a lesser extent, made-for-syndication movies and series, as the independent stations' primary programming tool, as it had been the networks' during the previous two decades. Film producers and distributors like MGM/UA, Columbia, and Warner Bros., with little network income for their films, and television syndicators like Viacom and Embassy resurrected the concept of "ad hoc" networks of independent stations to carry packages of recent feature films in prime time; to defray the huge initial costs to these stations, the distributors also resurrected the barter scheme, used when major studio features were initially released to syndicators in the 1950s, reducing the price in return for commercial time for sale to national sponsors. Indeed, such networks have proven such effective advertising vehicles, attracting decent audience shares at costs far below those regular network advertising would cost, that major national advertisers began to form their own networks—Proctor & Gamble, for instance, acquired the Time-Life film library to begin its own ad hoc barter network.

The networks, by withdrawing from the feature market, found themselves in the ironic position of providing the independent stations with fodder with which to combat the networks' own affiliates. By mid-decade, independent stations' showings of recent features began to win their time periods against network programming in markets large and small across the country, contributing, along with cable and VCRs, to the networks' loss of overall audience share. While the networks had historically used feature films to counterprogram their competitors' strongest programming, as in "sweeps" months, independent stations effectively used recent features against the networks' weakest prime-time programming, a ploy to increase the independent stations' aggregate viewer share. By 1987 feature films formed the foundation of independent station programming in the nation's top 20 markets, with over 90 percent of those markets' independents relying upon prime-time film, and despite an estimated 35 percent and 50 percent penetration nationally of cable television and VCRs, respectively, those stations in the top 5 markets had increased their share of viewers. Over the past 40 years, then, the status of feature film in prime time has come full circle, with their importance to network prime-time broadcasting marginal, but their importance to independent stations' prime-time programming again vital.

A NOTE ON PANNING, SCANNING, AND COLORIZATION

Commercial motion pictures and television represent two media based upon two distinct sets of technical standards but shared economic self-interest. To conform theatrical feature films to the technical constraints of television and to realize maximum economic return, the broadcasting and film industries subject these films to a variety of technological processes that render their televised image oftentimes radically different from what the films' creators initially intended and what theater audiences initially viewed. Films shot in wide-screen processes (virtually every feature shot in this country for the last 35 years) must be altered to fit the screen dimensions of a television set, while the ubiquitousness of color television has spawned a generation that regards black-and-white programming inferior, leading to the "colorization" of such films if they are to have any commercial life. Meanwhile, the time constraints imposed by scheduled broadcasting often require the deletion of portions of a film to reduce its running time, or as in some two-part presentations, the addition of material not seen in theatrical release, intended to pad the film for telecasting over two nights.

Panning and Scanning

The first features shown on television suffered alteration by stations paring the films' running times down to lengths that television's rigorously obeyed time slots could accommodate. Such editing could be as benign as shaving a few seconds off a panoramic establishing shot or a long dissolve, or as drastic as excising whole sequences of a film, often to the point of narrative incoherence. By the 1960s, such editing also embraced the removal of potentially objectionable material, especially nudity. However, by the time "Saturday Night at the Movies" appeared in 1961, the networks subjected feature films to another type of paring, this time of the image itself.

Older features shown on television, and the televised image itself, shared the same *aspect ratio*—the ratio between the image's width and height. During its technical evolution in the 1930s, American television adopted Hollywood's standard aspect ratio, 4:3; therefore, aside from some omission around the television screen's perimeter, little image loss occurred when feature films were presented. However, during the early 1950s Hollywood began shooting its films using a number of so-called "wide-screen" processes, like CinemaScope and VistaVision, hopeful that audiences would leave their television sets to marvel at the new, grandiose cinematic image. These processes involved aspect ratios ranging from 5:1 to 8:1. However, the American television industry still maintains a 4:3 ratio; when wide-screen films are shown on television, something has to go, and that something is large portions of the films' original image—around 50 percent for a CinemaScope film.

It is ironic that Twentieth Century-Fox, which pioneered wide-screen films with CinemaScope as a means to lure audiences away form television and back to movies, also pioneered the process by which audiences could see those films on television—and won an Oscar from a grateful film industry for each. The latter process, known as "panning-and-scanning," involves the actual recomposing of each frame of a wide-screen film. In scanning, an editor or technician selects (or "scans") from his or her console's screen the prominent field of activity within the frame and imposes a 4:3 frame over that area from one of as many as 60 available on the console computer, which then programs an optical, printer to print that selected portion of the frame. The resulting print adheres to the standard television aspect ratio, but any formal elements of composition of the wide-screen frame are utterly lost. In "panning," the image is scanned from side to side (as if being panned by a camera), preserving to an extent the original composition, but certainly losing its instantaneous visual impact.

With the importance of the television market, virtually the entire output of features from 1953 to the present must be panned-and-scanned for both television and videocassette release. The result is a loss of a crucial formal and aesthetic dimension of wide-screen films, particularly in the films of directors known for their imaginative and effective wide-screen compositions, like Nicholas Ray or Samuel Fuller.

COLORIZATION

As American television shifted to full-time color telecasting in the early 1960s, a primary allure of recent feature films for the networks was that they represented a large existing supply of color programming. In licensing and syndication for television, color films were more valuable to their distributors because of the demand for color programming; by the 1970s, with color television virtually the national norm and black-and-white programming considered archaic by viewers, the film industry confronted the possibility that huge portions of their film libraries might no longer have any television value. Beginning with a rudimentary Korean process that gave new economic life to venerable black and white cartoons, colorization is today a technically refined but controversial method to resuscitate the earnings potential of black-and-white films.

In colorization, different colors are assigned by a "colorist" to different fields within each frame of a black-and-white film; using computer graphics and video technology, each frame is then colored, like a black-and-white photograph being tinted by an artist, during its transfer to videotape. The color that results has no real relation to the original image: the colors are arbitarily selected and, to many, when compared to the brilliant, saturated colors of a Technicolor film, for example, are of no better quality than color Xerography. However, because the colors are so arbitary and represent creative work on the part of the colorist, the U.S. Copyright Office is willing to issue a copyright for certain colorized films.

Colorization has polarized the film industry, with claims that the process destroys the original compositions and aesthetic intentions of the films' directors, cinematographers, and lighting cameramen. On the other hand, the films' distributors (particularly Ted Turner, owner of superstation WTBS and the MGM/UA film library) claim that they own the films, and they are free to extract as much value from them through whatever means available.

Today, especially since the advent of colorization, there exists a heated controversy over the effects of television's alteration of feature films, rising from a fundamental conflict over what is the essence of a feature film. It is a conflict between commerce and aesthetics, and, some would even argue, between commerce and ethics. On one side of the controversy are the film and television industries, maintaining that feature films are industrial products and that those industrial organizations that control their production and exhibition are entitled to maximize the films' economic potential. On the other side are those who value these films as cultural and aesthetic objects, works of art, and who maintain that their creators be granted the privilege other artists possess, that their visions not be altered by crass commercial considerations. This side is composed of a variety of film industry creative personnel, particularly directors, many of whom, since from the time of Von Stroheim and probably before, have decried how their artistic visions have been violated by the greedy capriciousness of the film industry. Film historians and critics also occupy this camp, bemoaning that, should such alterations proceed unchecked, with the television or videocassette versions of scanned and colorized films becoming the accepted norm while their original, intended versions are lost, the nation will lose an irretrievable portion of its cinematic, and cultural, history. Their fear is that for those films for which there is a limited audience (early silent films, B movies, box office failures but critical successes, for example), there will no longer be any economic incentive to maintain their distribution or even their existence, culminating in a distorted view of the motion picture's aesthetic development.

NOTES

1. Television historians Earl Marsh and Tim Brooks in *The Complete Directory of Prime Time Network TV Shows, 1946–Present*, 3d ed. (New York, 1985), pp. 569–70, have identified over 30 network programs comprised of feature films to be broadcast in network prime time between 1948 and 1957. Most of these programs originated over ABC and DuMont, two networks whose precarious fiscal condition throughout the postwar decade limited their abilities to produce original programming, forcing them to rely intermittently upon features to occupy economically large segments of their network schedules.

2. "Sensational But Scarce," *Sponsor*, June 2 1950, p. 31.

3. By 1957 RKO's distribution network had been abandoned and its studio holdings sold to Desilu, among the foremost producers of programming filmed for television.

4. The Warner Bros. agreement also called for guild negotiations for release of several post-1948 features involved; the negotiations were unsuccessful, and those features were withheld from television.

5. "The Fight for Television Dominance," *Broadcasting-Telecasting*, December 17, 1956, p. 27.

6. Sylvester L. Weaver, "The Maturity of the Advertiser," *Television Magazine* 13 (January 1956): 39.

7. With a reinvigorated market for feature films prompted by the advent

of cable television and videocassettes, ABC resurrected its theatrical film unit by 1980.

8. "Curtain Falling on Theatrical Films on TV," *Broadcasting*, September 3, 1984), p. 42.

SUGGESTIONS FOR FURTHER READING

Little has been written expressly about feature film programming in prime-time television. The preceding chapter represents a synthesis of material gleaned primarily from trade periodicals, including *Broadcasting*, *Television/Radio Age*, *Advertising Age*, and *Television Magazine*, as well as *Variety*. These magazines are invaluable sources of information concerning all aspects of the broadcasting industry and have been indexed since the mid-1950s in the *Business Periodicals Index*, except for *Variety*, which has recently been indexed in the *Film/Literature Index*. These journals and indexes can be found in most public and university libraries.

Two outstanding sources concerning the relationship of feature films to television, and that have been used in preparing this chapter, are dissertations. Although dissertations are generally unpublished, they can occasionally be found in university libraries, acquired through a library's interlibrary loan service, and can always be purchased, in microfilm or hard copy, through University Microfilms in Ann Arbor, Michigan:

Schnapper, Amy. "The Distribution of Theatrical Feature Films to Television." Ph.D. diss., University of Wisconsin-Madison, 1975.

Dombkowski, Dennis Joseph. "Film and Television: An Analytical History of Economic and Creative Integration.' Ph.D. diss., University of Illinois at Urbana-Champaign, 1982.

A scholarly article that provides a broad perspective upon the economic determinants of feature film in television is:

Litman, Barry A. "The Economics of the Television Market for Theatrical Movies." *Journal of Communication* 29 (Autumn 1979).

The following are suggested readings on panning, scanning, and colorization:

Beck, Bernard. "Inglorious Color," *Society* (May/June 1987), pp. 4–12.

Belton, John. "Pan & Scan Scandals," *The Perfect Vision* 1 (Indian Summer 1987); 41-49.

"The Shape of Money." *Sight & Sound* 57 (Winter 1987–88): 44–47.

Berger, Arthur Asa. "Film Technology's Latest Frankenstein." *Society* (May/June 1987), pp. 12-13.

Kerbel, Michael. "Edited for Television. I: Scanning." *Film Comment* 13 (May/June 1977): 28–30.

"Edited for Television. II: Unkindest Cuts." *Film Comment* 13 (July/August 1977): 38–40.

"Edited for Television. III: A Loss for Words."
Film Comment 13 (September/October 1977): 34–37.

Part II ────────────────────

Responding to New Television Technologies

Introduction to Part II

Tino Balio

THE RECESSION OF 1969

I n 1969, the motion picture industry experienced a convulsion that was matched "in seriousness, dislocation and change by only two events in film history, the sound revolution of 1930 and the television upheaval of the 1950s," in the opinion of A. H. Howe, a Bank of America executive in charge of production financing.[1] The majors suffered more than $200 million in losses: United Artists led the pack with $85 million; MGM came in second with $72 million; and Twentieth Century–Fox was third with $65 million. Columbia became a candidate for receivership. Under pressure from the banks, Hollywood was forced into another period of retrenchment that lasted four years.

This state of affairs had its roots in the boom years of the sixties. The first cause was the blockbuster philosophy of the majors. At Twentieth Century–Fox, for example, the practice had been to produce one key picture each season to keep the company in the black. When *The Longest Day* revived the company in 1964 after the *Cleopatra* fiasco, Fox thereupon launched a succession of big pictures, beginning with *The Sound of Music*. Although the picture cost a hefty $10 million, it grossed over $100 million within two years of its release in 1965. Other studios jumped on the bandwagon and by 1968, practically all the majors were producing blockbusters.

The second cause was the entry of three "instant majors" into motion pictures. ABC, CBS, and National General, a theater chain,

259

were drawn into the booming motion picture business and started producing around ten films a year each. These newcomers succeeded only in bidding up the prices on talent and in glutting the market with pictures.

And the third cause was the insatiable demand of network television for feature films. As the number of movie nights increased and as rental prices skyrocketed, Hollywood became complacent. The thinking became that if a picture didn't make it in the theatrical market, it would break even or earn a profit from the network television sale.

Everything seemed to come apart by the end of 1968. Confronted with seven movie nights a week during the 1968–69 season, audiences became selective and ratings dropped. Audiences considered some movies too racy and too violent. Moreover, the networks had acquired enough product to last until 1972 and stopped bidding on theatrical films. Since there were more than enough pictures to meet the needs of exhibitors, many blockbusters with bloated budgets worked their way through the distribution system at staggering losses.

Hollywood nearly collapsed. ABC, CBS, and National General lost collectively over $80 million and dropped out of the motion picture business. The majors retrenched. MGM, for example, hired James Aubrey, Jr., the controversial former president of CBS-TV, to use Draconian methods to revive the ailing lion. Aubrey auctioned off the studio's old props, sets, and wardrobe; sold the backlot; put its studio in England on the block; and moved the company's New York head-quarters to Culver City. In addition, Aubrey cancelled $44 million worth of dubious production deals and, in an extraordinary move, closed down MGM's distribution arm. MGM continued to produce a limited number of pictures each year, but arranged with United Artists to distribute them. Other studios merged their production and distribution facilities, fired employees, and consolidated offices overseas. For example, MCA and Paramount formed Cinema International Corporation in 1970 to distribute theatrical films of both companies outside the domestic market. For the time being, the era of the blockbuster was over.

The majors learned some valuable lessons from the recession. The most important was that attendance had stabilized in size for all practical purposes, meaning that the market could support only a finite number of productions. During the seventies, the box office recovered somewhat as a result of ticket price inflation, but the decade was marked by short-term cycles of alternating strength and weakness. While the box office gross rose steadily from $1.3 billion in 1969 to $2.8 billion in 1979, admissions fluctuated from a low of 820 million in 1971 to a high of 1.1 billion in 1978. In response to this flattening of demand, the majors cut production in half.

Which brings up the matter of production costs. Production costs declined only briefly as producers hoped to emulate such low-budget youth-oriented hits as *Bonnie and Clyde* (1967), *The Graduate* (1967), *Easy Rider* (1969), and *Midnight Cowboy* (1969). The spectacular box office and critical success of such pictures revealed that a segment of the public wanted intellectually demanding and emotionally fulfilling pictures. Consisting mostly of the young, who had embraced the cinema as its favorite art form, this segment constituted the largest share of the market and had been hitherto ignored by the majors. But the youth audience interest in films exploring the dark side of America was short-lived. By 1971, the "youthpix" phenomenon was dead. Since films dealing with race problems, drugs, and the counterculture had lost their appeal, studios returned to more conventional fare.

The second lesson Hollywood learned from the recession is that only a few pictures, perhaps ten a year, will capture most of the box office dollar. The lesson was brought home in 1970, when two rather pedestrian pictures—Paramount's *Love Story* and Universal's *Airport*—broke box office records and were heavily attended by the under-30 age group. When Paramount's *The Godfather* broke the all-time box office record in 1972, the big-budget philosophy was reinstated. As a result, production costs for a typical motion picture rose from around $2 million in the early seventies to around $9 million by the end of the decade. Although a few hits, such as *American Graffiti* (1973) and *Rocky* (1976), had modest budgets, the majority, such as *The Sting* (1973), *The Towering Inferno* (1974), *Jaws* (1975), *Star Wars* (1977), *Close Encounters of the Third Kind* (1977), and *Superman* (1979), were big-ticket items.

As a third lesson, the majors learned to offset the risks of production by adopting defensive production and marketing tactics. During the seventies, the majors relied on sequels and series. Sequels solved a major promotion problem for the studios—how to make known to an audience what a film is about. Film titles with Arabic numbers, Roman numerals, years, or such phrases as "Return of," "Beyond the," and "Beneath the" appeared regularly after the successful release of such follow-ups as *The Godfather Part II*, *Trial of Billy Jack*, and *Airport 1975* in 1974. Thereafter, the majors devoted around 10 percent of their production efforts to sequels.

Unlike sequels, which repeat characters of an earlier film and take up the action where it left off, series films just repeat a set of characters over three or more pictures in succession. Each film is dramatically complete and there is no chronological order to the members of the series. Of all the ways to rationalize production, a series has the greatest potential of generating profits without much attendant risk. Once launched, a series creates loyal and eager fans who form the core of its audience. By keeping production costs in line with this ready-made demand, series pictures were guaranteed a profit. The James Bond series set the pace. Launched in the sixties by Harry Saltzman and Cubby Broccoli and released through United Artists, the series withstood changes of the star, a flood of imitations, and upheavals in the market to attract a mass audience worldwide year in and year out. Other profitable series of the period included the Pink Panther films, the Dirty Harry pictures, and the *Friday the 13th* series.

The new marketing practices adopted by the majors went beyond traditional channels of distribution by exploiting the entire leisure-time field. Book tie-ins, novelizations, sound tracks, and the merchandising of toys, games, and clothing were used no longer just as sources of free advertising but as "profit centers" that had the potential of generating significant additional revenue for hit films.

THE INNOVATIONS

The motion picture industry entered another era of prosperity during the eighties as a result of innovations in television technologies. Two new distribution outlets opened up—home video and pay television—each of which extended both the market and the revenue stream for filmed programming. It all started with the launching of commercial geosynchronous satellites in the mid-seventies. As Michele Hilmes states in chapter 10 "Satellite transmission capability finally began to transform television into a true 'broadcast' medium, loosening its dependence on the nineteenth-century technology of wired transmission and giving it the ability to offer an almost limitless variety of channels and services." Cable television was the first to benefit, and soon after, pay cable, pay-per-view, direct satellite broadcast, and other delivery systems to the home. Simultaneously, developments in videotape recorder technology spawned the VCR, which enabled viewers to store and retrieve programming either transmitted to the home or from other sources.

The first point to note is that the new technologies are in essence no more than hardware delivery systems for existing software. The second is that these delivery systems serviced the home. The third is that the public demonstrated its willingness to pay for convenient entertainment in the home. Which brings up the fourth point. The new technologies did not kill the movie theater, as some had predicted; in fact, the status of exhibition has actually improved. Pay cable and home

TABLE II.1

Domestic Distribution Pattern for Feature Films	
Time Period	*Market*
First 3 months	Theater exhibition
6 to 9 months	Home video and pay-per-view
1 year to 2½ years	Cable television
2½ years to 5½ years	Network television
5½ years	Re-release to U.S. cable
6 years	Television syndication

video need feature films, especially hits, which become so in only one place: the theater.

The creation of new markets changed the distribution pattern of motion pictures. Before television, motion pictures were distributed almost exclusively in the theatrical market. Afterward, motion pictures were released to theaters first, and then 18 months after the close of the theatrical run to network television, and then to syndicated television. By the time a picture had been played out, ten years or more would have passed. (See table II.1 for a breakdown of the life cycle of a typical hit feature film today.)

In releasing a new picture, the goal of the distributor is to wring top dollar from each market, or "window," as it is called in the trade. Going through the distribution pipeline, the picture is exploited in one market at a time, with the exception of home video, which has a window that remains open almost indefinitely. At each point, the price of the picture to the consumer drops. Economists call the process "price tiering," which can be explained as follows: Movies are first released to theaters at top prices to "high value" consumers, which is to say, those who are most anxious to see them and are willing to pay seven dollars and more a ticket; movies are then released to "lower value" consumers at prices that decline with time. Thus a consumer willing to wait two to three years for a picture can get it for "free" over network television. Distributing pictures in this manner allows a distributor to tap every segment of the market in an orderly way and at a price commensurate with its demand.

This section discusses how the new technologies created ancillary markets for feature films. The effects of the new technologies on the bargaining relationship between the producers and their existing outlets, such as motion picture theaters, network television, and foreign markets is discussed in the sections that follow.

Pay Television

Pay television came into its own when Home Box Office (HBO) staked its future on RCA's domestic satellite SATCOM I in 1975. A venture of Time Inc., HBO was the first of the so-called "premium services" that offered recent, uncut, and uninterrupted films, sports events, and other specially produced programming to cable subscribers. Since the venture had lost millions during its first three years, HBO's decision to lease transponders at a cost of $6.5 million to transmit regular programming by satellite was viewed at the time as foolhardy. The cost of leasing a transponder was only one factor. In order for a cable company to receive television signals from a satellite, it needed a receiving dish. In 1975, a receiving dish cost $125,000, a formidable outlay for a cable operator who could not be sure that others would follow HBO's lead or even that HBO would stay in business. But earth-station technology was progressing rapidly; HBO and the cable industry convinced the FCC in 1976 to relax its technical requirements and permit the use of a smaller, less expensive dish. Three years after going up on the bird, HBO was feeding its premium service to over seven hundred cable systems, with 2 million subscribers.

HBO programmed a continuous supply of differentiated programming—that is, product available nowhere else on television. For this service, HBO charged a monthly fee rather than a separate fee for each attraction. To implement this policy, however, HBO had to go up against the FCC a second time. In an attempt to protect "free" broadcast television, the FCC had issued regulations stipulating that a feature film shown on pay TV had to be either less than two years old or more than ten years old. The practical effect of these regulations would be to limit pay TV to either new pictures that flopped in the theatrical market or old pictures that had been played out on network and syndicated television.

HBO challenged the right of the FCC to protect broadcast television in the courts. On March 29, 1977, the U.S. Court of Appeals sided with HBO and struck down the protectionist regulations. Thereafter, any film of any age could be shown on pay cable. Other premium services such as Showtime, The Movie Channel, Cinemax, and The Disney Channel entered the market, creating a significant ancillary market for feature films. Roughly half of all television homes now subscribe to cable TV; over one-third of these customers receive at least one pay cable service.

Today, one company dominates the business—Time Warner Inc. The acquisition of Warner Communications by Time Inc. in 1989 created the world's largest international media conglomerate. Each company a media giant in its own right, the deal united Warner's strength in products to Time's channels in depth. Warner was a diversified, vertically integrated company engaged in recorded music, the production and distribution of film and television programming, and publishing. In addition to a long list of music stars, major Hollywood films, and hit television shows, Warner owned the distribution systems associated with each of its product lines, including Warner Cable Communications, the nation's fifth largest cable operator, with 1.5 million subscribers.

Time, first and foremost, owned Home Box Office, which operated the HBO and Cinemax cable channels. HBO, the largest pay cable service in the country, was sold to seven thousand cable systems; Cinemax, the third largest pay cable service, was sold to five thousand systems. To assure itself a steady stream of product, HBO had integrated upstream, to become the largest financier of motion pictures in the world. In addition to financing scores of independent productions, HBO had interests in Tri-Star Pictures and Orion Pictures. At the distribution level, HBO integrated horizontally by buying into Turner Broadcasting System, Cable News Network, and Black Entertainment Television. And lastly, HBO integrated downstream to the consumer level through its connection with the Time-owned American Television and Communications, the second largest cable multiple systems operator (MSO) in the country, with 4 million basic subscribers.

Viacom, HBO's principal competitor, operates the second and fourth largest pay TV services, Showtime and The Movie Channel, which have a combined market share of around 25 percent, compared to HBO's 58 percent. In addition to its premium services, Viacom owns basic cable services such as MTV Networks, Nickelodeon, and Lifetime, as well as a controlling interest in the tenth largest MSO in the country. To strengthen its position in the wake of the Time-Warner merger, Viacom joined forces with Tele-Communications Inc., the largest cable operator in the country, which bought a 50 percent interest in Showtime.

Seven other premium services constitute the remainder of the market, among them The Disney Channel, American Movie Classics, The Playboy Channel, and Bravo. Each specializes in certain types of films—family, classics, sex, and art—and target different audiences. As a group, the "seven dwarfs," as they are called, have 5 million subscribers, about the same as Showtime alone.

The key to HBO's success was its decision to finance feature film production. Since the Hollywood majors released only around 120 films a year, not nearly enough to fill HBO's demands, the company instituted the "pre-buy" in 1977. Instead of buying pay cable rights to a movie from a studio after the picture was made, HBO figured it would be cheaper to buy the rights from the producer before filming started. In a pre-buy, HBO typically put up 25 percent of the negative cost and in return acquired the exclusive cable rights to the picture and a share of the profits.

By forging partnerships with dozens of filmmakers and producers, HBO became a force to be reckoned with. Suddenly, the majors found themselves isolated "upstream" as product suppliers forced to deal with a highly concentrated distribution medium. As distributors of motion pictures in the theatrical market, the majors collected around fifty cents from each box office dollar. As producers of motion pictures for premium cable services, they collected an average of only 20 cents from each subscriber dollar. The difference in earnings resided in HBO's and Showtime's position as distributors, which enabled them to pocket a share of the take as distribution fees.

In her analysis of the film industry's response to remedy the situation, Michele Hilmes explains how other new television technologies, particularly home video, came to Hollywood's rescue (see chapter 10).[1] By making it possible for consumers to enjoy recent, uninterrupted films in the home even earlier than before, home video neutralized pay cable's clear product differentiation and thereby broke its hold on Hollywood.

Home Video

Although home video hit the market on the heels of pay cable, it did not become a force until the eighties. After nearly a decade of announcements and false starts by one U.S. company or another, Sony, the Japanese electronics giant, started the home video revolution by introducing the Betamax video tape recorder to the American consumer market in early 1976. Matsushita, a Japanese firm several times larger than Sony, introduced its VHS (for "video home system") recorder in 1977. Normally, Sony and Matsushita cross-licensed recorded and playback equipment, but for the home video market, the two Japanese companies went their separate ways by introducing systems that were incompatible. The VHS system used a cassette larger than Sony's Betamax and could record up to four hours, compared to Betamax's two.

Sony had originally promoted the Betamax on its ability to "time shift" programming—that is, to record a program off the air even while watching another show on a different channel. MCA, the highly successful Hollywood motion picture and television producer, and Walt

Disney Productions sought to stop the sale of Betamax machines by charging Sony with copyright infringement. The case was instituted in the Los Angeles federal court in November 1976. Sony believed the right of a consumer to record programs for his own use in his own home was absolute. It drew an analogy to the audio cassette recorder, which was introduced in the sixties and had made music tapers out of millions of American teenagers. Although the practice had not been tested in the courts, Sony believed a tradition had been established.

The rationale of MCA and Disney was ostensibly to protect film and television properties from unauthorized mass duplication and distribution. MCA may have also wanted to prevent Betamax from capturing a large segment of the market before MCA could start selling its DiscoVision laser disc system, which was to be test-marketed in the fall of 1977.

Handing down its decision in October 1979, the federal court ruled against MCA and Disney, stating that taping off air for entertainment or time shifting constituted fair use; that copying an entire program also qualified as fair use; that manufacturers could profit from the sale of VCRs; and that the plaintiffs did not prove that any of the above constituted economic harm to the industry. These rulings pertained to the court's interpretation of fair use as a concept of copyright. Equally important to home video dealers, the court let stand the First Sale Doctrine of the 1976 Copyright Act. The doctrine stated that the first purchaser of a copyrighted work (for example, a motion picture on videocassette) could use it in any way the purchaser saw fit as long as copyright was not violated by illegal duplication. This right extended to the rental of videocassettes purchased from Hollywood studios.

Until the arrival of the VCR, the majors had received a cut of the box office or a fee each time one of their films was shown. As the holder of copyright on their pictures, the studios were entitled by law to this remuneration. Since the First Sale Doctrine threatened to undermine Hollywood's control over its product, MCA appealed the case.

Originally, the majors believed that the only logical way to market videocassettes was direct sales, reasoning that the American consumer wanted to buy and "library" cassettes in much the same way as record albums. However, the average consumer preferred to rent titles from video and convenience stores. As the situation stood, a studio received only a tiny percentage of the rental revenues from one of its pictures. After purchasing a cassette for around $40 wholesale, a video store owner could rent it scores of times at, say, $2 to $5 a transaction. In contrast, the studio's profit would be small, less than $10 after materials, duplication, and distribution costs had been covered.

Hearing the *Betamax* case, the U.S. Court of Appeals reversed the lower court's decision in October 1981. But by then, the law was impossible to enforce. Since the start of the case five years earlier, the videocassette market had expanded enormously. VCR sales had increased from thirty thousand a year in 1976 to 1.4 million a year in 1981. More than six Japanese manufacturers had entered the business, both in their own names and as suppliers of machines to U.S. firms. In the interim, VHS had overtaken Beta as the preferred format for home video. The price of machines, which started out at around thirteen hundred dollars, had dropped by more than half and was still falling. Said James Lardner, "Not since the advent of color television had an appliance that cost so much sold so well, and the numbers fired the consumer-electronics industry with the hope that the VCR, like color TV, would become part of the standard equipment of middle-class American life."[2]

The *Betamax* case went all the way to the Supreme Court, which reversed the appeals court decision in January 1984. VCRs had been installed in 15 percent of American homes; by 1986, the percentage reached 50 percent and for the first time, the revenue from the sale of videocassettes equaled the box office gross. In its struggle with retailers to capture a dominant share of the market, the industry formulated a satisfactory policy for its software. As Bruce Austin explains in chapter 11, the majors introduced a two-tiered pricing policy. For the first six months after a new title went on sale, it would be priced relatively high on the assumption that the overwhelming majority of transactions would consist of sales to video stores for rental purposes. Then, as demand began to ebb, the same movie would be reissued at a much lower price to stimulate home sales. The majors used similar strategies overseas to dominate home video markets there as well.

For a while it seemed that home video rentals and sales would undermine pay TV's revenue base by skimming off its higher-value customers. But by making thousands of movie titles available on videocassette, the majors provided the necessary product diversity to differentiate home video from both the theatrical and pay TV markets, assuring optimum potential income from all sources. The tremendous revenues generated by the home video market had a significant effect on production. For the majors, home video has eased the burden of financing: a hit Hollywood film can earn at least $10 million from cassette sales worldwide, while an average entry might garner from $4 to $5 million. For independent producers, home video provided a godsend. Competition for product became so intense that independents could sell home video rights market by market to finance their pictures. This easy availability of funds created a boom in independent production during the eighties, as will be explained later.

Video Discs

The videocassette had the home video market pretty much to itself until RCA introduced its Selectavision videodisc player in 1982. Selectavision utilized the capacitance electronic disc—that is, a "needle-in-the-groove"—system that was simple to play. One merely had to insert the disc with the plastic sleeve still on, remove the sleeve, and press a button. This simplicity of design was supposed to differentiate Selectavision from the more complicated-to-operate VCR and attract a different buyer. RCA executives theorized that if the typical VCR owner was male, single, in his thirties, and earned over thirty thousand dollars a year, the average videodisc buyer would be a typical network-TV viewer with a family and moderate income, and fairly unsophisticated in things technological. Since the RCA discs were relatively inexpensive—around $25 each—consumers were supposed to buy them in much the same way as record albums. Years in development and devouring an investment of more than $200 million, Selectavision was RCA's biggest gamble in consumer electronics since color TV.

MCA's DiscoVision system, introduced in 1978, was the second videodisc system to hit the market. Jointly developed by MCA and N.V. Philips, a European-based manufacturing company, DiscoVision utilized a reflective laser optical—that is, laser disc—system that offered a top-quality picture, stereophonic sound, random access, and freeze frame, among other features. Pioneer and Magnavox manufactured the machines, which sold for half again as much as the RCA models.

Most industry insiders believed that VCRs and videodisc players could coexist, with the VCR used only to record programming off of television and the videodisc player used for showing prerecorded programming. Discs were cheaper to manufacture than cassettes at first and had better image and sound quality. In responding to the programming needs of the VCR and videodisc ventures, Hollywood decided to release their films in all media until the market chose which one would rule.

Although Selectavision, like DiscoVision, did not have the capability to record programming, RCA counted on the price advantage of the disc player and videodisc to carve a niche in the market. RCA's disc players sold for less than videocassette recorders; prerecorded feature films for both the RCA and MCA disc players sold for $24.95, which was less than a blank videocassette when the home video market first opened up. But from the start, consumers felt the ability to record was worth the extra cost. The price advantage enjoyed by the videodisc evaporated with the sudden growth of the rental market.

In 1982, about five thousand video boutiques had sprouted on street corners all over the United States. By 1986, the number of video stores skyrocketed to thirty thousand. RCA lowered the price on its machine from $400 to $350 to $200 to stimulate sales, but the demand was not there. Consumers preferred the flexibility of the VCR. RCA phased out its videodisc operations in April 1984, writing off $175 million on the project. MCA renamed its DiscoVision subsidiary MCA Home Video and went on to become a major force in the videocassette distribution business.

HOLLYWOOD IN THE EIGHTIES

The revenue generated by these new television technologies affected the industry in three important ways: (1) the entrenched companies improved their distribution capabilities to guarantee access to ancillary markets; (2) several smaller companies tried to attain "mini-major" status; and (3) a subindustry consisting of a new generation of independents emerged to fill the maw of the marketplace.

The Majors

The changes in the market had demonstrated to Hollywood the necessity of strengthening its distribution capabilities. The rationale, said financial analyst Harold Vogel, is as follows:

> Ownership of entertainment distribution capability is like ownership of a toll road or a bridge. No matter how good or bad the software product (i.e., movie, record, book, magazine, tv show, or whatever) is, it must pass over or cross through a distribution pipeline in order to reach the consumer. And like at any toll road or bridge that cannot be circumvented, the distributor is a local monopolist who can extract a relatively high fee for use of his facility.[3]

Four companies dominated business during the eighties: Warner Communications, Gulf+Western (Paramount), Disney, and MCA (Universal). The history of these companies reveals how they protected their entrenched positions while assuring themselves access to all the turnpikes and bridges.

Warner Communications and Gulf+Western (Paramount), perennially two of the strongest companies in the industry, responded decisively to the market by "downsizing" their operations to focus on a select group of core activities. Typical of U.S. business during the sixties and seventies, Warner and Gulf+Western expanded aggressively to become conglomerates engaged in a wide array of businesses. Gulf+Western, for example, became a textbook case of conglomeratization. Starting out solely as a manufacturer of bumpers for cars and trucks, it embarked on an expansion program in 1957 that took it into sugar, zinc, fertilizer, wire and cable, musical instruments, real estate, and motion pictures. By 1968, Gulf+Western owned 67 companies with assets of $2.8 billion.

If Gulf+Western was an example of a conglomerate that contained a composite of companies whose products and markets were unrelated, Warner Communications (WCI) was classified as a product extension type of conglomerate, in that its subsidiaries were functionally related but dealt in products that did not compete with one another. Its principal areas of activity were grouped around recorded music and music publishing, film entertainment, publishing, cable communications, toys and electronic games, and other operations.

By the eighties, this form of conglomerate business structure became too unwieldy to manage in any rational way. The turning point in WCI's operations occurred during the Christmas of 1982, when the company was inundated by returns of unsold Atari video games. Overnight, the video game business had collapsed, leaving the company with a huge $310 million loss. Subsequently, WCI decided to restructure its operations to take advantage of the new distribution technologies. Sold were Atari, Warner Cosmetics, Franklin Mint, Panavision, the New York Cosmos soccer team, and Warner's cable programming interests, including MTV and Nickelodeon. (In several cases, WCI retained partial interests in the former subsidiaries as investments.)

The "downsized" WCI became a well-diversified vertically integrated company engaged in three sectors of entertainment: (1) production and distribution of film and television programming; (2) recorded music; and (3) publishing. Diversification provided protection from the volatility associated with hits and flops; it also enabled the company to meet increased international demand for film and television programming, compact disc digital recordings, and cable TV. To position itself to meet the future, WCI bought out American Express's half interest in Warner Amex Cable, the sixth largest cable system in the country, and rewired and upgraded the system to make it addressable. Should pay-per-view, television's newest delivery system, make it, Warner planned to be there. And finally, WCI added considerable muscle to its distribution capability when it merged with Time Inc. in 1989.

In downsizing, WCI has remained a product-extension conglomerate. Downsizing for Gulf+Western meant creating a new identity. When Gulf+Western acquired Paramount in 1966, entertainment played a minor role in the conglomerate's activities. By the eighties, entertainment accounted for over a third of its total operating income. For the second year running, Paramount in 1987 had captured the largest share of the domestic box office, distributing such blockbusters as *Top Gun, Crocodile Dundee, Star Trek IV, Beverly Hills Cop II, The Untouchables, Fatal Attraction,* and *Planes, Trains. . . .* Paramount Home Video had captured the largest share of the home video market by selling nearly 14 million cassettes. Six Paramount titles ranked among the top ten best-selling cassettes of all time. Paramount Television had seven series on network TV, which included "Cheers" and "Family Ties," seven series on first-run syndication, and one on pay cable. Paramount Television also strengthened its competitive position in TV by acquiring a 50 percent partnership in USA Network, one of the top three advertiser-supported basic cable services. Strengthening its position in the entertainment sector further, Gulf+Western, which already owned the second largest circuit in Canada (Famous Players), spent close to $300 million to acquire several theater chains in the United States.

Meanwhile, Gulf+Western had shed more than 50 companies and had restructured its operation with the goal of becoming a global communications and entertainment giant. Capping its efforts in 1989, Gulf and Western changed its name to Paramount Communications Inc. and attempted to acquire Warner Communications. Warner successfully fought off the takeover attempt, and its merger with Time proceeded on course. Paramount Communications' operations thereafter consisted of two divisions: (1) entertainment, consisting of Paramount Pictures, Madison Square Garden, and motion picture chains; and (2) publishing and information, consisting essentially of Simon & Schuster, the nation's largest book publisher, and other trade and educational book publishing units.

Walt Disney Co., another perennial industry leader, adopted yet a different strategy. Going into the eighties, Disney had built an entertainment empire based on the family trade. Disney achieved the status of a motion picture major after switching from animation to live-action documentaries and features in 1953. Disney had the savvy to diversify into television and leisure time early and by the sixties, had carved a special niche for itself in the market. Becoming a broad-based entertainment-recreation company enabled Disney to get through the

1969 recession unscathed. Films accounted for only about one-third of Disney's business. About half of the company's revenues and a whopping 60 percent of profits came from Disneyland. The balance came from other entertainment activities, such as television, music and records, publications, and character merchandising—such as Mickey Mouse watches. Disney had demonstrated that diversification could stabilize the traditionally precarious motion picture business.

Producing wholesome family entertainment was no longer a viable idea for the eighties. Disney had churned out too many box office bombs, saw its revenues from Disneyland and Disney World leveling off, discovered that the growth rate of the Disney Channel, its new pay TV service, would be lower than anticipated, and suffered the indignity of having its lone television series, the hour-long "Walt Disney," canceled by CBS, leaving the company without a regular network show for the first time in 29 years. The only bright spot was Disney's film vault, which contained a treasure trove of animated classics such as *Snow White*, *Dumbo*, and *Pinnochio* that could be reissued to successive generations of youngsters.

In an attempt to get with it, Disney began making movies for adult audiences under the Touchstone label. Touchstone's first picture, *Splash* (1984), starring Daryl Hannah, was a hit, but the effort came too late to prevent an assault on the entrenched management, led by Disney's nephew, Roy E. Disney. The battle entailed a takeover attempt, greenmail, and lawsuits; the ouster of the old regime; and the installation of a new management team headed by Michael Eisner.

The philosophy, strategy, and scope of the company changed under the new management. Disney buttressed its theme park operations by building a $2 billion theme park in France and adding attractions to Disneyland in California and Disney World in Florida. The company also branched out into retailing to sell a plethora of Disney-brand merchandise. But the most successful strategy was to become a motion picture heavyweight. Disney doubled its film output to around 13 a year and aimed at the young adult audience. To hedge its bets, the studio kept production costs down in the beginning and looked for gifted but out-of-favor actors whose services could be secured inexpensively. By 1986, the new regime had turned the company around. As a result of a string of hits that included *Down and Out in Beverly Hills, Ruthless People, Three Men and a Baby, Stakeout* and *Who Framed Roger Rabbit?*, Disney became firmly ensconced at the top, capturing an incredible 20 percent share of the domestic theatrical market in 1988.

Of the top-tier companies, MCA's growth has been less impressive. Going into the eighties, MCA consistently captured a substantial share of the theatrical rentals. In 1982, MCA's *E.T. the Extra-Terrestrial* broke the seemingly unbreakable record set by Twentieth Century–Fox's *Star Wars* to become the all-time domestic rentals champ. On the strength of this picture, the company placed first in domestic rentals for the third time in ten years, which set another industry record. Television production and distribution also continued to prosper. Year in and year out, MCA's remarkably stable television operations traditionally accounted for over a quarter of the company's revenues. In 1985, MCA had more network prime-time shows on the air than any other rival. Among them were "Magnum P.I.," "Miami Vice," and "Murder She Wrote."

Afterward, MCA's track record declined; by 1987, the company's share of the U.S. box office amounted to only 8 percent. MCA saw its share of the television market shrink as stations stopped buying one-hour action programs—MCA's strength—in favor of half-hour comedies. And because MCA's recent releases contained few hits, the company could not count on sales of older films to home video. The one glaring exception was *E.T.*, which sold 15 million units on a sell-through basis in 1988.

Reacting to its decreasing share of the entertainment markets, MCA started on an acquisitions binge in 1985. In two years, the company invested $650 million to acquire toy companies, music companies, a major independent television station, and a half interest in a giant theater chain. The diversification strategy was designed to strengthen MCA's existing positions and to extend the company into contiguous businesses. The purchase of New York station WOR-TV, for example, was to ensure that MCA's old shows got on the air in the largest television market in the country. The acquisition of LJN Toys, Ltd., which MCA considered another leisure-time business, was to give MCA the capability of manufacturing and marketing toy lines tied in with its movies.

Of all its investments, the one showing the most promise is its venture to develop a $500 million studio and tour facility called Universal Studios, Florida in Orlando, near Disney World. Scheduled to open in May 1990, the facility is being counted on to repeat the success of the highly profitable Universal studio tour in Hollywood. If it doesn't, MCA might become a likely candidate for a merger.

The second tier of the majors consists of MGM/UA, Twentieth Century–Fox, and Columbia Pictures. Once the mightiest studios in Hollywood, MGM and United Artists became mere shadows of their former selves. Going into the eighties, the two companies were under the control of Kirk Kerkorian. Kerkorian's strategy, if it can be called that, was to sell and then buy back studio assets. Kerkorian made fortunes in the process, but he never succeeded in restoring the glory of those two great names.

After the 1969 recession, Kerkorian tried to revive MGM by getting back into distribution. As pointed out earlier, the company had dismantled its distribution arm during the recession as a cost-saving measure and in 1973, signed a ten-year pack with United Artists to handle its pictures. Believing that the risks of motion picture production had been minimized by the new television technologies, MGM acquired United Artists from Transamerica for $185 million in 1981 and formed a new company, MGM/UA Entertainment Company. The sale of UA to MGM was the end result of the resignation of UA's top management in 1978 in protest over Transamerica's administrative policies. Humiliated by the stunning failure of Michael Cimino's *Heaven's Gate*, which lost practically all of its $44 million investment, and by the inability of UA's new management to contain the runaway costs of the picture, Transamerica decided to get out of the motion picture business.

Despite the efforts of several management teams, MGM/UA never really got off the ground, but Kerkorian scored a coup in 1985 by selling the MGM film library, studio, and film lab, among other properties, to Atlanta broadcaster Ted Turner for over $1.5 billion. As a result of the increasing globalization of show business, Kerkorian nearly scored an even greater coup in 1989 when Christopher Skase and his Qintex Australia Ltd. offered more than $1.5 billion in cash for the remaining assets of MGM/UA. This deal would have marked the second sale of a major Hollywood studio to an Australian media giant, but the takeover collapsed when Skase failed to secure the financing. MGM/UA thereafter was left with "no throw," which in industry jargon meant no viable projects remaining in its development pipeline.

Twentieth Century–Fox's strategy has been nothing less than to challenge the three entrenched television networks by creating a full-blown fourth TV network. The audacity and the money behind this move belongs to media mogul Rupert Murdoch, head of Australia's News Corporation. The owner of newspapers and magazines in Australia, Great Britain, and the United States, Murdoch decided not to move directly into the television industry, but rather into television's source of programming, Hollywood. Murdoch had lost an earlier battle to take over Warner Communications in 1983, but his second foray into Hollywood succeeded. Under the sole ownership of Denver oilman Martin Davis, Twentieth Century–Fox had fallen on hard times. Although Fox had become a more aggressive player under Davis, forming a joint venture with CBS called CBS/Fox, an alliance that became the leading home video supplier in the country, and selling more series to network television than any other Hollywood studio in 1983, the studio lost $189 million from 1982 to 1985, the result of a dreary parade of box office bombs, and was forced to retrench.

In 1985, Murdoch bought a half interest in Twentieth Century–Fox for $250 million. Within weeks, Murdoch and Davis bought Metromedia Television, the nation's largest group of independent television stations, for $2 billion. The owner of six stations in top markets, the Metromedia group reached nearly 20 percent of U.S. television households. (In order to comply with FCC regulations governing the ownership of TV stations, Murdoch became a U.S. citizen.) A few months later, Murdoch bought out Davis's half interest in Twentieth Century–Fox for $325 million. Murdoch was then ready to create his television network, called Fox Broadcasting. After waging a three-year battle that cost hundreds of millions of dollars, Fox finally turned the corner in 1989. The details of this venture are described in a subsequent section.

In purchasing Columbia Pictures in 1982 for $700 million, Coca-Cola's goal was to introduce modern, scientific marketing techniques to the motion picture business, techniques that made Coke the leading soft drink brand in the country. In Coke's view, motion picture marketing had not progressed much beyond the "tush test" of the studio's founder, Harry Cohn, who measured the entertainment potential of a picture by its ability to mask any discomforts of sitting. Taking its cue from the consumer package industry, Coke monitored the effectiveness of Columbia's TV ads, tested consumer reaction to the basic ideas behind those ads, and experimented with pretesting script ideas.

To secure more shelf space for its pictures, which is to say more theater bookings, Coke created a new brand in 1982: Tri-Star Pictures. A joint venture of Columbia, HBO, and CBS, Tri-Star's goal was to produce a steady flow of movies that would be distributed to theaters by Columbia, to pay TV by HBO, and to network television by CBS. The venture was thought to create advantages for Columbia far beyond more theater bookings; the synergy generated by the interaction of the three companies was supposed to maximize revenues from all three markets.

In addition to forming Tri-Star Pictures, Coke invested in Weintraub Entertainment Group and purchased two television companies—Embassy Communications in 1985 and Merv Griffin Enterprises in 1987. Weintraub was the producer of such hits as *The Karate Kid* films, *Oh God!*, and *Diner*; Embassy owned an important feature film and television library; and Merv Griffin produced several of the top-rated game shows for first-run syndication.

Columbia's performance exceeded expectations, but its profits came from the syndication of its old movies and TV programs and not from new programming. Following Coke's philosophy with soft drinks, Columbia stepped up production from around 12 to 18 pictures a year. This frenetic production schedule resulted in a few hits early on—*Tootsie, Ghostbusters,* and *The Karate Kid Part II*—but after 1984, Columbia's share of the box office remained the same, just under 10 percent, or slightly below the average of its competitors. The strain on Columbia's creative resources was apparent as the company went through three management teams in as many years.

Tri-Star Pictures did not perform much better. To launch the company, the three partners put up a total of $100 million. Although the venture was designed to benefit each partner, it did not work out that way. Tri–Star released only two hits—*Rambo: First Blood Part II* and *The Natural.* Columbia earned back its investment in the company by collecting its distribution fees, but Tri-Star's pictures had lost much of their value to pay TV and network television. To recoup their investments, CBS sold its shares to Columbia in 1985 and HBO sold half its shares to the studio the following year.

Now befuddled by the motion picture business, Coca-Cola subsumed all of its production ventures, including Tri-Star, into a new entertainment subsidiary called Columbia Pictures Entertainment in 1987. Columbia "bumped along on a downhill path," in *Variety's* words, and experienced frequent management turnover. In 1989, just two weeks after Australia's Qintex offered to buy MGM/UA, Coca-Cola accepted a $3.4 billion bid from Japan's Sony Corporation to buy the troubled studio.

Sony entered the entertainment software business in 1987 when it purchased CBS Records for $2 billion. Branching out to records and motion pictures vertically integrated the consumer electronics giant by giving Sony sources of programming and the mechanism for distributing the programming. In so doing, Sony acquired a means of promoting the 8-millimeter video and high-definition television systems it had in development. Giving Columbia the management clout to regain its place as a Hollywood major, Sony hired producers Peter Guber and Jon Peters as cochairmen of the studio. The price tag for this decision cost Sony close to $1 billion, broken down as follows: $260 million to acquire the Guber-Peters Entertainment Co. and $500 to $700 million to buy out the contract Guber-Peters had with Warner Communications.

The Mini-Majors

The mini-majors consisted of Orion Pictures Corporation, the Cannon Group, and Dino De Laurentiis Entertainment Group. The financial underpinnings of all three companies rested on their ability to finance pictures by preselling the distribution rights to ancillary markets before production began.

Orion Pictures, the most successful of the group, was formed in 1978 by a management team that formerly headed United Artists. With backing from Warburg, Pincus, a Wall Street investment firm, and HBO, Orion's goal was to produce around 15 quality pictures a year. To minimize risks, the company made presale arrangements with HBO for pay TV, with RCA/Columbia for foreign home video rights, and with distributors overseas for foreign theatrical distribution rights. Concerning the latter, Orion figured the only way to compete with the majors, who had international distribution systems, was to created long-term relationships with distributors in foreign markets who would be willing to contract for Orion's full line-up. Money advanced from these sources covered the costs of every picture Orion produced in 1985.

Orion made it big in 1986 when three of its pictures received 18 Academy Award nominations—more than any other studio. These pictures—Oliver Stone's *Platoon*, Woody Allen's *Hannah and Her Sisters*, and *Hoosiers*—helped the company capture the biggest share of the theatrical market in 1987.

To stabilize its operations, Orion formed a subsidiary in 1986 to market its own pictures to home video. The company also branched out into television production and financed the extremely successful "Cagney and Lacey" series. And Orion aggressively entered the art film market by forming Orion Classics. Since foreign films could be picked up at low prices in the current market, the company started releasing one picture a month. By carefully handling these pictures, Orion planned to make a profit and maybe find a sleeper. Orion Classics found its first in 1986, Stephen Frear's *My Beautiful Laundrette*. Of the three mini-majors, Orion is the best managed and stands a good chance of carving a niche in the market.

Cannon has had a rockier history. In 1979, Cannon was a minor independent when Menahem Golan and Yoram Globus, two little-known Israeli filmmakers, took over the company. Cannon's revenue that year added up to a mere $1.8 million; in 1985, the year that its star shined brightest, revenues surpassed $150 million. Golan and Globus started out producing low-budget films for drive-ins, grind houses, and large multiplexes—"Cannon fodder," as they were known to the trade. Cannon's success, however, rested on their ability to trade successfully in the international marketplace, where scores of small distributors who were cut off from U.S. motion pictures were hungry for product.

In order to presell its output in foreign territories, Cannon churned out as many as 40 films a year that contained plenty of sex, action, and known actors. To minimize the risks to distributors who would be buying its pictures blind, Cannon kept production costs to around $5 million. Cannon claimed to have secured 85 percent of a picture's costs prior to completion of principal photography and to have made a profit by the time the production opened—all from presales.

To upgrade its product, Cannon started hiring major stars and directors in 1981. This strategy paid off when Cannon released *Death Wish II* in 1982, starring Charles Bronson. Containing almost nonstop violence, this $9 million entry quickly took in $40 million. Cannon's next blockbuster, *Breakin'*, was produced in 1984 and grossed $36 million on an investment of $1.3 million. During the eighties, a veritable constellation of stars worked for Cannon, including Katharine Hepburn, Faye Dunaway, Sean Connery, Roger Moore, and John Gielgud. The directors on Cannon's roster included Boaz Davidson, J. Lee Thompson, Menahem Golan, Michael Winner, and Tobe Hooper.

Flush with hits, Cannon was able to raise huge sums for expansion from Wall Street and European banks. To assure its films adequate exhibition, Cannon acquired theaters in Great Britain, the Netherlands, Italy, Austria, as well as the United States. Cannon also acquired production and distribution facilities abroad, to become a giant multinational conglomerate by 1986.

But the roof fell in when the Securities and Exchange Commission, which regulates the U.S. stock-market, launched an investigation of Cannon's accounting practices. Forced to issue a revised and corrected balance sheet, Cannon now reported large operating losses. Cannon nearly went under as its stock plummeted. After a life-saving infusion from Italian investors Giancarlo Parretti and Florio Fiorini, Cannon righted itself. By selling off its unprofitable assets and by retrenching, Cannon attempted to make a fresh start. However, in the restructuring, Golan and Globus lost control of the company. Today, Cannon is part of the European-based media enterprises headed by Parretti and Fiorini called Pathe Communications.

De Laurentiis is proof that preselling could not provide an absolute safety net for a fledgling company. The company was formed in 1985 by the expatriate Italian producer Dino De Laurentiis, who transferred his movie-making activities to the United States when the Italian film industry suffered a severe recession in the seventies. De Laurentiis operated out of Wilmington, North Carolina, where he had built a 16-acre studio. To acquire a film library and a distribution capability, De Laurentiis bought Embassy Pictures for $35 million. Then, with the proceeds from a public stock offering, the company started in on a full slate of pictures. Of the 11 pictures produced in 1986, only 1,

Crimes of the Heart, grossed over $10 million. Deeply in debt from the start, De Laurentiis was forced to sell its film library and other assets, streamline its operations, and ultimately file for protection from bankruptcy in 1988.

Independents

A new breed of independent producers entered the market during the 1980s, drawn by the growth of pay cable and home video, a sharp increase in the number of theater screens in the United States, and a cutback in production by the majors. Cannon and New World Pictures stood at the top of the independent ranks, with the former attaining mini-major status. These two firms released 20 films a year and more. The rest of the field consisted of scores of outfits that released from one to ten pictures a year. In this group were such firms as Atlantic Releasing, Samuel Goldwyn, Troma, Island Alive, Vestron, and New Line. Unlike the independents that populated Hollywood in the 1950s and 1960s, this new generation of independents did not receive any financial backing from the major studios and worked outside the mainstream. As a group, independents produced from two to three hundred pictures annually since the 1970s, which accounted for 50 to 70 percent of the industry's total output.

The opportunity provided by ancillary markets to presell pictures launched the independent effort of the 1980s. More than any other strategy, preselling was the most effective way to minimize risks. The practice entailed the selling of distribution rights to pay cable, home video, syndicated television, and foreign markets as soon as possible, even before shooting began.

Pay cable, with its four national movie channels operating around the clock, created an enormous demand for fresh material. The sale of pay cable rights yielded anywhere from a few hundred thousand dollars to a million and more. Although these sums were insignificant compared to what a Hollywood blockbuster could fetch, such ancillary income for a low-budget picture might make the difference between profit and loss. And deals could be struck even for pictures that received little or no theatrical exposure. In fact, pay cable companies started financing made-for-cable pictures that would be released theatrically only in foreign markets.

After pay cable reached a plateau, home video took off and provided independents another shot in the arm. Home video rights typically yielded 25 percent of the production costs; some projects received total financing. For those companies that came up with hits,

he home video proved extremely lucrative. For example, several of
New Line's cult favorites, among them Tobe Hooper's *The Texas
Chainsaw Massacre*, John Waters's *Pink Flamingos* and *Polyester*, and the
Nightmare on Elm Street series, sold over seven hundred thousand units
n the home video market.

Independent productions had only one thing in common—low
:ost. Whereas the typical budget for a Hollywood picture ranged from
;12 to $20 million, a typical independent feature cost well under $1
nillion on the average and utilized small crews (nonunion), light-weight
:quipment, direct sound, location shooting, and often nonprofessional
ictors. The most popular genres in descending order of box office per-
ormance from 1970 to 1983 were horror, drama, action, teen comedies,
locumentary, adventure, science fiction, and Western.

Among the independents, Samuel Z. Arkoff's American International Pictures (AIP) set the pace. The dominant independent
distributor of the 1970s, AIP distributed 64 pictures that earned more
han $1 million in domestic rentals. Among them were *The Amityville
Horror* (1979), $35 million; *Love at First Bite* (1979), $21 million; *Born
Losers* (1974), $12.5 million; *Walking Tall, Part Two* (1975), $9.5 million;
ind *Macon County Line* (1974), $9 million.

Picking up where AIP left off, independents of the eighties carved
a niche for themselves in the youth market using various strategies.
Typically, independents minimized risks with time-honored techniques such as producing sequels and remakes, distributing B pictures
nade by outside producers, and by preselling the ancillary rights to
heir pictures. They also specialized in one or maybe two genres.
3y specializing, producers could target their audience and exploit
hose ingredients of a proven formula that would guarantee at least
a modest return on the investment. Crown International's forte, for
:xample, was teenage sex comedy. *The Pom Pom Girls* (1977), Crown's
>reakthrough picture, grossed $7.5 million and spawned such pictures
is *Coach* (1979), *Don't Answer the Phone* (1980), and *My Tutor* (1983). Troma
specialized in horror films for pay cable and home video. In 1985 Troma
·eleased its biggest hit, *The Toxic Avenger*. Roger Ebert called it the worst
novie ever made, but it went on to become a cult classic.[4]

A shakeout in the independent market occurred in the late eighties
is many small independent producers went bankrupt. The lure of
>resales had created a product glut. From 1984 to 1987, annual output of
he mini-majors and independents grew by nearly a hundred pictures,
:ausing a logjam at the exhibition level. Marginal films—those judged
inlikely to recoup print and advertising costs—were shelved; others
were lucky if they got any playing time. Without national exposure
>r a theatrical run, few films found takers in the ancillary markets.

To get national exposure, a picture had to open in New York and be reviewed favorably. Because this meant going up against the majors, independents were forced to spend more on advertising for a longer period of time. Few firms had the muscle to pull this off.

CONTEMPORARY EXHIBITION

After the economic advantages of the multiplex were recognized, national and regional theater chains and independent theaters got on the bandwagon. The number of screens grew slowly but steadily, from 12,652 in 1963 to 13,750 in 1970; afterward the pace picked up, until today there are over 24,000 screens in the country. Because auditoriums in multiplex theaters are relatively small and because much of the multiplexing is the result of subdividing older theaters, the overall number of seats has increased only slightly.

The chains that pulled exhibition out of its slump were not the former affiliated circuits but the rising stars of the business, such as General Cinema, United Artists Theatre Circuit, Plitt Theaters, and American Multi-Cinema. The *Paramount* decrees severely restricted the ability of the former affiliated circuits to meet the dynamic changes in the exhibition market; these circuits "could acquire theaters to replace those that they sold after divestiture, but could not acquire new theaters unless they could convince the district court that the acquisition would not unduly restrain competition," said Michael Conant.[5] Any plans of the affiliated circuits to follow the demographic trend and expand into the suburban shopping centers were thus stymied. The old chains declined, as a result, as the downtowns of the major cities where most of their theaters were located decayed.

Although the names of the major players have changed, the exhibition market is still dominated by a few national chains. The top chains, such as United Artists Theatres, Cineplex Odeon, General Cinema, and American Multi-Cinemas, control nine thousand screens, or about a third of the total. However, in terms of clout, these same chains take in over 85 percent of the total box office.

The most dynamic company of the group is Cineplex Odeon. A Toronto-based theater chain headed by Nat Taylor and Garth H Drabinsky, Cineplex Odeon has grown through mergers and new construction to become the second largest chain in the United States, after United Artists Theatres. As described by Douglas Gomery in chapter 13, the key to Taylor and Drabinsky's success was the policy of upgrading the quality of the movie-going experience. Cineplex started out by creating "film bazaars"—theaters containing blocks of up to 20 screens, usually situated in upscale urban shopping malls across Canada. The strategy was to create a mall-within-a-mall that allowed people to browse and sometimes make impulse purchases, just like they did in stores. However, unlike the multiplexes that had sprung up during the sixties, these film bazaars contained all the creature comforts, including elegant interiors, comfortable seats, and quality concessions.

Cineplex entered the U.S. market in 1982 by acquiring the Los Angeles–based Plitt Theatres, consisting of three hundred theaters formerly belonging to ABC Television and the New York–based RKO theater chain, consisting of nearly a hundred screens, in addition to other chains. In less than a decade, Cineplex Odeon had become a leading force in exhibition in the North American market.

During the eighties, the exhibition market stabilized; each year, exhibitors sell around 1 billion tickets and the total box office revenue in constant dollars has stayed around $2 billion. Yet the number of screens has surged by over 20 percent since 1980, to an estimated 21,500 by 1986. Where the norm in the seventies was the quad-,6-, and even 10-plex theater, in the eighties it became 16 or more screens under one roof. The rationale for this seemingly irrational growth was this: the more screens in a single setting, the better chance the exhibitor has of booking a hit film. A "risk-reward ratio" implies that the greater the exposure in the market, the more predictable the earnings.

Although new theater construction continued apace during the eighties, the future of exhibition was assured ironically enough by new forms of competition. Observers at one time predicted that home video and pay TV would kill the conventional theater. But, on the contrary, the new ancillary markets generated increased interest in the movies. Because the demand for more films was met by the majors and a growing number of independents, theaters enjoyed not only a larger picture selection, but also an enhanced status in the distribution chain. In the minds of consumers, the success of a film on the big screen determined its value on pay TV and home video.

The vitality of the theatrical market, coupled with the relaxed regulatory environment of the Reagan administration, drew the major motion picture companies back into exhibition, reversing the intent of the 1948 *Paramount* decrees. MCA started the trend in 1986 when it bought a 49 percent share of Cineplex Odeon (1,880 screens in 1989). Today, in addition, Columbia Pictures owns Loew's Theaters (839 screens), and Paramount Communications, in partnership with Time Warner, owns the Mann, Festival, and Trans-Lux chains (466 screens).

According to Wall Street, the majors followed this logic in acquiring theaters: Since only 1 movie out of 20 makes it as a theatrical hit
why not go into exhibition and profit from whatever hit films are ir
release? Although nonaligned chains welcomed the trend, believing
that it underscored the commitment of the majors to the long-term
health of the exhibition business, some observers of the industry are
not as sanguine because of the antitrust implications.

HOLLYWOOD'S RELATIONS WITH TELEVISION

Network Television

ABC, CBS, and NBC continue to dominate commercial television
but their hold on the market has weakened. Before the new technol
ogies, the public's access to programming was restricted pretty much
to what the three networks and PBS proffered; afterward, the public
was presented with a multitude of alternatives, which weakened the
commercial base of commercial television. Helping the process along
was a freer regulatory environment at the federal level.

As waves of viewers defected to cable channels, independent stations, and videocassette recorders, the networks' share of the viewing
audience shrank from 90 percent a decade ago to the 60 percent
range today—a decrease in viewership of around 5 million households
Despite the loss of advertising dollars represented by this audience ero
sion, network television has remained extremely profitable; between
1982 and 1985, the networks actually saw their prime-time revenues
increase 50 percent, from $3 billion to $4.5 billion.

Nonetheless, the competition from the new distribution technol
ogies put enormous pressure on network profitability and on network
managements that were historically unaccustomed to managing in
such a competitive environment. The result has been changes in
ownership or management at all three networks. In 1986, two networks
changed hands: ABC was sold to Capital Cities Communications, and
NBC, along with its parent RCA, was acquired by General Electric
In 1987, managerial control of CBS was turned over to Laurence A
Tisch, the network's largest shareholder. Afterward, all three networks
entered an era of cost-consciousness.

The networks' grip on the TV audience had eased as a result of
heightened competition from three sources—cable television, super
stations, and independent stations. Cable television, the largest source

of competition, developed from a financially shaky, tightly regulated industry to an economic powerhouse during the eighties. The principal causes were the existence of reliable communications satellites that transmitted basic and premium programming to local television systems; the increased availability and variety of programming services; and the relaxation of regulatory restrictions, which permitted the distribution of television signals transmitted from distant cities.

From 1980 to 1989, the number of basic cable television subscribers rose from 15 million to more than 50 million of the nation's 90 million TV homes. Cable subscribers today have access to 30 or more channels of specialized programming. Simultaneously, the number of pay subscribers increased from 5 to over 25 million. Although the growth of pay cable flattened during the mid-eighties, basic cable rebounded by expanding into original and cable-exclusive programming and into pay-per-view.

The second source of competition for the networks was the superstation. The superstation phenomenon began in 1976, when Ted Turner realized that he could turn his fledgling Atlanta television station, now called WTBS, into a national station by feeding cable systems all over the United States. Renting a transponder on SATCOM I, Turner transmitted programming from his independent station to cable systems in distant markets and charged a monthly fee for each subscriber. The Supreme Court ruled on the legality of superstations in 1974 by holding that the broadcast of a program from a distant market is not an infringement of the producer's copyright. In transmitting programming across the country, WTBS originally remitted nothing extra to syndicators, but after the expiration of the contracts, WTBS's payments were adjusted to reflect market coverage.

To provide a ready supply of inexpensive programming for his station, Turner bought the Atlanta Braves baseball team and the Atlanta Hawks basketball team in 1976. He next created the Cable News Network in 1980, a 24-hour news channel, and the Headline News, a spinoff news channel that edits CNN's news footage into compact 30-minute segments.

Then this maverick broadcaster stunned the industry by making a hostile $5.41 billion offer for CBS in 1985. It was an outrageous move because, in essence, Turner attempted to buy a company much larger than his own without using any money, just junk bonds. CBS took him seriously, however, and killed the offer with a $954.8 million stock buyback.

Undaunted, Turner went to Hollywood and made a preemptive bid of $1.5 billion in cash for Kirk Kerkorian's MGM/UA Entertainment. Turner was after not only MGM/UA's film library, the largest in the business, but also both the MGM and United Artists production and distribution companies. But because Turner had trouble raising all the money, he sold back to Kerkorian the United Artists film library and the UA and MGM film companies and auctioned off the MGM studio and film processing lab. At the conclusion of the deal, Turner was left with the entire MGM film library and two smaller pre-1948 libraries from Warner and RKO. (The latter two libraries had come to MGM as part of the United Artists acquisition.)

Although many industry observers thought that Turner had gotten a fleecing, Turner immediately went to work to exploit the film library, which contained cartoons, shorts, and television shows in addition to 3,300 feature films. To ease Turner's debt load and to preserve the independence of one of their major product suppliers, a group of 26 MSOs, led by Time's American Television and Communications, invested $575 million in Turner Broadcasting in 1987. In exchange for the money, the cable operators received broad authority to over-see—and if necessary to veto—the management decisions of Turner Broadcasting System.

Turner gave the cable companies the programming they wanted by launching the TNT channel in October 1988. A basic offering rather than a premium service like HBO and Showtime, TNT prof-fered a steady stream of old movies from the MGM film library. With programming like this, the cable operators hoped to sign up more subscribers. Today, Turner's flagship station WTBS reaches over 38 million homes and is cable's biggest and most profitable advertiser-supported network. Turner's competitors are WGN in Chicago, with over 22 million subscribers, and WOR in New York with over 9 million subscribers.

The third source of competition for the networks was the inde-pendent television station. The number of independent stations more than doubled, rising from 120 in 1980 to 283 in 1987. Virtually all this growth occurred in the UHF spectrum. Before 1980, only the top 20 or 30 cities had independent stations, but afterward independents started up enough markets to reach 75 percent of American homes.

Here again, relaxed regulations played a key role. The FCC's Must Carry rules governing the carriage of local television broadcast signals by cable systems required cable systems to carry every television station within the franchise area regardless of the station's ratings and of whether the station duplicated another network or PBS affiliate. These rules, which expired in 1990, encouraged the start-up of new UHF independent stations, since the owner of a weak-signaled UHF station knew his signal coverage would improve by being carried on the cable system.

The growth of independent stations and the ease of distributing programming by satellite suggested the creation of a fourth network or, stated another way, a large-scale syndication effort that would provide an alternative to network programming. From time to time, loose confederations of affiliated and independent stations financed miniseries to run in place of or in competition with network offerings. But not until Australian publisher Rupert Murdoch formed the Fox Broadcasting Co. (FBC) in 1986 did the fourth network idea pack any punch.

Murdoch set the stage for his assault on the big three in 1985 by purchasing the Metromedia independent station group for $1.55 billion and by acquiring full ownership of Twentieth Century–Fox. With Metromedia as a start, Murdoch assembled a network of more than one hundred independent stations capable of reaching 83 percent of all TV homes. Since CBS reached 99 percent of all TV homes, FBC faced a serious disadvantage in the fight for ratings. Fox, therefore, hoped to improve its chances of spending upward of $80 million to develop counterprogramming aimed at young adults.

FBC began broadcasting in the spring of 1987. Like many previous fourth network tries, it initially limited itself to two nights of prime-time programming—Saturdays and Sundays. In addition, it offered a weeknight strip of "The Late Show Starring Joan Rivers." The programs were distributed by satellite. Given the size of its operations, FBC had to get a national rating of 6 to be profitable. (A rating point represented 874,000 TV homes). A network show, in contrast, has to receive a rating of at least 15 to survive. A phenomenal hit like "Cosby" scored an incredible 36. FBC's Sunday line-up, which launched the network and consisted of five programs, averaged only 3.7 in the ratings; "The Late Show" got a 3.0 in the ratings. Going into the fall 1987 season, Fox scrapped the "Late Show" and cut its weekly prime-time programming in half. Fox Broadcasting lost hundreds of millions of dollars the first three years, but in 1989 it staged a turnaround as a result of two hit series—"America's Most Wanted" and "Married . . . With Children."

Feature Films on Network TV

Network television remained the largest ancillary market for feature films until the eighties. Nearly every night was movie night on prime time. Feature films still meant high ratings and substantial advertising revenues for both the networks and the majors. The average rental fee for features dropped by nearly one-half during the 1969–71 recession because the frank language, violence, and sexual content of the films made them unacceptable for network broadcast. But later, bidding on films soared, and Hollywood saw its annual revenues from the networks rise from $65 million in 1970 to $475 million in 1979.

ABC, in its fight to achieve rating parity with NBC and CBS, led the bidding. ABC went on a five-day, $50 million buying spree during the summer of 1971 to pick up a package of blockbusters that included *Love Story, Lawrence of Arabia, Patton, The Ten Commandments,* and seven James Bond films. Broadcast early in the 1972–73 season, *Love Story* garnered the highest rating in television history up to that time. Thereafter, all three networks regularly used hit films to bolster their schedules during the November and February sweeps, the periods when rating services surveyed all the television markets in the United States to set advertising rates for local stations.

In addition to beating out the competition, hit films were used to target the youth audience. Boundaries between film and television began to blur as films, no longer constrained by the Production Code, began breaking ground for television's new candor in programming. Newer movies that appeared on network television dealt with pregnancy, abortion, homosexuality, prostitution, rape, adultery, and other sex-related themes and also with bigotry and other human vices that were previously taboo. Newer movies also chipped away at the old language barrier of the medium. Although network censors blipped unacceptable words from *Love Story* and *Patton,* for example, they left enough to preserve the flavor of the originals and discovered that only a few viewers objected.

ABC had paid $2.5 million for each of the Bond films, $3 million for *Love Story,* and $5 million for *Lawrence of Arabia.* NBC heated up the bidding in 1974 by paying a record $10 million for a single showing of *The Godfather.* The average price per picture reached $1 million in 1975 and more than doubled by 1977. But for reasons that will be explained later, prices afterward became skewed; hits continued to command top dollar, but mediocre pictures received less and less. The largest network deals included CBS's purchase of *Gone With the Wind* in 1978 for $35 million (for 20 runs over a 20-year period); CBS's purchase of *Rocky II* in 1979 for $20 million; and ABC's purchase of a package of 11 Columbia pictures in 1979 that included *Kramer vs. Kramer, Midnight Express,* and *California Suite* for $60 million. Thus, as the decade ended, network television was paying more than ever in the aggregate for features, but the lion's share of these fees went more and more to blockbusters.

Bargaining relations between Hollywood and the networks were conditioned by several factors. The first was a decrease in the availability of recent features. The recession put ABC Circle Films, CBS Cinema Center

Films, and National General Pictures—the three instant majors—out of business and forced the majors to cut back on production. The networks therefore had to compete for a smaller pool of features.

The second factor was the rapid growth of HBO, which exacerbated the product shortage. As pointed out earlier, FCC regulations tried to protect broadcast television by restricting pay TV to very new or very old films. But HBO outmaneuvered the FCC by challenging the regulations in court and by aggressively bidding on the full range of new feature releases. And by 1975, HBO had succeeded in altering the distribution pattern to accommodate pay TV second, after theatrical release and before network release.

The third factor was a drop in ratings for blockbusters. As pay TV exposed more and more movies—uncut and without commercial interruption—the ratings for features on network TV were affected. To justify paying higher rentals demanded by the majors, the networks expected to earn at least a 40 share for the first run. Beginning with the 1980–81 season, however, the market softened. *Saturday Night Fever*, *The Spy Who Loved Me*, and other blockbusters performed sub par, and the networks began to cancel movie nights. As home video grew, the networks used features as loss leaders to kick off a season or to batten down a night, and by the mid-eighties their function as a prime-time programming staple came to an end.

After the networks abandoned the practice of buying blocks of pictures that tied many lower-grade features to a few blockbusters, the majors had to devise a way to dispose of their marginal product. Beginning in 1984, companies like MGM/UA, MCA, and Paramount introduced bartering as a means of reaching program-hungry independent television stations. Typically, a barter arrangement was designed for an ad hoc syndication network that reached the largest markets in the country and offered a package of fresh features that could be promoted with the hook, "First time on commercial TV." The features were to be aired twice. For the first run, which would be on prime time, the distributor traded the films for commercial time—that is, the distributor held back 10 minutes to sell to national advertisers and accorded the stations the remaining 10 to 12 minutes of commercial time to sell on their own. To accomplish this, the films had to be edited down to around 95 minutes. For the second run, which could be in any slot, the distributor charged a straight cash fee. Distributors were able to generate up to eight hundred thousand dollars per title using the barter system, a far cry from the fees the networks used to pay; nonetheless, it helped to compensate for lost network deals.

The syndication market for features, meanwhile, held firm. Unlike the barter system, which made films available soon after the theatrical run, the syndication market was last in line, following the theatrical run, videocassettes, pay TV, and network television. Typically, the window between theatrical release and syndication was four to five years. During the seventies, estimated revenue for feature films released to syndication rose from $32 million to $110 million per year. The trend continued during the eighties as more independent television stations entered the market and as the demand for programming grew.

Made-for-Television Movies

The wild card in the relationship between the networks and Hollywood after 1970 has been the made-for-television (MFT) movie. An outgrowth of experiments in long-form television programming during the fifties, the MFT developed into two formats, the single-night feature and the multinight miniseries. Both were designed as inexpensive alternatives to the escalating costs of theatrical features.

This form of collaboration between the two industries began in earnest in 1965 when NBC signed a deal with Universal Television to cofinance more than 60 MFTs over the following five years. Called "World Premiere," the NBC series was launched during the 1966–67 season with "Fame Is the Name of the Game". ABC followed with a television movies series in 1969 called "Movie of the Week." Whereas the NBC series broadcast MFTs on an occasional basis, the ABC series broadcast new films each week for a 26-week season. CBS, the perennial ratings champion during this period, did not find room in its schedule for an MFT series until the 1971–72 season, with "The New CBS Friday Night Movie."

As Hollywood's feature output declined during the seventies, the networks put up complete financing and commissioned the major studios and independents to fill their programming needs. MFTs were made on a tight budget—around $250,000 per hour at first—and cost considerably less than the licensing fee for run-of-the-mill features. Shooting schedules were short, around 15 days for a 90-minute film and 20 days for a 2-hour film; a regular feature, in contrast, took 50 days and more to shoot. Networks usually acquired the right to broadcast MFTs twice, after which they reverted to the producers, who earned their profits through domestic and foreign syndication.

By 1974, telefilms surpassed features for the first time on network television. The popularity of MFTs increased until, by the end of the decade, they became the movie of choice for the networks, while theatrical features prevailed on pay TV, videocassettes, and independent television stations.

The primary form of the MFT, as explained by Laurie Schulze in chapter 12, consists of a high-profile social problem "torn from the headlines" or based on a controversial subject that is targeted at the younger-urban-female audience. Plots have run the gamut of topicality from the Holocaust (*Playing for Time*), Vietnam (*Friendly Fire*), and nuclear catastrophe (*The Day After*), to missing children (*Adam*), incest *(Something About Amelia)*, and battered women (*The Burning Bed*). MFTs consistently outrated conventional theatrical features during the eighties and sometimes even out-performed blockbusters. *The Day After* (1983), for example, attracted 100 million viewers; *Something About Amelia* (1984), more than 70 million; and *The Burning Bed* (1985), 75 million.

Spinoffs of the MFT—the docudrama and miniseries—proved just as popular. Docudramas, unlike the regular MFT, were based on "real" people, places, and events and became an entrenched made-for-TV staple during the seventies. Miniseries, as the name implies, were designed to be broadcast over a short period of time, either one episode a week or on several consecutive nights. After the stupendous success of *Roots*, which was aired on eight consecutive nights in January 1977 to 85 percent of the TV homes, the miniseries became the principal weapon the networks used to fight the incessant erosion of its prime-time audience.

Today, ABC, CBS, and NBC together underwrite more original movies each year than all the studios combined. The overwhelming majority of the MFTs are produced by independents and not the Hollywood majors. The economics of MFT production explains the cause. An MFT earns in domestic and foreign syndication—the only markets open to it outside the networks—only around three hundred thousand dollars, an amount of little consequence to the majors, who focus their efforts on the windfall potential of sitcoms and dramatic series.

Television Production and Syndication

The production of original programming for the networks and the syndication of off-network programs continued to be a lucrative source of revenue for the major motion picture companies. Going into the eighties, revenues from new technologies had yet to surpass most studios' television production profits. The majors regularly supplied 50 percent of the networks' prime-time programs. No single company benefited from the improved market more than MCA. At one point in the seventies, MCA produced 16 of the 63 weekly hours of prime-time television. Most of MCA's success stemmed from a single genre—action-adventure. Its hits included "Kojak," "Six Million Dollar Man," "The Rockford Files," "Magnum P.I.," and "Miami Vice." Today, MCA's revenues from television are nearly double that from movies.

Supplying the networks with the remainder of their prime-time requirements were a parade of independents led by MTM Enterprises ("Mary," "Rhoda," "Lou Grant"), Lorimar-Telepictures ("Dallas," "Knots Landing," "Falcon Crest"), Aaron Spelling/Leonard Goldberg ("Charlie's Angels," "Dynasty"), TAT/Tandem ("All in the Family," "The Jeffersons"), and the Carsey-Werner Company ("The Cosby Show," "A Different World").

New federal regulations ensured that the production business remained hotly competitive. As a result of findings published by the FCC during the sixties and an antitrust suit filed by the Department of Justice in 1972, the networks signed consent decrees that were designed to restrain the networks' control over program supply and distribution. The Prime Time Access Rule confined network entertainment programming to a maximum of three of the four prime-time hours. Network affiliates could fill an hour of their weeknights with locally produced programs, nationally syndicated nonnetwork programs, and, with the exception of network affiliates in the top 50 markets, off-network syndicated reruns. The Financial Interest Rule had two parts: (1) it restricted the number of hours a week a network could self-produce; and (2) it prohibited the networks from having a financial interest in the syndication of programming. The Syndication Rule prohibited the networks from syndicating off-network shows. In short, the rules limited the networks' power over prime-time television by keeping them out of program production and syndication. For the major studios and independent producers, this meant that ideas and programs could be developed without having to compete with the largest buyers, the networks.

The effect of these rules on first-run syndication has been to enlarge the market for original programming. First-run syndication had formerly been confined mostly to high-quality original programming, such as miniseries, for ad hoc networks. The Prime Time Access Rule opened the market to network affiliates and created a boon for inexpensive original programming. Talk shows, soap operas, game shows, and other inexpensive forms of programming fit the needs of affiliates because of their good ratings potential. In contrast to a network situation comedy, which might cost five hundred thousand dollars an episode to produce, a game show for syndication ran twenty-five thousand dollars. The market potential for this type of programming is best exemplified by "Wheel of Fortune," which generated more than $80 million in revenues during the 1987–88 season. King World Productions, which distributed the program along with "Jeopardy" and "Oprah Winfrey," was the champion of the first-run syndication business. Lorimar-Telepictures, an independent that supplied "People's Court" and "It's A Living," came in second.

The syndication market rode high for a while, as independent television stations and cable program services competed for off-network shows. For example, when "M*A*S*H" was initially syndicated in 1979, the series sold for $250,000 per episode; in 1984, when the series went on the market again, an episode fetched $900,000. When the market for action series peaked in 1986, "Magnum P.I." sold for almost $2 million per episode. When the immensely popular "Cosby Show" went into syndication in 1988, reruns were selling for from $3 to $4 million, making it the most lucrative syndicated show yet.

The part of the Financial Interest Rule limiting the number of hours per week a network can self-produce has a sunset provision in November 1990, leading to speculation that the networks will become more deeply involved in production and hence gain more leverage over producers. The other part of the Financial Interest Rule, prohibiting the networks from having an interest in syndication of programming, has no expiration date, but as will be discussed below, political pressure from Congress is likely to force a modification of the rule and pave the way for the restructuring of American entertainment industries.

THE COMMERCIALIZATION OF EUROPEAN TELEVISION

The European television scene is in a state of tremendous growth and change. At one time, European television was dominated entirely by state-owned networks, but today privately owned commercial television stations have sprung up and expanded rapidly in the major markets. So great is the potential for new revenues overseas that the Writers Guild of America went on strike in 1988 for 22 weeks—one of the longest strikes in Hollywood history and one that delayed the start of the fall season—to win a larger share of foreign profits for its members.

Although the United States is by far the principal supplier of imported television programming in the largest markets of the world, the value of this trade has been considerably smaller than the trade in motion pictures. For example, American films earned $1.1 billion overseas in 1984; whereas U.S. syndicated television programming earned less than half that. Looking at the majors separately, the difference is even more dramatic; theatrical films accounted for a 65 percent share of their foreign revenues, while television programming accounted for only an 8 percent share.

This disparity in earnings exists because in most major markets overseas, television until recently was state controlled. Take the case of Western Europe. Western Europe constitutes a market of some 320 million people comprised of 125 million households (versus 250 million people and 90 million households in the United States). Because European governments have traditionally exercised a good deal of latitude in deciding what is best for their citizens in cultural matters, they developed public, nonprofit television systems and erected trade barriers for television programming, similar to those imposed on motion pictures after World War II. Great Britain, for example, restricted foreign TV imports to a maximum of 14 percent of total broadcast time. France, West Germany, and Italy also limited the foreign television programming on their state-controlled television system. Today, new restrictions have been placed on American imports.

Given a choice, foreign audiences have demonstrated a preference for programming with greater appeal and more variety than their state broadcasting monopolies provide. This is vividly seen in the phenomenal growth of VCR sales in Western Europe. In 1978, VCR sales totaled around half a million; by 1987 sales topped 40 million, or nearly one-third of all households. Like their counterparts in the United States, European VCR owners wanted not only to time-shift programming to suit their own schedules, but also to enjoy different kinds of programming, particularly Hollywood movies. The message was clear: The demand for more entertainment on television had been left unsatisfied.

As explained by Edward Buscombe (chapter 14), a new climate of political, economic, and cultural openness has vastly increased commercial television in Europe. Italy, the first European nation to allow privately owned stations, has become one of the world's most commercial and competitive television markets. Britain will soon have a plethora of new commercial channels to add to its two BBC and two commercial networks. France, which ended its monopoly on broadcasting in 1987, sold off its national station (TF-1) and created several other commercial channels, including Canal Plus, an over-the-air national pay TV service that shows a mixture of films (both French and American) and regular programming.

The launching of communication satellites by several European nations, together with the abolishing of trade barriers among the 12 nations of the European Economic Community, scheduled to go into effect in 1992, will transform the Western European television market. Whatever shape European commercial television takes, American producers have much to gain, at least in the short term. If only a portion of the potentially available television channels were to begin operation, U.S. imports would increase in volume and in price, notwithstanding new or existing program quotas and the possible increase in the production capabilities of European broadcasters.

The industry coined the term "globalization" to describe the major trend in the entertainment business as it heads into the 1990s. The growth of foreign markets as a result of deregulation of broadcasting, the development of new electronic technologies, and the rise of living standards greatly increased the demand for entertainment programming—"software," to use another piece of industry jargon.

Because Hollywood makes films and television programs that are consistently successful all over the world, foreign companies have acquired American motion picture companies and invested in American film production both to participate in industry growth and to own a source of programming for existing broadcast outlets. Australia's Rupert Murdoch established a beachhead when he purchased Metromedia and bought into Twentieth Century–Fox in 1985. Afterward, Australia's Northern Star Holdings acquired Barris Industries, an independent film and TV producer; Britain's Television South acquired MTM Enterprises, the production company cofounded by Mary Tyler Moore; and Italy's Giancarlo Parretti acquired the Cannon Group. Japan, the country with the biggest stake in high-definition television and consumer electronics, entered the U.S. entertainment market in 1978 when the Sony Corporation purchased CBS Records and then Columbia Pictures two years later. These takeovers were part of what Wall Street analyst Harold Vogel calls "the first phase of entertainment industry consolidation."

To steel themselves from foreign encroachment, Time and Warner Communications participated in this first phase by merging in 1989, to create the nation's first global media colossus. After the Sony buyout of Columbia, political pressure increased to prevent additional pieces of America's cultural heritage from slipping away. Congress and the FCC are likely to soon modify the Financial Interest Rule by permitting the networks to share the potentially high profits from the syndication of programming. Deregulation would remove a significant barrier between the networks and program producers and provide the catalyst for what Vogel calls "the second phase of entertainment industry consolidation."[7] This phase will be defined by mergers between the networks and the three remaining major studios—MCA, Disney, and Paramount. The prediction is that unlike other U.S. industries that have been crippled by foreign competition and structural changes, Hollywood will retain its preeminent position in worldwide entertainment, but just what constitutes Hollywood remains to be seen.

NOTES

1. A. H. Howe, "A Bakner Looks at the Picture Business," *Journal of the Screen Producers Guild* 11 (March 1969): 15–22.

2. James Lardner, "The Betamax Case," *The New Yorker*, April 6, 1987, p. 70.

3. Harold L. Vogel, "Entertainment Industry," Merrill Lynch Report, March 14, 1989.

4. Jeffrey Trachenberg, "Low Budget," *Forbes*, March 26, 1984, p. 117.

5. Michael Conant, "The Paramount Decrees Reconsidered," in Tino Balio, ed. *The American Film Industry*, rev. ed. (Madison: University of Wisconsin Press, 1985), p. 564.

6. Harold L. Vogel, "Entertainment Industry," Merrill Lynch Report, March 6, 1989.

7. Ibid.

Chapter 10 ───────────────────────────

Pay Television:
Breaking the Broadcast Bottleneck

Michele Hilmes

───────────────────────────────────────

F or most of its history, the U.S. system of broadcasting has
built upon and profited from a distribution bottleneck: the
network structure, which effectively limited the number of national
channels in most markets to two or three. Though the economics of
broadcasting alone might not have allowed more than three stations to
thrive in most local markets, it is a technological rather than a purely
economic factor that both created and supported the network system
during most of its early years. This technology consists of the very
backbone of networking itself: the web of wires owned and operated by
the American Telephone and Telegraph company (AT&T), with which
first NBC, then CBS, and finally the spun-off NBC blue network that
became ABC strung together their affiliates across the country, and
through which their programming was distributed. Though radio,
and later television, might have been "broadcast" technologies at the
local end—using the publicly owned airwaves to carry their signals
from the local stations into the living rooms of the community—they
remained wire-transmitted technologies at heart. From the networks'
central transmission points to the local stations, broadcasting relied
on a government-regulated but privately owned system of long lines
controlled by AT&T.

AT&T's monopoly over wire transmission and the mutually beneficial series of agreements reached with RCA in the mid-1920s made
the entry of others into the broadcasting field difficult. Out of all other
applicants for national network lines after 1926, only CBS was granted
access to AT&T wires. This bottleneck affected the film industry as
well. Both Paramount and MGM attempted to start networks in the late
1920s, and although the reasons for their withdrawal are complex, one

factor seems to have been the unavailability of AT&T lines.[1] However, it is with the arrival of television in the late 1940s that the situation became acute, both for the film industry, whose ready supply of film programming stood poised to find a new broadcast outlet, and for the viewers at home. Not until 1975 does a truly viable alternative to the AT&T system emerge. But early efforts to circumvent the limitations of the network system took place on two fronts: by the film industry, in the form of over-the-air subscription television; and by home market entrepreneurs, in the form of cable television. These two concepts would later come together, with the help of a new transmission technology, to produce "pay television"—referred to variously as "pay cable" or PTV[2]—leading to the successful integration of film and cable that we see today.

To begin with the situation on the consumer end, radio's relatively low costs and greater carrying power had made operation and reception of local radio stations fairly widespread. Television stations were much more expensive to put on the air, and television signals were subject to greater interference and degradation over distance than those of AM radio. These factors, combined with the FCC "freeze" on the granting of broadcasting licenses in the early 1950s, left many U.S. communities with no available television service well into that decade. Communities isolated by geography or distance often found themselves unable to receive even one television signal, as the rest of the country moved into the television age. Local entrepreneurs acted to correct that situation, and by doing so drove in the initial wedge that eventually would split apart the three-network system and usher in the age of cable.

Across the country, in Pennsylvania, Colorado, Utah, and other remote and rugged locations, local businessmen erected large antennas on the highest available ground and strung cables to the homes of the town's residents, usually charging them not only a connection fee but a small amount monthly. These early "community antennas" provided no original programming, but merely relayed the signals of the closest existing stations. Though at first the nearby broadcasters encouraged cable connection as an additional market for their advertising, they soon raised objections to having their local market invaded by signals brought in from distant locations, as the community antennas allowed the cable operators to do. Appealing to the FCC for protection, broadcasters were able to keep cable's growth to a minimum through the sixties and early seventies. As long as cable had to rely on existing broadcast programming, distributed primarily through the existing system of AT&T long lines and subject to FCC regulation designed to protect the interests of broadcasters, cable remained a limited technology firmly ancillary to broadcast television.

The film industry, meanwhile, found itself locked out of television network operations and limited in its attempts to own and operate television stations as well. A few of the larger studios responded by investigating the possibilities of an alternative technology: subscription television, an early form of PTV, which used UHF frequencies (or various forms of non-AT&T wire connection) to transmit scrambled movies to paying customers. Several systems were developed, ranging from Paramount's 'Telemeter', a type of "coin box" operation that allowed customers to drop money into a box on top of the TV to unscramble the movie signal, to the Zenith Phonevision system, which first used telephone lines to transmit its signal but later adapted to a broadcast, punch card operation. The combined objections of broadcasters and theater owners, again appealing to the FCC, inhibited development of these systems. By the time the FCC authorized the subscription television interests to so much as test their alternative technology, 13 years had elapsed and cable television had already begun to look like a promising, ready-made substitute for over-the-air technologies.

However, in the early 1960s the FCC, finally subsuming cable operations under its full authority, began to lay down a system of guidelines for cable that, while at least allowing for its continued operation and growth, placed heavy restrictions on the new medium. Through rulings on importation of distant signals, must-carry legislation, and program-by-program consent from broadcasters for cable transmission, the FCC made it clear that cable television existed as a distribution service distinctly subservient to television broadcasting, limited in the amount of original or nonbroadcast material it would be allowed to supply. As long as the slowly but persistently increasing network of local cable lines continued to be dependent on over-the-air programming, the network bottleneck still remained, simply carried over onto the technology of cable—itself not really a new technology, but a makeshift, cobbled-together system of wires under new decentralized ownership. This state of affairs is reflected in cable TV subscription figures, which grew slowly during the 1960s and early 1970s. At the end of 1971, only 9.6 percent of U.S. TV homes subscribed to cable, through almost three thousand local cable systems.[3]

The first step in freeing cable from its restricted status came with the FCC's 1972 *Report and Order on Cable Television*. While maintaining strict controls over potential "siphoning off" of broadcast programming, this new set of rules did respond to increasing interest in the possibilities presented by cable by encouraging local franchises to make more creative use of vacant channel space. Though the FCC seems to have envisioned locally originated programs on these channels, it also allowed the systems to lease channel space to outside program providers. Soon after the 1972 ruling, the first pay cable services made their appearance. One of the earliest was a small subsidiary of media conglomerate Time Inc. called Home Box Office (HBO), operating initially over a cable system in Wilkes-Barre, Pennsylvania. HBO supplied programming unavailable over regular broadcast channels, mainly live sports and theatrical films, for a monthly fee, using a combination of microwave connection and physical transportation of videotape as its network expanded to cable systems in other pay TV locations. During the early to mid-1970s, a few other pay TV services were cautiously originated, including Viacom's Showtime service and one operated by Warner Communications that would later evolve into The Movie Channel. Pay cable grew slowly, reaching only 3 percent of cable subscribers by the middle of 1975.[4]

BREAKTHROUGH

The first real crack in the bottleneck occurs in 1975, perhaps unforeseen by those who made it possible. The launching of SATCOM I, the first commercially available geostationary orbit satellite, marks the beginning of a new era in communications that would eventually affect all aspects of the media industries—but perhaps none with more impact than cable television. Satellite transmission capability finally began to transform television into a true "broadcast" medium, loosening its dependence on the nineteenth-century technology of wired transmission and giving it the ability to offer an almost limitless variety of channels and services. Cable interests were not slow to perceive the possibilities in this new medium. One of these was HBO, which on September 30, 1975 began offering 12 hours of pay programming daily via two transponders leased by its parent company on SATCOM I. Satellite transmission allowed HBO to create the first "pay network," transmitting to cable systems across the country simultaneously, without awkward relays or distance-sensitive costs.

HBO differentiated its programming from that available on the broadcast networks by bidding more for exclusive or first rights to new theatrical films and major sports events and showing them uninterrupted by advertising. Cable customers proved willing to pay for this alternative programming, and a "two tier" system of cable arose, with a growing number of subscribers paying their basic monthly charge for a combination of local stations, superstations, and basic cable networks (those supported by advertising), plus a monthly fee for their "premium" HBO service. The local cable operator kept a portion of this premium—usually around half—with the balance going back to HBO. Though the FCC at first attempted to place restrictions similar to those in effect for broadcast programming on this new service, by 1978 a series of appeals and rulings had invalidated most rules on pay cable, leaving an open field.

As satellite distribution opened up new possibilities to the cable field, another trend began to emerge. In 1978 HBO's parent, Time Inc., purchased the American Television and Communications Corporation (ATC), a cable multiple systems operator (MSO) owning 98 cable systems serving over 675,000 subscribers. Time Inc. thus became overnight the second largest MSO in the country. Vertical integration had begun. That same year Viacom, another MSO, also became vertically integrated when it placed its subscription service on satellite. This new premium channel, Showtime, became HBO's main competitor and remains so today, throughout many ownership changes and mergers. The first jolt of competition hit HBO immediately when later that year the Teleprompter Corporation, the nation's largest MSO with over 1 million subscribers and heretofore one of HBO's best customers, purchased a 50 percent interest in Showtime. This caused a drop in HBO's subscriber rate of approximately 250,000, as Teleprompter's local operations dropped HBO from their channel line-up and switched to the new service.

Indeed, cable operators were not slow to take full advantage of their ability to control access to PTV services within their franchises. According to statistics compiled in 1980, 87 percent of ATC's pay television customers subscribed to HBO, leaving only 3 percent for Showtime and 1 percent to a third competitor, The Movie Channel; 75 percent of Teleprompter's customers subscribed to Showtime; and of Warner Amex Cable subscribers fully 79 percent received the Warner Amex premium service, The Movie Channel.[5] In other words, cable systems tended to promote their own vertically integrated premium services almost exclusively; very few systems even carried those of their competitors, and of those that did, the competing service's subscriber numbers were substantially smaller. HBO's dominance of the total market can be seen in overall PTV figures. By 1980 fully 4 million, or 60 percent, of the nation's 7 million PTV subscribers belonged to HBO. Showtime came in a distant second, with 20 percent of the market or 1.5 million subscribers.

Between 1978 and 1980 several other pay television services began satellite distribution, including Warner Communication's The Movie

Channel, HBO's supplemental all-movie service Cinemax, and a few more specialized or regional services; basic cable channels proliferated at an alarming rate. Movie release patterns, which had remained basically the same for years—first run, second domestic run, foreign run, network TV, and finally syndication, over a period that might take as long as 14 years—began to change. By 1983 that pattern had shifted to incorporate videocassette release immediately after, or even during, first run, with PTV exhibition following, sometimes within the same year. This virtually eliminated second-run houses and made broadcast network showings distinctly less profitable. In compensation to the studios, ancillary rights to these new outlets provided revenues that more than made up for the loss of traditional income. However, dependence on PTV in particular had its price.[6]

HBO's position as the dominant PTV service gave it considerable leverage in bargaining for program rights. While studios split box office profits 50/50 with theater owners, PTV revenues are divided three ways. For each $9.00 charged to an HBO customer, the cable operator keeps approximately $5.00 and HBO itself receives the balance, out of which $1.50 to $1.75 goes to the studios for films. This leaves producers only a 16 percent to 20 percent share of PTV profits, with HBO in control. In addition, HBO had begun as early as 1976 to finance theatrical films, in exchange for guaranteed PTV rights; by June 12, 1983, the *New York Times Magazine* could report, "Time Inc. has become, by far, Hollywood's largest financier of movies." HBO's increasing involvement in film financing affected the studios' hegemony in the field. It gave independent filmmakers another source of backing for their productions, often resulting in the sale of ancillary PTV rights to HBO prior to making a theatrical distribution with one of the studios.

This type of "pre-buy" arrangement limited the extent of profits a studio could possibly receive from picking up an independent project; previously, a film that bombed at the box office could at least break even through sale of PTV and broadcast rights. In the words of Richard Frank, a Paramount Pictures executive, "Most movies lose money on their theatrical run. Therefore, if the producer sells off exclusive pay rights to HBO before the project comes to a studio for financing, the studio has lost a key element in offsetting its risk."[7] Deprived of this fail-safe, studios became reluctant to risk backing independent projects, increasing the independents' dependence on HBO and consequently HBO's influence on the movie business. With its pay cable market assured, and a voracious schedule to fill up with films of nearly any description, HBO could afford to take risks where the studios could not. "When the studios make a movie, they don't

know if anybody's going to show up. . . . We don't live or die on any
individual movie," according to Frank Biondi, president of HBO. HBO
and its parent company, Time Inc., soon became an important force
in Hollywood, sparking a rise in independent film production backed
by HBO.[8]

Thus a situation comparable to the film industry's predivestiture
arrangement took shape, as large companies such as Time Inc.,
Teleprompter, and Viacom both financed and distributed programming,
with an assured outlet in wholly owned cable systems nationwide. The
film industry began to feel the squeeze. HBO's dominance in the pay TV
business allowed it to exert considerable pressure on its film suppliers,
especially since its acquisition in 1976 of Telemation Program Services,
a distribution company that bought pay television rights to films and
other properties for sale to "stand-alone" cable systems—those not
affiliated with an MSO, the equivalent of an "independent" broadcast
station. These developments put the film studios, in the words of one
movie executive, at a disadvantage in the market on these levels:

> one in terms of the local monopolies . . . the second in terms of MSO's and
> the projection that MSO's would increasingly constitute the bulk of the
> marketplace. And the third that HBO in particular, in terms of its control
> of the universe of subscribers, put the individual movie companies into
> a noncompetitive, untenable position.[9]

Another industry analyst claimed that, "The power exerted by the
duopoly of HBO and Showtime has enabled them to keep down the
fees paid to the studios," as the financial return on licensing agreements
shrank from $16 per subscriber a few years before to about $7 as of
1980.[10]

Again in the view of film industry sources, HBO in particular did
not hesitate to use its position in the market to drive film prices down.
According to an official of MCA/Universal, one of the first companies
to license films to HBO,

> We had numerous meetings with HBO representatives who indicated that
> they only had a need for five studios' product and there were seven
> studios, or words to that effect. And that if I didn't get on the wagon
> soon, it would leave without me.

In another case, it is reported that when Twentieth Century–Fox refused

HBO's bid for its hit film *Breaking Away*, choosing instead to sell to NBC, no Fox films appeared on HBO for a year in retaliation.[11]

To the film industry, the situation appeared depressingly familiar: discouraged from radio broadcasting, blocked from offering movies over subscription television, then virtually excluded from the major network schedules, history seemed to be repeating itself as the 1970s drew to a close. Starting in 1978, executives from the major film studios began to meet, formally and informally, to discuss a workable scheme that could compete successfully with the PTV giants.

> Our goals are basically the same. To erode HBO's ever increasing leverage and eliminate outside middlemen from our business. We know from the network television business what can happen to us and we don't want it to happen again. We cannot sit idly by watching HBO gobbling up the market with our product. The revenue potential is staggering.[12]

FILM INDUSTRY RESPONSE

For a variety of reasons—including its past experience with subscription TV, failed negotiations with Showtime and The Movie Channel, and the knowledge that to compete effectively with the entrenched services, a response involving more than one studio would be necessary—the film industry waited until 1980 to attempt to remedy this situation. In a series of meetings held in the latter half of 1979, representatives from Columbia, Paramount, MCA, and Twentieth Century–Fox reached an agreement to form a new pay TV service, to be called Premiere. A fifth partner was the Getty Oil Corporation, whose transponder on the COMSTAR satellite would provide distribution for the service. Premiere would be an all-movie service, operating only during evening hours and showing three films each night, Monday through Thursday, with four films on Friday, Saturday, and Sunday. About half of the approximately 150 films per year needed to meet this schedule would come from the four partners, with the rest from other producers on a nonexclusive basis. The primary concern of those involved in Premiere was to differentiate the service sufficiently from HBO to persuade cable systems to make room on their limited cable space for the new PTV channel. Since none of the Premiere partners were MSO's, they, unlike HBO, would be unable to enforce Premiere's inclusion at the local level and would have to make up the difference in product differentiation and aggressive marketing.

This insistence of differentiation led to the joint venture's downfall through the infamous "nine-month window" provision, designed to provide the service with exclusive programming. For nine months after the release of each film licensed to Premiere—and this would include the total theatrical output (except for X-rated films) of each of the four studios—they would belong exclusively to Premiere; no other service or outlet would be allowed to purchase rights or exhibit these films. With exclusive contract to over half of the total Hollywood output, Premiere could market itself as *the* Hollywood PTV network, virtually ensuring itself a space on any cable system. To placate the cable operator worried about losing HBO subscribers should 70 percent of its movies suddenly be cut, Premiere claimed that its nine-month exclusivity would eliminate the kind of duplication that currently existed on HBO/Showtime/TMC schedules. In other words, said the Premiere marketing literature, the subscriber will want at least two services: Premiere for movies, and HBO or Showtime for sports, specials, and other programming.[13]

Though Premiere's reasoning might have been valid, it should have come as no surprise that objections would be raised to such a plan; indeed, at the urging of HBO and Showtime, the Justice Department began an investigation in April 1980 and filed a civil antitrust suit in August of the same year, charging Premiere with violation of the Sherman Antitrust Act. Showtime representatives called Premiere "an illegal conspiracy" involving "price fixing and attempted monopoly," while HBO spokesmen noted, "it's simply illegal for companies to get together, to set up a mechanism of pricing and to boycott competitors."[14] Despite the studios' reply that the Premiere scheme merely responded to an existing market imbalance, the courts found against Premiere. In the colorful words of one MCA executive, "We may also control a number of toilets in Orange County. The relevant place to look at is the market we're trying to get into."[15] On December 31, 1980, Judge Gerald L. Goettel issued an injunction against the service, which had been scheduled to start on January 1.[16] One of Judge Goettel's reasons for this action was that initiation of the new service might have the effect of driving HBO's only two existing competitors, Showtime and The Movie Channel, out of business, thus reducing the overall number of pay channel competitors. Though the matter never came to trial, the Premiere partners were advised that a trial would probably lead to a decision against them. Plans for Premiere were formally abandoned early in 1981.

POST PREMIERE

However, even this severe and costly blow did not deter the movie industry from seeking another foothold in the PTV business. In the months following the Premiere debacle, Columbia Pictures took one route: tacitly abandoning the idea of an ownership position in cable, it decided to accept the current situation by becoming the first major studio to sign an exclusive five-year contract to supply pictures to HBO. In return, HBO agreed to invest up front in Columbia's films, besides paying a fee based on per-film theatrical revenues. Two of the other Premiere partners took a different approach, making one more attempt at ownership of a cable channel. In November 1982 Paramount and Universal began discussions with Warner Communications and American Express, owners of The Movie Channel, to purchase a partnership in that service. Before these plans had been finalized, Showtime's parent company, Viacom, became interested in the project, finally agreeing to merge Showtime and The Movie Channel under the joint ownership of Paramount, Universal, Warners, and itself. Each of these four companies would own 22.58 percent of the new service, with American Express holding the remaining 9.68 percent.[17]

But the Justice Department proved no more willing to condone this sort of cooperation between supplier and distributor than it had with Premiere. Contending that not only would substantial vertical integration result from this plan, but the merger of two secondary PTV services would again reduce the number of competitors in the pay television field, the Justice Department decided that this proposal was anticompetitive, objecting particularly to the involvement of the two movie studios in the venture. Paramount and Universal then withdrew from the proposal, and the Justice Department agreed to withdraw its objections. A merger of the two services was completed in August 1983 under the joint ownership of Viacom, Warners, and American Express. Warners and American Express later sold their interest to Viacom, which now wholly owns the merged Showtime/The Movie Channel service.[18]

This second indication on the part of the Justice Department that vertical integration between program supplier and distributor/exhibitor would not be allowed seems to have convinced the major studios that these tactics could not succeed. In their place, the film industry has pursued three major strategies for adapting to the new satellite-distributed marketplace: cross-ownership, in which film studios, PTV services, and even broadcast networks jointly produce, distribute, and exhibit films; package deals like Columbia's, whereby the film studios enter into exclusive or nonexclusive contract with one or another of the established PTV services; and investment in other aspects of cable distribution, especially basic cable services.

The most remarkable example of the first strategy was the creation in 1983 of the "first new major film studio since the 1940's," as it was billed by its owners. This was Tri-Star studios, formed by a partnership between Columbia Pictures, HBO, and the CBS television network. Tri-Star released 15 films in its first two years of operation, including such hits as *The Natural* and *Rambo*, all produced by Columbia, reserved for HBO pay television viewing, and finally aired on CBS. However, other pressures caused this unique partnership to dissolve after its two-year honeymoon. Originally owned by the three partners at 25 percent each, with the remaining 25 percent sold publicly, CBS sold its shares to Columbia in 1985. One reason for Columbia's purchase was the prospect of also producing shows for television, which Tri-Star was prohibited from doing as long as it was partially owned by a network.[19] In 1986, Time Inc. sold half its shares to Columbia, subsequently forming its own production house, HBO Pictures. This left Columbia 43 percent owner of Tri-Star, with another 43 percent of shares publicly held and the remaining 14 percent retained by Time. By the end of 1987, Tri-Star had indeed expanded into production both for network and syndication, in addition to ownership of the Loew's theater chain. Plans were announced late in 1987 for the merger of Tri-Star and the Coca Cola Company's entertainment divisions through a stock purchase agreement. Besides Columbia Pictures, Coca-Cola also owned, as of the end of 1987, Embassy Communications and Merv Griffin Enterprises, both television production houses, and was part owner of RCA/Columbia Home Video and the Weintraub Entertainment Group. In 1988, all of Coca-Cola's production ventures, including Tri-Star, were subsumed under a new subsidiary called Columbia Pictures Entertainment.[20] Another film studio partially owned by PTV interests is Orion Pictures, in which both HBO and Showtime have purchased a small equity through financing arrangements.

The second strategic option, the signing of distribution agreements with PTV services, was selected by Paramount Pictures in the aftermath of the failed Showtime/TMC venture. Paramount signed a five-year exclusive contract with the new combined pay service in December 1983, agreeing to release all of its films to Showtime/TMC after theatrical distribution and videocassette release. This agreement affected about 75 Paramount films over the five-year term and involved only pay cable distribution, with no investment on the pay channel's part in the production of the films. The distribution pattern consisted of release on videocassette about six months after the theatrical run,

with exhibition on Showtime/The Movie Channel possible after a furthe
six months. Widely heralded as the potential savior of the troublec
second-place service, Paramount's films did indeed help Showtime
The Movie Channel to gain subscribers during the 1983 to 1988 period
However, when the agreement expired in 1988, Paramount surprisec
industry analysts by switching to a nonexclusive agreement with HBC
for another five years. HBO also retains an agreement with Columbia
since that studio's original 1981 agreement was extended to last unti
1990 by subsequent negotiation. Other studios currently under nonexclusive contract with HBO included MCA/Universal, Warner Bros.
Orion, and Twentieth Century–Fox, with Fox also agreeing to handle
theatrical distribution of HBO-produced films.

The issue of concern for film studios in the late 1980s in thei
relations with the two major PTV services centers on exclusivity. By
offering only nonexclusive contracts, HBO can pay the film studios
less for their product, while leaving open the possibility that they may
simultaneously market their films elsewhere. However, given HBO's
dominance of the PTV market, it is unlikely that any competitor woulc
be willing to pay any substantial amount to duplicate programming
already available on HBO. So HBO's nonexclusive agreements become
defacto exclusives; the only difference lies in the amount paid to the
studios for this right. Showtime/TMC, on the other hand, prefers
exclusive agreements because of its fear that HBO could come in
with high offers for the most attractive films, cutting out any advantage Showtime/TMC could offer its customers. By mid-1988 Showtime
counted only Cannon Pictures, Atlantic Releasing, The De Laurentiis
Entertainment Group, and Disney's Touchstone Pictures among its
exclusive suppliers. A change in management in mid-1987, when
National Amusements Inc. bought Showtime/TMC's parent Viacom,
could bring about some changes in the PTV contract system.[21]

The third option, ownership interests of another sort in cable, are
becoming the rule rather than the exception in film industry/cable
relations in the 1980s. One of the more visible success stories is Disney
Corporation's The Disney Channel, which debuted in September 1983
under the sole ownership of Disney Studios, backed by an arrangement
with Westinghouse, then the owner of MSO Group W Cable. Disney's
venture avoided problems with the Justice Department and has met
with considerable commercial success, due to the unique characteristics of the studio and the service. Since only one studio was involved
rather than a possible "price-fixing" consortium, as in the Premiere
case, the Justice Department could not object on antitrust grounds;
this ability to form a one-studio PTV service in turn rests on the fact
that Disney films in themselves are sufficiently differentiated from the

bulk of film programming as to make the service easy to identify and sell. By the end of 1987 Disney had 3.2 million subscribers nationwide, making it the fourth-rated PTV service.

Other studios have invested in basic cable services. Paramount and MCA jointly own and operate the USA Network, an advertiser-supported entertainment and sports channel founded in 1980 and reaching over 39 million homes as of 1988. MCA also owns WOR, a broadcast/cable "superstation" operating out of New York with the potential of reaching over 9.5 million homes nationwide. Warner Communications, a diversified media company built on the foundations of the former studio, started early in cable. By 1988 its subsidiary Warner Cable operated 101 systems across the United States. In 1979 it formed Warner Amex Satellite Entertainment Company, with American Express as a partner. The new company, Warner Amex, took an interest in innovative uses of basic cable programming, purchasing the highly original and influential Music Television (MTV) channel and its adult-oriented spin-off Video Hits I (VH-1), as well as the nation's top children's cable channel, Nickelodeon. Warner Amex at one time also owned the merged Showtime/TMC, as mentioned above, but following heavy losses in its cable system division and from its Atari subsidiary in 1986, Warner sold its interest in The Movie Channel, along with all of its basic cable services, to Viacom. However, in 1987 Warner Communications—now divorced from American Express—purchased a part interest in the Turner Broadcasting System, as did United Artists Communications, Viacom, and several other cable companies, in the wake of Ted Turner's financial crisis following his aborted 1985 take-over of the CBS television network. TBS had previously purchased the MGM/UA film library (prompting the current "colorization" controversy), which forms the backbone of yet another basic cable channel, the TNT network, a 1988 entry into the basic cable sweepstakes. As for Warner, its 1989 announcement of a merger with media conglomerate and HBO parent Time Inc. promises the start of yet another phase of media industry economics, as will be discussed below.

While all of these ventures and agreements represent the most visible aspects of the film industry's response to the new era in cable communications, pay cable's effect on the film industry exceeds simple marketing and cross-ownership considerations. The emergence of cable, and particularly of satellite-distributed pay systems, had a far-ranging impact on all aspects of the media business, including the traditional broadcast networks and stations. Some of these, in turn, crept around through the back door of existing relations with the film industry to create new markets for traditional studio output, as well as opportunities to create new types of programs. For instance, the proliferation of cable systems after 1978—spurred by the growth of pay cable—had a side effect of boosting the viability of the former stepchildren of the broadcasting structure: independent television stations. FCC must–carry legislation mandated that cable systems carry any over-the-air station in their market, even the puniest UHF operation; cable carriage, in turn, brought new audiences to the small independents, enabling them to compete more effectively in the local broadcast market. The independents' new visibility sparked a need for more and better programming than their former diet of network reruns and old movies. Into this breach stepped the film studios and their television subsidiaries, with syndicated film packages and so-called "first-run syndication" programming, produced specifically with this new market in mind.

Most remarkably, the new strength of these independents produced the birth of the first new broadcast network in 30 years, as the former studio Twentieth Century–Fox, purchased by media magnate Rupert Murdoch's News Corporation in 1985, launched the Fox Broadcasting Network in October 1986. Fox began on a small scale, providing just one night of prime-time programming a week to unaffiliated stations across the country. By 1988 it had expanded to two, with a third forthcoming in 1989. A drop in overall network ratings in 1987—based in part on the new Nielsen "peoplemeter" system—has led some critics to question the viability of a fourth broadcast network at this time. Partially in response to this, Fox's Monday night schedule will consist of "The Fox Movie of the Week," to be supplied by Fox Film Corporation.[22] Though future prospects are still uncertain, its corporate affiliation with Metromedia, a broadcasting and television production company also owned by Murdoch, with several of the nation's largest independent stations in its stable, should contribute to the new network's success.

BEYOND PAY CABLE

Besides distribution directly related to cable, three other new technologies have had a considerable impact on film production and release in the late 1980s. One of these is the rapid growth of the home videocassette recorder, which is discussed in detail in another chapter of this book. Videocassettes have become a permanent and highly profitable step in the film distribution chain, traditionally occurring immediately after theatrical release and before pay cable exhibition. In

1986 videocassette revenues exceeded traditional box office income for the first time in history; in 1987 home video accounted for 30 percent of total consumer electronic media spending, against 19 percent at the box office and 18 percent for pay cable.[23]

The second "new" technology, pay-per-view, bears striking resemblance to the subscription television systems advocated by film interests in the 1940s, though it is based upon a far more sophisticated technology. Pay-per-view, or PPV, in the 1980s relies upon addressable converter devices, which have a two-way communication ability to allow a customer at home to select whichever film the PPV service is offering at a given time and be billed only for the cost of that film rather than at a monthly rate, as with PTV. The nation's largest PPV network, Request Television, is owned by Reiss Media Enterprises, but owes its existence to an investment of over $40 million over the last five years by several film companies: Columbia, Disney, Lorimar, MGM-UA, New World, Paramount, Fox, Universal, and Warner. Request currently serves 3.7 million homes, offering two to four movies per week along with special events such as sports and concerts. Other PPV operations include Viewer's Choice, owned by Viacom, second largest at 3.5 million addressable homes; Playboy; Home Premiere TV; Jerrold's Cable Video Store; and Graff PPV.

PPV networks operate virtually as middlemen between studios and cable operators. Viewers Choice splits its revenues three ways, with 50 percent of subscriber fees going directly back to the studios, 40 percent to the cable operators, and a 10 percent "fee" to the PPV service. Request Television goes even further by simply selling transponder time to studios, which they may program as they please. The PPV service then takes a smaller percentage of revenues, as the studio and cable operator divide profits 45/55. After five years of slow growth, PPV subscribership jumped 24 percent in 1988, due in part to a resolution of release-pattern difficulties. Previously, PPV release came immediately after theatrical run, before videocassette distribution, which in turn occurred before pay cable release. Pay cable operators such as HBO and Showtime originally regarded PPV as an "offensive weapon" against videocassette competition, since PPV exposure allowed newly released movies to be taped at home, thus weakening video sales and rentals and speeding up release to the pay cable networks. This situation changed dramatically with the 1988 shift in distribution patterns; now films are released to PPV after, rather than before, videocassette distribution, at once relieving video retailers, opposition to the medium and contributing to the downturn in pay cable subscribership. This is clearly a move in the direction of more control over posttheatrical release on the part of the movie studios, now that ownership of pay cable has been ruled out. In addition, the gradual dissemination of more sophisticated addressable converters in newly deregulated cable systems makes the spread of PPV possible; new, easier-to-use decoders also allow PPV consumers to make ordering decisions more impulsively, thus boosting sales.[24]

Of equal, and potentially related, significance is the 1980s boom in direct satellite distribution of all of the above cable, broadcast, and pay offerings, called DBS. Across the country, satellite receive-only dishes have blossomed in backyards and pastures, especially in rural areas unserved by cable. Though confusion over whether or not to scramble these signals, previously received for free by dish owners, disrupted dish purchase trends in 1986 and 1987, 1988 saw the figures climbing again. In March 1987 Viacom began offering a package of 12 cable channels—including Showtime/TMC, CNN, ESPN, Lifetime, and Nickelodeon—for a monthly fee of $17.95, and the VideoCipher II descrambling technology has become a standard part of the home satellite package. Currently, five companies have applied to the FCC to launch a total of ten satellites to be dedicated to DBS service, each capable of carrying up to 16 channels of programming developed specifically for the new medium. With development of new, higher-frequency KU band satellites, the size of the receiving dish has begun to diminish as well. In mid-1988 COMSAT and Matsushita jointly introduced a 15-inch flat plate antenna that could be mounted on a wall or sit near a door or window inside the house. For the film industry, the most important development in DBS may be the recently announced plans of Touchstone Video Network, backed by Uniden, the telephone and satellite company, for a PPV service to be delivered via direct broadcast satellite. Beginning in 1989, subscribers would be able to select from among ten simultaneously and continuously transmitted films, paying only for the one they select, to be received over their backyard or living room dish, with the charges appearing on their monthly telephone bill.[25]

As receiving dishes become more manageable and affordable, and with previous ordering and billing difficulties smoothed out by new decoders and telephone company involvement, DBS could become the primary method of reception for all those signals currently picked up through a combination of broadcast, microwave, and cable transmission, without the former technologies' limitations on channel space. Though it is hard to predict the combined effects of technology, regulation, and economics on the ultimate resolution of this service, it has the potential for finally freeing television completely from its restrictive roots in nineteenth-century wired transmission, thus opening up the number of potential channels to the almost limitless capacity of high-frequency broadcasting. If yet another new technology, high-definition television (HDTV), is to survive and prosper in the 1990s, KU band satellite transmission will be necessary to provide sufficient band width for the improved television pictures it promises to supply.[26]

High-definition television, still in its early stages of development in this country, is a technology for improving the resolution of the television picture by doubling the number of times each TV picture is "scanned," or read by the camera. Developed by laboratories both in the United States and Japan, several competing systems are currently in experimental use. Two factors have worked to slow adoption of this improved broadcast standard: First, as mentioned above, the doubled signals would require significantly more band width for transmission than current signals, and given the already crowded conditions in the normal broadcast spectrum, another means of distribution, such as DBS, would need to be cleared. Second, television sets employing the current 525-line picture would be incapable of receiving HDTV's 1125-line signal, requiring HDTV providers to offer duplicate services well into the future, or else requiring a considerable investment in new technology on the part of the consumer.

What does this mean for the movie companies? HDTV could finally bring a picture quality to the home screen to rival that of the theater. In fact, during 1988 a French movie distributor, Videac, announced plans to distribute films to movie theaters via HDTV, using France's TELECOM I satellite to reach cinemas in small towns across the country. With satellite distribution simultaneously, and at long last, removing the channel "scarcity" upon which so much of our current broadcast and cable economics and regulations are based, and with PPV technology bringing the direct sale economics of the box office into the home as well, the home may become the movie theater of tomorrow. Certainly an increasing number of channels of distribution implies an increasing need for programming, and so far the film companies have proved themselves more than adequate in retaining their hold on the supply end of the business.

Through investment in pay television, television production, syndication, basic cable, and videocassettes, alongside regular and increasing theatrical production, the film studios of today exist in a high-demand market. With the broadcast bottleneck finally broken, and the restrictive regulatory conditions of scarcity removed, they may be able to move more freely into the highly competitive distribution market of the satellite era. The success of videocassette sales and rentals in the 1980s, compared to the relative slump in PTV subscriptions and overall broadcast ratings, indicates that the consumer enjoys films above almost any other type of electronic entertainment and prefers to be able to select from a wide variety of alternatives rather than a limited menu, to be viewed at a time of his or her own choosing. This seems to be precisely what the current situation stands poised to deliver, to the ultimate benefit of the production companies.

Furthermore, evidence suggests that Hollywood may be succeeding in a sort of "pincer play" on its rivals. With pay-per-view and videocassette release capturing the posttheatrical market before PTV can get to it, earlier basic cable play dates, plus more original production, on studio-owned basic cable services, combined with deregulation-inspired hikes in cable subscription rates by local cable operators, PTV may find itself squeezed out of the market by studio-controlled alternatives. Thus, despite earlier defeats, the ultimate effect of the challenge of PTV may be to leave the studios in a more diversified position than ever before.

A NEW ERA

As the 1980s draw to a close, yet another era in film/television/ cable industry relations seems to be emerging, based in large part on the expanding international distribution structure. Developments in European broadcasting systems in particular promise to open up a vast new market for U.S.-produced programming, as well as opportunities for investment and competition on a new international scale. Besides the increased commercialization of broadcast networks and stations across Europe and the loosening of restrictions and quotas on foreign import programs,[27] the advent of direct broadcast satellite systems in England and across the continent strengthens the demand for American-produced programming. Rupert Murdoch's Sky Television began operation of five DBS channels across Europe in early 1989; a competitor, the British Satellite Broadcasting Company (BSB), announced plans to launch three channels of its own in the fall of 1989. Both of these, have aggressively pursued Hollywood studios for exclusive contracts. Sky Television, through Murdoch's cross-ownership, has access to the Twentieth Century–Fox catalogue and Orion films. BSB, owned by a consortium of Australian, British, and French media companies, includes MCA/Universal, Paramount, Columbia/TriStar, MGM/UA, and several independents in its stable of producers. This new European DBS market, combined with the ever-expanding number of terrestrial outlets in the United Kingdom, Italy, and West Germany in particular, provides a fortuitous source of additional revenue to American studios: "However it comes down, it's a major add-on to the U.S. revenue flow. Unlike cable in the U.S., which ate into network revenues, it's new money," according to MGM/UA chairman Norman Horowitz. European distribution will add one more step to the American film release chain, probably occurring about 12 months after videocassette release.[28]

Perhaps partly in anticipation of these events, and partly in response to the growing size of media conglomerates in the international media market, another visible characteristic of the media industry of the 1990s promises to be merger and consolidation on a large scale. The acquisition of Warner Communications by Time Inc. brings a U.S.-based company into line with other global media powers, companies which combine interests in all or most aspects of the media field. The deal has made Time-Warner the largest media corporation in the world, with interests in book and magazine publishing, film and television programming, broadcasting, cable systems, and the music industry. It can now compete worldwide with such integrated corporations as Bertelsmann A.G. of West Germany, Murdoch's Australian-based News Corporation, and Hachette S.A. of France, along with Capital Cities/ABC at home. According to *The Wall Street Journal*, "The leading media companies see the world dominated by a few giant concerns by the end of the century, each company controlling a vast empire of media and entertainment properties that amounts to a global distribution system for advertising and promotion dollars."[29] Already the global merger trend has sparked acquisitions in the U.S. market. Just a few weeks after Time-Warner, MGM/UA announced its partial purchase by Australian-based Qintex Corporation, owner of one of the Australian broadcast networks. Though this fell through, in October 1989 an acquisition of even larger import occurred when the Sony Corporation of Japan purchased Columbia Pictures, effectively adding another level to its vertically integrated empire in the communications industry. Meanwhile, rumors of a possible merger of MSO and program distributor Viacom with either Gulf+Western or MCA began to circulate, as U.S. media company stocks rose dramatically. This activity, combined with speculation that other major international corporations such as Sony are also looking for U.S. media investments, makes the future for Hollywood appear bright, as the words of one far-seeing Hollywood executive indicate:

When television started in the 1950's, there was a strong view that that was the end of Hollywood. When cable came, we thought that would kill our sales to the networks. None of these things happened. Every time the market expands, the combination is greater than before. After all, it should be immaterial to Hollywood how people see its product so long as they pay.[30]

NOTES

1. Michele Hilmes, *Hollywood and Broadcasting* (Champaign: University of Illinois Press, forthcoming). Though regional and cooperative networks such as the Mutual Broadcasting System, founded in 1934 by four powerful independent stations (WOR New York, WGN Chicago, WXYZ Detroit, and WLW Cincinnati), managed to survive into the 1940s, their success was hindered by the policies and rate structures then in use by AT&T, which gave precedence and more favorable rates to heavy users and prohibited interconnection of its lines with those of other wire providers. Occasional or part-time networks found themselves forced to contract for time on the wires far in excess of that which they could actually use—or find advertisers to pay for; the interconnection policy prevented them from contracting with another provider. See Committee on Interstate and Foreign Commerce, *Investigation of the Telephone Industry in the United States*, 76th Cong., 1st sess., House Document No. 340, 1939.

2. I will use the term "pay television" synonymously with "pay cable" throughout most of this chapter. Though pay television can include such related noncable distribution channels as over-the-air subscription TV or satellite master antennae services, such as those in hotels, it has come to refer primarily to its most visible and widely accessible component, pay cable, and I will be using the term in this sense except where otherwise specified.

3. Christopher Sterling, "Cable and Pay Television," in Benjamin M. Compaine, ed., *Who Owns the Media?* (White Plains, N.Y.: Knowledge Industry Publications, 1979), p. 295.

4. Sterling, "Cable and Pay Television," p. 311.

5. Christopher Sterling, "Cable and Pay Television," in Benjamin M. Compaine, Christopher Sterling, Thomas Guback, and J. Kendrick Noble, eds., *Who Owns the Media?* 2nd Edition (White Plains, N.Y.: Knowledge Industry Publications, 1982), p. 434.

6. "How TV Is Revolutionizing Hollywood," *Business Week*, February 21, 1983, pp. 78–79.

7. Tony Schwartz, "Hollywood Debates HBO Role in Film Financing," *New York Times*, July 7, 1982.

8. Robert Lindsey, "Home Box Office Moves In On Hollywood," *New York Times Magazine*, June 12, 1983, pp. 31 ff.

9. Lawrence B. Hilford, "Deposition taken in *United States of Americas v. Columbia Pictures Industries, Inc.; Getty Oil Company; MCA Inc.; Paramount*

Pictures Corporation; and Twentieth Century–Fox Film Corporation." Civil Action #8-Civ. 4438, United States District Court for the Southern District of New York, September 9, 1980, p. 62.

10. "Hollywood Battles for New Markets," *Dun's Review* (June 1980) p. 75.

11. Quote from Fred Dawson, "Waiting for Goettel," *Cablevision*, December 1, 1980, pp. 88–96; Jane Mayer, "Hard Bargainer: Show Buyer for HBO Is a Power in Pay TV, A 'Pain' in Hollywood," *Wall Street Journal*, August 15, 1983, p. 1:1; Pamela G. Hollie, "Hollywood Offers Pay-TV Challenge," *New York Times*, April 29, 1980, p. D1; Tony Schwartz, "New Pay TV Network to Offer Box-Office Hits," *New York Times*, May 19, 1980, D1:4.

12. Tony Schwartz, "Pay Cable Is Fighting for Movies," *New York Times*, August 22, 1981, p. C24:1.

13. Premiere publicity package, 1980.

14. "Time Inc. to Oppose Getty TV-Film Deal," *New York Times*, April 24, 1980, p D4:1; "Getty's Pay TV Venture Is Sued By Justice Unit," *Wall Street Journal*, August 5, 1980, p. 5:1; *Broadcasting*, April 28, 1980, pp. 22, 23; "Hollywood Challenges HBO Clout In Lucrative Cable-Movie Business," *Wall Street Journal*, August 11, 1980, p. 15:4.

15. Tony Schwartz, "New Pay-TV Service to Offer Box-Office Hits," *New York Times*, May 19, 1980, pp. D1, 10.

16. "U.S. Says 5 Companies Broke Law in Plan to Limit Movies on Pay TV," *New York Times*, August 5, 1980, p. 1:1; "Getty's Man on Pay TV," *New York Times*, August 7, 1980, p. D2:5.

17. Jack Banks, "A Survey of the Pay Cable Industry: Concentration and Integration in a Stagnant Video Market" (unpublished paper presented to the Regional Conference of the Union for Democratic Communications in Eagle Creek, California, October 23–25, 1987), pp. 16, 17.

18. "Justice Agency Approves Pay-TV Merge After 2 Distributors Removed As Investors," *Wall Street Journal*, August 15, 1983, p. 8:1.

19. Laura Landro, "Coke's Columbia May Increase Its Stake in Tri-Star; Sale of CBS's Share Is Seen," *Wall Street Journal*, November 14, 1985, p. 7:1.

20. *Broadcasting*, April 28, 1980, pp. 22–23; *View* (June 1983); *Channels 1988 Field Guide to the Electronic Environment* (December 1987), p. 47.

21. "Great Expectations: One More Time," *Channels 1988 Field Guide to the Electronic Environment* (December 1987), p. 117.

22. Fox Revamps Saturday, Will Expand with Movies," *Broadcasting*, May 23, 1988.

23. "At the Crossroads," *Channels 1988 Field Guide to the Electronic Environment* (December 1988), p. 102.

24. "Forcing Open a New Window," *Channels 1987 Field Guide to the Electronic Environment* (December 1987), p. 82; "Waging the Battle for Ultimate Consumer Comfort," *Channels 1988 Field Guide to the Electronic Environment* (December 1987), p. 121; "At the Crossroads," p. 102.

25. "The Birds Fly Low," *Channels 1988 Field Guide to the Electronic Environment* (December 1988) p. 122.

26. "The Dish Crowd Fights for a Pipeline in the Sky," *Channels 1988 Field Guide to the Electronic Media* (December 1987), p. 99; Stephen Brookes, "After Signals Get Scrambled, Home-Satellite Firms Adjust, *Insight*, September 26, 1988, pp. 38–40.

27. "Media Markets Around the World," *Electronic Media*, May 1, 1989, p. 46 ff.

28. Kevin Pearce, "Hollywood Reaps a Windfall From Television's Richest Endeavor," *Channels* (March 1989), p. 9.

29. "Plenty of Fish in Pond Time-Warner Wants to Swim In," *The Wall Street Journal*, March 7, 1989, p. B1.

30. *The Economist*, July 30, 1983, p. 73.

SUGGESTIONS FOR FURTHER READING

Channels Field Guide to the Electronic Environment. New York: C.C. Publishing. Yearly summary of activities published as December issue each year.

Drummond, Philip, and Richard Patterson, eds. *Television in Transition*. London: British Film Institute, 1985.

Hilmes, Michele. *Hollywood and Broadcasting: A History of Economic and Structural Interaction from Radio to Cable*. Champaign: University of Illinois Press (forthcoming).

Hollins, Timothy. *Beyond Broadcasting: Into the Cable Age*. Champaign: University of Illinois Press, 1984.

LeDuc, Don R. *Cable Television and the FCC: A Crisis in Media Control*. Philadelphia: Temple University Press, 1973.

Mosco, Vincent. *Broadcasting in the United States: Innovative Challenge and Organizational Control*. New York: Ablex, 1979.

Negrine, Ralph M., ed. *Cable Television and the Future of Broadcasting*. New York: St. Martin's Press, 1985.

Noam, Eli M., ed. *Video Media Competition: Regulation, Economics, and Technology*. New York: Columbia University Press, 1985.

Sterling, Christopher, "Cable and Pay Television," in Benjamin M. Compaine, Christopher Sterling, Thomas Guback, and J. Kendrick Noble, eds. *Who Owns the Media?* White Plains, N.Y.: Knowledge Industry Publications, 1982.

Tydeman, John, and Ellen J. Kelm, *New Media in Europe: Satellite, Cable, VCR's and Videotex*. New York: McGraw-Hill, 1988.

Chapter 11 ────────────────────────────

Home Video:
The Second-Run "Theater" of the 1990s

Bruce A. Austin

───

D espite the powerful influence of nostalgia, few things were truly simpler or necessarily better in the past. Although bread may very well have sold for only pennies a loaf in 1930, for the many unemployed individuals during the Great Depression, it might as well have cost a hundred dollars. So too the business of motion picture distribution was never simple. Theatrical film distribution was never just a matter of moving several reels of celluloid from Place A to Place B. Nevertheless, it is accurate to observe that movie distribution has become increasingly complex as the medium matured and as various new technologies and channels of distribution have been introduced. This chapter reviews developments in a relatively recently realized channel of film distribution: the videocassette. Included in the analysis is a discussion of the introduction of videocassettes as a distribution channel, the growth and demand for films on cassette, pricing and distribution strategies used to make cassettes available, and the importance of home video to Hollywood as an ancillary market for movie revenues.

VIDEOCASSETTES AS A DISTRIBUTION CHANNEL

Nurtured in the teens and 1920s and fully developed during Hollywood's 1930s Golden Age, movie distribution involved a release and pricing structure carefully designed to milk maximum money from each picture. Until the 1950s, there was, in essence, only

319

one variable the domestic film distributor needed to be concerned with: theatrical run. By the early 1960s Hollywood had adapted itself to television and was profiting as a result of its association. Interestingly, broadcast television initiated the change—some would say confusion—in meaning concerning the term "movies." With the introduction of TV, "having seen a movie" required clarification: a movie in the movie theater or on TV? In 1975 further confusion was added by the nearly simultaneous introduction of pay cable and the home videocassette recorder (VCR).

On September 30, 1975, Time Inc.'s Home Box Office (HBO) began using a SATCOM I transponder to deliver programming for a fee directly to subscribers' homes via cable television. A new two-tiered system of pay television was launched: basic and premium. Premium pay cable offered viewers uncut and commercially uninterrupted motion pictures as the primary incentives for subscribing. At virtually the same time, in November 1975, another media giant, Sony, introduced its home VCR, the Betamax, and within a year Matsushita had launched its own home VCR in a noncompatible VHS format. The fact that these two technologies were introduced virtually simultaneously is important. One without the other would have no doubt resulted in quite a different configuration in terms of each innovation's sales, growth, consumer use behaviors, and various other factors.

With the introduction of a host of new opportunities (although moviemakers did not initially perceive them as such) for motion picture distribution, changes in the previously standard methods for distribution were necessary for both practical and economic reasons. Practically, film distributors simply could not ignore the realities presented them by the various alternative means of public consumption of filmed product. Economically, the new means of film consumption potentially could prove to be a financial bonanza to distributors.

In essence, such technologies as videocassettes, video discs, cable television, pay-per-view, direct satellite broadcasting, and others are no more than hardware delivery services for existing software. A transportation metaphor is perfectly appropriate: These technologies do no more than provide new highways, or alternative routes, which one might use to travel from place to place. Moreover, like the Interstate highway system constructed in the United States in the 1960s, the new routes did not necessarily render obsolete the older state and county highway systems. While the experiential and aesthetic dimensions of movieviewing may very well differ between the theatrical and home video context, both viewing options remain open (though not necessarily simultaneously, as discussed below).

Following the acquisition of film rights by a distributor, a plan for the product's distribution (where the film will be available) and release sequence (when the film will be available) is created.[1] Whereas previously film distribution was a rather straightforward task involving only the selection and timing of theatrical sites, contemporary distribution plans differ significantly. More variable than previously must now be considered, analyzed, and plotted onto a complex map. Today, distributors speak of a series of distribution "windows" for film release plans. Each window represents another opportunity for the distributor to exploit the product. As David Waterman has noted, "the release sequence is essentially a method of price discrimination . . . or to use a less incriminating term, 'price tiering' [since] the value of a movie declines with its age."[2] The formerly standardized release sequencing involving subrun theaters has given way to pay cable, videocassettes, network television, and TV syndication, and with all of these, as was also true 50 years ago, the age of the film product has become the most important factor in determining price structure.

Today, a typical film release sequence involves the following pattern. First, the movie is released for exhibition in movie theaters for a period of six months or so. Theatrical exhibition, however brief, is viewed by distributors as a flag that represents the quality of their product and is proudly waved before the representatives of subsequent distribution windows. Pictures that have not received theatrical release are perceived as a second-rate product by operators of nontheatrical outlets. As was true 60 years ago, first-run theatrical release was felt to improve publicity and promotion of a picture beyond the capability of subsequent-run houses, resulting in enhanced revenues. Writing about theatrical distribution in the 1930s, John Izod notes that "films whose screen life began on the small circuits automatically seemed to the majors [distributors] to lack prestige."[3]

The second window is home video, primarily videocassettes (and to a much lesser extent, video disc and, at present, pay-per-view). This window remains "open" almost indefinitely; that is, rental or purchase of the film on videocassette or disc—but not pay-per-view—remains possible for years after the film's first appearance in this form. Third, the movie moves to the pay cable and subscription television release window for perhaps up to 12 months. Following a brief break of 3 to 6 months during which time the film is not available in any form except cassette, the movie next appears in its fourth window on network television, where it may be shown occasionally over a period of two years. The film may then make a reappearance on pay cable, followed by availability in the fifth window of syndicated television.

Each of the five major release-sequence steps is mutually exclusive to the others, with the exception of videocassettes and discs. That is, movie viewers may choose either to see a given film at the theater or wait for it to become available to them on HBO. This method of release offers the publicity and sales value of exclusivity to operators of each window and therefore enhances and maximizes the financial returns to the distributor.

Movie viewers may be classified by distributors as falling along a continuum, labeled at each end as "high" and "low" value customers. Conceptually the continuum resembles that of early-late adopters of innovations, as described by diffusion theory. At one extreme, high-value consumers are those who, for whatever reasons, are most anxious to see new films. They pay a premium price in order to see the film at the earliest possible time, since viewership is restricted to the theatrical venue at an average cost (in 1986) of $3.71 a ticket.[4] Thus the term "high value" applies equally to the amount of money returned to the distributor as well as the importance invested in the movie-viewing experience by the consumer. At about the midpoint on the continuum are the less eager, or perhaps more patient, viewers. They have an opportunity to rent the film on cassette for about one dollar or so, but pay the penalty of having to wait until the picture has played out its theatrical run. Finally, "low value" viewers are content to wait up to three years following theatrical release in order to see the movie for free on network TV.

There are additional windows available to film distributors as well. The form the film takes in distribution to these venues includes celluloid (for military bases and prisons), videotape (airlines), and microwave transmission systems, such as multipoint distribution service (hotels). Last, but certainly not least in terms of financial benefit, the nondomestic theatrical (as well as nondomestic ancillary) market has traditionally proven enormously receptive to U.S. film entertainment. In fact, prior to the introduction of cable TV and videocassettes, the nondomestic theatrical market accounted for about half (and in many cases substantially more) of a film's total revenues.

DEVELOPMENT OF THE VCR

The evolution and development of the VCR can be traced to the VTR (videotape recorder) and, before that, the audiotape recorder. Long before its entry into the home consumer market, videotape revolutionized the world of television and TV programming. Until the introduction of videotape, there were three modes of televised presentation possible: live, recorded on motion picture film, and kinescope recording. There were problems in terms of both program presentation and image preservation with each mode. Not all programs easily (in regard to technical or economic matters) or sensibly lent themselves to live presentation. Whereas film offered an acceptable image with some permanence, it was initially problematic insofar as matching a mechanical-optical medium (film) with that of an electronic medium. (This problem was resolved with the invention of the film chain.) Moreover, film was expensive, required processing, and did not afford immediate playability. Kinescope recordings were capable of capturing the picture and sound from a TV screen. This was valuable for the transmission of network programming to network affiliates not connected by microwave relay or wire. The downside, however, was an inferior image: Kinescope pictures were fuzzy and grainy.

The videotape recorder was invented by the Ampex Corporation as a device to be marketed to the broadcast industry.[5] The Ampex VTR, an important antecedent of the VCR, debuted in April 1956 at the National Association of Broadcasters convention in Chicago. If for no other reason, the event was auspicious in that for the first time "West Coast stations had a high-quality, practical means of delaying East Coast broadcasts without having to use film or kinescopes, or simply having New York repeat the show live."[6] Later that same year the Ampex VTR recorded Dwight D. Eisenhower's second presidential inauguration on NBC, and in January 1958 videotape captured (and perhaps even instigated) the famous Nixon-Khrushchev kitchen debate.[7]

Despite Ampex's extremely modest sales projections for their machine, they soon found themselves innundated with orders. The significance of the VTR and videotape, as it turned out, far exceeded Ampex's hopes. Using tape, editing could be performed far more rapidly, since tape did not require processing. Special effects could be easily accomplished with the push of a button and for considerably less cost than with film. The fidelity of taped images was superior to that of film or kinescopes. Mistakes in an actor's performance could be easily removed using the erase/rerecord mode of VTRs. The producer's and program standards department's fear of unanticipated on-air obscenity or libel occurring on audience participation programs was removed by virtue of the new medium. And, significantly, program production was no longer wedded to either the calendar (specific air dates) or clock (time slot).[8]

The VTR also offered salient advantages to the news departments of network and local broadcasters. Chief among them was that videotape required no lab processing (and hence no waiting time or expense), as did 16mm film; images captured on the magnetic tape could be broadcast as soon as the tape was physically wound on the playback machine and was up to speed. Moreover, these same news pictures could be used repeatedly. By the early 1970s, network entertainment programming as well had switched nearly entirely from film to tape. Ampex's first recorder, however, a bulky, expensive piece of equipment, was not the kind of machine consumers were likely to purchase for their living rooms.

Sony, a Japanese firm that had built its technological acumen and financial clout on the basis of tape recorders and transistor radios, entered into an agreement with Ampex in 1960 to design and provide transistor circuits for a portable model of the standard Ampex VTR. For Sony, the deal's real benefit was that Ampex agreed to permit Sony to manufacture VTRs for the retail consumer market. This Sony did, and quite rapidly.

Why did Sony want to market a portable version of the VTR? In large part, it seems, the firm's interest and motivation was largely a function of corporate philosophy coupled with their previous successes in the field of consumer electronics. In the first case, Sony's managers had determined early on in the company's development that rational risk-taking along with being on the technological cutting edge had enormous profit potential. In an ironic twist, a Japanese firm had taken on and internalized the "can-do" optimism of its nation's wartime opponents. Also, on a political-economic level, the Japanese government not surprisingly found distasteful the idea that its currency would be exported to nations whose products were being imported. Was there no alternative to the importation of Ampex recorders? Sony, with its 1960 Ampex agreement in place, was perfectly positioned to respond to this governmental concern.

In the second case, Sony's business acumen and history of success in manufacturing products for new consumer markets gave additional impetus to the idea of a portable model VTR. The firm's early experience with the tape recorder and radio were appropriate strategic models for the VTR. In both instances, each device had been tied to a rather limited—or at least not fully exploited—market. Schools had been the primary market for tape recorders, and the home consumer had been the market for radios. By introducing transistors for both machines, Sony had effectively broadened the market of each product. Tape recorders found new markets in business environments. Perhaps even more impressive was the case with radio: the portability made possible by transistor radios made them a spectacular success, resulting in families now owning as many as five or six radios, as opposed to only one or two. Likewise for the VTR, Sony correctly anticipated new nonbroadcast markets for a portable model. The airline industry would find such machines attractive for their in-flight entertainment. The education and instructional media market would replace their 16mm film operations with the more flexible videotape equipment. And the consumer market, it was felt, would be persuaded to purchase the machine if it was marketed as a device that would free them from the tyranny of television programmers' schedules. With this history, these ideas, and the Ampex agreement in place, all that remained was production and distribution of the home VCR.

The Sony SV-201, though not a resounding sales success, was on the market 18 months after the agreement with Ampex was signed. By 1965 Sony had produced a machine that could not only record television programs off the air, but would also do this job even if the owner was not at home at the time the show was being broadcast. Sony's machine could think—that is, it could be programmed by its operator. Still, despite these remarkable technological advantages, the machine remained by and large a sophisticated toy for the well-to-do. Moreover, it was a video*tape* recorder; one physically had to touch and wind the magnetic tape into the machine, much the way reel-to-reel audio tapes were wound on their recorders.

The cartridge format videocassette was perfected in 1969, using three-quarter-inch tape. Conceptually, the idea for videocassettes was an outgrowth of the audiocassette, a technology that was rapidly revolutionizing the way people purchased and listened to recorded music. Sony introduced this innovation in 1971 for its U-matic VCR. Still, the public response was cool. Within four years, though, on April 16, 1975, the half-inch format VCR was announced: the SL-6300 deck. This was a floor model Betamax with a built-in 19-inch Trinitron color TV. The retail price was a prohibitive $2,295 and, not surprisingly, the unit met with only marginal success. However, the February 1976 introduction of the stand-alone (no TV) Betamax deck at $1,295 was enormously popular. Indeed, retailers had a difficult time stocking enough videocassettes to meet the demand.

Not long after Sony's successful introduction of the Beta format VCR, another Japanese manufacturer, Matsushita, introduced its own line of VCRs, employing a tape format they called Video Home System (VHS). Differences between the two machines were, with one exception, marginal. However, tapes recorded on one system could not be played back on the other; the tape loading format and size of the cassette were not compatible. The most important difference, though, was the fact that at the time of its introduction the VHS system permitted users to record up to two continous hours of programming, whereas the Beta format was capable of only one hour's worth of recording. Although at the time Sony did not perceive this to be an especially salient product advantage, consumers did, and quickly endorsed the VHS format. Within a few years VHS format machines had captured better than three-quarters of the market. Soon, Sony was virtually alone as a manufacturer of Beta format machines and, eventually, even Sony had to acquiesce by manufacturing the VHS format. The market for blank and prerecorded VHS tapes has grown steadily, while that for Beta tapes has largely stalled (see table 11.1).

By the end of 1988 some 56 percent of all U.S. households owned at least one VCR. However, since demand for the VCR is finite, a slowdown in the growth of sales is to be expected; indeed, observers of the electronics industry predict a ceiling of 75 to 85 percent household saturation for the VCR. Nevertheless, as David Lachenbruch reports, an interesting and developing trend is that many homes are now adding a second VCR. On the software side, unit sales of prerecorded cassettes, at the wholesale level, expanded by 17 percent during 1988, which is the rate generated during 1987. At the retail end, sales were up a modest 8 percent in 1988, as compared to 20 percent the previous year. Still, sales of prerecorded videos realized a whopping $462 million in sales (26 million units) between November 1 and December 13, 1988.[9]

In the brief space of three decades, there developed not only new technology but also a new, rapidly expanding consumer market and fascination with electronic gadgetry, including such other devices as the compact audiodisc player, TV monitors, and other pieces of hardware that formerly appealed only to the rather narrow and shallow market niche of audio and video aficionados. Sarnoff's suggestion to his engineers, Ampex's development of a broadcast-quality VTR machine, and Sony's micro engineering know-how had resulted in a briefcase-sized machine that had taken a firm hold on the consumer electronics marketplace.

HOLLYWOOD'S RESPONSES TO THE INTRODUCTION OF VIDEOCASSETTES

As has often been said, history repeats itself. Such is largely the case with Hollywood's response to the introduction of videocassettes. Following its pattern of response to previous "threats" to its business, such as radio and television, the movie industry moved from a mixed initial response to full-blown, head-to-head competition and,

TABLE 11.1

Selected Home Video Trends, 1983–86

	Manufacturers' Shipments (in thousands)				Retail Value (in millions)			
	1983ᵃ	1984ᵃ	1985ᵇ	1986ᵇ	1983ᵃ	1984ᵃ	1985ᵇ	1986ᵇ
Videocassette recorders	4,020	7,143	11,912	12,685	2,303	3,444	NA	5,067
Videodisc players	312	188	179	125	106	54	51	25
Blank videotape	61,690	98,353	156,088	192,655	725	925	1,132	1,106
Beta	15,870	25,392	27,897	29,024	175	224	210	170
VHS	45,820	72,961	128,191	162,631	550	700	923	924
Prerecorded videotape	9,606	19,690	43,100	65,441	521	963	1,913	2,416
Beta	2,633	4,922	7,430	6,707	131	221	301	246
VHS	6,973	14,768	35,670	58,234	389	742	1,613	2,160
Videodiscs, lasers	5,368	6,000	7,200	10,040	NA	NA	NA	326

NA Not available
ᵃ Source: U.S. Bureau of the Census, *Statistical Abstract of the United States: 1986:* (Washington, D.C.: G.P.O., 1985 p.228).
ᵇ Source: U.S. Bureau of the Census, *Statistical Abstract of the United States: 1988:* (Washington, D.C.: G.P.O. 1987 p.217).

finally, economically sensible and advantageous cooperation with the videocassette industry.[10] Despite the rather clear outcomes and lessons that could be drawn from the events surrounding the introduction of radio and television vis-à-vis theatrical movies, with notable exceptions Hollywood chose at first largely to ignore the videocassette. According to the one report, in 1982 moviemakers initially were rubbing their hands in glee, since "the demographics of theater and home video audiences are thought to be so different as to rule out significant overlap."[11] But as sales of VCRs grew, due especially to increased affordability (see table 11.1), Hollywood changed its tune to a more adversarial one.

One firm in particular, MCA (parent to Universal Studios), reacted virtually immediately to the introduction of Sony's Betamax in 1976. On November 11, 1976, Universal and Disney brought suit against Sony on the grounds of copyright infringement and sought judicial relief in the form of an injunction. Universal and Disney's argument, essentially, was that the manufacture of a device that could copy their copyrighted material was a violation of the Copyright Act, and hence the device should not be manufactured. Nevertheless, three years later, in October 1979, the District Court found in favor of Sony and indicated that home use recording from broadcast TV was not an infringement on copyright; private in-home recording was not a breach of the "fair use" provision of copyright law. Judge Warren Ferguson wrote that even if such recordings were an infringement, "the corporate defendants [Sony] are not liable and an injunction is not appropriate." On appeal, however, Ferguson's decision was reversed. The October 19, 1981 decision by the U.S. Court of Appeals for the Ninth Circuit sided with the plaintiffs, finding that home video recording was an infringement and that Sony could be held responsible for it. Finally, on January 17, 1984, the Supreme Court overturned the 1981 appeals court's decision and ruled that home use of the VCR for time-shift viewing and other in-home uses constituted "fair use."

Over the eight years during which *Universal v. Sony* was being pursued through the courts, the film industry also sought relief from other sources. The Motion Picture Association of American (MPAA), through its president, Jack Valenti, attempted to persuade Congress to impose royalty charges, or a copyright fee, on the sale of videotapes and VCRs. The revenues generated by these charges would be distributed to movie producers to cover the royalties due them. Congress could not be convinced, and hence this strategy did not meet with success. Importantly, the outcome of *Universal v. Sony* not only established the legal basis for time-shifting in the home; it also left standing the First Sale Doctrine under the Copyright Act, thereby legalizing the rental of videocassettes through retail outlets. First Sale prevents distributors of copyrighted materials, such as videocassette versions of theatrical films, from exerting absolute control over retailers' eventual use of these materials. In other words, retailers are free to sell outright or rent a videocassette to their customers. First Sale specifies that the first buyer of a copyrighted work can use that work in any way he or she sees fit so long as no violation of copyright occurs (for example, duplicate copies of the work would not be permitted). In short, the Supreme Court's decision affirmed the right of video shops to sell or rent the videotapes they stocked.[12]

Recall that two important events were occurring at pretty much the same time: the introduction of both VCRs and pay cable services that offered uncut Hollywood movies. The movie industry found that it would have to accommodate itself to a medium that promised to further nibble away at the size of the theatrical audience by providing to consumers in their homes virtually the identical product for which they formerly had to leave home and pay. At least two profound consequences of this can be identified. First, Hollywood initially perceived there would be a direct negative effect on their revenues: Movies presented on pay cable would decrease theatrical returns. Perhaps equally important, the public might (further) diminish the value of the moviegoing experience;[13] the sense of specialness engendered by viewing a high-definition, large-screen image, complete with stereo sound, would be further eroded from the previous wave of commercial television by virtue of the fact that commercial-free motion pictures were presented on pay cable. Also, pay cable did not suffer the (self- and externally imposed) censorial structure of being a "guest in the home" as did network broadcasting, so that uncut movies became one of several salient product advantages of cable.

Moreover, the cost of pay cable subscription was such that on a per-movie basis, seeing a movie was now extremely economical, if not downright cheap. The attendant costs of going to the movies (in addition to the price of admission), such as gasoline for the car, parking fees, and babysitter expenses, were removed; all one needed to do was pay the monthly subscription fee and select the correct channel—all from the comfort of one's living room. Still, by itself pay cable could be seen by farsighted moviemakers as an important new (but not necessarily an additional or incremental) source of revenue, since the Hollywood product would serve as its primary programming. Rental arrangements with HBO and others, differing only modestly from the traditional arrangements made with theatrical exhibitors, would no doubt offset entirely, or at least in large part, the diminished theatrical returns that might be lost as a result of pay cable. (Unlike theaters, pay cable services may not charge distributors for "housenut" overhead and co-op advertising.)

The videocassette recorder, though, was another story entirely. Previously the sole providence of TV broadcasters, the home VCR clearly threatened to turn loose to the public that which belonged to the studios. People, in the comfort of their living rooms, could record for their own use any movie, or anything else, shown on television. Furthermore, with the programmability function of VCRs, televiewers did not even have to be at home while the movie was playing; instead, they could simply instruct the machine to do the work for them. Moreover, and of equal importance to filmmakers, Hollywood would physically lose control of its product, since consumers did not share contractual agreements with Tinseltown, as did cable services, broadcasters, and theater operators.

As became rapidly clear, the public enthusiastically endorsed VCRs. One writer charted the growth of VCR households and found that the diffusion pattern for VCRs mirrored nearly set-for-set the diffusion curve for color television in the 1960s. VCR sales also paralleled the growth curve of numerous other innovations. Following an initial period of limited adoption (that is, purchase) by "innovators" and "early adopters," a product's breadth of adoption may widen substantially. According to Lachenbruch, the case for this with VCRs (as was also the case for color TVs) was the "snowball effect in which potential buyers [were] introduced to the new product in their friends' homes." This explanation, of course, fit well with what diffusion of innovations theory predicts: The rate of an innovation's adoption is enhanced by such factors as its compatibility with personal values and needs, trialability, and observability. Moreover, in the specific case of the VCR, increased adoption also followed a decline in cost as well as the addition of such standardized features as scanning, which permitted users to skip over commercials ("zapping") or through segments of the program about which they were not interested. Thus sales of VCRs in 1983 more than doubled those of 1982. As table 11.1 illustrates, the pace of adoption begins to slow only once the innovation has topped the 50 percent penetration level.[14] In short, VCRs were not a technoflash in the pan.

In order to regain its hold on its product, Hollywood's first response following its recognition of the VCRs permanence was to create an outright sales strategy for films on videotape. Consumers, it was felt, could be persuaded to purchase movies on tape so that they might acquire a film library or collection. Basically, this strategy was similar to that of the recorded music industry, to which many of the Hollywood majors had strong and often direct corporate and financial ties: People will also want to own the music that they can hear for free on the radio. Whereas radio provided free musical entertainment and, especially since the introduction of TV, even specialized music formats tailored to various listener preferences, consumers continued to purchase recordings so that they might choose the specific music to fit their specific listening motivations at any given time. The consumer sales approach also preserved an important legal protection: copyright. Ownership of the original work remained with the manufacturer and was shared only with the consumer who bought a videotaped movie.[15]

By 1980 virtually all of the major Hollywood studios had created divisions of joint ventures to manufacture and distribute prerecorded entertainment and offered selected movie titles directly (or through various other distribution outlets, such as record stores) to consumers at $50 to $75 a title. As is true for the recorded music and book publishing industries, tape clubs also sprung up. Important differences, however, between the sales strategy for music and movies quickly became apparent. For one, the movie-VCR connection did not share the same kind of symbiotic relationship as the recorded music and radio industries do. Recorded music provides the bulk of most radio stations' programming, and new titles help maintain or improve audience ratings and hence revenues from radio advertisers. Radio play of new record releases calls the buying public's attention to a product that can be purchased for home use, thereby enhancing the revenues of record companies. The movie industry did not share either in strength or in kind an identical relationship with any other medium, since the distribution window between the theatrical release of a film and its eventual play on pay cable and broadcast TV was quite wide. In other words, cross-promotion of a movie via channels other than movie theaters was not possible in a timely fashion.

Perhaps a more important difference was that of cost. Whereas a 45 rpm record might be purchased for as little as $1.29 and a paperback book for $2.95, movie cassettes represented a significant financial investment to consumers. Simply stated, the issue of price elasticity was a difficult obstacle to overcome. Price elasticity refers to the sensitivity, or responsiveness, of the quantity demanded relative to changes in price.[16] Moreover, the sales-to-consumers strategy adopted by movie distributors further assumed that people would want to build a film library/collection. Whether or not this was in fact true was not determined in any empirical sense. Intuitively, though, many felt that whereas people might very well be disposed to listen to the same record a dozen or more times, such would not be the case for motion pictures. If for no other reason, movie viewing usually requires a two-hour time commitment; in contrast, 45s run about 3 minutes, albums 45 minutes, and books, of course, can be picked up and put down at the reader's discretion.

The sales approach also suffered another inherent disadvantage to moviemakers, this one technological. The videocassette recorder, like audiotape equipment, possessed the intrinsic characteristic—indeed its key purchase advantage—of recording, and hence the ability to duplicate prerecorded cassettes (as well as off-air/cable) at will and regardless of legal restrictions. All that was required were two VCRs: a master and a slave. Copyright, after all, protects the owner only to the extent that it can be enforced—ethical and philosophical concerns aside. Just as the introduction of photocopying machines played havoc with the publishing industry, so too would VCRs prove problematic for movie producers. An even more recent example is the debate over the introduction of DAT (digital audiotape) recording machines, which, the music industry believes, will further encroach on their revenues by making available a technology that can reproduce the fidelity and clarity of compact discs on magnetic tape.

With these concerns in mind, it was not surprising that Hollywood, especially MCA (the parent company to Universal Pictures), more enthusiastically endorsed yet another technology, one that precluded copyright infringement: the video disc. Indeed, MCA had led the charge against the VCR by initiating a lawsuit naming Sony as the primary defendent and claiming copyright infringement. Development of the videodisc began in the late 1960s, finally reaching the consumer in the late 1970s. At first, the innovation's potential to store 108,000 frames of information caused the discs to be heralded as the premier method for data storage and retrieval; the contents of an entire set of encyclopedias could, for instance, be stored on a single disc. Shortly thereafter, the disc's value as a medium for movies also began to be exploited, for good reason. Conceptually, and in contrast to VCRs, the videodisc offered the advantages of superior picture quality (image sharpness and definition), stereo sound capability, and lower cost—both the player and the software were less expensive than VCRs or cassettes. Moreover, the discs themselves were virtually indestructible.

Initial interest and sales were promising; media consultant David Butterfield estimated that "entertainment video discs [including not just movies but also games] could be a $6.75 billion industry" by 1990.[17] The primary software for videodiscs rapidly became motion pictures, and disc owners were reported as purchasing on average about 30 discs annually in the early 1980s.[18] However, videodiscs also had significant drawbacks from the consumer's perspective. Sales were hampered by three incompatible formats—the reflective laser optical disc, capacitance electronic disc, and video high-density disc—and, nore important, the videodisc was restricted to a playback-only format. Hollywood, of course, delighted in the latter item; absent a recording capability, the technology ensured that no unauthorized copies of their product would be manufactured, which left distribution and revenue control with the producer. Still, since Hollywood adopted a wait-and-see attitude while the contestants battled it out for the home video hardware market, their motion pictures were made available to both videocassette and video disc manufacturers.

With its headstart on the videodisc, VCRs quickly achieved economies of scale as well as a host of features that consumers deemed desirable. Retail prices on VCR players and tapes fell to levels that permitted average-income consumers to purchase them; longer record and playback formats were introduced; programmability functions were increased; and stereo high fidelity sound was added, along with enhanced image quality. After a brief period of market uncertainty, it became clear that VCRs would become the predominant form of home video, much to Hollywood's dismay. At the close of 1981, MCA's laserdisc arm, DiscoVision, had for all intents and purposes been dissolved. The cost to MCA was some $30 million.[19] More spectacular, RCA announced in April 1984 that it was dropping its disc system (Selectavision) at a loss of $580 million.[20] U.S. household penetration estimates for the videodisc in 1990 have subsequently been revised to only 5 to 10 percent, [21] while the actual penetration level for VCRs exceeded 50 percent in 1986. The final note on the disc-cassette competition belongs to Harvey Schien, president of Sony Corporation of America: "I don't think it was accidental that the company that took the lead in fighting the videocassette [MCA] was the company that had all the patents on the videodisc."[22]

TRENDS AND ISSUES

In 1980, five years after the introduction of the VCR to the consumer market, videocassette sales accounted for only 15 percent of all domestic revenues earned by the major studios. Four years later the figure had risen to 33 percent, and by 1986 fully half of all domestic revenues were being generated by videocassettes.[23] In addition, according to a report issued by Merrill Lynch in 1987, prerecorded home videocassettes will account for the overwhelming share of revenues to U.S. film producers by 1995, when VCR ownership will reach the 85 percent penetration level.[24] Plainly, the earlier fears of

TABLE 11.2

Cost Structure for Prerecorded Videotape, 1984	
Cost of blank tape	$6
Packaging and transfer costs	6
Royalties (15-20% of wholesale price)	7
Distribution cost	5
Advertising and marketing cost	3
Total cost	$27
Distributor's markup	$10
Retailer's markup	18
Retail price	$55

Source: Harold L. Vogel, *Entertainment Industry Economics: A Guide for Financial Analysis* (Cambridge: Cambridge University Press, 1986), p. 219.

Hollywood regarding VCR have proven to be unfounded. Moreover, with predictions such as these, should they come to fruition, we must begin to question whether or not the term "ancillary" is in fact the most accurate appellation for the videocassette market. As is now obvious, the videocassette market is enormously popular and economically advantageous for the studios. What was its evolution?

Hollywood's first strategy relied upon a sales format that was perceived by the studios as being low cost and high reward, since the movie had already been produced and paid for. Financial analyst Harold Vogel detailed the cost structure and profit potential for prerecorded videotape; his findings are presented in table 11.2. Pretty much all that was required in marketing prerecorded videotape was to transfer the information from celluloid to tape, create an attractive package, and distribute the tapes to retailers. In January 1980, Warner Bros. took a first step by releasing 20 pictures on cassette at the $50 to $65 retail level. Economically, this made perfect sense. For instance, investment analyst Mara Miesnieks of Smith Barney estimated that on average Hollywood earns $1.50 a head from theatrical attendance; pay TV generates $.25 per household; and network TV brings in $.05 a household. On the other hand, a $50.00 videocassette returns $5.80 to the studio.[25] However, by July 1980 it was clear that rentals rather than outright sales would predominate the market. In fact, rentals accounted for five times the frequency with which taped movies were consumed as compared with sales. By the mid-1980s the domestic ratio of sales to rentals of prerecorded tapes was about one-to-nine.[26]

Initially, tape rentals were primarily the province of small mom-and-pop operations. Individual entrepreneurs took the initiative and risk to open storefront video shops that featured equipment sales and tape rentals. With the studios providing the taped entertainment, these operations could purchase a number of titles at the wholesale price and then rent them out to eager customers. The growth of home video rental outlets was given both impetus and legal protection by the First Sale Doctrine of copyright law. In many ways, these early forays were strongly reminiscent of how the motion picture industry itself first developed. What Thomas Edison believed to be merely a gadget or gimmick that provided moving images to accompany his more important invention, the phonograph, was exploited by individuals who either possessed sharp foresight or were willing to undertake the necessary financial risk to feed a public that would prove to be hungry for a new commercial recreation. The hastily redesigned urban storefront nickelodeons for the exhibition of moving pictures at the turn of the century are the direct ancestors of the small shopping mall video store of the 1980s. As was the case 80 years earlier, the movie manufacturers first sold their product outright to retailers, who were then free to use it until it was physically "used up." Only later would rental arrangements with exhibitors become the established procedure for distribution.

Very quickly, the video stores initiated membership schemes whereby their customers joined video rental "clubs" for an annual fee in addition to a per-tape rental charge. Customers received a club membership card, thereby lending an air of exclusivity and privilege, and could sign out tapes for specified periods of time, much like public libraries do with their books. Club members also received preferred rental rates as compared to nonmembers. Gradually, as competition from drug and convenience stores (such as Fay's, Rite-Aid, 7-Eleven), supermarkets, and other large-scale mass merchandisers (K-Mart) intensified, membership fees (through not necessarily membership clubs) were dropped in an effort to maintain a customer base. Cassettes were also aggressively marketed by major distributors and independents by direct mail appeals and though bookstore chains such as Waldenbooks and B. Dalton's, as well as other nontraditional outlets. Inevitably, these new outlets forced some of the pioneering mom-and-pop operators to close up shop.[27] Nevertheless, despite the increased attention by major retailers, a 1986 survey of consumers found that most (83 percent) bought or rented their cassettes from video stores; 16 percent said discount stores and 9 percent indicated grocery stores were their source.[28]

Recognizing the futility (not to mention the income they were losing) of the sales-only approach, Hollywood undertook a second strategy for handling videocassettes. Virtually all of the major studios implemented elaborate and often confusing combination sales/rentals policies in which video dealers could either purchase a tape for resale-only or could purchase a tape to be used for rental-only. This two-tiered plan was not only perplexing in its complexity, it also engendered the wrath of video operators over a policy that was largely unenforceable, unworkable, and impractical for both parties. In point of fact, video dealers would simply buy a tape and then rent it out to their customers, claiming protection under the First Sale provision of copyright law.[29]

As a means of achieving the revenues lost through tape rentals, the distributors sought a third strategy and began dropping the retail (and wholesale) purchase price of their goods from a high of $89.95 to the $19.95–$29.95 range. This is a clear, practical example of the principle of price elasticity. In October 1982, Paramount released *Star Trek II* at $39.95, about half the usual price at the time, with great success. Indeed, this "sell-through" pricing strategy, which encourages consumer purchase rather than rental, seems to be among the most effective ones thus far promulgated. Although a lowered price necessarily means diminished revenue on a per-unit basis, the sell-through strategy seeks to offset this result on the basis of a greater overall volume of sales for the same title. That is, if a given movie on videocassette is capable of selling fifty thousand units at $89.95 via direct sale (through a tape club for example) and returning a profit of $100,000, how many units of the same title need to be sold at $39.95 to generate, at minimum, the same profit? Thus, for the sell-through strategy to "work" (that is, be profitable), distributors need to be convinced that there is in fact a sufficiently large buying market for the title and that lower pricing does result in stimulating sales in numbers beyond those expected at the higher price. Contemporary analyses suggest that the sell-through approach works particularly well for blockbuster movies that have demonstrated box office strength and, especially, for films aimed at children. The apparent success in the latter market segment is perhaps a function of a belief that children will tire less readily than adults of repeated showings of the movie.

Whereas rentals still dominate the tape market (as discussed below), exceptions do occur. MCA Home Video's *E.T., the Extra-Terrestrial* was successfully released in late 1988 at a retail price of $24.95; more than 10 million copies were preordered by video operators. This compares with the previous best-seller, Disney's *Lady and the Tramp*, which had sold 3 million units after a year on the market. *E.T.*'s video release at that price made it the first video title to generate more than $150 million for any studio.

The sales success of *E.T.* was not necessarily applauded by all and, thus, offers an instructive example of the many video industry vicissitudes. MCA was no doubt pleased with its sales of 15 million units of *E.T.* Yet not all small video retailers were equally enthusiastic. According to Harvey Dossick, director of purchasing for the West Coast Video chain, "The long-range effect of *E.T.* is negative. It brought the mass merchants into the video business on a large scale. With their volume business they can sell at low prices—even under the wholesale price. How can video retailers compete?" Because MCA had underestimated the demand for *E.T.*, smaller video operators quickly exhausted their inventory. As a result, consumers turned to the better-stocked mass merchandisers such as K-Mart and Target. Bob Klingensmith, president of Paramount's Video Division, asserts that "Most of the sales of these [blockbuster] titles will be through the mass merchants. The big video chains will know how to market these titles but a lot of the small retailers don't."[30] As a result we can expect to see further consolidation among video retailers and still fewer mom-and-pop operations.

Recent reports and conjectures suggest to some, at least, that the future of the home video business is in sales rather than rentals. Barry Collier of Prism Entertainment stated at Cinetex, an industry conference held in September 1988, that "by 1990 I fully expect video sales revenues to double rental market grosses."[31] Although in part this may be merely wishful thinking, the example of *E.T.* has served as compelling evidence and a source of reassurance for many.

The contemporary marketing strategy used by the major film producers for all but their most spectacular titles is in essence a compromise to the previous approaches. After the direct sales scheme failed and after the MPAA unsuccessfully tried to introduce a royalty bill in Congress, the majors developed a two-tiered pricing plan. For the first six months after a new title goes on sale, the price is set relatively high (for example, $89.95) on the assumption that rentals will account for the overwhelming majority of transactions. Then, after demand for rentals begins to ebb, the same title is reintroduced at a much lower price (around $29.95) in order to stimulate consumer sales. As may be seen, this strategy permits the majors to capture at least some of the revenues heretofore unavailable to them through rentals. As 1988 drew to a close, yet another marketing approach was being introduced. Called "pay-per-transaction," this scheme seeks to exploit consumer demand for blockbuster movies at their peak. According to Mayer, this method "has a studio or distributor leasing a copy of the tape to a retailer for a fee, plus a commission on every rental."[32]

Rentals of videocassettes, however, remain the dominant form of "purchase" for most consumers at present. According to a study conducted by Alexander & Associates, by 1988 rental receipts still accounted for more than 80 percent of all home video revenues.[33] For the most part, growth in the retail purchase of videocassettes was greatest for original programming such as educational, self-help, instructional, and other nontheatrical items. The same report found that nearly half (45 percent) of all videos purchased were nontheatrical. These findings suggest that consumers perceive the nontheatrical programming as more likely to become library material, valuable to them for repeated reference and consultation (not to mention a better "fit" with the library metaphor) as opposed to the "mere" entertainment offered by movies, which may be conceptualized as a disposable commodity.

Indeed, the sales approach taken by both major distributors and independents to nonentertainment cassettes is today a $1 billion market.[34] With cassettes being aggressively marketed by direct mail appeals and through bookstores and other nontraditional outlets, significant market niches for instructional, self-help, educational, hobby-related, do-it-yourself, and sporting fare has experienced enormous growth. Nonmovie titles include such popular items as *Jane Fonda's Workout*, *The Making of Michael Jackson's Thriller*, and so forth. One firm, Mediacast Television Entertainment, sold fifty thousand copies of *Battle of the Monster Trucks* at $29.95 each by direct mail.[35] Taking their cue from these entrepreneurs, the movie studio have also attempted to capitalize on the highly segmented videocassette market, offering deluxe packaging such as MGM/UA's 2-cassette boxed set of *Gone With the Wind* and Thorn EMI's 26-tape set of the TV series *The World at War*.

What types of motion pictures have done best in home video? While generalizations are seldom precisely accurate, table 11.3 indicates that successful box office films are successful in the home video marketplace as well. Still, inspection of the full listing of top 25 home video hits reveal strong, continued sales for film classics such as *Cinderella* (7.2 million units at $29.95) and, especially, instructional/self-help tapes such as the many Jane Fonda workout titles. The popularity of X-rated sexually explicit videos, long suspected of particular success in the home market, is difficult to track with any precision, since industry reports of such titles are either nonexistent or notoriously unreliable. Lastly, it is instructive to note that among the kinds of films that do not appear on the top-selling video list are foreign films, along with other nonmainstream product by independent producers such as John Sayles (*Matewan, Eight Men Out*). In short, as is emphasized by the listing of distributors in table 11.3, the traditional economic structure of the theatrical market is echoed in the home market.

What does all of this mean for the traditional structure of theatrical film production, distribution, and exhibition? For one thing, with

TABLE 11.3

Theatrical and Home Video Hits, 1988

Title	Box Office (in millions)	(Rank)[a]	Distributor	Video Unit Sales	(Rank)[a]	Distributor
Good Morning, Vietnam	120.0	(3)	Buena Vista	2,200,000	(5)	Disney
Three Men and a Baby	108.3	(6)	Buena Vista	535,000	(8)	Touchstone (Disney)
Moonstruck	79.4	(8)	MGM/UA	416,000	(11)	MGM
Beetlejuice	73.3	(10)	Warner Bros.	300,000	(19)	Warner Home Video
Willow	56.6	(12)	MGM/UA	340,000	(15)	RCA/Columbia
Rambo 3	53.6	(13)	Tri-Star	325,000	(16)	IVE
Young Guns	44.0	(18)	Fox	290,000	(20)	Vestron
The Last Emperor	43.9	(19)	Columbia	300,000	(19)	Nelson
Broadcast News	40.4	(23)	Fox	310,000	(18)	CBS/Fox

[a] Ranked (out of 25) according to placement by title relative to other titles within either the box office or video units column.

Source: "Top 25 Grossing Films of 1988," *The Hollywood Reporter,* December 30, 1988, p.4; "1988 Home Vid Top 25," *The Hollywood Reporter,* December 29, 1988, p. 4.

home video so prevalent, theaters that specialized in showing reviv
pictures are being forced to quit the business or to change their forma
One distributor estimated that there were 200 movie houses in th
United States in 1980 that showed revival films, 75 of them exclusivel
By mid-1987, the latter figure had dropped to a mere 15 sites.[36] As woul
be expected, videocassette entertainment has begun to usurp the plac
formerly held by 16mm film on college campuses. With lower-price
VCRs and inexpensive rentals, students are opting to view films in th
comfort of dorm rooms rather than traveling across campus to se
the same picture in an auditorium. More often than not, titles availab
on cassette are much more recent than campus film programmers ca
get from by going through the 16mm film distributors.

An extreme response to the "threat" of videocassettes to the movi
industry was offered at the June 1988 ShowBiz '88 conference in L
Angeles. Kit Galloway of Mobile Image asserted that rental vide
screening rooms in the Far East, coupled with VCRs, threatened t
"kill the theater business there" and that "without movie theater
who would pay for movies to be made? The whole economics coul
change."[37] The term "threat," of course, is loaded language and need
careful definition; what does the term refer to? A threat to a wa
of conducting business, or of gathering revenues, or experiencin
moving image entertainment, or of thinking about what is meant b
the word "movies"? As Syd Silverman, publisher of the industry trad
magazine *Variety*, once stated, "No one ever bought a ticket to watc
technology."[38] Few in the industry today doubt that Hollywood wi
retain its catbird seat insofar as it will remain the most prolific an
prosperous producer of movie (however it may be defined) entertair
ment. Moreover, the impact of home video (as well as pay TV) may hav
important positive consequences for independent (those not tied to th
studios) filmmakers. In particular, new markets for the products of th
Hollywood-outsiders could result. Already we have seen independer
production of horror/slasher films targeted to the teenage audienc
in the home. Still, at present it is too early to predict the long-terr
eventual success of these efforts.

The nondomestic market for U.S.-produced films on videocas
settes has likewise proven enormously profitable for manufacturer
and distributors. In terms of software—that is the filmed entertainmer
itself—Europe has long been an established market for U.S. produc
Indeed, many made-for-TV telefilms broadcast by the three U.
networks have subsequently been successfully released theatrical
outside the United States. In addition to the carefully cultivated an
extremely receptive market for Hollywood software, two other facto
significantly enhance the overseas marketability for U.S.-produce

videocassette entertainment. First, outside North America, pay TV is less prevalent form of ancillary distribution for motion pictures. Second, home video, especially in the form of VCRs, has grown at a rate far exceeding that in the United States. As a result, foreign sales of home video software has boomed, though at the cost of (modestly) diminished theatrical returns.

One example, however, of how the economic structure might change is illustrated by the onset of advertising incorporated in the videocassette. Nestle's placed an advertisement prior to the beginning of *Dirty Dancing*. Jeep did the same in *Platoon*. Best known is Pepsi, which created a conceptually clear link between its (diet) product and the filmic content of the enormously successful *Top Gun*. Moreover, the Pepsi tie-in with *Top Gun* lowered the tape's retail price from the $29.95 standard, set by *Beverly Hills Cop*, to $26.95.[39] Interestingly, the introduction of this form of commercial advertising into a new milieu did not seem to provoke negative consumer response. Research conducted by the Fairfield Group found that, in fact, consumers were receptive to ads inserted on videotape, especially when they lowered the tape's price.[40]

A corollary issue concerns people's availability and use of leisure time, for this is when movies (at the theater, on pay cable, or on cassette) are consumed. A recent report by pollster Louis Harris and Associates confirms findings about leisure that have been reported since the mid-1960s. Their survey of fifteen hundred U.S. adults found that, in terms of absolute hours, adults reported that their leisure time is increasingly being spent at home. Indeed, the home-bounded nature of leisure is traceable to as far back as the years following World War I when, concomitant with the baby boom, the population shifted from the large urban centers out to the suburban and rural sectors. The Harris study found that during the period from 1984 through 1987, high-brow leisure (such as attendance at dance, theater, classical and pop concerts, and opera and musical theater) all showed a marked decrease ranging from 14 to 38 percent. Movie attendance was up a modest 9 percent. Taking the largest leap was VCR ownership, which had increased 234 percent during the four years examined by the report.[41] Still, whereas American households were watching 8 billion hours a year of prerecorded video in 1988, this figure pales in significance when compared to the 221 billion hours of broadcast television consumed annually.[42]

What of the theatrical movie audience? In response to a survey of major studio marketing heads by *The Hollywood Reporter*, Peter Sealey, former president of the domestic marketing group of Columbia Pictures, offered the following concerning the impact of VCRs on movie audiences:

The VCR is opening up the over-30 audience to pay for movie entertain
ment. That means that you need a breadth of films. The world of hom·
video has opened up an enormous audience, for example the couple witl
two infants who cannot get out. We are making movies for them. They wil
not go to the movie theaters. The studios have to be adroit and selective i»
making a film visible and financially successful in the theatrical window
to validate it more for the home video market. That means you have t·
be smarter in the theatrical window.[43]

Nevertheless, the conventional (which is not to say empirical or sci
entific) wisdom has held that teenagers comprised the vast majorit·
of the theatrical film audience. Contrary to this, a November 198·
press release from Teenage Research Unlimited (TRU), a Lake Forest
Illinois, marketing research firm, proclaimed that "the living roon
has replaced the cinema as the place where teenagers go to watcl
movies."[44] Based upon survey interviews with 2,200 12 to 19 year olds
TRU found that teenagers spend more than twice the number of hour
watching films on videocassettes than in movie theaters. Although the·
spend 2.6 hours a week on average in movie theaters, the teens spen·
an average of 4.4 hours weekly viewing rented tapes and 1.8 hour
weekly viewing purchased tapes. At the same time, the study foun·
that as teens grow older, they tend to spend more time at the movi·
theater and less time at home watching tapes on the VCR. This, o·
course, is explained by dating behavior: The video date is not yet th·
prevalent form of behavior. There is little doubt that movie attendanc·
at theaters will continue. Instead, the questions that remain concer·
the *level* of attendance, the *opportunity* to attend, as measured by th·
number of theatrical screens available, and the kinds of movies tha·
will remain in theatrical distribution. Furthermore, as Vogel instructs
"One of the most noticeable trends of the early 1980s . . . has been th·
virtual dichotomization of the theatrical market into a relative handfu·
of 'hits' and a mass of also-rans." As a result, most films require "les·
immediate responsiveness" by the public (that is, low-value consumer·
who can wait for their film entertainment, as previously discussed) an·
the theatrical experience for such films is replaced by home viewing
The movie-in-the-home scenario, therefore, allows "people to becom·
more discriminating as to when and where they spend an evenin·
out."[45]

For motion picture producer-distributors, the advent of home vide·
offers yet another opportunity (along with cable, foreign theatrica·
and TV sales) to presell distribution rights, thereby offsetting th·
high start-up costs of film production. Whereas the annual numbe·
of tickets sold at U.S. box offices has remained relatively steady a·

ome 1.1 billion over the past two decades, ancillary markets are
ccounting for more and more of the revenue generated by filmed
ntertainment. (Box office dollar sales, of course, have increased due
ɔ higher ticket prices.) *Variety's* industry analyst Art Murphy stated,
More people are watching films than in the history of the medium."[46]
Vhat Murphy did not say was where and in what form people were
vatching the films.

Finally, what will happen to theaters as a result of home video?
Jo doubt a number of marginal theaters will disappear. However, this
ɔ not entirely a result of the videocassette "revolution." Instead, small
ndependent theaters and chains are increasingly being bought-up by
nd consolidated into the larger exhibition chains, such as General
ʿinema, or by the movie studios.[47] That the theatrical experience of
ᴉovieviewing is only one significant portion of a larger gestalt was
rticulated by Garth Drabinsky, president of Cineplex Odeon Corpo-
ation. In a speech delivered at the 1987 NATO (National Association
f Theatre Owners) National Convention in Atlanta, Drabinsky quoted
ritic Bosley Crowther:

> The total effect of a motion picture is conditioned to a greater or
> lesser extent by the environment in which it is shown. . . . The fun of
> movie-going, pleasure that is derived from the experience of spending a
> few hours in the movie theatre, includes a lot more than the experience
> of observing the film. It is the amalgamation of a series of pleasurable
> stimuli—the initial anticipation, the warmth of companionship, the con-
> geniality of the surroundings, the freedom to use and partake of all the
> facilities, the feeling of elegance. The final satisfaction is in the total
> experience.[48]

elf-serving as this statement may be (Cineplex Odeon is one of the
ɪrgest exhibition chains in North America), the theatrical ambiance
ɔ undeniably a culturally and historically important part of what we
ᴉean (or meant) by seeing a movie. Few, one suspects, would be quick
ɔ endorse or encourage the elimination of that element.

CONCLUSIONS

Historically, the film industry is characterized by an exceptionally
ɪigh degree of concentration. Separate research studies by Guback,

Gomery, and Waterman all reveal that the industry majors accoun
for up to 90 percent of all film revenues.[49] There is little reason t
doubt that this condition will change appreciably in the near future
All current indicators likewise suggest tight-knit symbiosis betwee
filmmakers and the videocassette industry. The addition of cassettes t
the distribution chain merely adds another avenue by which revenue
may be generated. Whereas the early distribution plans called for a
exhibition schedule beginning at the downtown Palace and slowl
branching out to the neighborhood Bijou, contemporary plans simpl
replace the subrun theater with cassettes and pay cable.

Research on owners' use of their VCRs has clearly, consistently
and repeatedly shown that recording movies is the most frequen
activity and that movies account for the most frequently played bac
recordings.[50] In short, the public is not giving up on movies as a forn
of entertainment as much as they are changing the place where th
entertainment is consumed. For the movie manufacturers, howeve
this does not necessarily mean advanced revenues. As Vogel states
what is gained in one market "may be at least partially lost in another,
since "new-media revenues [have] thus far . . . been an importan
prop (rather than a great new source of growth) for aggregate industr
profits."[51] At the same time, it is clear that the moviemakers hav
not—and most likely will not—lose any financial ground as a resul
of the introduction of videocassettes.

Moviegoing was once a communal ritual, often set in an opulen
ambiance. In 1946, more than one-third of the American public wen
to the movies once a week; by 1986, only 21 percent attended onc
a month. Today, moviegoing retains comparatively little of the socia
and experiential specialness it once had. Indeed, one suspects tha
few moviegoers today can discriminate between the large-screen the
atrical experience of movieviewing and the small-screen video version
People's television viewing behaviors have invaded the theaters to th
extent that theater operators have taken to running brief messages or
the screen reminding patrons not to talk while the movie is playing
Further, these messages offer the previously common sense rational
for the instruction: Talking disturbs other people in the theater. Th
same, of course, tends not to be true at home.

NOTES

1. This section relies on David Waterman, "Prerecorded Home Vide

nd the Distribution of Theatrical Films," in *Video Media Competition: Regulation, conomics, and Technology,* ed. Eli M. Noam (New York: Columbia University ress, 1985), pp. 228–35. See also Thomas Guback, "Theatrical Film," in *Who)wns the Media? Concentration of Ownership in the Mass Communications Industry,* d. Benjamin M. Compaine (White Plains, N.Y.: Knowledge Industry Publica-ions, 1979), pp. 193–201; and Harold L. Vogel, *Entertainment Industry Economics: A Guide for Financial Analysis* (Cambridge: Cambridge University Press, 1986), ·p. 75–80.

2. Waterman, "Prerecorded Home Video," p. 231.

3. John Izod, *Hollywood and the Box Office, 1985–1986* (New York: Columbia Jniversity Press, 1988), p. 92.

4. Richard Gertner, ed., *1988 International Motion Picture Almanac* (New 'ork: Quigley Publishing, 1988), p. 31A.

5. This section, except as noted, relies on James Lardner, *Fast Forward: Iollywood, the Japanese, and the VCR Wars* (New York: Mentor Books, 1987).

6. Christopher H. Sterling and John M. Kittross, *Stay Tuned: A Concise iistory of American Broadcasting* (Belmont, Calif.: Wadsworth, 1978), p. 321.

7. Eric Barnouw, *Tube of Plenty* (New York: Oxford University Press, 975), pp. 212, 240–42.

8. Sterling and Kittross, *Stay Tuned,* p. 322.

9. David Lachenbruch, "Here, Buy Another," *Channels* (December 1988), ·. 126. Information on cassette sales reported in Ira Mayer, "Good-bye, Easy irowth," *Channels* (December 1988), p. 106. Data on November-December assette sales reported in Paula Parisi, "Sell-Through Vid Takes Home $500 /illion in Holiday Sales," *The Hollywood Reporter,* December 19, 1988, p. 1.

10. For analyses of the impact of TV's introduction on the film industry, ee Lawrence L. Murray, "Complacency, Competition, and Cooperation: The 'ilm Industry Responds to the Challenge of Television," *Journal of Popular Film* , no. 1 (1977): 47–70; Frederic Stuart, *The Effects of Television on the Motion 'icture and Radio Industries* (New York: Arno Press, 1976; reprint of a Ph.D. Iiss., Columbia University, 1960); and Izod, *Hollywood and the Box Office,* pp. 35–38. Two reports by Austin review issues concerning the introduction ·f new media on film: Bruce A. Austin, "The Film Industry, Its Audience, nd the New Communications Technologies," in *Current Research in Film: Iudiences, Economics, and Law,* vol. 2, ed. Bruce A. Austin (Norwood, N.J.: iblex Publishing, 1986), pp. 80–116; and Bruce A. Austin, "Film and the New /edia," in *Film and the Arts in Symbiosis: A Resource Guide,* ed. Gary R. Edgerton Westport, Conn.: Greenwood Press, 1988), pp. 339–61.

11. Lee Margulies, "Will Movie Theaters Survive Video?" *Home Video* November 1982), p. 53. To characterize Hollywood's response to either he introduction of television or home video as complacent in an absolute ense is inaccurate. In the case of TV, for instance, reaction by the industry najors was mixed. Paramount, for example, invested in the new medium as arly as 1938 and was directly competitive with its theater television operation n 1949. Likewise, United Artists had set up a television department to distribute elefilms to stations in 1948 and, in 1949, Columbia formed Screen Gems to

produce telefilms and commercials. See Izod, *Hollywood and the Box Office* pp. 135–38.

12. For additional information on *Universal* v. *Sony*, see Lardner, *Fast For ward*, pp. 30–31, 98, 104–16, 128, 262–63. Ferguson quotation is from ibid., p 115. Useful discussion of Copyright, the First Sale Doctrine, and Fair Use ma^ be found in the following U.S. government publications: Senate Committe on the Judiciary, *Copyright Infringements (Audio and Video Recorders)*, Hearing on S. 1758, 97th Cong., 1st and 2d sess., November 30, 1981 and April 21 1982; House Subcommittee on Courts, Civil Liberties, and the Administration of Justice, *Audio and Video First Sale Doctrine*, Hearings on H.R. 1027, H.R 1029, and S. 32, 98th Cong., 1st and 2d sess., October 6 and 27, Decembe 13, 1983, February 23 and April 12, 1984.

13. For discussion of the experiential aspects of moviegoing, see Bruce A Austin, *Immediate Seating: A Look at Movie Audiences* (Belmont, Calif.: Wadsworth 1989), pp. 45–47.

14. David Lachenbruch, "Home Video: Home Is Where the Action Is," *Channels* (November/December 1983), pp. 42–43. For information on diffusio theory, see Everett M. Rogers, *Diffusion of Innovations*, 3d ed. ((New York: Th Free Press, 1983), esp. pp. 210–38.

15. Discussion of all copyright issues is beyond the scope of the presen chapter. For information on this important topic, see Waterman, "Prerecorde Home Video"; Lardner, *Fast Forward*; Vogel, *Entertainment Industry Economics* pp. 137–38; and Donald E. Agostino, Herbert A. Terry, and Rolland C. Johnson "Home Video Recorders: Rights and Ratings," *Journal of Communication* 3 (Autumn 1980): 28–35.

16. See Edwin Mansfield, *Microeconomics: Theory and Applications*, shorte 4th ed. (New York: W.W. Norton, 1982), pp. 25–27. The term is being use here in a comparative (to other media entertainment forms) sense rather than the absolute manner (e.g. a single product).

17. Quoted in Steve Behrens, "Shortcut to the Home," *Channels* (March/Apri 1984), p. 30.

18. Lynne Schafer Gross, *The New Television Technologies* (Dubuque, Iowa Wm. C. Brown, 1983), pp. 102, 105; Lachenbruch, "Home Video," p. 43.

19. Lardner, *Fast Forward*, p. 201.

20. David Pauley and Connie Leslie, "The Videodisc Strikes Out," *Newsweek*, April 16, 1984, p. 69.

21. Watson S. "Jay" James, "The New Electronic Media: An Overview, *Journal of Advertising Research* 23 (August/September 1983): 35–36.

22. Quoted in Lardner, *Fast Forward*, p. 32.

23. Richard Corliss, "Backing Into the Future," *Time*, February 3, 1986 p. 65. The U.S. film industry defines the domestic market as including no only the United States but, curiously, Canada as well.

24. James Melanson, "Merrill Lynch Sees Homevid Boom for U.S. Pi Producers," *Variety*, January 29, 1987, pp. 1, 34. According to Vogel, b^ 1990, licensing of movies for use in such ancillary markets as networ and syndicated TV, pay cable, and home video "will in the aggregate fa

vershadow revenues derived from theatrical release." *Entertainment Industry Economics,* p. 50.

25. Steve Behrens, "Home at the Bijou," *Channels* (November/December 984), p. 10.

26. Vogel, *Entertainment Industry Economics,* p. 216. Declining retail prices or tapes, however, is expected to raise the sales end.

27. See Stephen Koepp, "Clash of the Video Merchants," *Time,* November 7, 1986, p. 74.

28. Jeffrey Cohen, "Are Video Clubs for You?" *Consumers' Research* (April 986), p. 25.

29. See Lardner, *Fast Forward,* for a full discussion of these sales-ental plans.

30. Dennis Hunt, "Industry Weighs Effect of Video Purchases," *Los Angeles imes,* January 13, 1989, pt. 6, p. 25.

31. Paula Parisi, " 'E.T.' " Video Sales Take Flight for Other-Worldly 7 iil Mark," *The Hollywood Reporter,* August 31, 1988, pp. 1, 22; Paula Parisi, "'E.T.' " Goes Home Vid with Record 10 Million Preorders," *The Hollywood eporter,* September 16, 1988, pp. 1, 38. The wholesale return for the preorders in excess of $160 million. On the future of the video business, see Ron Delpit, Home Vid Future in Rentals Proclaim Experts at Cinetex," *The Hollywood eporter,* September 30, 1988, p. 4.

32. Mayer, "Good-bye, Easy Growth," p. 106.

33. Paula Parisi, "Original Titles Slice Up Larger Piece of Vid Sell-Through ie," *The Hollywood Reporter,* September 1, 1988, p. 1.

34. Parisi, "Original Titles Slice," p. 19.

35. Charles Kipps, "Sell-Thru Tapes on the Move, But Whose Bottom Line 'limbs?" *Variety,* September 2, 1987, p. 47.

36. Bill Barol with Mark Starr, Erik Himmelsbach, and Eric Scigliano, The Last Picture Shows," *Newsweek,* June 8, 1987, p. 76.

37. Jeffrey Jolson-Colburn, "Industry Stands at Crossroads as New Tech-ologies Take Hold," *The Hollywood Reporter,* June 13, 1988, p. 8.

38. Syd Silverman, "Entertainment in the Satellite Era," *Variety,* October 5, 1983, p. 13.

39. Chuck Ross, "Par's 'Top Gun' Vid Breaks Ad Barrier with Pepsi romo," *The Hollywood Reporter,* January 15, 1987, p. 1. See also Paula Parisi, Home Video Industry on Fast Track Toward Ad Sponsorship," *The Hollywood eporter,* September 29, 1988, pp. 1, 23.

40. See Jeffrey Jolson-Colborn, "Vid Ads Score High Marks in New tudy," *The Hollywood Reporter,* June 16, 1988, pp. 1, 13. Research on audience eceptivity to advertising presented on cinema screens, also a new milieu, as found similar results, See Bruce A. Austin, "Cinema Screen Advertising: n Old Technology With New Promise for Consumer Marketing," *Journal of onsumer Marketing* 3 (Winter 1986): 45–56.

41. "Americans and the Arts: VCRs Take Off," *Newsweek,* March 28, 1988, . 69. For additional reading on movies in the context of leisure, see Austin, *nmediate Seating,* pp. 25–43.

42. Jolson-Colborn, "Vid Ads Score High," p. 13.

43. Cliff Rothman, "Studio Trends Point Toward Streamlined Launch Promos," *The Hollywood Reporter*, October 16, 1986, p. 8.

44. Teenage Research Unlimited, press release, November 1987.

45. Vogel, *Entertainment Industry Economics*, pp. 50–51.

46. Murphy quoted in "The Return of Hollywood," *The Economist*, Octobe 29, 1988, p. 24.

47. See Andrea King, "Future Dim, Say Indie Exhibitors at Cinetex Panel,' *The Hollywood Reporter*, September 30, 1988, pp. 1, 46. See also Martin A. Grove "Hollywood Eyes Exhibition as Lucrative Business," *The Hollywood Reporter* October 21, 1986, p. 87.

48. Quoted in Garth H. Drabinsky, "New Strategies for the Future: Tw« Challenges Facing Exhibition," *Boxoffice* (February 1988), p. 11.

49. See Guback, "Theatrical Film," p. 221; Douglas Gomery, "The Ameri can Film Industry in the 1970s: Status in the 'New Hollywood' ", *Wide Angle* 5 no. 4 1983): 54; and Waterman, "Prerecorded Home Video," p. 229.

50. See Agostino et al., "Home Video Recorders"; and Mark R. Levy' research: "Program Playback Preferences in VCR Households," *Journal o Broadcasting* 24 (Summer 1980): 327–36, "Home Video Recorders: A Use Survey," *Journal of Communication* 30 (Autumn 1980): 23–27; "Home Vide« Recorders and Time-Shifting," *Journalism Quarterly* 58 (Fall 1981): 401–405.

51. Vogel, *Entertainment Industry Economics*, pp. 52–53.

SUGGESTIONS FOR FURTHER READING

"Americans and the Arts: VCR's Take Off." *Newsweek*, March 28 1988, p. 69.

Austin, Bruce A. *Immediate Seating: A Look at Movie Audiences*. Belmon Calif.: Wadsworth, 1989.

Behrens, Steve. "Home at the Bijou." *Channels*, November/December 1984 pp. 10, 12.

Izod, John. *Hollywood and the Boxoffice, 1895–1986*. New York: Columbi University Press, 1988.

Lachenbruch, David. "Home Video: Home Is Where the Action Is.' *Channels*, November/December, 1983, pp. 42–43.

Lardner, James. *Fast Forward: Hollywood, the Japanese, and the VCR Wars* New York: Mentor Books, 1987.

"The Return of Hollywood." *The Economist*, October 29, 1988, pp 21–22, 24.

Vogel, Harold F. *Entertainment Industry Economics: A Guide for Financia Analysis*. Cambridge: Cambridge University Press, 1986.

Waterman, David. "Prerecorded Home Video and the Distribution of The atrical Films." In *Video Media Competition: Regulation, Economics, and Technology* ed. Eli M. Noan, pp. 221–43. New York: Columbia University Press, 1985.

Williams, Wenmouth, Jr., and Mitchell E. Shapiro. "A Study of the Effects n-Home Entertainment Alternatives Have on Film Attendance." In *Current eserach in Film: Audiences, Economics, and Law,* vol. 1, ed. Bruce A. Austin, •p. 93–100. Norwood, N.J.: Ablex Publishing, 1985.

The following trade publications frequently report on issues relevant to he present chapter: *Boxoffice* (monthly), *Channels of Communication* (monthly), *)aily Variety, The Hollywood Reporter* (daily), and *Variety* (weekly).

Chapter 12

The Made-for-TV Movie:
Industrial Practice, Cultural Form, Popular Reception

Laurie Schulze

*T*he made-for-TV movie's initial reception by popular criticism was marked by a particularly vehement hostility. Despite the fact that NBC's 1966 "Fame Is the Name of the Game" (usually credited with being the first made-for-TV movie) captured 40 percent of the viewing audience, *TV Guide*'s Richard K. Doan labelled "Fame" a "non-movie," describing it as "Grade-B melodrama ... given the promotional trappings of a 'world premiere' because neither moviegoers nor TV audiences had seen it before."[1]

Variously referred to in popular critical discourse as "non-movies," "quasi-movies," and "quickies," made-for-TV movies were immediately positioned by reviewers as objects unworthy of serious considera-tion. The inevitable point of comparison was the theatrical feature, and made-for-TV movies were designated the "film industry's step-children." As television critic Judith Crist wrote in 1969, the TV movie "wouldn't ... earn a B rating on any theatrical meter bill."

Crist went on to say that "what separates the television movie from the theatrical film is, basically, production values-—cheap ones—not quite casts and hiccuping plots" that lurch "from climax to climax in time for the cluster of commercials at set intervals, allowing no subtle developments of character or story." Crist con-demned TV movies for their formulaic characteristics, and included a quote from a network executive admitting that TV movies are "all the same ... and they get the same ratings so who cares?" Early popular criticism like Crist's almost always justified its dismissal of the TV movie by pointing to the movie's mode of production—its limited budget, tight shooting schedule, and the sheer amount of text generated implicates the TV movie as the product of the "factory,"

351

not the "atelier." "Popularity," Crist concluded, "is small proof of quality."[2]

If the meaning constructed for the TV movie in early popular criticism might best be summed up as "junk," eventually reviewers attempted to make a space in which "exceptional" TV movies could be singled out and positioned against the background of the form. Articles like Dwight Whitney's "Cinema's Stepchild Grows Up" (*TV Guide*, July 20, 1974) situated themselves as an apologetic for made-for-TV movies, while acknowledging that most of them were "shoddy."

Whitney's attempt to recuperate some TV movies begins by pushing the made-for-TV movies as "mere potboiling trash" back into history: "in the beginning, the made-for-TV movie was . . . a repository for the deposed stars of former TV series." A few years later, Alvin H. Marill and Patrick McGilligan used similar arguments, Marill referring to "those escapist pieces of the early days" and McGilligan echoing Whitney's opening gambit: "in the beginning, most of the made-for-television movies were run-of-the-mill exploitation pictures."[3] This clears a space for the "good" TV movie by relegating the "bad" TV movie to the formative stages. That space is then filled by gesturing at the serious topics taken up by recent TV movies and making a case for the existence of TV movie auteurs.

Marill refers to the "more mature themes" (homosexuality, alcoholism, rape) dealt with by the contemporary TV movie, the kind approvingly labeled the "sociological film" by Whitney and the "public service drama" by McGilligan. The implication is that TV movies that deal with serious social problems themselves deserve to be taken seriously, much like David Thorburn's argument concerning television melodrama, which urges that melodrama deserves critical consideration because it acts as an "arena" for dealing with "disturbing" social and moral problems. These attempts to valorize the social-issue TV movie also emphasize its public service or informational value: Whitney singled out "The Morning After" because it "showed what it is like to be afflicted with alcoholism." If the public service seriousness of the TV movie was the basis of one of the earlier critical strategies used to make a case for the "good" TV movie, however, it seems to have become a point of potential dissatisfaction with the form. In a review of "The Burning Bed" (NBC, 1984), Richard Zoglin refers to social-problem TV movies as "TV's issue-of-the-week parade," arguing that they are so wrapped up in teaching viewers about social issues that they become very bad drama.[4]

If serious themes are no longer necessary and sufficient conditions for elevating the TV movie to a place in the popular canon, pointing to the identifiable presence of TV movie authors has been maintained as a critical strategy for legitimating some made-for-TV movies.[5] Some popular television critics, following the lines of the auteurist project in film studies, argue that the made-for-TV movie can be shown to be popular art because it can be shown to have authors. Those TV movies that can be linked with an authorial presence (and issuing source of meaning) are marked off as deserving serious critical study and critical acclaim. This strategy is implicit in Whitney's earlier article; those films that he singles out for attention are labeled "Christiansen and Hosenberg's "The Autobiography of Miss Jane Pittman,' or "Paul Junger Witt's 'Brian's Song,'" or "Roger Gimbal's 'I Heard the Owl Call My Name," Later "auteurist" critical work draws heavily on directors.'" who began in TV movies and then became recognized auteurs in film. Steven Spielberg is most often cited as an identifiable artist in the TV movie genre ("Something Evil," "Duel," "Savage"). Since Spielberg is now an acknowledged cinematic (and thus, from the point of view of traditional criticism, more prestigious) director, the invocation of his name in connection with the TV movie adds weight to the claims of critics who attempt to canonize a TV movie by attributing it to an author. Patrick McGilligan extends the visible presence of a single auteur to cover the entire field of TV movies, claiming that "it took a director like Steven Spielberg to legitimize the made-for-television movie."[6] At the least, the TV movie can be pointed to as a place where "real" auteurs serve their apprenticeship and graduate to "real" movies.

The auteurist project for TV movies, however, is limited to a few movies by a few TV movie directors. Tom Allen, for example, attempts to identify patterns of meaning and style marking the TV movies of John Sargent, Steven Spielberg, John Badham, Lamont Johnson, John Kerty, and William A. Graham as authored movies that therefore command critical attention. But while he valorizes the TV movies of the TV auteurs, he sets them against the "great bulk" of TV movies as a whole, which, he writes, is "impossible to imagine . . . anywhere but on subsidized, time-killing commercial TV." If the TV movie can be demonstrated to have "some golden talents," Allen claims, it has not produced a "golden age." Some TV movies are special because golden talents have managed to resist the institutional constraints of the television system, inscribing a personal vision in their movies that can be extracted from them by the critic. But the TV movie as a whole is characterized by Allen as "a common heap of dross."[7]

Faced with the immense popularity of the TV movie, which seems to fly in the face of reviewers' low estimations of the genre, critics often offer up the audience as a scapegoat. Sometimes the popular audience is conceptualized as merely unsophisticated, helpless to resist the machinations of the powerful and persuasive television system. Herbert Gold, for instance, speaks of the promotion of the TV movie as an "attack" on audiences, and cites the unquestioned ability of the TV movie's dramatic construction to "hold" and "grip" viewers in spite of themselves.[8] A recent essay in *Time* on the "dangers" of the made-for-TV movie based on real events worries that the public may not be capable of understanding that "a network may have one standard of fidelity to fact in its 7 p.m. newscast, and another an hour later in its docudramas."[9]

More often, however, traditional criticism holds the audience itself responsible for its low sensibilities. Television critic Tom Shales (*The Washington Post*) bemoans the fact that TV movies like ABC's "awesomely stupid" "Lace" and "ludicrously smarmy" "My Mother's Secret Life" received much higher ratings than the "wholesome movie hits" *Star Wars* and *Chariots of Fire*. Shales quotes an independent producer who charges that "the public deserves some of the blame for these programs. They always flock to the trashy things." The trashy things Shales in concerned about trade in "stereotypes" that are "most demeaning to women." Significantly, Shales goes on to argue that the female audience is at fault. "Such programs," Shales claims, "would not be on the air if they didn't appeal to women." This implicates the female audience in either feeblemindedness, reactionary antifeminism, or a kind of masochistic aesthetic, all of which Shales appears to imply. The moral turpitude Shales attributes to the TV movie is traced to some deficiency on the part of its female viewership, setting up a kind of "us" and "them" opposition. Made-for-TV movie "trash" is something that "they" (presumably uneducated, ideologically defective, or self-destructive women) want to watch. "We" (the implied reader of Shale's essay) would like to see what Shales approvingly labels "serious, intelligent, unsmutty TV movies," which won't be made because the (female) audience wants trash. (The "we" is presumably educated, liberal, and male.)[10]

Although popular criticism does not seem to explicitly categorize the TV movie as a women's genre, it lurks around the edges of the common complaint about the TV movie's reliance on melodrama, a genre historically linked with female viewership. When critics like Richard Corliss comment that "for a cathartic sob one must go to TV for a Movie of the Week" instead of to the cinema, a connection is clearly drawn between the TV movie and the woman's film—the "tearjerker" or the "weepie."[11] There are also frequent allusions to the similarities between TV movies and the soap opera, a narrative strongly connected with the female audience in popular and academic discourse. The TV movie, with its reliance on the family melodrama and the romance, its tendency to take up domestic issues, and its penchant for female protagonists and female stars, may indeed lean toward what has come to be called a feminine narrative form. The point is that a female audience for the TV movie is taken to task by popular criticism to strike another blow against what is perceived to be a nonaesthetic and morally defective form of popular culture.[12]

Incapable of constituting the typical TV movie as an aesthetic object and thus incapable of attributing any positive aesthetic or social pleasures to the viewing experience, popular criticism pushes the TV movie even closer to the edges of its discourse by positing an audience that is also marked as "different," and in some way as aesthetically and morally bankrupt and as incomprehensible as the TV movie is thought to be. Traditional aesthetic criticism refuses to make a space for the possibility of legitimate meanings or pleasures on the part of the typical made-for-TV movie audience, except for the sophisticated pleasures of the "schlock buff," whose superior sensibilities can legitimately be trained on trash. But if reviewers, on the whole, have not taken to the TV movie, the popular audience has, and the history of the made-for-TV movie is largely the history of a television form that has been increasingly profitable for networks and that has taken on a significant role in competitive programming strategy.

In the 1950s, Hollywood's major motion picture companies released their pre-1948 feature films to local television stations for broadcast. The major Hollywood studios were already involved in producing programs for television, but until 1956, the only theatrical features shown on television came from foreign studios or from B-movie American producers. Their "cheap production values" notwithstanding, these theatrical features became, according to Douglas Gomery, a "mainstay of local television programming practice" by 1955. In 1956, C & C Television, which had acquired the rights to the RKO features, released the first theatrical titles from a major Hollywood studio to local markets and within a year pulled in an estimated $25 million. The other major studios soon followed, and by 1958, all of the majors' pre-1948 features were in heavy circulation on local stations. Yet the networks, although occasionally including a feature film in their prime-time schedules, did not take up Hollywood films until the 1960s, when the consistently high local ratings for pre-1948 films convinced them that Hollywood movies on network prime time might generate an even more impressive share of the audience. In the 1960s, television successfully negotiated for recent feature films, and by the early 1970s the three networks were broadcasting ten prime-time "Movie Nights" each week. The ratings were high, and the recent

Hollywood feature became, as Gomery puts it, "one of the strongest weapons" the networks could deploy in the ratings wars, especially during the rating period called "sweeps weeks," which determine the rates local stations and networks will charge advertisers for commercial time.[13]

This programming practice, saturating prime time with Hollywood films, rapidly led to a shortage of available and appropriate features: television broadcast them faster than Hollywood could produce them. In May 1966, *Television Magazine*, describing the "seller's market" created by the movie shortage, reported that the stations were so desperate they were buying "anything with sprocket holes." Opportunistic studios used the impressively high ratings commanded by their features to exact even higher prices from the networks for the right to broadcast their more popular films. When *The Bridge on the River Kwai* went to ABC for $2 million in 1966, the television industry began to realize that there might be no limit to what studios could demand for their product.[14]

With the increasing costs of Hollywood features cutting away at their profits, the networks began to commission the production of films exclusively for television. MCA, Inc. and its subsidiary, Universal City Studios, were influential players in the development of TV movies. Lew R. Wasserman, chairman of MCA, the top talent agency in the 1940s, had long been interested in getting into film production, but Screen Actors Guild regulations prevented a talent agency from moving into the movie business. When television came along, however, the union allowed MCA to produce filmed material for television, and MCA's Revue Productions, with programming chief Jennings Lang, was turning out popular programs like "Alfred Hitchcock Presents," "General Electric Theater," and "Bachelor Father" by the late 1950s. In 1962, Wasserman bought the Universal Pictures lot, modernized the run-down studio, and then Wasserman, Lang, and MCA began pitching the concept of one-shot movies made just for television to the networks. CBS and ABC were skeptical, but NBC was more optimistic. In 1965, NBC contracted with MCA for more than 30 "World Premiere" movies to be produced over a several year period. The first, "Fame Is The Name of the Game" (Universal, 1966), turned out to be a "back-door pilot" for a subsequent series, as well.[15] What critic Patrick McGilligan terms a "declaration of independence" from the Hollywood theatrical feature by the networks had begun.[16]

For the next three seasons, movies made for television appeared intermittently in the networks' prime-time programming, but they were, according to McGilligan, "infrequent" and considered "risky business." In 1969, ABC introduced its "Movie of the Week," a regular series of films made exclusively for television. No one, according to arry Diller, who created the "Movie of the Week" format, expected the genre to be that popular. But the made-for-TV movie demonstrated that it could command extremely large audiences, sometimes even overstripping the ratings power of popular theatrical features.[17] In addition to its rating potential, the made-for-TV movie was also more economical to produce than the theatrical feature and often cost less than the rights to broadcast popular Hollywood films (in the early 1970s, production costs were typically under $1 million). By 1972, the popular and profitable made-for-TV movie, was, as Gomery puts it, "established as a force on network television," with all three major networks placing made-for-TV movies in their prime-time programming. ABC's "Brian's Song" (1971), a docudrama about the friendship between Chicago Bears' football players Gale Sayers and Brian Piccolo (Piccolo, tragically, died of cancer in 1970), made the top ten list of all movies (theatricals and made-for's) ever shown on television, winning Emmies and critical acclaim, as well as the highest rating yet achieved by a made-for-TV movie.[18] TV movie production more than doubled between 1970–71 and 1971-72.

In the mid-1970s, producers and networks expanded the made-for-TV movie form to include novels for television and miniseries. "Rich Man, Poor Man" in 1975, "Roots" in 1977, and "Holocaust" in 1978 proved to the industry that the long-form television movie could produce spectacular ratings. The long-form movies became what McGilligan calls the "command items" of the genre. These special events, however, have equally special production costs compared with the average TV movie. Currently, a typical made-for-TV movie costs about $2 million to produce, while the CBS miniseries "Space" (1985) reportedly cost over $32 million and the recent ratings hit "Lonesome Dove" (1989) over $20 million. Since the long-form movies need high ratings to recoup their high production costs, they represent more of a gamble than the ordinary movie of the week, and the two-hour made-for-TV movie continues to be the backbone of the genre. Not that the average made-for-TV movie is uncompetitive. In 1979, ABC's "Elvis" (a biography of Elvis Presley) captured the largest share of the audience, against *Gone With the Wind* on CBS and *One Flew Over the Cuckoo's Nest* on NBC. In the 1983–84 season, two ABC made-for-TV movies, "The Day After" (a drama about a nuclear strike on Lawrence, Kansas, starring Jason Robards and JoBeth Williams) and "Something About Amelia" (a made-for about incest, starring Ted Danson and Glenn Close), ranked second and fourth in the ratings for all television shows of the season. NBC's "Adam" (missing children) and "Policewoman Centerfold" (a police officer's career is at stake after she poses for a centerfold) both out-performed ABC's "Monday Night Football," while blockbuster theatricals like *Star Wars* and *Chariots of Fire* failed to win their time slots.

Since its entry into broadcast television, the made-for-TV movie has become a major part of network programming practice. The three networks together commission, on average, over a hundred movies each year, sometimes outstripping domestic feature film production. The made-for-TV movie occupies about 20 percent of network prime time.[19] Since the growth of cable and pay TV, made-for-TV movies may be more important to the networks than ever, because cable and pay TV are getting the first-run deals for theatrical features. In 1983, Lew Erlicht, president of ABC Entertainment, reported that the first-run exposure of theatricals on cable and pay TV cost the eventual network run of the same theatricals at least 10 to 15 share points. Erlicht said, "there's no reason we should be buying 24-share films, why should we?" The TV movie, with real first-run status, represents a network programming alternative to overexposed theatricals. ABC chose to open the 1983–84 season with "The Making of a Male Model," getting a 33 share. Steve Mills, CBS vice president/motion pictures for TV, claims that CBS's TV movies perform well in "defensive" programming, going up against the competition's top-rated shows and coming away winners. Made-fors also have a highly desirable flexibility. Functioning as television's "switch-hitters and designated schedulers" in the programming game, TV movies can come off the bench to undercut the other networks' feature films, special events, or series.[20] CBS, currently running third behind ABC and NBC in prime time, recently announced that since series are not pulling viewers to the CBS schedule, their programming strategy for the 1989–90 season would focus on "high concept" made-for-TV movies to attract the audience.[21]

The TV movie is undeniably a mass-produced text. The networks underwrite the production of over two hundred hours of made-for-TV movies every year, and the economic constraints on made-for-TV movie budgets as well as the demand for quantity limit the actual shooting schedule of the average TV movie to about three weeks, although there may be months in which to develop a concept and write a script. Months spent in preproduction and three weeks in production might seem a rather leisurely pace in comparison with the production schedules of television's other narrative forms: an episode of a soap opera, for example, must be shot in a single day.

In critical discourse, however, made-for-TV movies were invariably compared to the "real" movies, and the comparison resulted in a characterization of made-for-TV movies as "quickies." Judith Crist, perhaps the most influential television critic, labeled them "nonmovies." Crist, like many other critics, claimed that the mode of production of the TV movie consigns it (with rare exceptions) to the trash heap of formulaic mass-produced narratives. Made-for-TV movies, Crist wrote, "don't bear detailing" because they are "all the same," identical products of the "assembly-belt system" of the television "factory."[22]

Popular aesthetic discourse on the made-for-TV movies as mass-produced culture does have a point: made-for-TV movies are organized according to an industrial system of production, have limited production funds, and restricted production schedules. But leveling all made-for-TV movies to the same narrative text and deducing the way the text will be read and its aesthetic value from the mode of production obscures a necessary difference between mass-produced consumer goods and "mass-produced" texts. As Robert Allen points out, the analogy breaks down at a crucial juncture, often lost on traditional critics.

The absolute standardization required for the mass production of consumer items is inapplicable to the production of narratives. The consumer expects each bar of Ivory soap to be exactly like the last one purchased, but he or she expects each new movie or episode of a television program to bear marks of difference.[23]

While the mode of production and the institutional function assumed by television texts—the establishment of a regular audience habituated to a particular program—does demand that programs exhibit marks of similarity so that viewer familiarity will ensure repeated and predictable return to them, they must also exhibit marks of difference. Television's fictive narratives must be both the same and yet not the same. Their differences, ignored by much traditional criticism, are as essential to their popularity as their similarities. Meaningful differences among TV movies may include generic variations: there are TV movie versions of hard-boiled detective genre ("Calendar Girl Murders"), the screwball comedy ("Maid in America"), science-fiction ("V"), the family melodrama ("Family Secrets"), the docudrama ("Flight #90: Disaster on the Potomac"), the biography ("The Jesse Owens Story"), the historical romance ("Mistress of Paradise"), the suspense-thriller ("Through Naked Eyes"). TV movies take up different social issues, from alcoholism ("The Boy Who Drank Too Much") to union activism ("Heart of Steel"). Some TV movies experiment with visual style (NBC's "Special Bulletin," a 1983 made-for about protestors threatening to detonate nuclear warheads in Charleston, South Carolina, was shot on videotape as a simulated newscast).

Alongside their differences, made-for-TV movies have also developed identifiable similarities that have solidified into "codes" that distinguish them from, for instance, the theatrical feature. Critics and audiences both exhibit a sense for what those distinguishing characteristics of the TV movie genre are, although they may not necessarily articulate them. But almost everyone would understand what is meant when, for example, a film reviewer remarks that the 1988 theatrical release *The Good Mother* (starring Diane Keaton and Liam Neeson, about a divorced woman who risks losing custody of her daughter when her exhusband charges that the six-year-old's exposure to the relationship between Keaton and her lover is damaging the child) "looks like a standard Issue-of-the Week TV-movie that somehow wandered onto the big screen."[24]

Shooting for the box rather than the big screen makes a difference in the visual style of the TV movie. Because the television image is much smaller, and because the image has relatively low resolution and permits less detail than the cinematic image, the medium shot and the close-up dominate TV movie practice, combined with a tendency to use relatively shallow focus: compared to the cinematic image, television's mise-en-scene is stripped down. Limited budgets also restrict the TV movie's scope: huge crowd scenes and on-location spectacles cost money, money that may not be available to the typical movie-of-the-week. But the TV movie has fashioned an aesthetic from its limitations. Horace Newcomb identifies "intimacy" as one of television's aesthetic principles, pointing out that stylistic intimacy is appropriate for television's reduced visual scale and for TV's normative viewing conditions: television is watched in private spaces, in the home. TV movies extend the principle of intimacy into their narrative material as well, concentrating heavily on the personal story.[25] (The TV movie's preference for melodrama as the generic vehicle for intimate human interest stories will be discussed at greater length below, as will the TV movie's reliance on hot social issues for topical material. Both "melodramatic" and "topical" are practically synonymous with the cultural connotations indentified with the TV movie genre.)

Television's viewing situation is generally a distracted one, and viewers' attention to the small screen is often intermittant. John Ellis argues that watching TV is organized by a "regime of the glance," rather than the concentrated gaze at the image encouraged by the theatrical film viewing situation. Television sound is audible, however, even when the viewer may not be looking directly at the screen. So TV places a greater emphasis on sound to attract the viewer's glance and to carry the message.[26] Thus, TV movies tend to rely on dialogue more than their theatrical counterparts.

Unlike theatrical films, TV movies are interrupted by commercials. Made-fors must structure their narratives around commercial breaks, resulting in what David Thorburn terms "segmented dramatic structure," each act achieving a "localized vividness," with dramatic mini-climaxes occurring just before the commercial breaks, so viewers will stick with the story across the interruptions. Thorburn goes on to point out that one key strategy functioning to achieve this segmented vividness is an aesthetic of performance: the actors must be "intense" and "energetic," so that their highly emotional performances give each segment "independent weight and interest."[27] The effects of segmentation on narrative structure and the actor's performance is perhaps most clearly evident in the opening act of the TV movie. As Todd Gitlin puts it, "all salient [narrative] elements have to be established with breathtaking haste" and characters' traits must "leap out of the screen," or the TV movie risks losing its audience.[28]

TV movie acting seems to have produced, as one critic observes, its own "galaxy of stars," with names that seldom appear in theatrical features but that are almost guaranteed to win high ratings for made-fors. Lindsay Wagner, Elizabeth Montgomery, Mariette Hartley, Angie Dickinson, Richard Thomas, Robert Wagner, and Richard Crenna, for example, have or have had TV movie star power comparable to the box office clout of a Meryl Streep or Sylvester Stallone. While movie stars occasionally appear in made-fors, the TV movie has its own independent star system, marking the made-for off from theatrical films. Both the aesthetic of the close-up and narrative segmentation, as well as the reliance on melodrama, invest the TV movie heavily in the actor's performance, and the TV movie star is a significant aspect of the genre's popularity.

Most made-for-TV movies are the product of independent producers. The networks are the buyers. According to independent producer Frank von Zerneck ("Katie: Portrait of a Centerfold"), the initial determination on the production of a made-for-TV movie is the development of a "concept" that will interest a network. Network interest is predicated on generating the maximum audience of the right demographic kind to deliver to advertisers. Networks will make the decision to underwrite TV movie projects based on whether or not they think the movie can be marketed in such a way as to ensure a sizable share of the audience.[29]

Todd Gitlin notes that the case of the made-for-TV movie presents the networks with a rather unique problem of promotability. Since TV movies anchor the relatively closed end of television's spectrum of narrative closure/openness, and since they are seen only once—sometimes twice if rerun in the summer—their audience cannot be developed by word of mouth or critical acclaim, as can the audience for a theatrical feature or a television series or serial. The TV movie cannot constitute, in effect, it own advertisement, as a series or serial or soap opera can.[30]

The marketing strategies available to the networks to bring an audience to a made-for-TV movie are limited to a few sentences in *TV Guide* and a brief trailer broadcast the week before the movie is scheduled to air. Von Zerneck says, "the audience [for the made-for-TV movie] is fresh, it's new each time. You have to convince them that there's something in this movie they want to see."[31] Being able to persuade an audience that "there's something in this movie they want to see" with a short series of clips and a sentence in *TV Guide* practically demands what one former network vice-president in charge of TV movies refers to as "hot concept" movies, already invested with "high promotability."[32]

In the absence of continuing characters and situations, which build an audience for the series and serial forms, the TV movie must depend on a brief, condensed one-shot narrative image to solicit its audience. As Gitlin puts it, to be marketable to networks in the first place, the concept for the TV movie has to be "sensational."[33] The TV movie therefore depends on a high degree of responsiveness to whatever issues are currently in heavy cultural circulation for its economic survival and effectiveness in commanding an audience. It must provide curiosity by the promise of the unusual or the scandalous and immediately mark itself off as different. Yet it must be familiar at the same time, and reassure by its reference to the instantly recognizable. If the concept proposed to the network by the independent producer cannot be condensed into this brief sensational/familiar narrative image, the project stands little chance of being developed. Von Zerneck sums up the situation from the network point of view: "No matter how good or bad a movie is, for television, if you can't summarize it in a sentence that will appear in *TV Guide*, and if you can't describe it in a paragraph, then you'll have a great deal of difficulty selling the project."[34]

If a network feels that the concept will be promotable—sometimes a random sample of viewers are surveyed to find out if they would watch a TV movie on the basis of a brief plot summary like the one that would appear in *TV Guide*—the independent producer will hire a writer to construct a treatment. If the treatment is approved by the network, a writer will proceed with a script. The producer, according to von Zerneck, usually pays for the script, but is reimbursed by the network if the network wants to fund the project. (Von Zerneck's company must develop 20 to 25 scripts for the networks to produce three or four made-for-TV movies per year. The development of a script does not guarantee that the network will eventually decide to bankroll the movie.) If the network accepts the script, it pays the producer a license fee, which will finance the production of the movie. This license fee gives the network the right to broadcast the finished movie twice.

The advantage to the independent producer is that after the network broadcasts the movie, the rights then revert back to the producer, who may sell it into syndication, release it on videocassette or theatrically in foreign markets, or sell it back to the networks for late-night programming. The producer also has the option of entering into partnership with a studio that provides production and postproduction facilities and the services of its marketing organizations to sell the movie into syndication or foreign release after the network has given the movie back to the producer. The studio exacts an overhead, built into production costs, which means that the producer must expect more of a delay before profits from syndication or foreign or videocassette sales are returned. The studio might also make it more difficult for the producer to go over budget or over schedule.

The greater determination, however, is exerted by the network, which first decides, in effect, whether or not the project will be produced at all. Von Zerneck admits, "they control the money and the network. The also have a point of view about what they want on their network, what kind of movie they want. So you're essentially writing it to order. The script is custom made for them." The bottom line for the networks, von Zerneck claims, is, "is it going to be a movie they can exploit? Will it get an audience? Will it have footage that they'll be able to put into a trailer to entice people to watch it?"[35]

The economic basis of the commercial broadcast television system is delivering the largest, most desirable audience to advertisers. So the networks tend to underwrite movie projects with a high degree of exploitability, projects for which the popular audience can be presumed to have the necessary "cultural capital," in Pierre Bourdieu's useful term, required for its narrative image to be immediately salient and relevant. The network notion of where popular sensibilities are to be monitored is summed up by a former network vice-president in charge of TV movies: "I look at TV commercials to look for a trend. Or places where money is spent, not free stuff like television. What's on the covers of magazines? What are the advertisers using to sell soap? What are they saying about what's going on in the country?" Hot concepts are mined from national magazine covers or from television's reality programming, talk show issues and tabloid television scandals that provide the narrative skeletons that can be fleshed out into what Gitlin rather sarcastically calls "little personal stories that executives think mass audiences will take as relations of the contemporary."[36]

The made-for-TV movie, perhaps because its story world begins and ends in two hours, because its narrative situations and characters do not come into the American home week in and week out, appears to be capable of pushing at the limits of the controversial without losing its audience. As Les Brown observes, when NBC broadcast "My Sweet Charlie" in 1970, a TV movie about an intimate relationship between a black man and a white Southern girl, it received a 53 share in the ratings; very few viewers complained that the movie was offensive.[37] Almost 20 years later, interracial sexual relationships between continuing characters on series, serials, or daytime soap operas seem to be very difficult for the networks to risk. Television's practice implies the assumption that the mass audience is more willing to tolerate sensational or controversial subjects for a single evening than on a continuing basis. Nevertheless, networks (in search of ratings) are reluctant to chance deeply offending even the TV movie audience. *TV Guide* reports that NBC "toned down" the recent "Roe vs. Wade" (1989), a TV movie about the again controversial Supreme Court decision legalizing abortion, to avoid criticism by antiabortion groups, who felt that the docudrama might be too sympathetic to "Jane Roe" (the woman denied an abortion under Texas law whose case eventually came before the Supreme Court). According to a senior vice-president in charge of TV movies, changes were made in the script to make "Roe vs. Wade" less "pro-choice."[38]

In broadcast television practice, the made-for-TV movie emerged as a privileged site for the negotiation of problematic social issues. What has been variously termed the issue-of-the-week movie, the public service drama, and the social problem TV movie by popular critics became the primary form of the TV movie genre. The issues taken up by the TV movie, however, tend toward the hot concept problems that can be transformed into salacious, highly promotable trailers: housewives turned afternoon prostitutes, lesbian mothers, gay fathers, venereal disease, rape, white slavery, addiction, abortion, domestic violence, incest, adultery, bisexuality, child pornography. If some critics complain that TV movies "take a spicy topic . . . and publicize it with a lot of juicy, lead in advertising," they also argue, as Richard Zoglin does in a review of "The Burning Bed" (NBC, 1984), a TV movie about domestic violence starring Farrah Fawcett, that "one by one, TV movies take up a topic, adorn it with stars, and promote it as another prime-time break through. As drama, these TV crusades have such familiar faults—too simplistic, too preachy, too ponderously 'educational'—that a good one can easily get lost in the shuffle."[39]

Whether the controversial issues the made-for TV movie appropriates are easily marketed as "provocative" (teenage hitchhikers, male strippers) or more "serious" social problems (missing children, teenage suicide, toxic waste, the homeless, union activism, racism), both criticisms found in popular reviews—too sensational, too educational—point to interesting functions the TV movie has assumed in prime-time broadcast television. The issue-of-the-week movie, the center of the genre, already constitutes a response to points of social struggle. It opens up the site of an immense and intense ideological negotiation, limning, as it does, the more salient and disturbing phenomena on the social agenda.

That the topics "torn from the headlines" (a promotional slogan used to market "The Burning Bed") are capable of being sensationalized in the movie's narrative image can be traced to the function any television text must assume in the economic system of broadcast television—getting the maximum audience of the demographic kind attractive to advertisers—and to the unique problem of promotability attached to the TV movie. That movies made for television also take on what I will call a pedagogical function with respect to the issues they organize—educating the audience by having characters cite the latest statistics on whatever subject is taken up, describing a social problem with presumed accuracy (if within a fictional context), and indicating the solution to the issue—brings up what Stuart Hall has called the "framing" function of popular television.[40]

Todd Gitlin, among other academic critics, argues that the made-for-TV movie, while taking up sensational and disturbing problems, strongly tends to organize or frame these issues in a way that domesticates them. Gitlin writes that "if the networks like a dollop of controversy now and then, they usually want it manageable: social significance with a lifted face." The TV movie's social issues are "routinely depoliticized" when turned into "little personal stories," and the made-for-TV movie ends up as "mass culture's equivalent of the squarish, hard-skinned, tasteless tomato grown for quick, reliable, low-cost machine harvesting, untouched by human hands."[41] Douglas Gomery, in his analysis of "Brian's Song" (ABC, 1971), concludes that made-for-TV movies simplify complex social issues at best and more often than not, through narrative structure and mythologizing stereotypes, manage to make the social issues they invoke "non-controversial."[42] Gitlin's analysis points to the effects that framing social issues in the context of the melodramatic personal story might have on a TV movie's ideological edge. The pedagogical stance frequently adopted by the made-for-TV movie might have a similar domesticating function.

"Something About Amelia," for instance, spends the balance of its narrative energy in depicting the steps that need to be taken in a case of incest: believing the child, alerting the proper authorities, removing the father from the home and temporarily placing the child in a treatment center for abused children, counseling with qualified professionals to enable the family to deal with the consequences in ways that will lead to "healing" and the reformation of the family. All the facts and statistics about incest are oddly comforting, as if by simply knowing them we gain control over the problem. And the movie seems to reassure us, in a teaching sort of way, that existing social institutions and professionals already in place can and do provide solutions, that the problem is being handled.

Some TV movies bring in extra-textual material to educate the audience about issues and suggest ways in which they might be prevented or managed. "Adam" (NBC, 1983) was followed by a broadcast of photographs and descriptons of missing children, with a public appeal to call a special telephone number with any information that might help locate them. More than 30 missing children were found, and the solution indicated in the movie—the establishment of a nationwide network for finding missing children—was eventually put in place on the strength of public awareness generated by the TV movie. (Adam's real-life father, John Walsh, went on to host "America's Most Wanted.")

"Surviving" (ABC, 1985) was broadcast accompanied by a number of extra-textual programs on the issue of teenage suicide, including a 30-minute documentary on the problem, local and national news features, and educational material made available for use in schools in conjunction with the movie. The movie itself was bracketed with direct appeals to teenagers considering suicide, encouraging them to seek help. One network executive described the movie as "preventive medicine" for teenage suicide.[43] Whether it brings in extra-textual informational programming, or whether the shape of the problem and its solutions are left to the movie alone, the TV movie's pedagogical strategies do potentially work to pull the disturbing issue it takes up toward socially manageable limits. The problem can be understood, statistics cited, fictive representatives of professionals consulted, solutions spelled out, the issue reassuringly negotiated.

It is also always the case that articles in national news magazines and newspapers, stories on local and national news programs, and educational materials operate as part of a marketing strategy as well, putting a specific made-for-TV movie on the agenda, promoting it as a socially significant television event. For example, although the full-page ad in *TV Guide* reads "She had only just begun . . . and suddenly her world was falling apart. The life and death of a superstar" to promote "The Karen Carpenter Story" (CBS, 1989), the close-up emphasizes that Karen had a "serious health problem," anorexia nervosa, a "life-threatening eating disorder." Immediately following the close-up, in the Denver edition of *TV Guide*, is a full-page advertisement for the Rader Institute for the treatment of all eating disorders. The caption, above a drawing of an emaciated young woman staring into a mirror filled with an overweight reflection, reads "The Agony of Anorexia." The young woman is saying, "If only I were thinner, then I'd be happy." The advertisement gives the institute's address and telephone number, under the phrases "It's not your fault . . . you're not alone." In the same *TV Guide*, an article by Karen's brother, Richard, discusses her anorexia, and an article by staff writer Susan Littwin offers an analysis of the eating disorder by a psychiatrist specializing in the treatment of anorexia. The 5.00 P.M. news on the local CBS affiliate (KMGH, channel 7) broadcast a story on anorexia and bulimia the day the movie aired. The movie was also a "Read More About It" book project selection, and in this case "it" was eating disorders.[44] Whatever informational aspects all this material surrounding "The Karen Carpenter Story" might have had, it also certainly functioned to add another layer to a hot concept and to promote the TV movie as a social issue must-see. And in fact, as of mid-March 1989, "The Karen Carpenter Story," with a 26.4 rating and a 41 share, was the top-rated made-for-TV movie of the season.

The TV movie, then, typically activates what might be termed referential codes—codes that tie an issue depicted in a fictive narrative to the shape the problem and its possible solutions assume in social reality. However, the made-for-TV movie also depends on certain fictional codes. The made-for-TV movie, like much of fictional television, relies heavily on the family melodrama as a generic code that pulls whatever issue is taken up into familiar terrain.

Melodrama, in particular, is a preferred fictional context for addressing disturbing social materials. Peter Brooks, in his study of melodrama, defines the genre in terms of its tendency toward "excess," the unmasking of things that might otherwise be repressed. As Brooks writes, "the genre's very existence is bound to [the] possibility, and necessity, of saying everything."[45] If melodrama involves itself with the excessive, its function consists, many critics have argued, in invoking desires or anxieties only to put them back into the box again. John Cawelti describes melodramas as narratives whose worlds "seem to be governed by some benevolent moral principle," presenting a "moral fantasy". . . showing forth the essential 'rightness' of the world order," an order that "bears[s] out the audience's traditional patterns of right and wrong, good and evil."[46]

While there is something to be said for conceptualizing melodrama as a "fantasy of reassurance," some critics step back from Cawelti's definition of the genre. David Thorburn, for instance, in his definition of television melodrama, argues that while the genre's "reassurance-structure," its "moral simplification," and its "topicality" are among its generic conventions, TV melodrama is not escapist fantasy that sensationalizes the controversial only to neutralize it by arbitrarily invoking the established moral and political order in the end. TV melodrama, Thorburn claims, functions as a "forum" or "arena" in which "forbidden or deeply disturbing materials" may be addressed; melodrama is "not an escape into blindness . . . but an instrument for seeing."[47]

That the made-for-TV movie has a distinct preference for melo-dramatic codings of the issues it takes up, especially those issues that center around the family, has not escaped the attention of popular critics. Crist, for example, complains that made-for-TV movies are sunk in the "melodrama rut," a rut that mires the genre in predictability, exaggerated sentimentality, and shallow characters.[48] While Crist is quite right to point out that the TV movie does indeed almost invari-ably use melodrama, and the family melodrama in particular, as its central fictional code, what Crist calls a rut I would call a generic convention. It is, however, a generic convention not without possible consequences.

Ellen Seiter, in her analysis of television's family melodramas, identified some of the key characteristics of the genre: "convention-ally, the structure of melodrama limits it to the presentation of only those conflicts which can be resolved within the family." Further, the family melodrama presents its problems as privatized ones that can be managed by privatized solutions, domesticating what are in fact profound social conflicts by pulling them down to the personal level of the individual character.[49] Todd Gitlin's critique of the made-for-TV movie centers largely around this point: The "iron embrace of the little personal story" smothers the social issues the TV movie would like to think it is dealing with.[50]

Not surprisingly, the made-for-TV movie, concentrating as it does on the family and domestic issues, frequently features women centrally in its narratives. From "Sybil" to "Money on the Side," from "The Auto-biography of Miss Jane Pittman" to "Katie: Portrait of a Centerfold," TV movies are one of the few prime-time programming forms that permit a woman's story to be the story being told. Prime-time series and serial melodramas—"Dynasty" and "Dallas," for example—tend to place a community of male characters more centrally in their narratives. The made-for-TV movie may be filling a gap left by the "woman's film" of the Hollywood studio system. A statement concerning the affinity of the TV movie for the woman's story has come, interestingly enough, from television producer Aaron Spelling ("Charlie's Angels"), who claims that TV movies are one of the few prime-time contexts in which women can be stars. Spelling remarked, in an interview, "tell me one woman who has carried a regular dramatic series since the days of Loretta Young and Barbara Stanwyck. Women like to watch women and they seldom got a chance on prime time before the TV movie."[51]

That the made-for-TV movie appears to address itself to the female audience is not without its advantages to the broadcast television system. The audience most attractive to most television advertisers are women between the ages of 18 and 54, since they make the balance of consumer decisions, purchasing goods not only for themselves but for all members of the household. There may be, however, a certain paradox in the way in which the family melodrama places women at the center of its narratives and in the way it addresses the female audience.

Ellen Seiter argues that the "obsessive questioning of the characters in terms of their family relationships and a delineation of what is appropriate for mothers and fathers, wives and husbands, daughters and sons" is one of the main preoccupations of the genre. The "examination" to which women in melodrama are subjected typically reveals that the burden placed on them is an "impossible" one, for which they must nonetheless bear the responsibility. Caught in contradiction, the women in melodrama are "never let off the hook," either loving too much or not enough, caring too much about the home or too much about a career. Male characters in television's melodramas, on the other hand, are "treated with a remarkable degree of permissiveness." If they are cold and ambitious, the narrative suggests that these qualities are necessary masculine strategies for survival. Underneath the veneer men in the family melodrama are really sensitive and vulnerable, and the responsibility for bringing out those qualities rests with the female characters, who must understand their fathers, husbands, or lovers and win their trust if this essential male tenderness is to emerge. The history of the family melodrama is heavily weighted down with patriarchal values that locate a woman's place in the traditional roles of "nurturing, patient, forgiving . . . wives, mothers and daughters." Even when a melodrama puts women at the center of the narrative, men, Seiter claims, are "the heart" of the genre.[52]

In an earlier article, I explored some of these issues with respect to "Getting Physical" (CBS, 1984), a made-for-TV movie about female bodybuilders (a hot topic at the time). And, although I would hesitate to extend the analysis into a general claim about melodrama and the TV movie, it does appear that one way of reading "Getting Physical" reveals that its use of the family melodrama exerts considerable influence on narrative and characters. For example, "Getting Physical" at first seems as if it will be, perhaps, a feminine version of *Rocky*, the story of a female underdog who, with hard work and strong will, transforms herself into a winning athlete. However, the movie quickly turns into a story about how Kendall's commitment to bodybuilding upsets her family in general and her father in particular, and her romantic relationship with her boyfriend, Mickey. Kendall's father charges her with being a rebellious, inconsiderate, and unfeminine daughter, who has disrupted the family's unity, while Mickey forces a break-up because Kendall is ignoring him to concentrate on her sport. Most of the movie's narrative energy is spent on the problems Kendall's bodybuilding causes in terms of her position as daughter in the nuclear family and as woman in the heterosexual romance. And, in the end, Kendall's choice is rephrased into compliance with her father's prime directive, to "pick one thing to be good at and stick to it." Kendall's father, realizing that Kendall has been a good daughter, comes to see her compete in a contest, and it turns out that he is really a benevolent and caring father, after all. Mickey, in a similar move, decides to take Kendall back, and supports her dedication to the sport. "Getting Physical," using the family melodrama and the romance, transcribes Kendall's story into a story that concentrates on her relationships with men, a story that not so subtly insists that her choices are valid only if they are compatible with being the kind of daughter her father wants her to be and the kind of girlfriend Mickey wants her to be.[53]

If popular critics are less than happy with the TV movie's investment in melodrama because of what they take to be melodrama's aesthetic defects, academic critics tend to be skeptical of melodrama's ideological tendencies and the effects that they have on the TV movie's politics, perhaps its gender politics in particular. However, we cannot underestimate the possibility that melodrama may, in some contexts, work to expose the problems that some critics argue it works to repress. As Geoffrey Nowell-Smith argues, "the importance of melodrama lies in its ideological failure. Because it cannot accommodate its problems either in a real present or an ideal future, but lays them open in their contradictoriness, it opens a space which most . . . films have studiously closed off."[54] For their female audiences, melodramatic TV movies may very well lay bare more conflicts and contradictions in the culture's ideologies of masculinity and femininity, and of the family, than they lay to rest. Further work around the made-for-TV movie audience needs to be done, to explore this possibility.

The made-for-TV movie, then, in current broadcast television practice, assumes a certain general function and a certain ideological shape. Within the television system, made-for-TV movies are both popular and profitable. Relatively inexpensive, quickly produced, they are financed by the networks, which brings institutional and economic pressures to bear on their form. Because the economic point of programming is to delivery the largest, most profitable audience to advertisers, the conditions of its production dictate that the TV movie possess a certain saliency. It must be sensational, because its limited promotion must provide enough interest to command a sizable share of the audience. Yet it must not be offensive enough to provoke viewers into changing the channel or never tuning in at all. Typically shown on the networks only once, the made-for-TV movie anchors the closed end of broadcast television's spectrum of narrative closure/openness. In addition to its topicality, the TV movie's narrative form is also used as a promotional device. With respect to broadcast television's other narrative forms—the soap opera, the serial, and the series—the TV movie assumes a sort of urgency. It is a "special event," a "tonight-only world premiere."

Made-for-TV movies have merged as a privileged site for acknowledging and negotiating some of the most contested issues in American society. The social issue TV movie, the backbone of the genre, has taken on a pedagogical function with respect to the problems it organizes, educating the audience about the issue and indicating ways of managing the conflict. Melodrama, the preferred fictional code of the TV movie, which focuses on familial and domestic issues, functions to enable the expression of disturbing material, while working to contain it within traditional frames of meaning.

Nevertheless, the TV movie's politics cannot be taken for granted. The made-for-TV movie, responding as it does to the most salient points of sociocultural strain, opens itself up to the possibility of alternative or subversive readings on the part of its vast audience. In its search for ratings through the controversial, the TV movie frequently brings the socially marginalized—women, people of color, gays and lesbians, the working class, the homeless and unemployed, the victims—onto popular terrain. Despite critical charges that it does so only to domesticate or depoliticize social issues or emerging ideologies, the TV movie may very well, for some audiences, make a space for progressive or even radical perceptions of the conflicts and fault-lines in American culture. Many critics of the made-for-TV movie seem to underestimate both the essential contradictoriness of the TV movie and the audience's role

in actively making meanings and pleasures from popular texts. Unles
we are to suppose that popular audiences are indeed simply helpless
stupid, and capable of being duped into watching (and taking pleasur
from) television that is not in the best interests, we must suppose tha
even the typical TV movie is more than escapist trash or depoliticize
fluff. As Richard Dyer argues in "Entertainment and Utopia," popula
entertainment is "escapist" in the sense that it "offers the image o
'something better' to escape into, or something we want deeply that ou
day-to-day lives don't provide." And, as Dyer goes on to say, the wa
in which popular entertainment points out the gaps between what w
actually have and what we want, between what society promises u
and what it gives us, plays with "ideological fire."[55] The popular TV
movie, in terms of its possible meanings, pleasures, and politics fo
the audience, deserves a second look.

NOTES

1. Richard K. Doan, "The Name of the Game Is Quickies," *TV Guide*
December 10, 1966, p. A1.

2. Judith Crist, "Tailored for Televison Movies," *TV Guide*, August 30
1969, pp. 6–9; Douglas Stone, "TV Movies and How They Get That Way: Ar
Interview with TV Movie Makers Frank von Zerneck and Robert Greenwald,"
Journal of Popular Film and Television 7 (1979): 146.

3. Dwight Whitney, "Cinema's Stepchild Grows Up," *TV Guide*, July 20
1974, p. 21; Alvin H. Marill, *Movies Made for Television* (New York: DaCapo
Press, 1980), pp. 21, 26; Patrick McGilligan, "Movies Are Getting Better Thar
Ever on Television," *American Film* 5 (1980): 52.

4. Richard Zoglin, "A Domestic Reign of Terror," *Time*, October 8
1984, p. 85.

5. See Tony Bennett, "Text and Social Process: The Case of James Bond,"
Screen Education 41 (1982): 3–14, for an analysis of the relationship between the
concept of the "author" and the process of canon-formation.

6. McGilligan, "Movies Are Getting Better," p. 52.

7. Tom Allen, "The Semi-Precious Age of TV Movies," *Film Comment* 15
(1979): 22–23.

8. Herbert Gold, "Television's Little Dramas," *Harper's* (March 1977), p
88.

9. William A. Henry III, "The Dangers of Docudrama," *Time*, February
25, 1985, p. 95.

10. Tom Shales, "Networks Refuse to Acknowledge Sexual Revolution,"
The Sunday Oregonian, March 18, 1984, pl 41

11. Richard Corliss, "The Revenge of the Male Weepie," *Time*, April 20
1985, p. 65.

12. See Terry Lovell, "The Social Relations of Cultural Production," in One Dimensional Marxism, by Simon Clarke, Victor Jelenieski Seidler, Kevin McDonnell and Kevin Robbins, and Terry Lovell (London: Allison & Busby, 1980), pp. 232–56, for an interesting discussion of how women and children are inevitably positioned as the social groups most susceptible to the supposed ill-effects of mass culture. See also Robert C. Allen, Speaking of Soap Operas (Chapel Hill: University of North Carolina Press, 1985), esp. pp. 25–29, for how popular criticism and academic research has constructed the (female) soap opera audience as somehow "abnormal," and pp. 11–18 for a clear explanation of why "traditional aesthetics" discourse can find little good to say about popular television.

13. Douglas Gomery, "Television, Hollywood, and the Development of Movies Made for Television," in Regarding Television, ed. E. Ann Kaplan Frederick, Md.: University Publications of America, 1983), pp. 124–25; Douglas Gomery, 'Brian's Song': Television, Hollywood, and the Evolution of the Movie Made For Television," in Television: The Critical View, 4th ed., ed. Horace Newcomb (New York: Oxford University Press, 1987), pp. 197–200.

14. Bruce Edwards, "Co-production: Ready When You Are TV," Television Magazine (May 1966), p. 56.

15. Peter J. Schuyten, "How MCA Rediscovered Movieland's Golden Lode," Fortune (November 1976), pp. 122–23.

16. McGilligan, "Movies Are Getting Better," p. 126.

17. McGilligan, "Movies Are Getting Better," p. 52; Gomery, "Television," p. 126.

18. Gomery, "Television," p 126; Gomery, "'Brian's Song,'" pp. 197–98.

19. Todd Gitlin, Inside Prime Time (New York: Pantheon, 1983), p. 157.

20. Fred Silverman, "Made-For-TV Movies: Seen Playing Greater Role in Web Strategy," Television/Radio Age, November 7, 1983, pp. 34, 104.

21. Jeff Kaye, "CBS Plans 'High Concept' TV-Movies," TV Guide, December 31, 1988, p. A-1.

22. Crist, "Tailored for Television," pp. 6–9.

23. Robert C. Allen, "Speaking of Soap Operas," p. 46.

24. Art Durbano, "This Week's Movies," TV Guide, September 23, 1989, p. 51.

25. Horace Newcomb, "Toward a Television Aesthetic," in Television: The Critical View, ed. Newcomb, pp. 614–20.

26. John Ellis, Visible Fictions (London: Routledge and Kegan Paul, 1981), pp. 126, 143.

27. David Thorburn, "Television Melodrama," in Television: The Critical View, ed. Newcomb, pp. 633–34.

28. Gitlin, "Inside Prime Time," pp. 161–62

29. Stone, "TV Movies," pp. 147–48.

30. Gitlin, "Inside Prime Time," pp. 158–59

31. Stone, "TV Movies," p. 148.

32. Albert Auster, "If You Can't Get 'Em Into the Tent, You'll Never Have

a Circus: An Interview with Len Hill," *Journal of Popular Film and Television* 8 (1981): 13.

33. Gitlin, *Inside Prime Time*, p. 161.

34. Stone, "TV Movies," p. 148.

35. Stone, "TV Movies," pp. 150–51.

36. Gitlin, *Inside Prime Time*, pp. 161, 163–164.

37. Les Brown, *Television: The Business Behind the Box* (New York: Harcourt Brace, Jovanovich, 1971), p. 30.

38. Joanna Elm, "NBC Tones Down 'Roe vs. Wade' TV-Movie to Avoid Angering Abortion Pressure Groups," *TV Guide*, May 6, 1989, pp. 49–50.

39. Auster, "If You Can't Get 'Em," p. 10; Zoglin, "A Domestic Reign of Terror," p. 85.

40. See Stuart Hall, "Culture, the Media and the 'Ideological Effect,'" in *Mass Communication and Society*, ed. James Curran, Michael Gurevitch, and Janet Woollacott (Beverly Hills: Sage Publications, 1979), pp. 315–48. See also Todd Gitlin, "Prime Time Ideology: The Hegemonic Process in Television Entertainment," in *Television: The Critical View*, ed. Newcomb, pp. 507–32.

41. Gitlin, *Inside Prime Time*, pp. 163, 194.

42. Gomery, "'Brian's Song,'" pp. 213–16.

43. Richard Zoglin, "Troubles on the Home Front," *Time*, January 28 1985, p. 65.

44. *TV Guide* (Denver ed.), December 31, 1988, pp. A-53, A-54, A-58, pp. 26–29.

45. Peter Brooks, *The Melodramatic Imagination* (New York: Yale University Press, 1976), p. 42.

46. John G. Cawelti, *Adventure, Mystery, and Romance* (Chicago: University of Chicago Press, 1976), p. 45.

47. Thorburn, "Television Melodrama," p. 630.

48. Crist, "Tailored for Television," p. 8.

49. Ellen Seiter, "Men, Sex and Money in Recent Family Melodrama," *Journal of the University Film and Video Association* 35 (Winter 1983): 19.

50. Gitlin, *Inside Prime Time*, p. 179.

51. Whitney, "Cinema's Stepchild," p. 26.

52. Seiter, "Men, Sex and Money," pp. 23–26.

53. See Laurie Schulze, "'Getting Physical': Text/Context/Reading and the Made-for-Television Movie," *Cinema Journal* 25 (Winter 1986): 35–50, for a more detailed analysis of the relationship between melodrama and ideology in this particular made-for-TV movie.

54. Geoffrey Nowell-Smith, "Minelli and Melodrama," in *Home Is Where the Heart Is: Studies in Melodrama and the Woman's Film*, ed. Christine Gledhill (London: BFI, 1987), p. 74.

55. Richard Dyer, "Entertainment and Utopia," in *Genre: The Musical: A Reader*, ed. Rick Altman (London: Routledge and Kegan Paul, 1981), p. 177.

SUGGESTIONS FOR FURTHER READING

Alder, Dick, and Joseph Finnegan. "The Year America Stayed Home for the Movies; How Films Have Burgeoned on TV and Why." *TV Guide*, May 20, 1972, pp. 6–10.

Allen, Tom. "The Semi-Precious Age of TV Movies." *Film Comment* 15 (1979): 21–23.

Auster, Albert, "If You Can't Get 'Em Into the Tent, You'll Never Have a Circus: An Interview with Len Hill." *Journal of Popular Film and Television* 9 (1981): 10–17.

Crist, Judith. "Tailored for Television Movies." *TV Guide*, August 30, 1969, pp. 6–9.

Doan, Richard K. "The Name of the Game Is Quickies." *TV Guide*, December 10, 1966, p. A1.

Edgerton, Gary. "The American Made-for-TV Movie," in *TV Genres*, ed. Brian G. Rose. Westport, Conn.: Greenwood Press, 1985.

Edwards, Bruce. "Co-production: Ready When You Are TV." *Television Magazine* (May 1966), pp. 31, 56–61.

Gitlin, Todd. *Inside Prime Time*. New York: Pantheon Books, 1983.

Gold, Herbert. "Television's Little Dramas." *Harper's* (March 1977), pp. 88–93.

Gomery, Douglas. "Television, Hollywood, and the Development of Movies Made for Television." In *Regarding Television*, ed. E. Ann Kaplan, pp. 120–29. Frederick, Md.: University Publications of America, 1983.

"Brian's Song': Television, Hollywood, and the Evolution of the Movie Made for Television." In *Television: The Critical View*, 4th ed., ed. Horace Newcomb, pp. 197–220. New York: Oxford University Press, 1987.

Henry, William A. III. "The Dangers of Docudrama." *Time*, February 25, 1985, p. 95.

McGilligan, Patrick. "Movies Are Better Than Ever—On Television." *American Film* (March 1980), pp. 50–54.

Marill, Alvin H. *Movies Made for Television*. New York: DaCapo Press, 1980.

Schulze, Laurie Jane. "'Getting Physical': Text/Context/Reading and the Made-for-Television Movie." *Cinema Journal* 25 (Winter 1986): 35–50.

Schuyten, Peter J. "How MCA Rediscovered Movieland's Golden Lode." *Fortune* (November 1976), pp. 122–27.

Schwartz, Nancy. "TV Films." *Film Comment* 11 (March/April 1975): 36–38.

Shales, Tom. "Networks Refuse to Achnowledge Sexual Revolution." *Sunday Oregonian*, March 18, 1984, p. B3.

Silverman, Fred. "Made-for-TV Movies: Seen Playing Greater Role in Web Strategy." *Television/ Radio Age*, November 7, 1983, pp. 33–35, 102–6.

Stone, Douglas. "TV Movies and How They Get That Way; Interviews with TV Movie Makers Frank von Zerneck and Robert Greenwald." *Journal of Popular Film and Television* 7 (1979): 146–57.

Whitney, Dwight. "Cinema's Stepchild Grows Up." *TV Guide*, July 20, 1974, pp. 21–26.

Chapter 13

Building a Movie Theater Giant: The Rise of Cineplex Odeon

Douglas Gomery

M edia observers in the United States have labeled the 1980s the age of the new television technologies. We have seen the phenomenal rise of cable television, pay television, and home video, with pay-per-view and high-definition television seeming to be on the immediate horizon. All these television delivery systems proffer movies into homes day and night, and as they have been introduced, they have been expected to cut dramatically into business at America's movie theaters. But they have not. Indeed, the number of folks going out to the movies has remained steady in the face of temptations from the new television technologies. And as ticket prices have increased, so has box office take.

The innovations of one corporation, Cineplex Odeon, have kept millions coming to movie ticket booths. During the 1980s this Canadian enterprise significantly altered the form and style of going to the movies in North America. Following the economic logic of product differentiation, Cineplex Odeon replaced the dominant mode of showing films in drab "cookie-cutter" multiplexes with vast complexes of whimsical, postmodern "picture palaces" offering a seemingly boundless number of different cinematic choices to the public. And in the process, this company, founded in Toronto, Ontario, Canada, in 1979, became one of the giants of the movie business in North America.

Cineplex (the original name of the company) commenced business as plain, cheaply constructed multiplex cinemas were spreading across the United States and Canada during the 1970s. These auditoriums were simply screening rooms, stressing the attractions of the films presented, not the surroundings or ambience. By the 1970s, old-timers remembered the splendors of the movie palace, where

it was as much fun to enter these cathedrals of cinema pleasure as to
see any one particular feature film.

Cineplex broke with the tradition of the drab multiplex and startled
the movie world in April 1979 with the opening of its ornate, $2 million
Toronto complex, comprising some 18 different auditoriums (with as
many choices of films) under one roof. This original Cineplex, from
cinema plus com*plex*, was part of a new postmodern downtown billion
dollar city-mall, the Eaton Centre. The Eaton Centre's three hundred
stores were directly linked to the Toronto subway as well as to a
massive parking structure, thus offering it an advantage in Canada's
cold winters for helping to reattract shoppers downtown.

Cineplex's auditorums were small, ranging from 60 to 130 seats, all
monitored from a central, computerized box office. This was typical of
multiplexes in North America. Other aspects of the Cineplex operation
were not. For example, staffing needs were cut to the bone. At the
Eaton Centre, a maximum of 3 employees were needed to sell tickets,
and with cooperation from the projectionist's union, only 2 operators
were needed in the booth. A staff of 58 ran the whole operation.

To generate increased revenues, Cineplex expanded concession
operations as had no other theater chain before it. Built into its operation were massive stands featuring the usual popcorn, candy, and soft
drinks as well as large-sized cafe operations offering "upscale" pastries
and yuppie beverages. One did not have to go out for a bite to eat after
the show; it was more fun to remain within the theater complex.

The offerings at the original Cineplex ranged the gamut of second-
run revivals and repertory favorites to the best in foreign films. In 1980
Canada had two dominant theater chains, both of which held long-
standing relations with the major Hollywood film companies. Famous
Players and Odeon, a duopoly (economic power by two), embraced
all first-run bookings of top Hollywood feature films. Cineplex had little
other choice but to maximize its returns from art film and repertory
classics, absent any first-run Hollywood product.

With 18 screens, films could be moved and double-booked to
maximize revenues. For example, an extremely popular film might be
screened in three auditoriums. Cult films played on weekends, classics
midweek. Cineplex could take full advantage of changing, fragmented
audience tastes. If the shopping center offered a variety of merchandise
in its stores, Cineplex sought to tender its young customers a wide
variety of movie shows.

In the beginning, Cineplex even tried screening short subjects, many
from the National Film Board of Canada. But soon, like most mainline
commercial operations, Cineplex completely embraced feature films to
fill all possible seats. No seats should be empty; that is, it was better to

have a 75-seat house turn away 25 potential patrons than to have 100 fans take up only one-quarter of the space in a 400-seat auditorium. The analogy that Garth Drabinsky and Nat Taylor, the founders of the company, made focused on the airline industry: "When the movie starts or the plane takes off, the income from any empty seats is lost forever."[1]

Saturday proved to be Cineplex's busiest night of the week. Often half its auditoriums sold out. Moviegoers could consult a giant lighted marquee on the wall outside the main entrance to match the film with the proper auditorium. They could purchase their ticket, go away and shop, and return in time for the movie. During the Christmas and Easter school holidays Cineplex made going to the movies even easier by offering the equivalent of free baby-sitting service. Parents could buy tickets for their children, trust the Cineplex staff to monitor the movie show, and return after two hours of uninterrupted shopping in the adjoining mall.

Offbeat mainstream films tendered the chain's first big hits: *Midnight Express* (1978) ran for 68 weeks, *Life of Brian* (1979) even longer. These "move-overs" (after first-runs) made Cineplex pots of money, since rental fees were so low. By the end of its second year the Eaton Centre Cineplex was grossing an average of $50,000 per week. *Life of Brian* earned more than $175,000 gross in 75 weeks on one screen, all after the film finished its first-run engagement in Toronto. Fans under age 30 made up three-quarters of the average Cineplex audience.

The Cineplex innovations were the product of two long-time Canadian film exhibitors, Nat Taylor and Harry Handel, united with a newcomer, a 29-year-old lawyer, Garth Drabinsky. Their first few months of Cineplex at the Eaton Centre proved troublesome, as computers broke down, staff became confused, and the projection equipment broke down from constant use. But within six months Taylor and Drabinsky started to make money, principally with art house films; *The Marriage of Maria Braun* (1978), from Germany, was the first film that demanded showings in multiple auditoriums.[2]

Taylor and Drabinsky had raised the necessary monies by tempting investors with low capital requirements and the promise of future riches. By 1980 business in the Eaton Centre had proved so good that it was decided to expand. Taylor and Drabinsky would take their formula to Vancouver, Calgary, Montreal, and Winnipeg, to challenge Famous Players and Odeon for control of the movie exhibition market in Canada. Cineplex began to seek sites in downtown shopping centers or well-positioned suburban shopping centers, but could not count on booking the best that Hollywood could offer. It was one thing to counter program in a large city like Toronto; it was another to take that strategy across the breadth of Canada.[3]

By late in the following year, 1981, Cineplex was operating 124 screens in 16 locations throughout Canada. Although yearly grosses had climbed to $20 million (Canadian), there were more doubters than believers. Anthony Hoffman, financial analyst for Wall Street's A. G. Becker, Inc., noted in 1981 that Cineplex "seems to be going in exactly the wrong direction in terms of trends in the motion picture business."[4] Not only did the company have the "proper" Hollywood connections, most film industry pundits believed that pay television and videodiscs would soon eliminate the second-run film audience Cineplex was courting.

The prognosticators underestimated the flexibility and innovative skills of Taylor and Drabinsky. Cineplex was still able to woo away a sizable audience to go out to the movies. It did this by seeking out specialized niches. Reggae movies were promoted to Toronto's Caribbean audience, Yiddish movies to its significant Jewish population. In this way Cineplex was able to differentiate its marquee attractions from rival Odeon and Famous Players, which showed only Hollywood films.

Encouraged by their success in Canada, Drabinsky and Taylor looked southward. After scouting several sites in the United States, they selected the movie-mad westside of Los Angeles and opened a $3 million Cineplex in the chic new Beverly Center, which opened in July 1982 with 14 screens. Los Angeles was not dominated by a single theater circuit, and so Cineplex had a chance to move in and compete with the half dozen powers on the scene. Moreover, West Los Angeles represented one of the most "movie-mad" population clusters anywhere in the United States.

But to make a mark in the Canadian film business was one thing, to break into the United States was quite another. There were major business competitors with which to deal. General Cinema, United Artists Entertainment, American Multi-Cinema, and Plitt Theatres each controlled more than five hundred screens and were multimillion dollar operations with long-standing ties to the major Hollywood studios. In Los Angeles, in particular, Plitt and the regional powers Mann Theatres and Pacific Theatres together held command of the marketplace. In any case, everyone claimed to know that the theater end of the business was going to wither away in the face of the emergence of cable television, home video, and all sorts of unforeseen new television technologies that would turn everyone's home into their own movie house. And so why add more theaters?

But Cineplex boldly moved in, replicating the strategy that had worked so well in Canada. Up north it had successfully taken on the duopoly of Famous Players and Odeon, two chains that were directly tied to the Hollywood moviemaking powers. Pundits doubted Cineplex would succeed in Los Angeles, but did agree it took a special brand of movie to test the Cineplex idea first in Hollywood's very own backyard.

As at the original Eaton Centre Cineplex, feature films at the Beverly Center were in and out quickly to accommodate changing audience tastes. Three projectionists could handle the 14 auditoriums using automated platter systems with single continuous loops. Special soundproofing eliminated the usual complaints of noise spill-over. The Beverly Center Cineplex opened with a mixture of art films and second-run Hollywood favorites. No more than four films were started within 15 minutes of each other in order to optimize consumer selection.

Film scheduling was honed to an almost exact science. Cineplex took direct aim at the fickle mentality of the American shopper. If mallgoers loved to browse and make "impulse" purchases for items from shoes to records, why shouldn't they be able to do the same thing for movies? To offer a tempting array of selections, Cineplex evoked a formula. It opened popular, well-advertised films at two or even three of the available screens. Then slowly, over time, bookers cut back to one auditorium as the popularity of the film waned. The timing of moves from good-sized auditoriums (about 400 seats) to screening-room-like facilities (often with only 75 seats) was carefully monitored.[5]

But Taylor and Drabinsky needed something special to catch the eye of cinema-saturated fans in Los Angeles. They added creature comforts not seen since the Golden Age of the movie palace. The Beverly Center Cineplex, going beyond the Canadian operations, offered a splendid art deco–inspired architectural design for lobbies and auditoriums. Cineplex meant their movie show should be a fun place to visit, even "hang out." They also further extended the appeal of the concession stand, constructing a massive cafe offering not only the usual popcorn, soft drinks, and candy, but also exotic coffees, upscale imported waters, and upscale candies such as Cadbury's fruit and nut bars.[6]

The Beverly Center was an immediate success. Cineplex's innovations became the talk of the movie business. Studio heads took notice of the new complex "just around the corner" from their studio offices. And Cineplex rested nary a moment on this impressive accomplishment. Drabinsky announced to anyone who would listen that his company would continue to expand until it became truly the equal of a General Cinema or American Multi-Cinema.

To immediately swell in size and influence, Cineplex sought to take over other chains, transfer its exhibition strategy to these new subsidiaries, and rake in millions. The first blockbuster merger came thousands of miles from the Beverly Center. In May 1984, for $49 million (Canadian), Cineplex bought one of Canada's two important circuits, the Odeon chain, and with it took control of new screens. At the time Cineplex itself controlled but 149 screens.[7]

The newly named Cineplex Odeon chain suddenly had 446 screens and "overnight" had become one of the top ten largest circuits in North America. It had not yet reached the ranks of the Plitts or General Cinemas, but was certainly on the way. For Canadian moviegoers in particular, the new Cineplex Odeon had become the new coequal of Famous Players, the new "partner" in the Canadian movie theater duopoly. The influential film trade paper *Variety* called it a case of "Mighty Mouse swallowing an elephant."[8]

Cineplex, which had long unsuccessfully sought bookings of first-run Hollywood product, suddenly stood as one of only two possible outlets in nearly every Canadian city. Famous Players had slightly more screens (34 more), in slightly more locations (27 more), but took in no more at the box office. Hollywood had to (and did) come to Drabinsky and Taylor; Cineplex became a major circuit, with ties to the major Hollywood studios.

In 1985 the new Cineplex Odeon kept expanding. In April it took over three theaters situated in the trendiest parts of Los Angeles: the Fairfax (three screens with one thousand seats), the Gordon (one screen with nine hundred seats), and the Brentwood (two screens with nine hundred seats). Cineplex turned the Gordon into the Cineplex Odeon Showcase Cinema by adding a new 70mm projection system and Dolby sound equipment, while refurbishing the original 1938 art deco design, including a classic ticket booth, a lavish marquee, and vast ceiling murals in the auditorium. With 20 well-placed screens, Cineplex Odeon had to be taken seriously by Plitt, Mann, and Pacific Theatres, its rivals in the Los Angeles filmgoing market.[9]

But the takeover of three independent theaters in Los Angeles, however important, paled by comparison when compared to the takeover accomplished in August. Cineplex Odeon swallowed another giant, paying $130 million for the vast Plitt Theatre chain. Plitt had been created out of the old Paramount theater chain, and at the time of the Cineplex acquisition, Plitt ranked as the fourth largest theater chain in the United States, with more than six hundred screens. Cineplex Odeon, the Canadian upstart, now was far more than a "new kid on the block"; it dominated moviegoing throughout the states of Texas, Illinois, North Carolina, South Carolina, Minnesota, Florida, Utah, and Georgia. Concentrations of more than one hundred former Plitt screens could be found in and around Houston, Dallas, and Chicago.[10]

But as the leaders of the U.S. film industry were beginning to appreciate the far-reaching implications of the Cineplex takeover of Plitt, in early December of 1985 rumors of an even bigger merger began to spread. Officially, all that was known at the time was that MCA, parent company of Universal Studios, and Cineplex Odeon would jointly build and operate the world's largest freestanding 18-auditorium theater operation, to be located in Universal's parking lot in California. The cost would be $10 million, shared equally, and the complex would hold more than six thousand patrons when full.

Few doubted the importance of the fastest growing movie chain, Cineplex Odeon, linking up with one of Hollywood's most powerful makers of movies and television programs. This was an important deal because it was blessed by Hollywood's most powerful mogul, Lew Wasserman. Wasserman appreciated Cineplex's accomplishments, and after months of talks, early in 1986 the movie world learned that the upstart Cineplex would be a full partner with MCA, a company already churning out $2 billion in revenues every year.

The announcement of the MCA–Cineplex Odeon alliance came on January 15, 1986. The formal agreement called for MCA to pay $75 million for an equity position in Cineplex Odeon (which later would rise to nearly a half share). But few doubted that Wasserman held the upper hand, even though at the time Cineplex Odeon operated more than eleven hundred screens in the United States and Canada, in nearly four hundred locations. As expected, the deal easily cleared the U.S. Department of Justice.[11]

The MCA deal would seemed to have offered Cineplex the time to "catch its corporate breath." (The company had achieved a measure of growth as rapid as any in the history of the film business.) Instead Taylor and Drabinsky used the MCA link as a base from which to launch the largest set of takeovers in American film industry history since the heady days of expansion in the 1920s.

The key year was 1986. In early April of that year Cineplex Odeon purchased the Atlanta-based Septum Theatre circuit of 48 screens for $11 million. In May 1986 it purchased the Essaness Theatres Corporation, with 41 screens, all based in greater metropolitan Chicago, for just under $15 million.

These two purchases filled in gaps in the former southern and northern divisions of the Plitt circuit, giving Cineplex Odeon even stronger positions in the growing Southeast and the third largest city in the United States. Septum added a growing presence in the hot market of Atlanta. Cineplex Odeon immediately announced plans to add 54 new screens in the Chicago area, thus establishing dominance unseen in one major American city since the days of Balaban & Katz in Chicago of the 1920s. The elegant Esquire theater, an art deco masterwork, was refurbished, creating a flagship in the upscale Chicago northside.[12]

Through the remainder of 1986, the deals came fast and furiously.

On the last day of July, Cineplex Odeon announced it was moving into the largest movie market in the United States, New York City. Cineplex Odeon had agreed to acquire 97 screens from the RKO Century Warner Theatre chain for nearly $180 million. Cineplex had thus made it into Manhattan, as well as Queens, Brooklyn, Long Island, Westchester County, and northern New Jersey. In Manhattan it now controlled 22 screens, including the prestigious Cinema Five theaters, located on Manhattan's Upper East Side, the center of New York film business since the 1950s. But this only whetted Drabinsky's appetite. The *Wall Street Journal*, the financial newspaper of record, quoted Drabinsky (nicknamed by this point "Grab"-insky) positing Cineplex Odeon's long-term goal as attaining "a major position in all the important film markets in North America."[13]

He began this task in Washington, D.C., one of the most affluent movie markets in North America. The capital of the United States ranked as only the eighth largest metropolitan region in terms of population, but its wealth and prosperity vaulted it into the top three in terms of movie attendance. On July 28th, two days before the announcement of the RKO Century Warner deal, Cineplex Odeon told the world it had purchased Neighborhood Theatres for $21 million. Neighborhood Theatres had a prominent position in the metropolitan Washington, D.C., market, with screens in suburban Maryland and north Virginia. With this acquisition, as best as anyone could tell, Cineplex Odeon would operate nearly fourteen hundred screens in North America, a total considered all but impossible a decade earlier.

In December of 1986 Cineplex Odeon took over the Sterling Recreation organization, a theater circuit in the Northwest with some 99 indoor screens and 15 drive-ins. This $45 million deal gave Cineplex Odeon a substantial presence in Seattle, Tacoma, and the state of Washington in general. Seattle was a particularly valuable territory, argued by some to be only behind New York, Los Angeles, and Washington, D.C., as a moviegoing city.

With this deal, during the final month of 1986 Cineplex went over fifteen hundred total screens in nearly five hundred locations. The bulk had come through the acquisition of the Plitt chain. But during 1986, even outside the Plitt deal, Cineplex Odeon had taken over nearly four hundred new screens in key locations in the best movie markets in North America. At the end of 1986 the company employed some 12,500 workers in 20 U.S. states and 6 Canadian provinces, the largest employer in the movie business.

But Drabinsky kept on dealing in 1987. On March 19, 1987, Cineplex Odeon acquired, for $32 million, all the outstanding shares of the Walter Reade Organization from the Coca-Cola Corporation, which, through

Columbia Pictures, owned this chain at the time. The Walter Reade Organization operated only 11 screens in eight locations in New York City, but these were among the most important, most visible movie houses in the United States, including the flagship Ziegfeld theater, home of any number of premieres, located in the heart of Times Square. Combined with the earlier RKO Century Warner acquisition, Cineplex now ranked as the major force in the movie business in America's largest city.

To make sure that everyone in the media capital of the United States stood up and took notice, Cineplex restored and expanded the Carnegie cinema, long one of New York's top art theaters. Accompanied by dozens of full-page advertisements, particularly in the influential *New York Times*, Cineplex reopened the Carnegie in June of 1987. Skeptics praised the glowing new colors, the new marble floors in the lobby, and red floral carpeting elsewhere. The intimate capuccino and pastry bar seemed to add just the right accent. Few complained that a second smaller screening room was added. This restoration cost more that $1 million, but won praise from all quarters of the influential New York press.

Later in 1987 Cineplex accomplished what would be its last major takeover. In December 1987, Drabinsky solidified his domination of the Washington, D.C., market with a $51 million buy out of Circle theatres, an 80-screen outfit, based solely in the District of Columbia and nearby Maryland. With this acquisition Cineplex Odeon, a Canadian corporation, held dominion in the environs of the District of Columbia. Films shown in Washington's most important theaters were selected more than a thousand miles to the north in Toronto, Canada.[14]

As in New York City, Cineplex Odeon presented a new theater to its newly adopted community. In December of 1987 it opened a splendid brand new six-plex on upper Wisconsin Avenue in northwest Washington, near the homes of any number of influential politicians and policy makers. (Indeed, President George Bush, neighbor Vice-President Dan Quayle, and their families showed up for a well-publicized premiere only days after their election.) Beneath a modern new office, shopping complex (a sort of miniature Beverly Center), Cineplex Odeon skillfully positioned six auditoriums, ranging from less than two hundred seats to nearly five hundred. Again skeptics praised the tasteful, spacious lobby with its real marble floors and columns, a clever sequence of spaces leading to the auditoriums, the carefully positioned, comfortable seats, the good-sized screens, and the refined decor, all accented in a light purple. The site was convenient to the majority of Washington's most fervent film fans.

Although Cineplex Odeon accomplished most of its expansion in

1986 and 1987 through acquisitions, it did open new theater complexes around the United States. During the first half of 1987, for example, it premiered 12 new complexes with 78 screens, including 2 in Los Angeles, 2 in Atlanta, 1 in Portland, Orlando, near the studio tour, and 2 more at home in Canada, in London, Ontario, and Vancouver, British Columbia.

But surely Cineplex's biggest triumph came in mid-1987 with the opening of the long-planned theater complex on the studio parking lot at Universal City. Ground breaking had taken place in October of 1986, after more than ten years of off and on again proposals, plans, and almost-deals. The $16 million complex opened to massive crowds over the fourth of July weekend. With 18 theaters, ranging from two hundred to eight hundred seats, the 120,000-square-foot complex featured marble floors, vast glassed-in spaces, a floral garden, stars and clouds in the ceiling of the lobby, two football field length concession stands, and even balconies in two of the auditoriums.

Pundits in Hollywood said Los Angeles was over-built in terms of the numbers of theaters. And besides, no one would drive all the way out to Universal City for a movie, with theaters in every mall in town. Again the conventional wisdom proved incorrect. The Universal Studios complex proved an instant success, with some thirty-eight thousand folks showing up during the first weekend alone. The complex, set smack in the middle of a parking lot, lacked for adequate parking that first weekend! For top prices of six dollars one could see a wide selection of films in "clean and comfortable" surroundings, noted the Los Angeles Times. Schedules had to be readjusted that summer to handle the overflow traffic.

Cineplex's growth during 1986 and 1987 pushed the then eight-year-old company's total number of screens to in excess of sixteen hundred. The statistics at the end of 1987 were nothing less than staggering. In that single calendar year Cineplex Odeon had opened some 31 new complexes, with some 163 screens in North America. In addition it completed major refurbishments of some 16 complexes with nearly 50 screens. At the end of 1987 Cineplex Odeon had nearly 500 multiplexes in 20 states in the United States plus the District of Columbia and six Canadian provinces.[15]

Through the years of this merger activity, Cineplex Odeon did not ignore its existing theatrical enterprises. It substantially refurbished eight theater complexes across Canada, from the Oakridge Centre in Vancouver to the vast West Edmonton Mall (then reputed to be the world's largest) to the Royale Theatre in Toronto. To handle an increasing number of architectural restorations and plans for new theaters, in 1985 Cineplex established its own in-house professional design unit, directed by architect David Mesbur and engineer Peter Kofman. Working closely with other Cineplex Odeon personnel, the design division assigned theaters clustered in one region a single set of architectural themes and colors. Carpets were custom designed to match recurring motifs found in the ceilings, columns, and archways, and were imported from England. Elegant inlaid marble floors added a touch of class in lobbies inspired with art deco motifs. Touches of neon helped highlight theaters that Cineplex wanted to be "reminiscent of the movie palaces of the 1920s."

To add further elegance, Cineplex Odeon commissioned new sculpture and paintings for its newly constructed theaters as well as its restoration projects. In November 1984 it hired David Burnett, then Curator of Contemporary Canadian Art at the Art Gallery of Ontario, as a consultant. With his advice, it commissioned Alan Wood's "The Movies" for the Oakridge Mall, Vancouver, and Phil Richard's "Once Upon a Time" for the Woodbine Centre in Toronto. Designs ranged from high realism to color-field abstraction, artifacts from pure painting to mixed-media constructions. Cineplex Odeon required artists to be distinguished Canadians who were willing to create works relating somehow thematically to the movies.

The business operations of Cineplex Odeon reminded movie industry veterans of the centralized operations of the old Hollywood theater circuits. Drabinsky supervised everything, regularly scanning required managers' reports, district supervisors' summaries, and even going out for on-the-spot inspections. All supplies, in particular candy, popcorn, soft drinks, and other goodies sold at the concession stands, were bought in bulk. Each theater's inventories for concession sales were monitored weekly to eliminate shortages, overstocking, spoilage, and waste. Record keeping was computerized, so costs were kept as low as possible.

Indeed, the revenue boost from concession sales stood at the heart of the economies of scale Drabinsky sought for the company. In 1985, according to company figures, patrons regularly purchased $1.30 worth of various items, believed to be one of the highest figures in the industry. Cineplex Odeon prided itself on its attractive concession stands, featuring ultramodern, technically advanced equipment, with the largest selections in the industry. Simplicity of service allowed the company to hire inexperienced workers at low wages, like a fast food outlet. Speed and efficiency of sales were emphasized in all company manuals.

Through rigorous testing and experimentation, Cineplex perfected an "ideal" assortment of package display, designed by the front office to maximize sales. Drabinsky swung a favorable deal to exclusively sell and promote Coca-Cola products, including Diet Coke, which for its upscale patrons accounted for nearly one-quarter of the soft drink sales at a typical Cineplex Odeon concessions counter. But the star attraction was always the "real" butter on the popcorn. Indeed, in 1984 Cineplex purchased Kernels Popcorn Limited to supply needed quantities of traditional popcorn as well as savory and sugar-glazed gourmet popcorn.

Several (but not all) of the Cineplex Odeon's complexes have cafes in their lobbies, where capuccino and expresso coffees, fine pastries, and fancy, upscale sandwiches are served. This was initiated at the Carlton Cinemas in Toronto and, with success there, initiated in selected upscale sites in other cities in the United States and Canada. This helped reinforce an upscale image, but equally as important contributed to the pots of profits to the bottom line.[16]

And by 1987 Cineplex's substantial increases at the bottom line finally caught the attention of analysts and investors. Cineplex had been considered a regional corporation, listed on the Toronto stock exchange. On March 26, 1987, Cineplex Odeon filed to sell stock on the New York Stock Exchange. Two Wall Street giants, Merrill Lynch and Allen & Company, underwrote the initial offering of 1.75 million shares of common stock, which generated in excess of $40 million. On May 14, 1987, the journey that had begun at the Eaton Centre less than a decade earlier reached the pinnacle of North American capitalism as Cineplex Odeon was listed on the New York Stock Exchange for the first time.[17]

But as its buying spree was reaching its acme, those who followed the string of successes of Cineplex Odeon began to notice cracks in the armor of this new movie theater giant. Drabinsky, insiders for once correctly argued, too often seemed willing to pay far above prevailing prices for multiplexes he considered vital to his vision of a national chain. Where would the additional revenues and profits come from to cover this ever-accumulating debt?

At times corporate difficulties spilled over from the pages of the business section into the world of entertainment news. In late 1987 and into the first months of 1988 Cineplex began to raise prices to meet expenses. Moviegoers balked, but soon realized they had no choice. Seemingly overnight, in community after community across North America, Cineplex Odeon had become the only game in town. In New York City, during the prime Christmas moviegoing season of 1987, Cineplex increased ticket prices from six to seven dollars. New York mayor Ed Koch proposed a boycott. Cineplex Odeon claimed that the increase was necessary, and with no alternative, fans soon learned to ante up the necessary amount.

But Cineplex Odeon's problems always came back to the nearly two-thirds of a billion dollars in debt it had taken on during the heady days of expansion. Wall Street wanted to make sure Cineplex could and would meet its payments. So did partner MCA. In the spring of 1989, Cineplex, innovator of so much during the remarkable past ten years, went "up for grabs."[18]

Early in December 1989 an eight-month struggle ended as Garth Drabinsky resigned, after failing to take full control of Cineplex Odeon. Drabinsky was unable to raise the necessary millions to buy Cineplex outright. Then MCA forced him out. Allen Karp, who had headed the chain's North American theaters, was named president. The plan, as the company entered the 1990s, was to sell subsidiaries not related to film exhibition and concentrate on making money from movie theaters. With the backing of MCA, few doubted Cineplex Odeon would not continue to be a power in the movie business well into the next century.[19]

Whatever its future, Cineplex Odeon introduced significant long-run changes in the movie theater business in the United States and Canada. This company led the way, and should be praised for bringing elegance back to North American moviegoing. Before Cineplex Odeon, the multiplex cinema-going experience was defined by plain, drab auditoriums, lacking any architectural elegance. The feature film provided the sole attraction. Moviegoing in the 1970s, most often associated with an ever-present sticky auditorium floor, became a thing of the past.

Cineplex Odeon's complexes were carefully crafted, postmodern Xanadus of pleasure, reminding film buffs of the glories of the 1920s movie palace era. Auditoriums were built with the creature comforts of the patrons in mind and maintained as built by a staff with pride in being part of the fastest growing theater chain in the world. But costs of operation were kept low through huge-scale operations of 10 to 20 auditoriums under one roof. Concession areas the size of basketball arenas only made the experience of going out to the movies that much more special.

Cineplex brought about significant, lasting changes in the movie business in the United States and Canada, the world's largest market for moviegoing. In the 1980s, when many thought that the movie theater business would soon die (killed off by cable television and home video), Drabinsky and company taught the world that with architectural splendor, careful monitoring of costs, the addition of a multitude of films, restaurant-like concession stands with trendy snack foods, all in convenient locations, it could lure millions away from their televisions sets to the fun of going out to the movies.

NOTES

1. Quotation form *New York Times*, November 22, 1981, sec. 10, p. 11; *Boxoffice*, April 23, 1979, pp. 10–12.

2. *Wall Street Journal*, November 9, 1981, p. 31; *Variety*, November 21, 1979, p. 51.

3. *Variety*, June 11, 1980, pp. 3, 38.

4. *Wall Street Journal*, November 9, 1981, p. 31.

5. Karen Stabiner, "The Shape of Theaters to Come," *American Film* (September 1982), pp. 51–52.

6. *Variety*, July 21, 1982, pp. 5, 25; *Boxoffice* (July 1982), p. 26; *Boxoffice* (October 1982), p. 20.

7. *Wall Street Journal*, May 30, 1984, p. 10.

8. *Variety*, November 21, 1984, p. 62.

9. *Variety*, May 30, 1984, pp. 1, 121; *Variety*, November 21, 1984, pp. 62, 84; *Variety*, April 24, 1985, p. 7; *Boxoffice* (December 1985), pp. 139–40.

10. *Wall Street Journal*, March 31, 1978, sec. 4, p. 9; *Variety*, April 5, 1978, pp. 7, 40; *Boxoffice* (November 1980), p. 10; The Cineplex Annual Report for 1985, pp. 2, 3, 20; *Boxoffice* (November 1985), p. 22; *Variety*, November 27, 1985, p. 3; *Variety*, December 4, 1985, p. 86.

11. *Variety*, January 22, 1986, p. 3; *Wall Street Journal*, January 16, 1986, p. 86. Later MCA bought more, to up its share to nearly one-half.

12. *Variety*, December 14, 1983, p. 13; The First Quarter Report, Cineplex Odeon Corporation, 1986, p. 4; *Film Journal* (April 1986), p. 8; *Film Journal* (May 1986), p. 4.

13. *Wall Street Journal*, July 31, 1986, p. 12.

14. *Variety*, July 30, 1986, pp. 3, 87; *Variety*, November 12, 1986, p. 3; The Annual Report, Cineplex Odeon Corporation, 1986, p. 3; *Variety* December 17, 1986, p. 5, 105; *Variety*, March 25, 1987, pp. 7, 35; *Film Journal* (April 1987), p. 6; *Boxoffice* (June 1987), p. 6; *Film Journal* (January 1988), p. 6; *Variety*, February 17, 1988, p. 5.

15. Annual Report, Cineplex Odeon Corporation, 1987, pp. 2–6; *Los Angeles Times*, June 16, 1987, sec. 6, pp. 1, 8; *Los Angeles Times*, July 7, 1987, sec. 6 pp. 1, 10.

16. The Annual Reports, Cineplex Odeon Corporation, 1985, 1986, and 1987.

17. *Wall Street Journal*, May 7, 1987, p. 59.

18. *Variety*, May 27, 1987, p. 24; *Variety*, June 10, 1987, p. 23; *Variety*, June 24, 1987, pp. 1, 108; *Variety*, January 6, 1988, p. 6; *Wall Street Journal*, December 19, 1988, p. B3; Chuck Hawkins, "Upteen Screens—And Oodles of Debt," *Business Week*, October 10, 1988, p. 148.

19. *Wall Street Journal,* December 4, 1989, pp. A3, A9; *The Wall Street Journal,* December 7, 1989, p. B10; *Variety,* December 6, 1989, pp. 3, 7.

SUGGESTIONS FOR FURTHER READING

There has been little written, in comprehensive book or article length form, about the recent changes in motion picture exhibition in the United States. For an understanding of the situation as of the early 1980s, see Harold L. Vogel, *Entertainment Industry Analysis* (New York: Cambridge University Press, 1986); Gary R. Edgerton, *American Film Exhibition and an Analysis of the Motion Picture Industry's Market Structure, 1963–1980* (New York: Garland Publishing, 1983); and Jason E. Squire, ed., *The Movie Business Book* (New York: Prentice-Hall, 1983).

The best source of current information remains the business and trade press. *Variety* regularly reports on changes in the exhibition business. (Indeed, for the official corporate history see, "Cineplex Odeon 10th Anni," *Variety,* April 26, 1989.) *Boxoffice* and *Film Journal* provide monthly reports for the film exhibition business. But the best source of corporate news remains the *Wall Street Journal.* Consult its second section on "The Media Business" for details of the business implications of all phases of the mass entertainment business.

Finally, Cineplex Odeon was not the only movie theater company to ever employ a concerted product-differentiating corporate strategy with a major degree of success. Indeed the pioneer in that regard was Balaban & Katz, a Chicago company that developed a new system of business practices for movie theater operation and in the process, created the Paramount Publix theater chain during the 1920s. For a historical analysis of that business expansion and influence, see Douglas Gomery, "U.S. Film Exhibition: The Formation of a Big Business,' in *The American Film Industry,* rev. ed., Tino Balio, ed. (Madison: University of Wisconsin Press, 1985), pp. 218–28.

Chapter 14

Coca-Cola Satellites?
Hollywood and the Deregulation of European Television

Edward Buscombe

THE LEGACY OF PUBLIC BROADCASTING

Until the beginning of the 1980s, television in Western Europe was ruled by the ethos of public service broadcasting. The organizational model varied from country to country according to differing historical legacies and more immediate political imperatives. But by and large there was agreement about the objectives of broadcasting and the means by which those objectives could be secured. In the major Western European democracies—Italy, West Germany, Great Britain, and France—and in most of the smaller ones too, the development of means of electronic communication had been carefully controlled by governments pursuing common goals.

The edifice of public broadcasting is founded on four supporting pillars. First, the complete range of broadcast services should be available to the whole population. Irrespective of their geographical isolation, all citizens should have the right to receive the service in its entirety and at an affordable cost. Second, broadcasters have a duty to provide a balanced schedule containing the full diversity of programming possibilities. All tastes shall be catered to. In particular, minorities and the disadvantaged shall be granted special provision. Third, the political content of programs must be balanced and impartial, favoring no one side of the political process. The fourth principle concerns finance. In order that the first three goals shall not be compromised, public service broadcasting is financed, either wholly or in large part, by a license fee. Thus it is paid for neither directly out of government tax revenues, which would render it vulnerable to political pressures, nor is it at the mercy of commercialism, as would arise were revenues derived principally from advertising.

Public service broadcasting, at least in its pure form, is a kind of public monopoly, just as the various utilities have been in most European countries. The telephone system, gas, water, and electricity, and to a great extent transport systems, except those powered by the internal combustion engine, have all traditionally been under the control of the government, a situation quite different from that in the United States. In Europe the social benefits of extending the availability of utilities, independent of market forces, have outweighed the possible price economies that would come from allowing private enterprise and competition to determine availability.

However, more is at stake than simply the ensuring of supplies. The four pillars are erected upon a foundation of assumptions about the very nature and purpose of broadcasting. Radio and television programs are regarded not simply as commodities, to be produced with the maximum economic efficiency and sold for what the market will bear. Instead, broadcasting is viewed as an aspect of the public good, as necessary in its way as education, political liberty, or secure defense. One concept that is never very far away when public service broadcasting is discussed is that of quality. In this context, quality generally includes not only the goals of high technical and artistic standards, but also diversity across the full range of genres. Quality may be said to inhere not just in individual programs, which may be good or bad of their kind, but in the service as a whole. A quality television service would include not only "entertainment," such as drama series, sitcoms, sports, and game shows, but also news, current affairs, arts programs, documentaries, and programs for special interest groups such as gardeners, amateur astronomers, and so on. Not only does the public have the right to the best television that can be produced, the broadcasters have a duty to provide it; even, and this is a key point, when the public does not seem particularly to want it. Public service broadcasting is nothing if it is not a campaign of public improvement.

It is clear, then, that while public taste cannot be ignored, the extent to which the market is allowed to intrude is limited. "Giving people what they want" (which usually means in practice selling people what is profitable) is incompatible with the objective of ensuring that all tastes, not just majorities, are provided for. And yet other media of communication, also important to the cultural and political health of the nation, are not the object of such attentive regulation by the government. In no Western European country are the press, the film industry, the theater, or the music industry under public ownership. Why is broadcasting such a special case?

One answer might be that broadcasting, and particularly television, is so much more central to a national culture than any of these other means of communication. Television both contains all of them and has to a great extent supplanted them. It has replaced newspapers as people's primary source of information about daily events and as the principal means for conducting political debate. It has to a marked extent absorbed the cinema's role as the main provider of dramatized fictional entertainment (the cinema having similarly, in its turn, already largely incorporated the theater). The rise of the music video has only accelerated the convergence between the visual and audio industries. If this is so, and television occupies center stage in the formation of a national culture and of national consciousness, then is it any wonder that European governments, traditionally so much more interventionist than that of the United States, should wish to bring television under their wing?

The problem with such an argument is that government regulation of television predates its rise to such a position of strategic importance within the nation-state. In Britain public service broadcasting dates back to 1922, when no one could have fully foreseen the importance of radio, let alone television. And yet clearly there was something about the new medium that excited the interest of government. The justification for state intervention is usually that the frequencies available for transmission are strictly limited, and that public regulation is essential if anarchy is not to prevail. This may well fit the case of the United States, where the government has never been involved in the provision of broadcasting but only in the procedures of handing out the franchises. But the argument of spectrum scarcity cannot be a sufficient explanation of why in Europe governments should have set up national bodies not only to allocate frequencies but also to produce programs.

The reason, of course, is that while it may not have been evident at first that radio and then television would come to play such a key role within national culture generally, it did not take politicians long to see the implications of the new media for the control of information, a vital weapon in the political battle. The history of the BBC shows this clearly. The famous episode of the 1926 General Strike, in which the head of the BBC, John Reith, effectively deployed his forces on behalf of the government against the striking miners, demonstrated what a key factor the new medium could be in political struggle. Since then, a series of crises in relations between the BBC and the government, occurring at moments of maximum political tension, such as the Suez crisis, the Falklands/Malvinas campaign, and the continuing troubles in Northern Ireland, have tested the precise limits of the BBC's independence from government policies.

By and large, the BBC has managed to keep the government of the day sufficiently at arm's length to satisfy the third principle of public service broadcasting, that the party political content of programs be impartial. Elsewhere in Europe this has not always been the case. In France and Italy particularly, there is a tradition of far more direct government intervention in programming policies and of government control of appointments, particularly within news and current affairs. The line that is supposed to divide public service from state control has at times been obscured. In the absence of a countervailing ideology such as exists in the United States and that is opposed to government involvement in anything that can be made profitable, governments in Europe have sometimes been able to highjack the ideals of public service and turn them to their own ends. Yet despite occasional failures to live up to its lofty principles, the ideal of public service broadcasting remained vigorously alive.

DEREGULATION TAKES HOLD

Quite suddenly, toward the end of the 1970s, the idea of public service broadcasting, which had seemed so well established and which had appeared to serve both broadcasters and viewers well, found itself under threat. In Italy, broadcasting had, since the end of World War II, been under the close control of the dominant political party, the Christian Democrats. The Italian national broadcasting company RAI (Radiotelevisione Italiana-Societa per Azioni) had a monopoly on the airwaves, and the ruling party kept a firm grip on senior appointments and on the content of news and current affairs. However, by the mid-1970s the Christian Democrats' domination of all aspects of Italian political and cultural life was becoming eroded. Other political parties, especially the socialists, were forcing concessions on broadcasting policy, which would oblige a more equal division of power. Just at this moment, however, in 1976, the Italian Constitutional Court declared that the state monopoly of broadcasting was legal only at the national level, and that local radio and television stations were permissible. The privileged position of RAI was undermined. In the next few years a myriad of small radio and television stations began transmissions, completely unregulated by any apparatus of state control.

By 1981, Italy had reached the highest density of radio and television stations per capita in the world: one radio station for every 16,000 inhabitants (1:25,000 in the United States) and one television station for every 93,000 inhabitants (1:274,000 in the United States).[1]

Their ability to control events now weakened by long-term shifts in political allegiances, the Christian Democrats were unable to prevent events from taking their course. Over the next few years the privatization of Italian television became an established fact. Though the Constitutional Court's ruling dictated that local television meant decentralized television, thus outlawing the formation of networks, in practice commercial operators have been able to get round this obstacle. As a result, Silvio Berlusconi has created Canale 5, a network company that in 1988 managed a 37.7 percent share of the audience. RAI's share was 47.3 percent, and other private stations shared the remaining 15 percent.)[2]

In France the rush toward privatization was less precipitous, but changes were nonetheless radical. Up until 1974, broadcasting in France had been under the control of a single body that performed all the functions of production and distribution. The ORTF (Organisation de Radio-Télévision Française) was, like RAI in Italy, a state-run monopoly. When Valery Giscard d'Estaing was elected president in 1974 with the support of a Centre-Right coalition, he instituted a reform that split the ORTF into separate companies. Though the television service would continue to be state-run, henceforth the three television channels would compete with each other for audiences and for revenue.[3]

When the Socialist Party took office at the beginning of the 1980s they initially continued with the existing system, except that in 1984 a new channel, Canal Plus, was created. This channel, with some private capital involved, was to be financed by subscription. After a shaky start, it has now become extremely successful, in large part due to the feature films it programs, including pornography in the early hours of the morning. A change with more profound implications came in 1985, when two more channels were created, La Cinq and TV6 (later rechristened M6). Both were privately owned and were financed by advertising. The next step along the privatization road came in 1987 when the conservatives under Chirac, who had by now replaced the socialists, decided to privatize one of the state-run channels, TF1. Thus, in 13 years France had moved from a total state monopoly in broadcasting to a situation in which the airwaves had been substantially opened up to market forces and private financial interests.

In West Germany private television came in a rush in the mid-1980s. Up until 1984 all broadcasting was publicly controlled. Mindful of the use that Hitler had made of radio, the Allies after the war had imposed a decentralized system of broadcasting under the control not of the federal government but of the separate states (or "Lander"), which make up the federal republic. The two public networks, ARD and ZDF, are formed from the broadcasting organizations of the 11 Lander. These Lander also run, on a regional basis, their own third channels.

On January 1, 1984, the situation was transformed overnight, with the introduction of no less than four commercial channels: Sat-1, RTL-Plus, Tele-5, and Pro-7. Technical factors have so far limited the ability of some of these new networks to reach wide audiences, and Tele-5 and Pro-7 have been largely dependent on cable for distribution. They also have to compete with the public channels for advertising revenue, since, as in several other Western European countries, state ownership and financing through a license fee does not preclude topping up the revenues of public service broadcasting with some carefully controlled advertising time.

Finally, to complete the picture in the largest countries of Western Europe, we turn to Britain. Here, the process of privatization goes back to 1955, when the Conservative government of the day allowed a second channel, Independent Television (ITV), to compete with the BBC. ITV was wholly privately owned and financed totally by advertising. The BBC continued to be financed by the license only, so that ITV enjoyed a monopoly of advertising revenue. Profits were consequently large, and the government was therefore able to lay on ITV a number of quasi-public service obligations, such as the requirement to provide for minorities, to produce programs of regional interest, to provide programs for schools, and so forth. There was no further opening to the private sector until 1982, when Channel 4 was launched. (The BBC had been given a second channel in 1964.) This channel is financed by subscriptions from the ITV companies, levied by the Independent Broadcasting Company (IBA), the government agency charged with regulating the commercial sector. In return the ITV companies get to sell Channel 4's advertising time. Channel 4 itself makes no profits and is owned by the IBA itself. The programs are made not by Channel 4, but by independent companies with whom it contracts.

At the end of 1988 the British government published a White Paper setting out its proposals for the future of television in the United Kingdom.[4] After a lengthy debate and an official investigation into methods of financing the BBC (the so-called "Peacock" report),[5] the government decided against the introduction of advertising on the BBC, but it now intends that the license fee should eventually be phased out and the BBC financed by subscription. This is likely to imperil the public service commitment to the provision of programming for minorities.

In addition, the government proposes to introduce a fifth, and perhaps a sixth, commercial channel. These new channels will not have imposed on them the public service obligations of ITV, and the latter will also have some of its public duties lifted, giving it "greater freedom to match its programming to market conditions." Another move toward privatization is that television transmission, which has up till now been carried out by the BBC and the IBA and is wholly publicly owned, will be sold off. As a result of these changes, the BBC, which has until now been far and away the dominant force within British broadcasting, and indeed within British cultural life generally, will find its position considerably eroded, possessing only one-third of the terrestrial channels and increasingly dependent for financing not on the security of the annual license fee but on the vagaries of the marketplace as expressed through the subscription meters.

So far, in Britain, public service broadcasting has not had to face significant competition from cable television. The spread of cable has been extremely slow, and to date only some 5 percent of homes have cable. In Italy, where private transmitters have mushroomed, cable has been equally retarded. In some European countries, however, cable has reached the great majority of homes (80 percent in Belgium, 70 percent in the Netherlands).[6] The resulting proliferation of available channels, including many delivered from outside the country by satellite to a ground station before being piped into the cable system, threatens further to undermine the dominance of the national broadcasters.

Even this is not the whole story. As the 1980s draw to a close, a whole new dimension has been added to the broadcasting picture by the innovation of DBS (Direct Broadcasting by Satellite) channels. At the World Administrative Radio Conference in 1977, Britain was allocated five high-powered DBS channels, and these have all been awarded to British Satellite Broadcasting, a wholly privately financed company, which will be launching its own satellite later in 1989. Besides the five forthcoming BSB channels, Britain already possesses, since February 1989, the four channels of Rupert Murdoch's Sky Television, transmitted via the medium-powered ASTRA satellite, owned by Société Européene des Satellites, a private company based in Luxembourg. In Britain, therefore, this important new development in the history of broadcasting has been left entirely to private enterprise. A number of international media conglomerates, including the Bond Corporation of Australia, Pearson, Reed International, and some ITV companies, such as Granada and Anglia, have so far subscribed £400 million, which makes this after the Channel Tunnel the largest single capital venture currently under way within the UK economy.

By and large this pattern is likely to be repeated in the rest of Europe. The five channels on the French DBS satellite, called TDF1, have been awarded to La Sept (a new channel similar to the British Channel 4), Canal Plus, Canal Plus Enfants/Euromusic (a children's and music channel), Sport and Canal Plus Germany. The expense of initiating satellite broadcasting, it seems, is not a burden governments are anxious to assume. And so the extension of satellite channels will further dilute the public service constituent of broadcasting provision.

Why, after decades of apparently stable public monopoly, should Western European countries have moved so rapidly and so far toward the privatization of their broadcasting services? The answers to this question must vary from country to country, because in each case, there are special circumstances. Nevertheless, certain general patterns emerge. In the first place, one may observe that broadcasting is not unique in displaying these tendencies. In Britain in the 1970s, the Conservative government embarked on a program of wholesale transformation of the state sector of the economy. In the course of this, it has so far removed from public to private ownership such diverse businesses as telecommunications, British Airways, the British Gas Corporation, British Leyland cars, British Steel, the British National Oil Corporation, the Trustee Savings Bank, and most of the government's holdings in British Petroleum. Soon to come are the privatization of water supplies, the electricity industry, British Rail, and the coal industry. The reasoning behind this policy is not hard to find. The government has a firm belief in the bracing disciplines of the free market economy and an extreme hostility to anything that smacks of socialism. Its campaign of privatization amounts to a crusade on behalf of old-style capitalism. Broadcasting should no more be protected from market forces than any other kind of production. There is also, particularly within Britain, a flourishing political rhetoric around the evils of monopoly. Hence the proposal in the White Paper to separate the ownership of the means of television transmission from the business of producing and selling programs, a move reminiscent of the U.S. government's action after World War II in divorcing Hollywood studios from the ownership of chains of movie theaters.

This process of rolling back the tide of socialism is not, of course, confined to Britain. It extends to other European countries, even countries such as France in which the conservatives have not had it all their own way during the 1980s. Indeed, one may say that the whole basis of the Treaty of Rome, the document that enshrines the tenets of the European Economic Community (EEC), the group of twelve nations that forms the most powerful economic grouping in Europe, is a commitment to the doctrines of the free market.[7] Of equal significance as part of a general move away from socialist economics is the retreat in Eastern Europe from the policies of central state planning which have dominated economic thinking since World War II.

Coupled with a belief in the economic correctness of opening up broadcasting to exploitation by private capital is a tendency on the right to see public service broadcasting as harboring nests of radicals dedicated to conspiracies against "freedom." Of course, governments of all political complexions nurse suspicions of the media, though in France and Italy, for example, the traditional means of dealing with this has been to pack the broadcasting institutions with known government supporters. In Britain, with its different model of the role of the state, this has not been an option. Instead, the tactic has been, ever since the introduction of commercial television in 1955, progressively to cut the BBC down to size. The present White Paper may be regarded as another stroke of the axe.

There has also been something of a populist ground swell against the high-minded few who claim to know what is best for the many. The politicians of the right may have a point when they criticize the lack of responsiveness in public bodies to the wishes of the very public they are supposed to serve. All too easily public broadcasters come to assume an identity between the interests of the public and the interests of the organization for whom they work. Without countervailing pressures, broadcasters may begin to see the continued well-being of their institution as an end in itself: Because the BBC stands for public service broadcasting, what is good for the BBC is good for the public. So when the White Paper talks of the way in which market disciplines can protect broadcasters from "sterile elitism or precious self-indulgence", it may strike a chord with some of the audience.

Still, one may wonder why governments in France and Italy, which have enjoyed considerable benefits from a system of broadcasting allowing them to exercise direct political influence, should voluntarily renounce their power. Does a crusade in favor of free market principles adequately explain their actions? Not all governments are as ideologically fervent in the free market cause as that led by Mrs. Thatcher. The French government, for example, continues to pursue interventionist policies in the field of telecommunications and electronics.

Was it simply that the logic of the case for privatization was irresistible? As Vincent Porter has shown, an intellectual argument against public broadcasting and in favor of deregulation was mounted systematically and with some determination during the 1970s and 1980s in the United States.[8] But debates in American academic and legal circles do not often have much influence on the policies of European governments. What may have concerned them at this time was the perception that public service broadcasting was undergoing a long-term economic crisis. By the mid-1970s services financed by license fees had for the most part reached a plateau of expansion in terms of their audience. Once television had been brought to virtually all the potential viewers, revenues from the license fee were no longer expanding through the addition of more license payers. Inflation generally was high at this time, and governments were reluctant to add to it by increasing any prices that formed part of people's cost of living. At the same time the cost of producing programs rose inexorably, as a consequence of Baumol's disease.[9] This is a condition that affects labor-intensive industries such as broadcasting. In most industries the cost in real terms of products continually falls, because improvements in technology and hence productivity result in constantly falling labor costs. The fewer workers it takes to build a car, the cheaper the car. But in industries such as broadcasting, technological innovations are limited in their capacity for saving labor. Opportunities for replacing workers by machines are rare. Since the wage rates in broadcasting have roughly to keep pace with those elsewhere, costs rise faster than in other industries. In public service broadcasting in the 1970s, the two sides of the equation, costs and revenue, had ceased to add up.

This problem was also present for the commercial broadcasting sector, in those countries where such a sector existed. But commercial broadcasters had the option of increasing their prices to offset higher costs. Thus, between 1975 and 1985 in Britain the BBC's expenditure on television was able to rise from £120 million to £554.6 million. But in the same period ITV's expenditure rose from £128.1 million to £896 million.[10] This imbalance between the commercial and public sectors presented governments with a problem: how could they avoid having to find ever-larger sums of money from the public's pocket to enable public broadcasting to keep pace with the commercial sector? The only answer that could be found was to water down the commitment to the public service.

At the same time that governments were being pulled along by economic forces, they were also being pushed by a powerful combination of interests dedicated to seizing the commercial opportunities that seemed to be opening up. As the 1970s advanced, the tendency within media industries toward concentration of ownership into ever fewer and bigger companies joined with a parallel tendency toward diversification, so that companies active in one field spread themselves into others. Television companies bought publishers, newspaper owners bought film studios, and products originally designed just for one market could be sold through into many. Books could be serialized in newspapers, made into films, their music scores packaged as records, and then the films released all over again on video and then on television.

As the companies got bigger and more powerful, they began to

:ast covetous eyes on the sector of television that was still in public
1ands. To governments already looking favorably on private enterprise
)r anxious about public expenditures, the offers of the media barons
:o take their problems off their hands became increasingly seductive.
In Britain, Rupert Murdoch's newspapers, which included *The Times*
and the *Sunday Times*, conducted a campaign of open hostility against
:he BBC that was clearly designed to soften up the government
and the electorate for the dismemberment of public broadcasting.
Though the goal of privatizing the BBC was not achieved, nevertheless
in Britain, France, West Germany, and Italy it is, by and large, the
big conglomerates that have largely reaped the spoils of privatization.
Twenty-one of the 24 additional television services introduced into the
EEC since 1983 are private companies funded solely by advertising.
Only the two West German channels, Eins Plus and 3-Sat, run by
the German organizations ARD and ZDF, and the French TV5 have a
public service remit.[11] The private companies are not, for the most part,
owned by the small shareholders who are the darlings of right-wing
politicians. In Britain, Robert Maxwell's MCC is heavily involved both
in terrestrial television and in cable, both in Britain and elsewhere in
Europe. Murdoch has his four Sky channels. As we have seen, BSB is
owned by major media multinationals. In Italy, Silvio Berlusconi has
the largest private network and is a major shareholder in France's
La Cinq. Berlusconi also has 45 percent of West Germany's Tele-5.
Another commercial channel in Germany, Sat-1, is partly owned by
the powerful Springer press and other publishers, while RTL-Plus is
owned by Bertelsmann, one of the world's largest media corporations,
and by WAZ, a newspaper company, and CLT, the hugely successful
television company based in Luxembourg.

THE EFFECTS ON PROGRAMMING

What kind of television will the new commercial services provide?
Specifically, what will the programs be like? And where will they come
from? The answers to these questions have to be sought in the finances of
the television industry. The first thing to consider is what the level of
demand will be for programming to fill the spaces on the new channels.
As with so much else in the field of international communications, the
evidence is sketchy and not always consistent. The magazine *Europe*
states: "Current consumption of television programmes in EEC
countries amounts to about 125,000 hours per year, but in the near

future the demand will skyrocket to 300,000 hours."[12] According to
the trade journal *Broadcasting*: "[European] Commission officials say
their calculations indicate Europe will need some 120,000 hours of
programming in the 1990s."[13] The context, unfortunately, does not
make it clear whether this means *additional* programming. The British
trade paper *Broadcast* quotes a figure of 470,000 hours needed by 1990.[14]
EBU Review, the journal of the European Broadcasting Union, states:

> A British trade journal [not named] has calculated that a total of 186,000
> hours of programming were broadcast in 17 European countries in 1985
> In the near future, when up to 40 satellite channels are each broadcasting
> for an average of 12 hours a day, another 175,000 programme hours will be
> needed. The E.E.C. Commission even expects demand in the Community
> to rise to 300,000 to 400,000 hours a year at the start of the 1990s.[15]

Even allowing that Europe and the EEC are not coterminous, the
variation in these estimates points to extraordinary vagueness in the
predictions about what will happen in European broadcasting in the
immediate future. But on one thing there is agreement: demand will
increase. It is also certain that current production capacity in Europe
is not adequate to meet that demand. According to *EBU Review*, that
capacity is only five thousand hours of new programming per year
(though again it is not clear from the context whether this is programming of all types).[16]

Since the new channels are for the most part financed by advertising, they will be compelled to maximize audiences. It seems likely,
therefore, that most of their programming will be entertainment rather
than informational or educational, and that a large part of it will be
dramatized fiction, since this is what, the world over, consistently
tops the ratings. Fiction is also the most expensive kind of television
to produce. In 1986 *Variety* estimated that the cost of producing an
hour-long episode of top-rated shows such as "Dallas," "Dynasty,"
"Magnum P.I.," and "Hill Street Blues" was in the $1 million to $1.2
million price range.[17] Costs in Europe are, of course, lower; currently
in the United Kingdom the BBC spends around £350,000 an hour on
drama, and ITV around £400,000.[18] But these are still very considerable
sums of money. Will the new channels be able to find the resources to
make their own drama productions?

Estimates of the likely revenues of the new advertising-financed
channels vary as much as the other statistics in this field. However,
we do know that in Europe not only is a lower proportion of the Gross

National Product spent on advertising, but also that television captures a smaller proportion of total advertising spent than it does in either the United States or Japan. Whereas in these latter two countries television accounts for around one-third of all money spent on advertising, in Europe as a whole it represents only 20 percent. And the figure also varies widely between countries. In the United Kingdom the proportion achieved by television approximates that in the United States and Japan. But in West Germany, before the creation of four new channels at the beginning of 1984, television was a mere 10 percent of total advertising spent. The possibility exists that if television in Europe can eventually secure a percentage of advertising revenues somewhere near that of the USA and Japan, then considerable sums of money would be unlocked. In 1987 the *Columbia Journal of World Business* estimated that if Europe achieved U.S. levels in its ratio between GNP and television advertising, revenue might increase from $4 billion to $14.4 billion.[19]

This is a big "if" because it supposes that the new channels can find audiences large enough to attract advertising on this scale. The new channels will have to compete for audiences with those that are already established. This will not be an easy task. It will be difficult to break out of the vicious circle in which low audiences mean little revenue, which means little money for attractive programming, thus keeping audiences low. The problem will be particularly intractable in countries such as Britain, where television's share of the advertising spent is already comparable to that in the United States and Japan and cannot be expected to increase. Richard Collins quotes a source in the *Financial Times* in March 1989 to the effect that by 1993 the new satellite channels in the United Kingdom will share between them some £265 million a year of advertising revenue. By comparison, the combined income of the established commercial system (ITV and Channel 4) will be over £1 billion.[20]

Failing some quite spectacular breakthroughs, either in terms of increasing the share of advertising spent for television overall or stealing audiences away from established broadcasters, the new channels will find themselves looking for extremely economical programming. They will not have far to seek. Drama may be very expensive to produce, but it can be cheap to buy. The economics of media products differ markedly from other consumer goods. Economies of scale are possible in most industries, but the costs of raw materials are always an important factor in the total cost of production, since the materials are consumed in the product. Thus if each car requires half a ton of steel, that steel cannot be used again to make the next car. In the media, a very large proportion of the costs of production go to make the first copy of a book, a record, a television program. Once that copy has been made, subsequent copies can be made for very little extra, since the price of paper or vinyl or videotape is minimal by comparison. This means that markets can be saturated for very little extra cost. In particular, it means that exporting is highly profitable, even at very low prices.

American television and film production companies have a particular advantage when it comes to exporting: the sheer size of the American domestic market. One estimate puts the world turnover for television, radio, and motion pictures in 1986 at $65 billion, of which the United States was responsible for $30 billion.[21] This means that U.S. companies can make expensive programs with high production values, of great appeal to audiences, and still recoup most if not all of their costs in the domestic market. "Miami Vice" currently costs about $1.5 million per episode. The deficit after it has been sold to NBC, the network that will show it, is $300,000. This can easily be recouped in sales abroad (and later in syndication), for only a marginal additional outlay for extra copies and sales expenses.[22]

The prices European countries pay for U.S. productions vary in proportion to the size of their audience. Small countries pay comparatively little, whereas the cost of producing their own programming does not reduce according to the size of the population. This means that the smaller the country, the more attractive imported programming can be. In Norway, for example, the cost of imported U.S. programming varies between three thousand and five thousand dollars per hour.[23] It has been estimated that the ratio of costs of home-produced programs in Norway to those of imported programs is of the order of 15:1.[24] Other things being equal, this is a powerful disincentive to domestic production.

The logic of these economic facts is clear. The new channels will be reluctant to invest in new programming made in the country to which they are transmitting. A recent estimate of the likely budgets of the new channels in the United Kingdom puts the expected average expenditure on programming per hour at £5000, as against £45,000 per hour for Channel 4 (easily the cheapest to run of the established channels).[25] The new channels will therefore be driven toward programming that is cheap and that has a proven record of attracting audiences: in other words, American fiction. And this is indeed what has happened in several European countries already. In Italy, the onset of privatization resulted in a huge increase in imports of foreign programs:

In 1982, the public and private television stations spent a total of 136 million dollars or 200 billion lire (double that of 1981 and four times that of 1980) to buy about 21,000 films, TV-films and plays from abroad. The

Italian broadcasting industry has been unable to meet the great increase
in demand from the television networks, which are obliged to resort above
all to the United States (80 per cent), Japan and Brazil.[26]

Though imports from the United States fell to 137 billion lire in
1987, American programs comprise much the larger part of all foreign
imports.[27] *Broadcast* reported that during the first six months of 1988,
Italian imports of foreign television programs more than trebled, with 75
percent of the money being spent on American programs.[28] In France
it has been estimated that since 1984, there has been a 400 percent
increase in the number of American programs.[29] In Britain the new
satellite channels are spending huge sums of money on American
material, especially feature films. BSB and Sky Television have been
competing against each other for the most desirable titles. According to
Screen Digest, in 1988 BSB signed deals worth over $460 million, bringing
its total U.K. satellite film rights to over 1,750 titles costing in excess
of $700 million over five years. The latest deals involve a $160 million
package of 175 first-run plus 200 classic feature films from Columbia
Pictures Entertainment; a $300 million-plus five-year package of 800
to 1,000 Universal and Paramount films from UIP; and a 16-film deal
with Fries International. Sky has meanwhile added a five-year output
deal with Warner Bros. to a similar arrangement with Disney/Touch-
stone/Hollywood Pictures and Murdoch's own Twentieth Century–Fox.
It has also lined up a 150-title package from Orion, an 80-film, $8 million
deal with New World Entertainment, and is negotiating deals with Rank,
Vestron, Virgin, and independent producer Jeremy Thomas.[30]

Admittedly, much of the hectic recent activity by the new channels is simply "pipeline-filling," and this level of purchasing will not be
sustained. Nevertheless, it is apparent that the privatization of European
television is giving a powerful boost to the film and television production industry in the United States. The *Financial Times* reported that
in 1988 foreign television stations spent more on U.S. movies than did
stations in the United States itself. Total foreign spending on American
films has grown by 63 percent from 1986 to 1988, against a mere 22
percent growth in the United States. [31]

Many of these large payments for movies are to provide for premium programming, most of which will be available only through
subscription. The run-of-the-mill round-the-clock advertising-financed
channels will, we may assume, be stocked with more routine fare at
less spectacular prices. Nonetheless, Hollywood's coffers should, in
the short term at least, be swelled as "The Lucy Show," "Bonanza,"
and "M*A*S*H" make yet another outing in syndication.

The question is, how long is the short term? If the tide of U.S. imports swells to a flood, will there be calls to man the dikes to preserve the purity of national culture? There is a phrase that has become current in England and that represents the worst nightmares of those who fear yet another wave of invasion by the products of American showbiz. The threat, we are told, is that before very long, British television will be furnished with nothing but "wall-to-wall 'Dallas.'" The fear, deep-seated in many cultural guardians, especially those who don't watch much television, is that American imports will swamp indigenous culture, which will be helpless before the onslaught. It is based on an assumption that in television, Gresham's law always applies—that bad (American) television will drive out good (British). Such a view tends to overlook the feelings of some who do watch a lot of British television, that if Benny Hill is good then the sooner the good is driven out the better. But it has many supporters, including some in high places in Europe. The French equivalent of "wall-to-wall 'Dallas'" has been coined by Jack Lang, the high-profile socialist minister of culture, who referred to Luxembourg-based ASTRA satellite as "a Coca-Cola satellite attacking our artistic and cultural integrity."[32]

There are, of course, legitimate concerns about the degree to which it is healthy for any country to import its culture from elsewhere, though unfortunately the poorer a country is the less it is able to do about the situation. The arguments advanced for protective measures are both economic and cultural. If, without an excessive waste of scarce resources in domestic product substitutions it cannot afford, a country can limit its unfavorable balance of trade in media products, then it can hardly be blamed for doing so. If at the same time this can be defended as securing the integrity of the national culture, so much the better. But the case against the deleterious effect of American programs on European screens is not proven. Statistics about the numbers of programs imported do not tell us very much about their effects on the audience. The assumption would seem to be that American programming inculcates American social values. Doubtless many Americans would like to think so; that democracy, the rule of law, the benefits of free enterprise, and other essential ingredients of "the American way of life" are imbibed along with the car chases and the shoot-outs. Conversely, those who are hostile to American programming accuse it of fostering aggressive social behavior and actual physical violence, excessive competitiveness, an obsession with money at the expense of human values. But whether American programs do in fact produce any of these effects, and to what extent and with what consequences, is a subject on which researchers have yet to provide much useful analysis.[33] Of course the effects may not be only on the audience. It is certainly possible that the success of American imports tempts native program producers to foresake indigenous models and emulate their style or content, or at least persuades them to work in similar genres. But again, this is not an aspect of the question that research has addressed. Whether British television is now different from what it would have been had there been no American programs on British screens these past 40 years is an interesting question, but it is hard to know how one would go about answering it.

There is a good deal of hypocrisy in politicians' expressions of valor in the cause of national culture. M. Lang does not explain why American culture is a danger to France, but not apparently German or Italian imports, which under the regulations of the EEC he will soon have no power to stop at the border. In 1984 the European Commission issued a Green Paper entitled *Television Without Frontiers*, which was designed to bring television under the same regime of regulation as other kinds of economic activity. By 1992, the European Community is pledged to remove all barriers to free trade among the 12 member state. Henceforth any television service that circulates in one country must be allowed, if it so wishes, to circulate in all countries.

The EEC is, however, as suspicious of free trade outside its border as it is in favor of it inside. Thus the Green Paper included discussion of quotas for non-European programming, designed to secure a larger measure of the developing trade for European producers. These suggestions were cautious in the extreme. The 1986 version of the proposals suggested that 30 percent of broadcasts should be reserved for EEC programs and that this should be increased to 60 percent within three years. But even the higher figure is below many existing quotas. In Britain there has been for years a quota far more stringent than this. Both the BBC and ITV operate on the basis of no more than 14 percent of non-EEC material, a figure that was originally imposed on the commercial channel by a strong trade union and that the BBC decided to honor as well, under an unwritten gentleman's agreement. Yet the new quota proposals were greeted with cries of horror by representatives of American film industry trade organizations. Jack Valenti, president of the Motion Picture Association of America, threatened the Europeans with a "commercial war" if the threat of quotas was not removed.[34] One must assume that the campaign against the quotas was not directed at the established broadcasters, but was rather a preemptive strike against any attempt to constrain the new channels from stocking up on cheap American fare. The problem was defused when the Europeans could not agree among themselves, even about whether the European Commission had jurisdiction over cultural matters. M. Lang was eventually reported as saying that instead of quotas, the EEC would probably now attempt to protect European television through a variety of measures designed to stimulate domestic production.[35] But the issue of quotas seems unlikely to go away, since it invokes a powerful combination of economic and cultural nationalism. It is also tempting for Europeans to tell Valenti to go and jump in the Atlantic, on the grounds that while Hollywood has 44 percent of the total imports of television into Europe, the United States imports less television from abroad than virtually any country on earth (currently around 2 percent).[36]

It may be that quotas are a sledgehammer to crack a nut. There is a body of expert opinion that seriously doubts that Hollywood will be able to achieve in television anything like the domination it has achieved over the world's cinema screens. Preben Sepstrup believes that the existing impression of U.S. domination of European television screens does not stand up against the facts (though he admits that the statistics are "limited and not very reliable"). He argues, on the basis of a 1983 study, that the significant figure is not that the United States supplies 44 percent of imports, but that on average 73 percent of each European country's national supply is domestically produced, and of the rest, 13 percent comes from the United States, 12 percent from other European countries, and 4 percent from coproductions and other countries. As he remarks, it is a subjective judgment whether 13 percent in U.S. imports is too much. Sepstrup concedes that U.S imports are nearly all fiction and are often concentrated into prime time, hence the impression that they form a larger proportion of programming than in fact they do. But he takes the view that a degree of transnationalization (that is, its diversity of national sources) is no bad thing in broadcasting.[37]

In a study of attitudes toward American programming by British audiences, Geoffrey Lealand found that, contrary to the cultural chauvinism often manifested by critics and reviewers, the viewers on the whole welcome American fare. But they are not so enamored of it as to suggest that American programs would ever supplant British ones in their affections.[38] Michael Tracey has also poured cold water on those who get hot under the collar about the tides of trash they foresee arriving from across the Atlantic. He points out that American programs, though popular, do not top the ratings in other countries. Almost invariably home-produced programs outperform even such chartbusters as "Dallas." In Britain, such quintessentially British soap operas as "Coronation Street" and "EastEnders" are consistently the most popular shows on the air, and owe nothing in their style or format to American imports. All the evidence, suggests Tracey, is that people prefer programming that arises out of their own culture. In the

Netherlands, where cable penetration is over 70 percent, giving access to several satellite services, and where most of the population can speak both German and English, 89 percent of total viewing nevertheless goes to domestic Dutch channels.[39]

The authors of *East of Dallas*, a study of the European reception of the popular U.S. series and of attempts within Europe to produce domestic rivals to it, confirm that domestically produced fiction out-ranks American imports:

> In all the countries studied (Italy, France, West Germany, Great Britain and Ireland) and presumably also in others, national fiction normally comes first in the audience ratings. *Dallas* and other American series normally do not go higher than second place at best. . . . This appears to suggest that the penetrating force of American culture conveyed by television has shown itself to be weaker than expected. Quite apart from audience ratings, our research has also shown how television series in European countries have preserved strong national traits, a distinct and original social and cultural identity, basically uncontaminated by the American model.[40]

Yet the economic attractions of American programs for European schedulers, their combination of high production values and low prices, are bound to remain. *East of Dallas* is skeptical about the extent to which a pan-European market can be created for European national productions. Because "American is now consolidated as the 'lingua franca' of television fiction," there is less resistance to it than there is to programs from other foreign countries. Italians would rather watch American programs than German ones, especially if both are dubbed into Italian. "The more a programme has a national flavour, the more difficult it will be to export it."[41] The possibilities, much touted among hopeful television executives, of greatly expanded European coproduction seem likely to founder on this rock. If this pattern continues, Hollywood should not hope for a long-term dramatic increase in its share of European markets; but it can expect a continuing steady sale of its wares.

Finally, one ought to take account of some of the more gloomy prognostications about the long-term financial viability of some of the new channels. Richard Collins, in a detailed study of the prospects for privately owned European satellite channels, concludes that their finances are shaky in the extreme. Because they start with small audiences, their revenue from advertising will be slow to grow. They will therefore be obliged to use the cheapest form of programming: recycled American material. But if, as seems possible, this has only a limited appeal to Europeans, and if, as seems likely, public service broadcasters fight back vigorously, then the satellites could be in trouble. Sky's annual budget to run four new channels for British audiences is a mere £115 million, approximately equivalent to the economical Channel 4's budget for one channel.[42] No less an authority than Ted Turner has pronounced that "Both [BSB and Sky] will hemorrhage for a long time to come. A lot of fine people are going to lose a lot of money."[43] So far sales of the new DBS equipment in Britain have been well below initial predictions:

> A wave of realism is sweeping through Sky Television. The reason is simple; three months after its launch the satellite broadcaster has to confront the fact that it has failed to make the expected inroads into the market. . . . In the face of low dish sales, Sky has been forced to recalculate its projected penetration levels and now estimates that only 500,000 to 700,000 dishes will be sold by the end of its first year.[44]

Even that figure now looks like an optimistic target. Though many privately financed channels are now well established in Europe, the possibility exists that several of the newest entries onto the scene will not in fact survive. Hollywood should enjoy the boom while it lasts.

POSTSCRIPT

This article was written before the full significance of the recent extraordinary transformations within Eastern Europe became clear. It now seems highly likely that one consequence of the political changes taking place will be that the state broadcasting systems of Eastern Europe will become much more open to Western programming, and may indeed become largely deregulated if state control of the economy is abandoned. If that happens the potential market for Hollywood product will expand dramatically; always supposing, of course, that the East Europeans can find the money to pay.

NOTES

1. Donald Sasson, "Italy: The Advent of Private Broadcasting," in Raymond Kuhn, ed., *The Politics of Broadcasting* (New York: St. Martin's Press, 1985), p. 121.

2. *Broadcast*, April 21, 1989.

3. See Jill Forbes, "France: Modernisation Across the Spectrum," in Geoffrey Nowell-Smith, ed., *The European Experience*, Broadcasting Monograph no. 2 (London: British Film Institute, 1989), p. 25.

4. *Broadcasting in the '90s: Competition, Choice and Quality*, Cmnd. 517 (London: HMSO, 1988).

5. *Report of the Committee on Financing the BBC*, Cmnd. 9824 (London: HMSO, 1986).

6. Klaus Wenger, "European Television—Pandora's Box?" *EBU Review* 39 (September 1988), p. 27.

7. The 12 countries of the European Economic Community are Belgium, Denmark, Eire, the Federal Republic of Germany, France, Greece, Italy, Luxembourg, the Netherlands, Portugal, Spain, the United Kingdom. The total population is 320 million, and the combined Gross National Product is larger than that of either Japan or the United States.

8. Vincent Porter, "The Re-regulation of Television: Pluralism, Constitutionality and the Free Market in the USA, West Germany, France and the UK," *Media, Culture and Society* 11 (1989): 5–27.

9. See W. Baumol and W. Bowen, *Performing Arts: The Economic Dilemma* (New York: Twentieth Century Fund, 1966).

10. *Report of the Committee on Financing the BBC*, p. 50.

11. Wenger, "European Television," p. 29.

12. *Europe* (April 1989).

13. *Broadcasting*, April 17, 1989.

14. *Broadcast*, April 22, 1989.

15. Wenger, "European Television," p. 29.

16. Ibid., p. 29.

17. *Variety*, September 24, 1986, quoted in Gareth Locksley, *TV Broadcasting in Europe and the New Technologies* (Luxembourg: Office for Official Publications of the European Communities, 1988), p. 211.

18. *Television*, October 6–12, 1988.

19. Steven S. Wildman and Stephen E. Siwek, "The Privatization of European Television: Effects on International Markets for Programs," *Columbia Journal of World Business* (Fall 1987), p. 73.

20. Richard Collins, *Satellite Television in Western Europe* (London: John Libbey, 1990), p. 51.

21. Locksley, *TV Broadcasting in Europe*, p. 3.

22. *Television Business International* (February 1989), p. 86.

23. Ibid., p. 88.

24. Sissel Lund, "Satellite Television and Media Research," *European Journal of Communication* 3 (1988): 351.

25. *Television*, October 6–12, 1988.

26. Giuseppe Richeri, "Television from Service to Business: European Tendencies and the Italian Case," in Phillip Drummond and Richard Paterson, eds., *Television in Transition* (London: British Film Institute, 1986).

27. Mauro Wolf, "Italy: From Deregulation to a New Equilibrium," in Nowell-Smith ed., *The European Experience*, p. 56.

28. *Broadcast* (December 1988).

29. Forbes, "France," p. 33.

30. *Screen Digest* (January 1989).

31. *Financial Times*, April 22, 1989.

32. Collins, *Satellite Television*, p. 3.

33. James Hay has also argued that the changed context of presentation and viewing when an American series is shown on Italian television means that the audience is no longer consuming quite the same product. See James Hay, "Neo-TV' and the Cultural Politics of National Identity," unpublished paper.

34. *Variety*, June 21–27, 1989.

35. *Variety*, July 5–11, 1989.

36. See the study for UNESCO by Tapio Varis, "The International Flow of Television Programs," *Journal of Communications* (Winter 1984): 143–52.

37. Preben Sepstrup, "Implications of Current Developments in West European Broadcasting," *Media, Culture and Society* 11 (1989): 29–54.

38. Geoffrey Lealand, *American Television Programmes on British Screens* (London: Broadcasting Research Unit, 1984).

39. Michael Tracey, "A Taste of Money: Popular Culture and the Economics of Global Television," paper presented at the Conference on The International Market in Film and Television Programs, Columbia University, October 23, 1987.

40. Alessandro Silj, with Manuel Alvarado, Régine Chaniac, Antonia Torchi, Barbara O'Conner, Jean Bianchi, Michael Hofmann, Giancarlo Mencucci, Michel Souchon, Tony Fahy, *East of Dallas: The European Challenge to American Television* (London: British Film Institute, 1988), p. 211.

41. Ibid., p. 213.

42. Collins, *Satellite Television*, p. 51.

43. Quoted in Collins, *Satellite Television*, p. 115.

44. *Broadcast*, May 12, 1989.

SUGGESTIONS FOR FURTHER READING

Burns, Tom. *The BBC: Public Institution and Private World*. London: Macmillan, 1977.

Drummond, Phillip, and Richard Paterson. *Television in Transition*. London: British Film Institute, 1985.

Kuhn, Raymond. *The Politics of Broadcasting*. New York: St. Martin's Press, 1985.

McQuail, Denis, and Karen Siune. *New Media Politics: Comparative Perspectives in Western Europe.* London: Sage, 1986.

Negrine, Ralph, ed. *Satellite Broadcasting: The Political Implications of the New Media.* London: Routledge and Kegan Paul, 1988.

Nowell-Smith, Geoffrey, ed. *The European Experience.* Broadcasting Monographs no. 2. London: British Film Institute, 1989.

Smith, Anthony. *The Shadow in the Cave: The Broadcaster, the Audience and the State.* London: Quartet, 1976.

Tunstall, Jeremy. *The Media Are American.* London: Constable, 1983.

The Media in Britain. London: Constable, 1983.

Tydeman, John, and Ellen Jakes. *New Media in Europe: Satellites, Cable, VCRs and Videotex.* London: McGraw-Hill, 1986.

Contributors

Bruce A. Austin is the William A. Kern professor of communications at Rochester Institute of Technology. He has written extensively on movie audiences and is the founder and editor of the annual series *Current Research in Film: Audiences, Economics, and Law*. His most recent book is *Immediate Seating: A Look at Movie Audiences (1989)*.

Tino Balio is professor of communication arts at the University of Wisconsin, Madison. He is the author of numerous articles and books on film and television history, most recently *United Artists: The Company That Changed the Film Industry* (1987).

James L Baughman is associate professor of journalism and mass communication at the University of Wisconsin, Madison. He is the author of *Television's Guardians: The Federal Communications Commission and the Politics of Programming, 1958–1967* (1985), and *Henry R. Luce and the Rise of the American News Media* (1987). His articles on television history include "Television in the Golden Age: An Entrepreneurial Experiment," *Historian* 47 (February 1985).

John Belton is assistant professor of film at Rutgers University. He has published widely in the area of film and technology, and is currently writing a history of American wide-screen cinema.

William Boddy is assistant professor of speech at Baruch College, City University of New York. He is the author of *Fifties Television: The Industry and Its Critics* (1990) and has written on film and broadcast history for *Screen; Cinema Journal; Media, Culture, and Society; The Historical Journal of Film, Radio and Television;* and *Communications*.

Edward Buscombe is head of trade publishing at the British Film Institute. He has taught film and television at universities in Britain, Canada, and the United States. His publications include studies of sports on television and television drama. His most recent book is *The BFI Companion to the Western* (1988).

Brad Chisholm is assistant professor of communication studies at the University of Nevada, Las Vegas, where he teaches courses on the influence of business and technology on screen aesthetics. He has published in the *Journal of Film and Video*, the *Journal of Popular Film and Television*, and the *Velvet Light Trap*.

417

Douglas Gomery is professor of radio-television-film at the University of Maryland and lives in Washington, D.C. He has written *The Hollywood Studio System* (1986), *The Art of Moving Shadows* (1989), *American Media* (1989), and *Film History: Theory and Practice* (1985) as well as articles for the *Village Voice, SMPTE Journal*, and *Critical Studies in Mass Communication*.

Michele Hilmes is assistant professor and chair of communication arts at Spring Hill College in Mobile, Alabama. Her book, *Hollywood and Broadcasting: From Radio to Cable* (1990), discusses the history of film and broadcasting relationships from the 1920s to the present. Her writings on film, television, and radio have appeared in the *Quarterly Review of Film Studies*, the *Velvet Light Trap*, and the *Journal of Film and Video*.

Vance Kepley, Jr. is associate professor of communication arts at the University of Wisconsin, Madison. He has published several essays in the areas of film and broadcast history.

William Lafferty is associate professor and chair of theatre arts at Wright State University. His articles and essays, focusing upon the technological and economic development of the American and European film and broadcasting industries, have appeared in a wide range of journals and anthologies. He is currently preparing a book-length study of the rise of recorded programming in American radio and television.

Barry R. Litman is professor of telecommunication at Michigan State University. His current research interests include studies of the economics of telecommunication and entertainment industries. He recently testified before the U.S. Senate during the hearing on media concentration.

Laurie Schulze is instructor of film and television studies and popular culture at the University of Denver. She is the author of articles on Madonna fans, female bodybuilders, and made-for-TV movies.

Timothy R. White is professor of film studies at Auburn University. He has previously published in *Film History*, and has presented papers at conferences of the Society for Cinema Studies and other professional organizations.

Index

ABC: acquired by Capital Cities, 284; and the FCC freeze, 53, 96, 105–7, 127, 131; feature film production, 249, 259–60; finances, 106–8; merger with UPT, 19, 91–4, 153; programming strategy, 10, 19–20, 37, 38, 52, 54, 79, 82–3, 227–8, 244, 246–7, 288, 290–1; station ownership, 70; switches to color, 227–8
ABC Circle Films, 249, 288–9
Academy of Motion Picture Arts and Sciences, 150, 225
Airport, 261
Airport 1975, 261
The Alamo, 201
'Alfred Hitchcock Presents,' 34, 79–80, 356
'Alfred Hitchcock's Mystery Magazine,' 80
Allen, Fred, 73
Allen B. DuMont Laboratories, 13–14, 20, 146, 220–1. *See also* DuMont, Allen B.; DuMont Television Network
'All in the Family,' 292
All the King's Men, 11
'Amahl and the Night Visitors,' 47
American Express, 271, 306, 309
American Federation of Musicians, 237
American Graffiti, 261
American International Pictures, 281
American Movie Classics, 265
American Multi–Cinemas, 282, 380
American Optical Company, 201
American Telephone & Telegraph (AT&T), 22, 65, 154, 223, 299–300
American Society of Cinematographers, 206, 225

American Television and Communications (ATC), 265, 286, 301
'America's Most Wanted,' 287, 366
Amityville Horror, 281
'Amos 'n' Andy,' 71, 73–4
Ampex Corporation, 323–4, 326
'Andy Griffith Show,' 83
Antitrust: AT&T's monopoly over wire transmission, 299–300; *Betamax* case, 266–8; investigation of MCA, 173; investigation of Premiere, 161, 305–6; MPAA suit against networks, 249; network monopsony power, 54, 135–40, 292–3; network radio, 92; option–time clauses, 130–1; *Paramount* case, 4–9, 19, 21, 93, 134, 145–9, 165–7, 202, 221, 282–3; *Technicolor* case, 218, 221; vertical integration, 117–31, 138–40, 306; withholding of feature films, 237–8
The Apartment, 174
Apocalypse Now, 205
ARD, 398, 403
Arkoff, Samuel Z., 281
Around the World in 80 Days, 201, 203, 204, 225
Art theaters, 7–8
'Arthur Godfrey and His Friends,' 98
'Assignment Foreign Legion,' 80
Association of Motion Picture Producers, 236–7
ASTRA, 399, 400
Atlantic Releasing, 280, 308
Aubrey, James, 41, 105, 109, 260
'Autobiography of Miss Jane Pittman,' 353, 368

419